A Study
In Austrian Intellectual
History

From Late Baroque to Romanticism

by Robert A. Kann

OCTAGON BOOKS

A DIVISION OF FARRAR, STRAUS AND GIROUX

New York   1973

a study in austrian intellectual history

Reprinted 1973
by special arrangement with Praeger Publishers, Inc.

OCTAGON BOOKS
A DIVISION OF FARRAR, STRAUS & GIROUX, INC.
19 Union Square West
New York, N. Y. 10003

The illustrations appearing in this book, except for Plates IV
and V, are reproduced by permission of Bildarchiv der Österreichischen Nationalbibliothek. Plates IV and V have been
reproduced from engravings in the author's private collection.

Library of Congress Cataloging in Publication Data

Kann, Robert A.   1906-
    A study in Austrian intellectual history.

    Reprint of the ed. published by Praeger, New York.

    Bibliography: p.
    1. Austria—Civilization.   2. Abraham a Sancta Clara, Father,
    1644-1709.   3. Sonnenfels, Josef von, 1732 or 3–1817.   I.
    Title.
[DB30.K3   1973]   914.36′03   73-16356
ISBN 0-374-94504-7

Manufactured by Braun-Brumfield, Inc.
Ann Arbor, Michigan

Printed in the United States of America

To
Alois Glingar
as ever

Acknowledgments

This study could not have been published without generous grants in aid of research and publication by the Research Council of Rutgers University. I am greatly indebted also to the John Simon Guggenheim Memorial Foundation for the award of a fellowship and a subsequent grant in aid of publication.

Thanks for editorial assistance are due to Mrs. Frances B. Greene, of Princeton, New Jersey. I am much obliged to Miss Beatrice H. Miers of Princeton for the preparation of a very difficult manuscript.

Finally, I am greatly indebted to the Director-General of the Austrian National Archives, Dr. Gebhard Rath, and several members of the staffs of these archives as well as of the archive of the University of Vienna for facilitating my research in every possible way. Special thanks are due to State Archivar Dr. Johann Christoph Allmayer-Beck for his counsel and aid in selecting the illustrations for this book.

R. A. K.

Contents

V
The Swing of the Pendulum
(Era of Francis I, 1792-1835)

ERRATA

p.150, line 19—Frederick William I (instead of Frederick Wilhelm I)

p.173, line 10 from foot of page—Wien (instead of Wein)

p.343, line 4—Wien (instead of Wein)

p.346, line 9 (ref. Sealsfield, Charles)—title is:
Österreich wie es ist (instead of Österreich wie es war)

p.288, line 15 from bottom of page—to read:
with the early revolutionary spirit of Kossuth (instead of with the spirit of early Kossuthianism)

p.358 (Index) entry to read:
Kossuth, Louis, 288; and pre-March era, 248. (omitting early Kossuthianism of)

List of Illustrations

INTRODUCTION:

Of Tradition and Change

The object of this study in Austrian intellectual history and its method of presentation are simple, albeit somewhat unusual. It attempts to combine a biographical with a social approach. The two main figures discussed at some length in these essays—the court preacher of the late seventeenth- and early eighteenth-century Baroque period, Abraham a Sancta Clara, and the reformer of the eighteenth-century Enlightenment, Joseph von Sonnenfels—have been selected not for their intellectual achievements, though those were substantial, but because of the type-forming character of their ideas. The three general essays which introduce and connect the biographical studies and survey in retrospect the accomplishments of these men are designed not merely to provide a historical setting; their aim is also to discover the typical elements and to show the cyclical pattern of Austrian intellectual development.

It should be clearly understood that a project of this kind does not claim to be a full-fledged history of intellectual development within a given time and place. It should, however, show the flow of development with reference to certain distinct and highly characteristic facets of history. This will be done within the narrow limits of a few specific case studies, which are discussed within their historical setting. The study would still be far from comprehensive if even twenty cases were analyzed instead of two. On the other hand, the very wealth of material then presented might obscure the principal aim: to trace the rise of the ideas of certain men within their social environment and the evolution of these men and of their ideas in time.

In order to achieve this purpose, certain standards must be met in regard to the individual men chosen for closer scrutiny and in regard to those ideas whose historical development is to be traced. For the first, the obvious choice would be that of a genius of extraordinary brilliance and vitality, whose impact on future generations, one way or another, has been so powerful that their intellectual standards can be measured largely in terms of their reaction to his image. Friedrich Gundolf's famous *Caesar: Die Geschichte seines Ruhmes** is a pioneer study of this sort. Another possibility would be to go to the opposite extreme and to select a man whose historical import rests on a fantastic incongruity between his personal insignificance and the tremendous force of his political and social influence. Obvious examples are several of the right- and left-wing dictators of our time. Support for selection of this kind of figure would be found in the widespread assumption that if a man of inferior character possesses an extraordinary appeal for the masses, he has it because he and his ideas are typical of the age—the theory being that, in a critical historical situation, viable political ideas are picked up by a trivial person as easily as ripe apples are plucked from a tree.

By necessity as well as intent, this study does not follow either method of selection. In the period and the area under discussion here—the German-speaking Austrian lands from the late Baroque at the end of the seventeenth century to the Romantic era in the early nineteenth—there is no individual man of genius who expresses completely the spirit of any major phase of it. The two greatest artists, Mozart and Beethoven, were too far removed from specific problems of their times to be considered entirely representative of the social climate of the age. What is more (and this certainly speaks well for the cultural history of Austria), throughout the entire era there was not a single intellectual leader of the "big drummer" type.

In any event, since the purpose of these essays is not to present the best or the worst aspects of a period but to show general trends, neither of these types of men would serve as appropriate examples. The two figures selected are men of considerable accomplishments. They are not common types, but they are exponents of type-forming patterns of ideas that can be discerned throughout the realm of social-intellectual development. As this writer sees it, Abraham of Sancta Clara exemplifies ideas and patterns of thinking that are found well into the twentieth century in a Catholic Action program of broad popular and spiritual appeal. Joseph von Sonnenfels represents a climate of thought that seems to be distinctly reflected in the growth of

*In English: *Caesar's Mantle* (New York, 1928).

nineteenth-century Austrian liberalism. In both cases we are dealing with the growth of the image of a man in succeeding generations and with later reactions to that image. In neither case is it suggested that the men intentionally formulated programs of social action; had they done so, this would have been a study not in intellectual history but in politics.

The fact that the study is strictly confined to intellectual history also explains why no third person has been selected whose pattern of ideas might be reflected in the growth of the powerful Austrian labor movement in the nineteenth and twentieth centuries. Certain elements of Christian and liberal social action and thought in Austria can be clearly traced to seventeenth- and eighteenth-century intellectual history. It would be artificial to look for a similar pattern in regard to the labor movement at that period in a country where as yet the Industrial Revolution had made little headway. Quite apart from this, Catholic and liberal social ideas have been traced here not because they happened to be developed into political programs but because they are reflected in the mental climate of early modern history in Austria. Various ideological connections notwithstanding, this was not true of socialist thought, even in its early Utopian form. Before the nineteenth century it played no direct part in the general development of ideas, which is the very essence of intellectual history.

This brings us to the second main aspect of this study—the framework of ideas to be discussed for the most part in the chapters that introduce and connect the biographical essays. According to the social climate during various phases of cultural development, the Baroque period, the Enlightenment, and the Romantic era of course differ substantially from one another. It is the contention of this writer, however, that they all express the underlying theme of the Austrian cultural tradition, a tradition made up of three main elements: first, adherence to the orbit of the German language and of Austro-German culture in general; second, the Christian heritage; third, the peculiar geopolitical and ethnic position of Austria. Standing as she does at the European multinational crossroads, she is at the gateway of a two-way cultural traffic between East and West and, to a lesser degree, between North and South.

These three factors are interdependent. The orbit of the German language and Austro-German culture, to be sure, does not include the entire Austrian cultural tradition, but only its most powerful stratum. But provided that one considers the lands of the Hungarian crown as a historico-political entity per se, Austro-German culture throughout the period under discussion, at least up to the beginning of the Slavonic cultural Renaissance, so far outweighs any other in importance that it seems quite legitimate to confine this study to that particular area. This does not mean that extraneous influences and complex background conditions of a different kind can be disregarded. In fact, the German-Austrian cultural inheritance in early modern times was conditioned by two main factors: the declining might of the Holy Roman Empire, and the rise of a predominantly non-German Habsburg power complex. Ottoman-Slavonic-Magyar, French-Flemish, and for a time Spanish influence and pressure played a part. To this must be added the steady influence of a North-South, German-Italian political and cultural interrelationship that was apparent even at the end of the early Middle Ages. At the point where this discussion starts, the high and the late Baroque period, all these factors exerted a strong, though unequal, impact on Austro-German cultural development. At the point where it ends, at the beginning of the nineteenth century, the Spanish-Flemish factor had ceased to be effective in the West, and the Ottoman in the East—the Ottoman, however, being more than replaced in potency by Slavonic influence. Furthermore, while well into the reign of Maria Theresa the Western influence outweighed the Eastern, and during the Renaissance and high Baroque southern Italian influence outweighed the northern German, in both cases the situation has gradually been reversed since the end of the eighteenth century. West must now yield to East, South to North.

In terms of cultural advancement these facts are not negligible. Western influence in Austria was strongest at the time of the emergence of the new national states, the high Renaissance, the golden age of the French monarchy. Eastern Slavonic influence was on the rise when, at the end of the eighteenth and the beginning of the nineteenth centuries, the Slavonic cultural Renaissance gained an amazing momentum. Italian influence was most vigorous at the time of the greatest achievements of the Italian Cinquecento and high Baroque. In the period of comparative cultural stagnation in eighteenth-century Italy, the impact of the northern German era of Enlightenment and later of German Classicism and Romanticism became increasingly important.

The Catholic Christian element, very deeply rooted in Austrian culture, limits to a degree the extent of German intellectual influence. The universalism of the all-embracing Church could not and would not submit to predominantly emotional demands that she confine herself within a national framework. Nationalism battered vainly against the ramparts of the universal Church, long before the late nineteenth century, when the conflict flared up throughout the arena of public affairs.

It may well be asked why the Church and German nationalism in Austria could not have come to a permanent understanding like that which has been achieved, though with difficulty, in major Western countries. The answer is supplied, at least in part, by the historic connection between the German-Austrian lands and the Holy Roman Empire of the German nation, the largely fictitious German universal empire. This tradition of world religion in a world empire helps to explain why a movement similar to Gallicanism could never make any real headway in Austria. This same tradition was instrumental in frustrating the victory of the Protestant Reformation in the core of the later imperial power, the German-Austrian Habsburg lands. Thus in spite of numerous temporary alignments and *quid pro quo's*, the fact remains that the universal character of the Church has helped to further and to sustain the supranational element in Austrian culture.

To assume, however, that the multinational character of Austria has in turn helped strengthen the position of the Church would be erroneous. Her comprehensive claims to spiritual authority were not based primarily upon the polyglot character of the Empire's national composition. The strength of the Church resides in religious doctrine and the political tradition of universality. The great concept of one stadholder of God on earth and of one emperor who, according to the two-sword theory, is to hold his stirrup is bound to collide with petty national interests. The Church found herself forced, much against her will, either to take sides in an all too mundane political conflict or to accept the role of mediator in an intranational struggle. But neither of these alternatives was acceptable, because she was supposed and intended to be a supranational force. Nationalism, moreover, was not only an external political factor which harassed the Church from outside; it was also at work within the Church organization itself. Contact with Catholics of the West, where the Church more nearly accommodated herself to a national framework, and relations with Protestants from the North and with Orthodox and Uniates from the East and the South all played an important part here. Nationalism, whether in the nationally homogeneous or in the heterogeneous area, thus represented a challenge that could not be evaded by the Church. It involved the Church in contested political matters; it threatened to impair her uncontested spiritual universality.

The concept of universality does not apply to Austria's geopolitical crossroads position or to her multinational composition. It is obvious that in the political sphere each of these factors acted, and increasingly so, as a divisive force. She has been exposed, on the one hand, to the threat of foreign aggression from the East and the North and, on the other, to internal national conflict. The fact that the multinational empire for a long time met this challenge with a certain degree of success is a considerable achievement in itself. Contrary to a distorted line of reasoning, however, the multinational character at no time helped strengthen and maintain the union of the Habsburg lands.

In the cultural field the issue is somewhat more complex. There the positive significance of the fact that the character of the people indigenous to Austro-German lands, their social institutions, intellectual abilities, and ideas, have been shaped by many different national traits cannot be denied. To do so would be to misunderstand entirely a culture whose contributions to Western civilization are as unchallenged as its complex background conditions are problematical. But these influences are in turn modified by the two other factors—adherence to the German linguistic and cultural orbit, and Christianity in its Roman Catholic form. They provide the specific features of Austrian-German intellectual development and limit the effect of the multinational and geopolitical crossroads position.

It has been noted previously that these three interdependent factors—the linguistic-cultural, the Christian Roman Catholic, and the multinational and geopolitical crossroads element—have operated continuously throughout German-Austrian cultural development and form the very basis of that intellectual history. To say that there has been unmistakable historical continuity, however, is not to imply that the main ideas have developed at the same pace, with the same momentum.

It is the contention of this study that these ideas, while present throughout the period under discussion, emerge more strongly at certain times than at others, and that this can be demonstrated in a clearly discernible cycle of intellectual development. Therefore not only is a given spiritual movement analyzed at its height, but its later ideological repercussions are studied as well. The counteraction to it is shown, and the return of the movement in a different form. In other words, we shall follow the full swing of the pendulum, the path of the wave from crest to crest, the pattern of action, counteraction, and fresh action. In fact, it may not even be necessary to analyze the new action, once it becomes evident that the breakdown of the counteraction will lead inevitably to it. Contrary to a Hegelian-Marxist interpretation of history, however, it is not suggested here that the new cycle necessarily operates on a higher level than the previous one, nor is it assumed that socio-economic motivations play a predominant part in it.

The five essay topics are thus to be understood in a cyclical sense. It is the purpose of the first two to show the spirit of the triumphant Austrian Counter Reformation and Catholic Reformation* in their later Baroque setting, just before their decline. The general intellectual aspects of these movements as well as their embodiment in a most brilliant representative, Abraham a Sancta Clara, and the impact of his life on the future are analyzed. The third essay contains some general reflections on the transition period between semi-conservative Baroque and semi-progressive Enlightenment. This leads to a discussion of basic trends in Austrian history during the Enlightenment. They are elucidated and further elaborated in the fourth section, a biographical study of the reformer Joseph von Sonnenfels and of the later ideological repercussions of his life work. The result of this work, in a way the "failure of a mission," will reveal the advent of neo-conservative and Romantic movements. These trends, discussed in the fifth essay, resemble in spirit, though not in

---

*The term "Counter Reformation" is used here in the traditional sense of reaction to the Protestant Reformation in the ecclesiastic and political sphere. The concept of "Catholic Reformation," on the other hand, refers to an original spiritual movement of religious rejuvenation especially manifest at the time of the Counter Reformation but actually rooted in the medieval world.

thought and action, the atmosphere of the historical situation
with which the study begins. Concentration on these few topics
in the last essay will help to accent clearly the high points of
the cyclical development.

The selection of this particular late-seventeenth-, eighteenth-,
and early-nineteenth-century cycle, when a progressive or semi-
progressive movement was hemmed in by two that were conservative or semi-conservative, may appear somewhat arbitrary.
Undoubtedly it would have been possible to trace a cycle wherein the reverse motion, a conservative era followed and preceded
by progressive ones, took place. Thus the Renaissance and the
Reformation in Austria might be viewed in several respects as
progressive movements superseded by the counterreformatory
Baroque period but resumed again in the Enlightenment. Or
again, it might be possible to consider the restoration period
after 1814 as a transition stage between Enlightenment and the
revolution of 1848, with all its ideological repercussions. Finally,
within the period with which this study is concerned, one might
find, on closer scrutiny, that there are smaller cycles within each
larger one. In other words, within the conservative as well as
within the progressive phases there is a constant shift between
stable and dynamic positions.

Historical development in large areas, however, as well as in
relatively limited ones, follows a certain rhythm. The structure
of Austrian intellectual history, as this writer sees it, clearly indicates that the conservative and relatively stable periods are
fairly long; the dynamic—often only relatively progressive—ones
are brief. For that reason a conservative to progressive and again
conservative cycle has been selected. However, the reasons that
dictated the choice of the period from the late-seventeenth to
the early-nineteenth centuries as a particularly significant example of such a cycle will not be argued in this introduction.
The following analysis must speak for itself.

A Study in Austrian
Intellectual History

AUSTRIAN CHRONOLOGY
Baroque to Romanticism
[*h* = emperor of Holy Roman Empire; *a* = emperor of Austria]

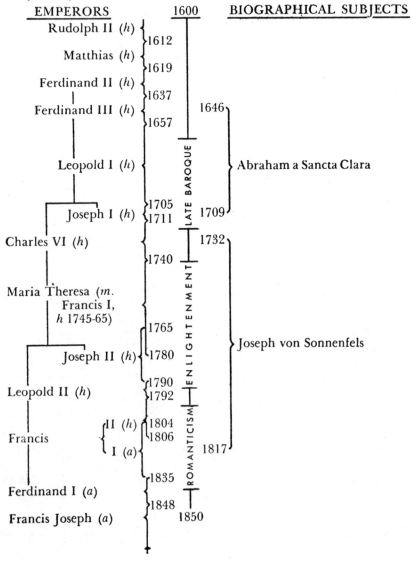

EMPERORS		BIOGRAPHICAL SUBJECTS

EMPERORS   1600   BIOGRAPHICAL SUBJECTS

Rudolph II (*h*)
1612
Matthias (*h*)
1619
Ferdinand II (*h*)
1637
Ferdinand III (*h*)
1657

1646

Leopold I (*h*) — LATE BAROQUE — Abraham a Sancta Clara

1705
Joseph I (*h*) 1711 — 1709

Charles VI (*h*) — 1732

1740

Maria Theresa (*m.* Francis I, *h* 1745-65)

1765
Joseph II (*h*) 1780 — ENLIGHTENMENT — Joseph von Sonnenfels

1790
Leopold II (*h*) 1792

Francis { II (*h*) 1804 / I (*a*) 1806 — ROMANTICISM — 1817

1835
Ferdinand I (*a*)
1848
Francis Joseph (*a*) 1850

I

THE CRISIS OF THE
BAROQUE ERA

The Age of Leopold I, 1657-1705

a. *The Baroque Concept*

The extension of the Baroque concept has not helped to clarify it. Whether it is perceived in the sense of the penetrating Heinrich Wölfflin as a cyclical movement that manifests itself in antiquity as well as in modern times, or whether its scope is extended from the field of the arts to the entire social body, as has been brilliantly attempted by Egon Friedell and others, many problems remain unsolved and still more have been added.

The reasons are simple. Unlike the Gothic, which was the emanation of an era in the Christian world of Western and Central Europe dominated by ideas of an enduring and universal character, the Baroque, even in its purely artistic aspects, is the offspring of a far more complex, far more contradictory world situation. The militant and ecstatic spirit of the Catholic Counter Reformation is not to be confused with that of medieval piety; to a certain extent it represents a reaction to the sobering effect of the Protestant Reformation. Even if one goes back as far as the melting pot and vulgarization stage of Greek art during the Hellenistic and late Roman imperial period, there is nothing truly comparable to the decorative character, the grandiose make-believe, the new approach to the problem of space, the curves and spirals of the new art, the splendor and elaborateness of courtly etiquette, the pomp of Italian opera. These are truly original responses to the ideological upheaval of

1

the Renaissance and the Protestant Reformation. The close connection between the statecraft of absolute despotism in its subtlety, intricacy, and conciseness and the occidental Christian inheritance of rule by divine right is, of course, undeniable; yet this statecraft does not operate within the framework of an imagined or desired universal empire but within the narrower fabric of the national or would-be national state. The mysticism and the irrationalism, the superstitions and the witchcraft proceedings, the revelations and the tortuous spiritual exercises in which the new era abounds, are not directly connected with the asceticism, the flagellantism, and the pietism of high and late medievalism. They are again responses to and reactions from the scientific revolution from Bruno and Copernicus to Kepler, Bacon, and Pascal and, to an even greater extent, the great deductive systems of Descartes and Spinoza and, to a scarcely lesser degree, the ironclad didactics and rigidly controlled emotions of the Jesuits. These phenomena have a *raison d'être* of their own quite independent of their ties with past and present.

The effect of all these forces is clearly traceable in the Baroque, even if it is regarded only in the relatively narrow nineteenth-century sense as an artistic-literary style. It is a tall order indeed to compress so conflicting an ideological heritage, so bewildering a product of diverse spiritual and sensual trends, into an even relatively homogeneous ideological picture. Nobody as yet has wholly accomplished this task satisfactorily. It is thus somewhat less than surprising that the problem becomes truly unsurmountable when the Baroque concept is expanded to include the full range of social action.

It is, however, a natural desire of the human mind to perceive the whole spirit of an era in one well-rounded concept. This may even be accomplished with a certain amount of success if, as has been done by Scheffler in his *Geist der Gotik* and more than a century before by Winckelmann in his *Geschichte der Kunst des Altertums,* such a concept is based on the philosophies that prevailed in the writers' own lifetime. We may differ today with their standards of aesthetic values and their historic analysis of the ancient and medieval world, but at least they manage to establish a logical connection between their ideas of historic art styles and their conceptions of the character of Hellenic and Gothic life.

The Crisis of the Baroque Era

Yet almost without exception the historiography of the Baroque has followed a different procedure. It has (on the whole rather uncritically) adopted the findings of art history and has set them up as general laws of historical development from the late sixteenth to the early eighteenth century. In so doing it has employed neither a deductive nor an inductive method, but plain and simple analogy.

To seek an analogy between Jesuit style, mystic sensuality, the great deductive philosophic systems, make-believe decorations, persistent Machiavellian statecraft, and the identification of state and individual in the mercantilist system—to mention only a few points—is obviously unsatisfactory. Yet all of these are linked together in the comprehensive histories of the Baroque period as emanations of the same spirit. In order to explain away contradictions, this kind of historiography frequently falls back on such theories as the assumed interrelationship of contrasts, thesis and antithesis, action and reaction, in the sense either of Hegelian dialectics or of Toynbee's challenge and response.

Thus this method endeavors to profit from its very failure to supply proof. In essence it can easily be reduced to *credo, quia absurdum est*. The best that can be said for it is that it at least makes an attempt, however misguided, to establish causation.

Even this fails if one descends from the realm of royal despotism, statecraft, art, and philosophy to that of the social problems of the masses. Here the historians of the Baroque era face not merely a *non sequitur* but a blank. On the whole, the problem of bridging the ideological gulf between the spirit of politics, art, and philosophy and the still-feudal structure of agricultural labor and, to a point, also of the lower urban classes has been ignored. In general, the thesis is that what cannot be fitted by hook and by crook into the new era is purely and simply a residue of the Middle Ages. The fact that this residue embraces the overwhelming majority of the people, that without their incorporation into the system of the new era one can hardly speak of this new era, is conveniently bypassed.

Attempts to bring any kind of order to this historiographical chaos will fail if these contradictions are to be smoothed over by arbitrary deductions. The first step toward finding the remedy is not therapy but diagnosis—in other words, to focus upon the contradictions ever more sharply. This will be attempted here, at least in the limited field of the Austrian high Baroque era of the second half of the seventeenth century.

b. The Habsburg Power in Baroque Europe

It must be recognized clearly at the outset that for the era represented by the reign of Leopold I (1657-1705) it is almost impossible to find a common denominator. In the domestic field it was a period of obvious crisis. The same may be said of the realm of foreign affairs, although, while much more has been written on this subject, it has remained actually more controversial. An anonymous English historian, having in mind this second aspect of those troublous times, describes them rather well, as follows:

> It being universally agreed on by the Learned, and found by daily experience to be true, that the most Turbulent Times afford the best Material for History; and seeing the Life of the Emperor Leopold has been in a manner but one continued and uninterrupted Scene of Trouble, there can be no tolerable Reason given why the same should not meet with as favorable a Reception as those of other Princes, his Contemporaries.
>
> It's true as for himself in Person he was a Prince very active in Council, much less so in the Field, seeming naturally to have an Aversion to War and Bloodshed. Notwithstanding all which, there scarce ever was any Reign of such a Length, engaged in heavier and bloodier wars, nor any of his predecessors, or any Potentate whatsoever, served by more consummate Generals and brave Soldiers. . . .[1]

This strange, deeply religious man was, according to reliable sources, highly diffident and slow to make up his mind, though he undoubtedly possessed a certain shrewdness and did not lack in erudition. Irresolute in action but tenacious in the defense of the *status quo,* narrow and yet with an artistic mind, impecunious and splendor-loving, homely, unheroic, and unmartial, he was indeed the true antithesis of his more brilliant opponent and cousin, Louis XIV. But he too, in that almost mystic Habs-

---

[1] Bibliographical notes follow the last essay, at the back of the book.

4

burg fashion, was just as deeply imbued with a consciousness of his own dignity; he is truly Grillparzer's emperor "who never dies."[2] Is this, then, the genuine paradigm of the contradictory Baroque man? At this point, before the pattern of the era has been delineated, it can only be said that Leopold, whatever else he stands for, was the product and representative of a deep political and social crisis, and in this sense the thesis of his English biographer that his reign was "but one continued and uninterrupted Scene of Trouble" is certainly well justified.

This is more obvious, though no more true, in foreign affairs than in any other field. Leopold was the contemporary not only of Louis XIV but of Cromwell, of Charles II and James II, Queen Anne, John Sobieski, and William III. Not only was he the passive antipole of Mohammed IV and Kara Mustafa in the drama of 1683, but his reign coincided with that of Peter the Great, the Great Elector, and King Frederick I of Prussia. Whether great or small, most of these rulers stand, if not for a new idea, at least for a new approach to the problems of government in their various countries. Yet the dominant feature of Leopold's Habsburg realm in the domestic field—though certainly not in foreign affairs—is the will to preserve the *status quo* in a changing world.

It would be wrong indeed to sum up the situation in such terms as "progress versus reaction." The struggle for a new order had not yet become a struggle for a new ideology; rather, it was a battle between conflicting systems. The Habsburg power did not represent such a clear-cut system, notwithstanding the fact that it stood for a powerful tradition and most certainly in more than one way for an idea.

This contrast is apparent across the whole of Europe. From the Puritan revolution to the Stuart restoration, the Glorious Revolution, the Irish pacification, and the Act of Settlement, English history paved the way for the entrenchment of the national constitutional state. French despotic absolutism, the revocation of the Edict of Nantes, Gallicanism and mercantilism, the military reforms, and colonial experiments manifested in different forms the new pattern of the national state. French imperialism in the Wars of Revolution and even the War of the Spanish Succession conformed to this pattern. The manifestations of French imperialism, viewed in this over-all context, are thus indeed an intrinsic part of a design extending far beyond traditional Great Power interests. This is as obvious when the new order failed as when it met with success. The France of Colbert and Louvois was as different from that of Richelieu and Mazarin as was the Spain of the eighteenth-century Bourbons from that of the seventeenth-century Habsburgs. The Prussia of the Great Elector and his lesser successor gave not only to the empire but to the Continent as well a new Protestant center. It cut through the feudal system not only in the German North but in wide areas of Central Europe. It initiated the consolidation of a new Germany. In the East we see the great spectacle of the entry into the concert of European Great Powers of a Russia modified by the early reforms of Peter the Great. From the vantage point of contemporary history it was too early to tell where these tremendous events would lead; that they would decisively shape the order of eighteenth-century Europe gradually became clear to keen observers of those days.

The great waves of the future rising in the East and the West were temporarily held in check by the breakwaters extending through eastern Central Europe from Scandinavia to Turkish-dominated Greece. From North to South, Sweden fought its death struggle as a Great Power, and Poland's intermittently successful struggle against Turkey only contributed to her destruction in the Russian holocaust. The Ottoman empire, in its contested western glacis a truly eastern Central European power, fought soulless and pointless wars to maintain and strengthen its undefendable western borders. The fleeting success of its forays into western Hungary and beyond the walls of Vienna could not hide the fact that those efforts were doomed to failure, that the driving power of the Saracene mission and even the grand imperialism of Suleiman the Magnificent were dead, and that further successes would be abortive. Aggression, to be sure, was still rampant, but its motivation was gradually changing from an ideological one to that of preventive warfare against the rallying West.

The geographical and political core of that broad eastern Central European girdle was the Habsburg power. Her position was in some respects not very different from that of Sweden, of Poland, or of Turkey, though often by offensive strategy she fought essentially a defensive struggle for preservation. Yet it was not really a fight for the survival of a system, the death knell of which had sounded at Münster and Osnabrück in 1648;

it was merely an attempt to keep alive the illusion that, at least in a limited sphere, the effects of Renaissance, humanism, Reformation, and the anti-feudal absolutism of the North could be undone.

To be sure, the reign of Leopold initiated the growth of that Habsburg Great Power, an impressive power, quite independent of the imperial position. It was also the reign of Leopold that initiated a stormy development of the Eastern Question, which within a generation, from 1683 to 1718, was to sweep the Turks from the suburbs of Vienna to the central parts of Serbia and Rumania and to destroy forever the Ottoman East-Central European position. Those were certainly events of the first magnitude and of lasting importance. Yet the authoritative historian of that dramatic and proud phase of Austrian history, Oswald Redlich, admits that the great territorial gains, particularly in the West, in Italy and the Spanish Netherlands, were heterogeneous, problematic, and altogether questionable. He rightly considers the notion that the world empire of Charles V had been seemingly revitalized at Rastatt and Baden in 1714 as wishful thinking.[3] This applies not merely to the impending loss of the Kingdom of Naples, the exchange of Sicily for Sardinia, sovereignty over Belgium severely restricted by the Barrier Treaties, and the undoing of the major gains of the eastern treaty of Passarowitz in 1718 barely twenty years later at Belgrad: those were only symptoms of failure, not causes, and by no means ultimate consequences. None the less, the Habsburg empire remained a great power in the West even after the death of Eugene of Savoy, the champion of its external good fortune, and the treaty of Belgrad did not permanently restore the Ottoman position in Europe.

The deciding facts were, however, of a different kind. The Habsburg alliance was deeply involved in the great anti-French alliance culminating in the War of the Spanish Succession. But it was connected only with the external aspects of the struggle, the fight against continental one-power hegemony in Europe, with further endeavors to establish a system of balance of power. It was scarcely concerned at all with the conflicts centering around colonial expansion, new markets, the attempts of either a streamlined absolutism or a semi-constitutional monarchy to test the strength of disparate reforms. The Austrian oriental mission, the notion of the bulwark of Christian civilization checking the Eastern, Moslem onslaught, does not compensate for this failure, nor does it bear even a faint resemblance to early medieval developments. The lifting of the siege of Vienna in 1683 was no true parallel to the battle of Poitiers almost a millennium before, not even to the serious attack on the Habsburg capital in 1529 under Suleiman the Magnificent. The Turkish empire was now on the decline, badly shaken by Janissary revolts, the wars with Venice, with Poland, and since 1677 with Russia. Even for Austria, Montecucculi's victory of St. Gotthard in 1664, leading to Transylvanian autonomy, is historically a more important though less dramatic event than the actions in and after 1683. Western civilization was still greatly harassed but, from a long-range point of view, by no means seriously threatened by the Turks in the war of 1683-99. What Austria had to meet was not a thrust but a counterthrust. That she could meet it successfully means much in terms of the defense and preservation of cultural achievements. In regard to Hungary it has even more significance in terms of alleviation of human sufferings. But in any event, this war did not represent a decision between the rule of the Cross or of the Crescent in eastern Central Europe. The subsequent oriental wars from St. Gotthard to Passarowitz were thinly idealized conflicts of power far more than of ideas. Neither the Habsburg empire nor the Ottoman power represented regimes sufficiently dynamic and strong at that time to enter into sweeping ideological warfare of crusading character.

Yet cognizance of these facts only raises further questions. Why did the Habsburg power, drawn into a great war by virtue of her geographic position, political ambition, and the pressure of external forces, play such an ambivalent role—i.e., why was she in the thick of the fighting and yet at the mere fringe of contemporary ideas? The answer is to be found in the complex crisis of the Baroque era, in the case of Austria a national, religious, social, and cultural crisis.

c. The National Problem

The question whether a national problem existed in the Habsburg lands before the late eighteenth century is extremely complex. Certainly the concept of ethnic nationalism was not consciously formulated at that time; hence, political demands based upon it did not exist. Pan-Germanism, Pan-Slavism, the Southern

Slav problem, and Italian Irredentism were of course ideas alien to the Baroque period. A Rumanian, or in terms of Transylvania a *Vlach,* national entity was only slowly emerging and was not as yet a political factor of significance. The Poles and the bulk of the Ruthenians as well were not yet included in the Habsburg empire. Czech nationalism was, so to speak, "frozen" after the battle at the White Mountain in 1620. Magyar national consciousness certainly was evident, though it was far more political than ethnic in character. However, whether recognized or not, whether conscious of their national character or not, nine of the eleven principal national groups represented in the Habsburg empire after the first partition of Poland were already within Habsburg lands in the period under discussion. The religious problem, to a certain extent the language question, and definitely that of the historico-political entities already existed in the Baroque period. Whether or not these factors are to be called "national problems" is an interesting sociological and psychological question; politically it is a moot one. The Habsburgs had to face the problem of more or less loosely organized groups of people whose interests to a very large extent coincided with those of the ethnic national groups of later days.

The Habsburg power had to face these problems at that time chiefly within the framework of the so-called historico-political entities, the *historisch-politischen Individualitäten.* As the Magyar statesman, Count Szécsen, put it in 1860:

> The historico-political entity of the different lands of the monarchy is exactly the expression and reunion of the whole development and all the activities of the diverse parts of the monarchy in a national historic and political sense; this concept comprises not only a kingdom of Hungary, a Danube, Tisza, Carpathian district, but also, instead of a district Troppau or Salzburg, a land of Salzburg, a land of Silesia; no district of the Moldava or the Adriatic, but a city of Trieste and a kingdom of Bohemia. But in varying degrees the attachment to the historico-political entity exists throughout the whole monarchy.

One of the keenest analysts of the Austrian national problem, Josef Redlich, perceives the functions of these entities thus:

These living historico-political entities were meant to have become the foundations of the Austrian monarchy. It was their task to conciliate the demands of the present time with the just tradition of the past. It was their task to strengthen the modern institutions by attaching them to those historically developed in the various lands. The principles of the system are recognition of the historico-political entity of the various lands, equality between the various lands of the monarchy, their administrative and legislative autonomy to the widest possible extent, full guarantee of the rights and privileges of the crown, respect for the ancient historic institutions.

Indeed, as the great Magyar nineteenth-century reformer Eötvös put it, "Austria owes her existence and her present greatness neither to her national homogeneity nor to her geographic frontiers; she is to be conceived solely as a product of her history."[4]

To be sure, these are nineteenth- and twentieth-century formulations adapted to the situation prevailing in the period in which they were written. Yet these are not nineteenth-century concepts. On the contrary, they were far more vital, far more a living reality in the seventeenth century, the century following the subordination of the lands of the Hungarian and Bohemian crowns and the triune Croatian kingdom to Habsburg rule, than after 1848, when the historico-political programs were gradually forced to yield to ethnic nationalism.

Thus in the reign of Leopold I, outside the hereditary Austrian lands we face the problems of the distinct historico-political units of the only partly freed lands of the Magyar-dominated holy Hungarian crown of St. Stephen, of the lands of the Bohemian crown of St. Wenceslav, of the triune Croatian kingdom, of the autonomy of the Transylvanian principality, and, after 1690, of the chartered rights of the Serbs in the Voiwodina. The strength or weakness, success or failure, of the Habsburg eastern "mission," while necessarily not cognizant of the problems of modern nationalism, can be and must be measured in terms of these historico-political concepts. The problem of the relationship of the Habsburg rule in the Baroque age to these concepts is central and decisive.

10

The Crisis of the Baroque Era

d. The Hungarian Position

As far as conditions in Hungary, unquestionably then the most important of the historico-political units, are concerned, the entire period from the peace of Vásvár in 1664 between the emperor and the Ottoman power to the end of Leopold's reign and well beyond was one of practically uninterrupted revolt against Habsburg rule. The situation was intermittently and sectionally relieved only by the fact that, compared to Turkish domination, Habsburg rule appeared to the Magyar Estates the lesser of two evils. The Habsburg power, in Magyar eyes, stood for Christianity as against Moslemism, but at the same time, and particularly in Transylvania, it also stood for the oppression of the substantial Lutheran, Calvinist, and Unitarian religious groups and their guaranteed rights, whereas the Ottoman Turks—chiefly for reasons of expediency—had been indifferent in those matters. Habsburg rule was considered a constant violation of Hungarian constitutional rights and the still-existing electoral monarchy, whereas the Ottomans, again for obvious political reasons, had offered at times recognition of Magyar-Transylvanian state rights. Habsburg rule was perceived as an intermittent but frequently violent attempt to subject Hungary to the rule of German officialdom and a *soldateska* under the ruthless leadership of Count Caprara, forerunner of the Windischgrätz and Haynau of 1849, whereas the Turkish administration, ruthless and economically destructive as it was in war, had interfered little in times of military truce.

All this did not, of course, obviate the values of Western, Christian civilization for Hungary, even in those trying times. From a long-range point of view, the very fact that Hungary, the foreground of military operations in the struggle between West and East, allied itself with the West in spite of imperial maladministration is of great significance. There is little reason for viewing Hungarian-Habsburg relations in terms of black and white. Politically it may indeed be argued that high treason was committed in negotiations, agreements, and subsidy contracts between Magyar magnates, the Ottoman empire, and the French government. From a legal point of view, however, there is a serious question as to whether—at least in more than two-thirds of seventeenth-century Hungary, the directly Turkish-dominated

11

part and autonomous Transylvania—Habsburg rule had not *de facto* lapsed, and whether the Hungarian Estates were not entitled to be free agents of the destiny of the nation. This, however, is a highly controversial matter, and a case can be made for both sides. Again from a long-range point of view, these claims are indeed more in line with the ideological development of the future than are those of the emperor's Ottoman and French opponents. All this explains and to a certain extent justifies the general objectives of Habsburg Hungarian-Transylvanian-Croatian policy. Yet it does not justify the ways and means employed, the questionable judicial procedure against the controversial rebels, particularly of the military tribunals, the trampling of Hungarian constitutional rights, the clear violations of the guaranteed privileges of the evangelical denominations in Hungary and Transylvania. In particular, the treatment of Transylvania during the first period of the War of the Spanish Succession caused the Protestant allies of the Habsburgs, the English and the Dutch, serious embarrassment—a situation not dissimilar in some ways to the German reaction to Turkish atrocities against the Armenians in the first World War and to Western attitudes toward Russian persecutions of Poles, Ests, and Latvians in the second.

Western historiography is inclined to interpret all this in the light of the unwarranted bickerings of the Magyar aristocracy, gentry, industrialists, and pseudo-intellectuals after 1867. Why should what was largely unjustified then (so runs the implied argument) have had a better case two centuries before? This argument is tenable in one respect only. The classes leading the opposition against Habsburg rule, in the seventeenth as well as in the nineteenth century, were by no means representative of the people as a whole. The Estates of the seventeenth and early eighteenth century up to the peace of Szatmár in 1711 between the emperor and the Magyar insurrection—the formal settlement of the conflict—were in a way even less representative than the pseudo-liberal parliamentarians of the era after 1867. Yet this is only one way to look at the problem. Magyar parliamentarianism of the nineteenth century was a distortion of constitutional government. The rights of Magyar feudal Estates of the seventeenth century represented far more adequately the forces which then, for better or worse (and more for the worse than for the better), formed the political nation. In this matter

Catholics and Protestants alike, however much opposed to each other in many respects, stood united in times of truce against the Austro-German military administration in Hungary in defense of their autonomous institutions. They also stood united, it is true, against administrative reforms and against any revision of the oppressive taxes levied on the common people. Yet at this very point where the imperial administration had a chance to prove the morally superior rights of its cause, it failed lamentably. The octroyed tax decrees of 1699 and 1700, after much stormy bargaining, imposed fifteen-sixteenths of the land tax on the unfree peasants and small, free landowning gentry, one-sixteenth on the landed aristocracy. A basis of agreement between imperial administration and Magyar aristocracy was thus found on at least one important issue. It was and remained the tragedy of the Magyar people that more often than not such agreements were bound up with the morally weakest issues.

All things considered, it would be rash indeed to conclude that the Magyar position was desperate at the time of the end of the second Rákóczi rebellion, the peace of Szatmár, and the acceptance of the Pragmatic Sanction in 1723. The electoral character of the Hungarian monarchy had been lost in 1687, it is true, and with it the more important right of resistance against unconstitutional government. On the other hand, Hungary remained a separate though by no means independent political unit within the Habsburg lands. Enough of Hungarian constitutional rights and traditions, above all the *Comitat* constitutions, were preserved to make a further evolution of the nation possible in matters political, religious, linguistic, and generally cultural. The autonomy of Transylvania, the then relatively most-advanced political unit in the Habsburg lands, continued on the whole unimpaired. The same applied to a lesser degree to Croatian autonomy, though there Magyar suzerainty—as was not the case in Transylvania—was preserved as intermediate agent between local and imperial control. Serb autonomous institutions in Hungary —granted, much to the displeasure of the Magyar Estates, by Emperor Leopold—were set up in the Vojvodina, Syrmia, and various Hungarian municipal communities. Even in the remote corner of imperial-controlled Hungary, in the Slovak districts, the people withstood to a limited degree the equalization efforts of the Counter Reformation. Here in particular growth of national consciousness and preservation of religious liberties, in

13

spite of and perhaps in a sense as a result of the counterre-formatory attack, is certainly worth mentioning.

Altogether, social group development in Hungarian lands was not as much repressed as it may appear if one perceives political life only as continuous series of plots, conspiracies, and revolts on the part of aristocrats like Stephen Bocskay, Sigismund Báthory, Gabriel Bethlen, Emery Thököly, Peter Zrinyi, Francis Frangipani, Francis and Georg Rákóczi, and their like. The gentry, the chartered-town representatives, may have had little influence within the framework of the badly mauled constitution, but their voice within the *Comitat*'s was not negligible. There is above all the armed peasant movement of the Kurucok, which was clearly of a class character. The peasants, the true source of strength behind the great Rákóczi uprising during the War of the Spanish Succession, may have been entirely ignorant of the game of power politics between Habsburg, Bourbons, and sultan, but they were conscious of the cause of a national, independent, "de-feudalized" Hungary. Although they were left in the lurch in the final settlement between magnates and emperor, the effect of their action was strong enough to establish a new and powerful tradition that was to have portentous significance in times to come.

Separatist revolts on the part of Magyar nobles had occurred even before the battle of Mohács in 1526, which brought that part of Hungary for one and a half centuries under Turkish rule. They certainly established a pattern for later risings. Yet the main reason for the violent political and social conflicts after the end of the Turkish occupation was probably the previous tri-partition of Hungarian lands into imperial, Ottoman-dominated, and autonomous Transylvanian territories. It prevented the early, uniform, and unrestricted rule of one power. One or the other force had always been compelled to make concessions to the political nation in their threatened domains.[5]

e. The Lands of the Bohemian Crown

Far less dramatic but far more desperate was the lot of the Czech nation, prostrate since the battle of the White Mounain in 1620. Bohemia, under Ferdinand II, after much suffering was officially reduced to roughly the same status as Hungary in relation to the Habsburg power by the diet of 1689. Yet internally the *vernewerte Landesordnung* of 1627 not only changed the ancient lands of the Bohemian crown to hereditary fiefs of the ruling house; it virtually converted them into mere provinces, and did so with the avowed intent of punishing them for their rebellion. The Bohemian Estates, though not formally abolished, had been reduced to so meaningless an institution that when the nation began to revive in the late eighteenth and nineteenth centuries it was no longer possible to convert them into the conservative pattern of a nineteenth-century revised Bohemian *Staatsrecht*. A live tradition may be revised, as in the case of Irish history, or distorted, as in that of Hungary; but a dead tradition such as that of the ancient Bohemian Estates can never again become the foundation of a nation's political rebirth. Czech revival was to flow through other, more enlightened channels.

It would be shortsighted to look upon the destruction of the Czech political nation in the seventeenth century as simply the product of constitutional oppression which brought about the ruin of the national nobility. Neither does it suffice to point to the ravages of the Thirty Years' War (worse in Bohemia than in almost any other part of Central Europe), to the confiscations of urban property, to the increasing pressure of the agricultural *robota* system, to penalizing taxation, twice as heavy in Bohemia as in German-Austrian lands. Even the relentless drive of the Counter Reformation under Jesuit leadership bent upon the eradication of the Bohemian Reformation provides only a small part of the story. Yet the extirpation of Bohemian liberties and wealth, the harsh treatment of the peasants, cultural reaction symbolized by the conquest first of the University of Prague and later of Olomouc, are in a way merely typical methods employed by a victorious alien regime to suppress a long-standing national revolution.

The crux of Czech-Bohemian misery in the seventeenth century was their subjection not only to an alien regime but to a German minority, for almost two centuries the uncontested "master race" in the conquered lands. Hungary was at times under foreign military occupation and civilian administration. Not only were the Bohemian lands oppressed by the government, but the Czechs themselves were second-class citizens in relation to a German minority. Their inferior position extended from the political into the social-cultural field. The fresh influx of German immigrants having a privileged status after the Thirty Years' War was, it is true, far more conspicuous in urban communities than in the country, yet the new distribution of the great estates among the German aristocracy had an important bearing on the national paralysis in agriculture as well.

Unquestionably there are certain attenuating factors worthy of mention. The new aristocracy—not wholly German, by descent at least—adopted in time an attitude on the whole more pro-dynastic, supranational, than outright Germanic. Religious intolerance and cultural restrictions were not confined to the Czechs; the German population suffered from them as well. In the formative arts, and even in the liberal ones, to take only the example of the seventeenth-century Jesuit historian Bohuslav Balbín, the influence of the new regime was not quite as negative as it appeared. Yet by and large the Germans suffered chiefly from political, and only to a far lesser degree from religious and cultural, suppression; the Czechs suffered intensely from all three. Above all, they were also subject to social and national discrimination. Moreover, while the second half of the eighteenth century at least brought about salutary modifications in all other respects, national suppression, though not actually worse, was far more strongly felt in an era of awakening nationalism. However little one may rate the spirit of national resistance in those otherwise much darker days of seventeenth-century Czech history, it would be more than naïve to assume that these people in a moral, spiritual, political, and economic sense could have been expected to take an active part in the drive of Habsburg Great Power expansion, be it in the East or in the West. The Czech position in the late seventeenth and early eighteenth centuries forms part of the incongruity between material and spiritual forces that is very characteristic of Habsburg expansion of the day.[6]

f. *The Austro-German Position*

In many ways the German-speaking people in the Habsburg realm, who after 1526 were the relatively largest group, had to face the same problems, though to a far lesser extent. But they had to meet others of a different kind as well, and formidable problems they were.

Harsh and unjust taxation was by no means confined to the Hungarian and Bohemian domains. While the taxes levied on hereditary Austrian lands were on the whole lower than those on the others, the distribution within the German lands was just as much in favor of the landed nobles and just as much to the disadvantage of the oppressed peasantry. Inflation, continued debasement of currency, hit both classes. The hardships of the *robota* system were of course felt most severely after the economic crisis of the Thirty Years' War. Peasant riots not only in Hungary and Bohemia but in Moravia, Silesia, and Upper Austria as well are only feeble indications of the true state of affairs, because they were easily and cruelly suppressed. The allegedly protective imperial *robota* legislation, weak in its intentions and entirely inadequate in its application, merely shifted the ordinary *robota* obligations to the field of unrestrained extraordinary ones.[7]

In view of the composition of the Estates in the hereditary lands—of prelates, lords, knights, and princely (not free imperial) towns and markets—an increase of the sovereign's power would hardly have alleviated the lot of the peasant. In principle, the imperial administration of course realized that the selfish policy of the Estates was just as responsible, and perhaps even more so, for the existing economic misery as the government was. The administration failed, however, to act according to that easily gained insight; yet strengthening the Estates system and its eventual expansion, at least to the free peasantry, might have pointed the way to reform. Actually, the significance of the Estates decreased continuously from the time of Ferdinand II to that of Leopold I. It boded ill for the character of Austrian representative institutions that reform ultimately came about not through modernization of the Estates system but through almost complete curtailment of its political freedom of action under Maria Theresa and Joseph II.

Austria, well into the second half of the nineteenth century ruled chiefly from above, was eventually to a certain extent reformed also from the exalted imperial platform. During the reign of Leopold I, however, viewed even from the most conservative standpoint, it was merely ruled, and inefficiently at that.

g. *The Armed Forces*

A further case in point is the military organization. The hereditary lands and Hungary, being directly exposed to Turkish onslaughts, had in a way more to suffer from its deficiencies than Bohemia had. Hungary, however, though in the forefront of Turkish attacks, was to a greater extent protected from the burdens of the imperial recruiting system by virtue of the permanent Ottoman threat. There the strengthening of the sixteenth-century Military Frontier organization at the end of the great Turkish War in 1699 (roughly speaking, along the southern border of the Hungarian lands) played a constructive part. In general, however, this system of semi-military colonies was fully developed only by the early Maria Theresan reforms, at a time when the Turkish danger was clearly on the decline.

At the time of the great French military reforms of Louvois and Vauban, Austria was still far from establishing a standing army. As far as recruiting mercenaries was concerned, authority in military matters was divided between the constantly wrangling forces of emperor and Estates, though in conquered Bohemia the Estates' power had to yield in that respect as well. The appointment of officers below the rank of colonel was still, as in the days of Wallenstein, left to those on whom the emperor conferred a regimental patent, as much or more for reasons of noble birth, connections, and wealth as of military proficiency. Montecuccoli, it is true, initiated certain changes that led to the establishment of a standing army, but it was Eugene of Savoy who actually brought it about, a generation later, on a large scale. Even then, however, the standing army was more or less confined to large-scale military operations, particularly on foreign soil. The defense of the home country was left primarily to the peasants, conscripted by the lords on the basis of agreements with the Estates. They were equipped and supplied in a niggardly fashion and were given no regular training.

Corresponding to the poor and burdensome military organization was the administration in a technical sense, in particular the chain of command. While the supreme authority rested in theory in the emperor, the actually commanding agency was a collegiate body, the Hofkriegsrat, or supreme war council, a cumbrous institution possessing strategic, administrative, and judicial powers. It also conducted diplomatic negotiations with the East, with the Turks and the Russians. There is abundant evidence that this organization, composed of civilian bureaucrats and "court generals," was on the whole slow, timid, inefficient, and unimaginative. As is frequently the case in councils of this kind, it was ruled by intrigue and was extremely jealous of its authority. It was in spite of that organization that Raimund Montecuccoli, Charles of Lorraine, Louis of Baden, Eugene of

Savoy, and Guido Starhemberg and their brave troops managed to win their brilliant victories.[8]

h. Political Administration and Administrators

The setup of the political administration in the Habsburg realms was extremely complex. In view of the dual position of the ruler as sovereign in the Alpine hereditary lands and as emperor of the declining Holy Roman Empire of the German nation, this could hardly have been otherwise. The fact that the lands of the Bohemian and Hungarian crowns were not truly integrated with the hereditary lands of course complicated matters still further. Certain progress had, however, been made in the sixteenth century by the comprehensive administrative reforms of Ferdinand I, the brother of Emperor Charles V.

In outline, this is the situation as it shaped up in the sixteenth and seventeenth centuries. The administration of the hereditary lands was divided between that of the Lower Austrian lands (northern lands) in Vienna and that of the Upper (southern) Austrian lands in the Tyrol in Innsbruck.* In each of these two principal administrative domains, general administrative as well as military affairs were handled by collegial boards consisting partly of nobles and partly of professional lawyers. Financial administration was under the control of separate "chambers." The supreme authority in administrative and judicial affairs was invested in the newly created Hofrat (Aulic Council), which dealt also with imperial agenda. In 1559 this board became the Reichshofrat (imperial council), in which the German princes were represented by the lieutenant of the imperial chancellor. This dignity, by then of little practical significance, was still held by the archbishop of Mayence.

The deputies of the emperor in the individual lands were governors of noble descent, jointly responsible in a rather involved way to sovereign and to Estates. They were entrusted with administrative as well as judicial responsibilities. In both areas they were considerably limited by the patrimonial (feudal) administrative and judicial authority of the nobles within their domains and that of the towns, held on the basis of special privileges granted to them individually. Numerous special courts

---

*This nomenclature must not be confused with that of the crown lands of Lower and Upper Austria, the two northern domains of the Hereditary Lands.

for ecclesiastic and feudal matters existed as well. Ecclesiastics, nobles, court employees, higher government and court officials, university teachers and students, and military personnel were exempt from general jurisdiction and were subject to that of special courts.

In the Bohemian lands the power of the king until 1620 was far more limited than in the hereditary lands. A number of autonomous institutions existed. The reduction of the Bohemian lands to provincial status, legalized by the *vernewerte Landesordnung* of 1627, increased the power of the sovereign enormously but did not actually simplify the channels of administration to any great extent, because the court chancellery for the Bohemian lands and other separate agencies were preserved. Essentially that was even more true of the Hungarian lands. These, apart from a separate court chancellery, had a district (*Comitat*) administration on the local level of more than merely patrimonial status and a court system that was more clearly separated from the administration. There also existed such powerful institutions as that of the Palatine, who possessed vice-regal status, his alternates, and the *Banus,* the head of government in Croatia-Slavonia. There too, though to a far lesser extent than in the Bohemian lands, autonomous institutions were curbed and the royal power strengthened after 1687; but in neither case did that lead to formal elimination of those institutions, but merely to reduction or permanent suspension of their power.

In view of the close connection between the Alpine hereditary lands and the Holy Roman Empire, as well as to the interrelationship between the Habsburg lands themselves, the emergence of joint institutions is of particular importance. As early as 1527 Ferdinand I had created the Privy Council in the name of the emperor Charles V. It consisted originally of three to five of the highest dignitaries and was particularly concerned with foreign affairs, although to a certain extent it dealt with major military and financial questions as well. In practice, this extremely important advisory board co-ordinated common policies of the Habsburg realms with those of the empire, insofar as— and this is an important restriction—those of the empire were under the control of the emperor. Under the following emperors the body was consistently enlarged until, almost by the time of Leopold I, it was comprised of more than sixty members.

Since such a large and unwieldy council could hardly be expected to perform its original functions, the emperor set up the

Privy Conference, which might be considered a "steering committee" of the original body as well as a kind of council of ministers. Other small committees dealing particularly with regional aspects of foreign affairs, relations with the Estates, and *ad hoc* problems such as the Hungarian revolt were likewise set up.

The general court chancellery was another control agency of considerable importance, which in the sixteenth and the early seventeenth centuries dealt with imperial as well as hereditary affairs, but which under Ferdinand II was set up separately for the Austrian hereditary lands. Even afterwards, the agency handled much of the agenda of the dynasty relating to all of the Habsburg lands. Similarly, the Court Chamber dealt not only with financial affairs of the hereditary lands but also with the empire's meager subsidies and general expenditures for central agencies and the armed forces, despite the fact that there existed separate financial chambers as well as the court chancelleries of the Bohemian and Hungarian lands. Finally, there was the previously mentioned Hofkriegsrat, the court war council for all of the Habsburg realms.

Jurisdiction in regard to all these institutions was, though in varying degrees, restricted by the Estates. Those of the Alpine hereditary lands consisted of the four curias of ecclestiastic lords, secular lords, knights (lower nobility), and cities and market towns. The very fact that every one of the hereditary lands had its own diet substantially limited the influence of these representative institutions. The major power of the Estates consisted in the right to approve or disapprove the levying of taxes, though certain sources of income, particularly the so-called regalia (those from mines, mint, and toll) and after the seventeenth century others as well, were under the exclusive control of the sovereign.

Major factors in the marked decline of Estates' power and that of secular nobles and towns was the turning of the tide in the war against the Turks and the triumph of the Counter Reformation in the Alpine lands. Both of these factors made the sovereign less dependent on Estates' power. The Counter Reformation in particular, which had the effect of eliminating for all practical purposes the Protestant Estates' representation, also deprived the adherents of the old faith of much of their bargaining power in relations with the sovereign.

The reduction of the Estates' power is a primary consequence of the Counter Reformation in Inner Austria. In the Bohemian lands it amounted to their destruction. That is not to say, however, that the Estates were formally abolished as an institution. The outer shell of the institution was preserved intact, but it was forcibly converted from a lawmaking to a law-accepting body.

In spite of severe curtailment, particularly in regard to free election of the king and resistance to the arbitrary exercise of royal power in 1687, the Hungarian Estates—and within it not the lords but the gentry—remained the only representative body of any sort in the Habsburg domains that could still claim genuine political significance.

A word must be said about the training and selection of government officials. As yet no civil-service system had been established in the Habsburg lands, but undeniably considerable improvements were made upon the medieval system. The most sensitive positions in the administration were now held by appointment and, for the most part, were no longer based on a feudal relationship between sovereign lords and their retainers. Nobles, in particular the high court aristocracy, were given an inordinate share of the top positions, but there were notable exceptions. Cases in point under Leopold I are the court chancellor Paul Hocher, his right-hand man Christoph von Abele, and Hocher's successor Theodor von Strattmann. Professional legal training, as in the case of Hocher, was beginning to be considered an important qualification.

A scrutiny of administrators' national origin in an age preceding that of conscious nationalism would seem to be of little significance, particularly in view of the fact that the powerful court aristocracy, whether of German, Italian, Spanish, or even Czech and Magyar origin, in contrast to the landed nobility residing on their domains assumed more and more a truly supranational character. They were bound primarily to the Habsburg emperor and sovereign and what he stood for, and no specific historico-political unit had any claims upon them.

On the other hand, the influence of the spiritual advisers of Leopold I, such as his confessors, the Jesuit Paul Müller, the two later bishops, the Capuchin Emeric Sinelli and the Franciscan Christoph de Royas y Spinola, and the powerful preacher Marco D'Aviano, must not be overlooked. This influence is generally conceded to have been great, although not easily definable. As the Venetian Ambassador Michiele put it in a diplomatic report of 1878, "One cannot overstate what power beyond the realm of conscience the fathers exercise at this court. It surpasses by far the influence of the ministers." A well-informed French observer wrote in 1688, "The emperor listens to the whole world and many monks take part in government."[9]

To sum up: Austria in the seventeenth century made slow but undeniable progress in making the transition from political feudalism to a centralized bureaucratic state. On the issue of representative government, the position of the Habsburg lands was somewhere between the strict absolutism of France and English-Dutch constitutionalism, but closer to the second than to the first. Undoubtedly the political trend moved increasingly in the direction of French absolutism. The few civil liberties that existed must be credited to institutions of the only slowly yielding old order: they are not due to the impact of the new ideas of political philosophy in the West and the North. The governmental transition process entirely lacked the efficiency of the French system, though outside the religious sphere there was less encroachment on the rights of individuals. A notable phenomenon of Austrian conservatism is the fact that new institutions continued to operate within the old, at times seemingly meaningless framework. Whatever the faults of governmental inertia were, smooth and speedy accommodation to despotism was not among them.[10]

i. Religious Conflict

Unabated religious conflict is a serious cause of general delay in cultural development. Austrian history in the time of Leopold I is the history of a Counter Reformation artificially prolonged far longer than elsewhere in the West. From a superficial standpoint, this does not appear to be borne out by the facts. During the second half of the emperor's reign, the struggle between Jesuits and Jansenism was still being fiercely waged in France. The revocation of the Edict of Nantes in 1685, which dealt a deathblow to the Huguenots, certainly did not indicate that the spirit of the Wars of Religion had passed. The question of Gallicanism was for the time being settled only in the political sphere by Louis XIV's acceptance of the papal encyclical *Unigenitus* of 1713, two weeks before his death in 1715—a decade after Leopold had died. The English Glorious Revolution of 1689-90 and the preceding reign of James II likewise indicate that the issue of the Catholic Reformation was anything but dead in the West.

Yet there is little real resemblance between these events and the contemporary Austrian Counter Reformation. The question of Jansenism was then considered an ideological issue within the Church. Renewed persecution of the Huguenots and Gallicanism, on the other hand, were primarily political problems, though they had a religious basis. Gallicanism directly involved the fundamental structure of the French absolute, centralized monarchy; Huguenot persecution, far less important in political significance, was simply the final chapter written at the opportune moment with the intention of eliminating separatism within France. Neither of these problems and their controversial settlements had at the time a direct connection with the Protestant Reformation. The same cannot of course be said for the English revolution, centering around the expulsion of the Stuarts and the accession of William and Mary. There the issue of the Catholic Reformation was indeed involved, but involved only as one factor within a politically much farther-reaching conflict. The question of Catholic restoration was a releasing cause of the revolution; its primary and lasting issue was, however, that of semi-absolutist versus constitutional monarchy. The problem of Catholic restoration itself—of the undoing of the English Reformation as such—never actually came to the fore.

The situation in the Habsburg lands was different. There the conflict, as a religious as well as a political issue, went straight back to the Westphalian peace treaty. Furthermore, as a direct consequence of the suppressed Magyar rebellion of the 1660's, discrimination against Hungarian Protestants, foremost among them Magyar and Slovak Lutherans rather than the more deeply entrenched Calvinists, changed into outright persecution. Lutheranism was considered treasonable. The only salvation from confiscation of property and even imprisonment or capital punishment for the "heretic" ministers was abandonment of ministerial functions altogether. While those actions did not violate the letter of the Westphalian peace treaty of 1648, since it did not apply to the Hungarian lands, they undoubtedly ran counter to its spirit, and they certainly conflicted with the provisions of the controversial treaty of Vienna of 1606 between the emperor, Prince Stephen Bocskay of Transylvania, and the

24

Magyar Estates. Not only were these measures unjust and cruel; they were ineffective as well. In 1681 the status of 1670, with express reference to previous concessions to the Protestants of 1606, had to be restored. Yet this again was only the prelude to and partly the price paid for establishment of the hereditary Habsburg succession in Hungary in 1687, with its severe curtailment of ancient constitutional rights.

In comparison with the far more serious character of the Bohemian revolt from 1609 to 1620 and its long and stormy background, the policies of the triumphant Counter Reformation were even more stringent. Protestantism in Bohemian lands, no longer protected by the provisions of the religious peace of Augsburg and the Letter of Majesty of Emperor Rudolf II, was not curbed but completely crushed.

In the hereditary lands there were obviously conflicting policies at work. While the nursing of the weak plant of Austrian mercantilism led to the toleration of a limited immigration of foreign Protestant skilled workers, merchants, and professional men, measures restrictive of their activities were not lacking. At the same time the government did not exercise its influence to prevent wholesale evictions of Protestant communities from Salzburg and Tyrol by order of the archbishop of Salzburg— a prince of the empire, to be sure, but hardly one of far-reaching independent power. Similar contradictions can be seen between mercantilist tendencies and the wholesale, brutal expulsion of the Viennese Jews—the majority of them traders and merchants. At the close of Leopold's reign his former conversion policy in Hungary also collided strangely with the religious and political autonomy granted to the orthodox Serbs in southern Hungary and the Rumanian Vlachs in Transylvania. Here well known considerations of expediency, namely that of the support of non-Magyar nationalities against the rebellious master nation, probably played a decisive part.[11]

Yet all things considered, it would be erroneous to assume that the religious policy in the Habsburg lands was on the whole more intolerant than that in other Catholic countries, even though by the end of the seventeenth century the harsh *cuius regio eius religio* principle of the religious peace of Augsburg and the Westphalian peace treaty were no longer enforced in German lands outside the Austrian domains. Neither can it be maintained that government measures regarding religious questions were completely controlled by the Church. There is abundant evidence that the imperial power at certain points rather severely restricted the freedom of action of ecclesiastical orders in such matters as raising religious funds and shipment of bullion out of the country to Rome. Even the promulgation of papal encyclicals and bulls was controlled by the government. On the other hand, on such major issues as the pacification of Hungary, economic measures, taxation, and migration, the government's church policy collided so often with its own interests and even avowed declaration of intent that one cannot help wondering whether the Habsburg power had even the faintest homogeneous religious policy. This indeed is the salient point. Whereas religious policy in the West—irrespective of its merits —formed an integral but on the whole fairly well controlled part of governmental philosophy and long-range objectives, the Habsburg power in practice was entirely undecided on the medieval issue of Church-State relations and on the evaluation of the Counter Reformation as an instrument either of church policy, of government policy, or of both. Ultimately this ambivalence could strengthen neither force. Here as in other fields (again irrespective of merits) the Habsburg power conveyed the impression of uncertainty and weakness. This aroused the opposition of its subject nationalities and the suspicion of its allies, and it was a source of delight to its enemies.

j. *Public Finance*

German historians frequently regard the self-willed isolation of the Habsburg lands from western and northern Protestant influence as one, if not the chief, reason for their relative backwardness at that time. This, however, is too broad an assumption. For one thing, the opening of a large part of the non-Habsburg Germanies to French Huguenots in particular and the relatively liberal Catholic policies of Prussia made themselves distinctly felt only during and after the reign of Frederick William I (1713-40). In the cultural sphere they became conspicuous only under Frederick II. Secondly, the suggestion that Austria, compared to late seventeenth-century Prussia and Saxony, could be considered backward at all is very much open to doubt, unless judged by the standards of despotic absolutism. Finally— and this is the decisive issue—it is rather questionable whether the problem of mercantilist policies or non-mercantilist policies is as important a factor in the development of the Habsburg lands as it is frequently asserted to be.

In fact, outside the important sector of the rural-agricultural order, the Austrian lands were not simply under a feudal economy when mercantilist policies were initiated under Leopold I. In the urban sphere the trends leading away from feudalism were inevitable, in any event, and were far less affected by mercantilism than is commonly assumed.

The basis of the Austrian fiscal system was the land tax, which, whether levied on the Estates or on individual nobles, was indirectly paid by the peasants. Income from the royal domains originated from exactly the same sources. Conflict between Estates and sovereign, and above all continuous military expenditures and the devastations of war, however, made these contributions less and less effective. They had thus to be increasingly supplemented by the regalia (the income from the mines, mints, customs, and tolls), special taxes levied on the Jews, etc. There were town and administrative taxes outside the feudal economic order. To this group belong the excise taxes on drinks, meat, and industrial products such as lime, brick, leather, mill wheels, the new tobacco monopoly, and the luxury taxes on wigs, lace, imported cloth, etc. All these taxes go back well into the sixteenth century.

A specific "contribution" of the seventeenth is the continuous devaluation of the currency through the debasement of coins and the mortgaging and pawning of government land and movable property. Here, in an entirely different way from that envisaged in mercantilist theories, the old order was changed. Monopolies were either sold or mortgaged to traders and great nobles or, rather, to great nobles trading by proxy. They gradually took over the lumber and iron trade and production; the first tobacco and coffee monopolies were leased to them; these *privilegia privativa* applied in parts of the Habsburg lands even to the supply of basic foodstuffs. The lucky recipients of those privileges controlled prices; they controlled the tariffs and the tolls pawned to them. Among these speculators we find in practice the shift from a semi-feudal to a badly distorted capitalist system, while the arduous and ingenious work of the Austrian mercantilists still remained largely in the realm of theory.[12]

A Study in Austrian Intellectual History

k. Austrian Mercantilism

Austro-mercantilism must not be underrated, none the less. In many ways it established the pattern for further Austrian development—a pattern, however, that matured only in the second half of the eighteenth century, when mercantilism in the West was already very much qualified by physiocratic theories. Evaluations of the contribution made by Austrian mercantilists will differ widely according to whether they are judged by their excellent thinking or by their limited accomplishments in the practical field—limited, to be sure, through no fault of their own.

Their intellectual leader was not, as has often been claimed, Philip Wilhelm von Hörnigk, author of the popular *Österreich über alles, wenn es nur will*, of 1684, but his brother-in-law, Johann Joachim Becher, a converted Protestant from the Rhineland, and probably in later years a reconverted Catholic. Becher was a real economist, not merely an ingenious dabbler in economic affairs, like many of his contemporaries. As one of the earliest promotors of populationist theories, he considered that the real wealth in society lay in population increase, a doctrine applied more widely almost a century later by Sonnenfels. He saw two basic classes in society: the non-producing class made up of civil servants, professional men, and army men; and the producing class of peasants, artisans, and merchants. Like most populationists, he considered the peasant class as the producer par excellence, after him the craftsman, and only last the merchant. All classes are linked together by the necessity of consumption. "Consumption is the soul of the three Estates, the only key which ties them to each other; consumption makes the merchant class vital in the community, the greatness of the peasant class notwithstanding."[13] Becher, still in a way an orthodox mercantilist bullionist, nevertheless perceives money as a commodity like any other. According to him and his Western predecessors, its value is not properly made use of by hoarding, but only by circulation. He persistently stresses the point that population increase is more important than storage of bullion. He still fights the import of foreign merchandise—rather indiscriminately. He also takes a strong stand against private business monopolies and the unequal distribution of wealth to the advantage of the privileged few and to the disadvantage of a potentially strong middle class. In many ways his practical proposals are unquestionably contradictory. He favors less restrictive trade practices—a demand difficult to correlate with his mercantilist premises and his aversion to international trade, which allegedly destroys domestic competition. His denunciation of the retail peddling trade, particularly directed against Jewish merchants, is probably inspired by emotion and prejudice rather than by reason. On the other hand, his campaign against guild restrictions is based on actual experience. Also, in his promotion of wholesale-trade stock companies he draws to a certain extent on the example of the British and, above all, the Dutch. His plans for governmental storage of agricultural products and for their limited price control—or, rather, price guarantee—are quite original. On the other hand, his conception of the public workhouse as an institution providing useful labor for the needy hardly differs from the one-century-older Elizabethan poorhouse legislation. Nevertheless, there is a definite social trend in Becher's thinking. He argues against oppressive taxes and heavy tolls, out of a sincere concern for the popular welfare. Economic policy and reform should be taken over by a collegial board in which should be represented not only government officials with legal training but also merchants, manufacturers, and, on behalf of the peasants, cameralists as well.*

Hörnigk, also Protestant, from a Rhenish converted Catholic family, in his *Österreich über alles, wenn es nur will,* and other writings is a stricter mercantilist and a less original thinker than Becher. His writings are largely inspired by the desire to promote a war economy in preparation for the decisive contest with France. He is not an extreme bullionist, however, because bullion guarantees wealth but not economic independence. And this economic independence of a truly isolationist brand is Hörnigk's primary aim. He therefore develops a nine-point program which Austria, favored by natural resources and, according to Hörnigk, highly developed consumer demands, might well carry through. The program, anti-French in its political objectives, faithfully copies French reforms. It attempts to encourage the production of industrial goods in the country, to train people in useful trades, to ban as far as possible the export of bullion and the import of goods, above all of finished products. Essential imports should be paid for in goods, not coin, and none that can be

*"Cameralists" in the seventeenth and eighteenth centuries are students of the more practical aspects of economics and political science.

produced at home should be permitted to enter the country. Exports should be furthered at all costs. This is indeed the most orthodox mercantilist program, from which Hörnigk, probably under the influence of Becher, deviates only in regard to bullionism.

Third in importance among the Austrian cameralists (all Austrians not by birth but by choice) is the Saxon Wilhelm von Schröder. More like Hörnigk and unlike Becher, he is primarily interested in the absolute power of the state, irrespective of considerations of social welfare. The prosperity of the subject is to Schröder the premise of a well-working tax system. Its justification and end is the welfare of the princes. Without a higher standard of living of the many, higher income for the few is not possible. His idol is Louis XIV; his *bête noire* is Cromwell. He advocates the import of precious metals by virtue of foreign trade, but within the country money should circulate as freely as possible. Extravagance on the part of the sovereign is wholesome so long as the money stays within the country and is promptly circulated. As to the amelioration of agriculture, he proposes the import of cheap labor, such as Negro and Ottoman slaves. Far more important, however, is the promotion of manufacturing. Like Becher and Hörnigk, Schröder is a severe critic of the guild system. In his restrictions on the embargo of bullion, he is more subtle than Hörnigk. He is primarily an expert on banking and envisages a rather original scheme of export trade financed by a public bank. Klenck, a disciple of Schröder, improves in some ways on these techniques of semi-public financing of export trade, whereas other mercantilists like Paul Johann Marperger from Nürnberg and Johann Georg Leeb are on the whole merely popularizers of Becher's and Hörnigk's ideas, though as such they are certainly not without merit.[14]

Unquestionably the ideas of these men are often constructive, their elaboration of the schemes of others skillful and certainly well intentioned. Their prejudices may easily be excused by the narrow ideological climate within which they worked, their intellectual mistakes by the French and Dutch pattern that influenced them. One might, of course, argue that economic reforms feasible in a fairly well-centralized country like France could not be easily imitated in the more backward and far more heterogeneous Austrian lands. On the other hand, Austria's failure to realize the bulk of the reform projects under Leopold saved the Habsburg lands from many of the mistakes of French policy. When ultimately introduced on a larger scale under Maria Theresa and Joseph II, the new economic ideas were already reasonably modified by physiocratic ideas.

The point is, however, that in general these men failed to achieve their purpose not because their policies under given conditions turned out to be wrong but because they had no chance to test them on a large scale. The practical influence of the new economy on Austria under Leopold has been greatly exaggerated, as can be seen from a brief survey of contemporary Austrian industrial accomplishments.

l. *Industrial Policies and Accomplishments*

It is very much to the credit of the Austrian administration that those learned Germans, frequently in spite of their Protestant background, as in the case of Becher and Schröder, were called to Austria at all, and that they were given positions on the board of commerce and as directing agents of new commercial enterprises. Almost every one of them, however, ran into difficulties with the conservative Austrian administration, and none of them stayed permanently with the administration in Vienna.[15] None of them was entrusted with a governmental position high enough to empower him to institute general reforms. All of them worked only on specific projects of limited significance and even more limited duration.

Becher, for instance, is to be credited with the establishment of the silk industry in Austria. The single enterprise established by him proved, however, to be unprofitable and was soon abandoned, and for this he himself may have been partly to blame. Much more important was his establishment of a *Kunst- und Werkhaus* in Vienna in 1676. This institution was to include a chemical laboratory, largely for the purpose of conducting alchemistic experiments in which Becher, who was an adventurous spirit, put great faith. There were also plans for the production of high-quality china and furniture, somewhat questionable drugs, and Venetian glassware and for a metal foundry. Native workers were to be trained in these new industries and tenements were to be provided for them. Objections to these allegedly too-sweeping plans on the part of the administration, coupled with pressure for immediate profits on the one hand and unwillingness to grant necessary funds on the other, embittered Becher and within a year he gave up and left Austria for good. With him the country lost the services of one of the most ingenious spirits of the time. A typical Baroque man full of contradictions, he believed simultaneously in such medieval superstitions as the philosopher's stone and the strangest kind of alchemistic processes of production and in long-range economic planning. He developed training and production methods, price control for the export trade, new commerce relations with the Levant, and blueprints for a public banking system. With all his faults, his departure would have been a real loss for Austria—if his retention in government service could really have secured the success of his projects. That, however, was not the case. It was not Becher's shortcomings but the unwillingness, the timidity, and the sterility of the government that were chiefly responsible for the failure of his projects.

This is proved by the fact that his far more stable successor, Schröder, was no more successful. Under him the production of the *Werkhaus* actually got under way, but when it was destroyed during the Turkish siege in 1683 all plans for continuation of the promising experiments were dropped. Others of Schröder's schemes concerning the registration and training of skilled labor, as well as an impressive project of trade statistics, were likewise never given a fair try. He ended his career in an insignificant government position in the Hungarian Zips district. Hörnigk fared hardly better than Schröder. Scarcely any of the reform proposals of his famous *Österreich über alles, wenn es nur will,* were put into practice.

Undoubtedly the development of the Bohemian glass industry and Bohemian and German-Austrian textile factories were to some extent furthered by the invigorating influence of these men. But again, they were hampered by the discriminatory administration in Bohemia and Austrian anti-Protestant political practice. How could the influx of skilled craftsmen from the Protestant North and West be successfully promoted if discrimination and, in some instances, even religious persecution continued at the same time? How could the new national Giro Bank of 1703, soon to be converted into a more modest Viennese *Stadtbank,* succeed when the government had destroyed its credit by failing, either by intention or out of carelessness, in its obligation? When the chief creditor of the government, the Jewish banker and "court factor" Samuel Oppenheimer, the controversial chief financier of the Austrian war economy, was driven into bankruptcy, public opinion could again be easily swayed against the Jews, but new capital could not be raised by this cheap and even then well-worn scapegoat device. Thus the *Stadtbank* was as stillborn as the Giro Bank and folded within a generation. However, long before the government's financial experiments were begun, and soon after the failure of Becher's and Schröder's manufacturing experiments, Hörnigk had left the Austrian service to find a less frustrating career as economic adviser to the mighty prince bishop of Passau.[16]

Ultimately the failure of the mercantilist reforms on a large scale was not, as pointed out before, as detrimental to Austrian economy as it seemed. Neither can the whole responsibility for failure be laid at the door of the government. The almost incessant wars, particularly the long-drawn-out struggle for the Spanish succession, also played a very important part. The fact, however, remains that Austrian economic development under Leopold I did not, on the whole, proceed according to the plans so liberally furnished by reformers. It developed rather more or less naturally according to the greater demands of a society influenced by the rising industrial standards of the West. This process was already well under way before the reformers started their laudable work, and they could do virtually nothing to change or to accelerate it. The semi-feudal order in the urban atmosphere was on its way out, in any case. But since economic change in Austria was not accompanied by any kind of systematic planning, it did not, as in the case of the West, entail an immediate social change. For more than a generation to come, the development of capitalism, industrialization, and the rise of consumer demands did not influence to any appreciable degree the character of the existing social structure. On the whole, the government of Leopold I met new conditions with old means. This, and not the conflict between feudalism and new doctrines, is the dilemma of the Austrian high Baroque in the economic sphere. It is not primarily a question of conflict between a declining feudal and an already powerful commercial class, as it was in England. There was no major collision, such as took place in Holland, between patricians and petty bourgeoisie. Nor was there a bitter contest, like that which occurred in France, between state and waning territorial power, between state capitalism, feudal separatism, and medieval guild interests.

A Study in Austrian Intellectual History

The crisis in Austria was of still a different nature. As yet it was connected with the rise neither of a new class nor of a new social system: it was a conflict strictly within the existing social order. The feudal class of old intended to take over the functions of a gradually evolving industrial and commercial society, yet it had no intention of changing its pattern of life, or of making the necessary reforms in the Estates and the guild system. The Austrian Baroque system, with the exception of attempts at mercantilist reform and unsuccessful ventures in state-controlled foreign-trade companies, did not ride the waves of new social conditions; it was swept along by them. It faced problems similar to those of the West, but it was slower to do so. This system too was moving in the direction of an increasingly centralized state, but more timidly. Unable to reform its social structure, it merely applied the old means to the new ends.

m. Education

All of these facts have a bearing on cultural development. But before this aspect of Austrian Baroque civilization can be discussed, it is necessary to ask the question: Culture for whom?

Any discussion of this issue must avoid the obvious pitfall of focusing too much attention on the evolution of the formative arts, frequently referred to as "the glory of the Austrian Baroque." For very simple material reasons, broad strata of the population are excluded *a limine* from participation in the achievements of the new era. Thus the student of the problem is on solid ground if he tackles first the more complex problem of the evolution of the humanities and science, in which this exclusion does not pertain to so great an extent.

Culture for whom? Certainly not for the peasant, and beyond and above the most elementary training in the three R's and in trade, it was only for a selected few in the urban middle class. It was accessible to a relatively larger segment of the clergy and to those members of the higher nobility who wished to avail themselves of cultural opportunities, though they were by no means forced to do so for economic or political reasons. This, however, except for the simple issue of the desolate peasant, does not clarify the problem. The basis of selection for higher advancement in the liberal arts and the learned professions is not primarily social stratification but subordination to the dominant

34

ideology in education—in Austrian late-seventeenth-century terms, primarily Jesuit education. Only the man who went through this kind of schooling possessed an admission ticket to the further pursuit of intellectual interests. The prerequisite for admission to this schooling, however, was not so much upbringing and status in society as submission to and faith in the Order itself.

One of the most positive achievements of the Protestant Reformation in the Habsburg realms, particularly in Bohemia, in Moravia, in the hereditary lands, and to some extent in Hungary was the advancement of education. Again, this did not apply in any appreciable degree to the village school and its peasant children, or to the universities, which at the time of the late Renaissance had blossomed, but were, in the last decades before the Thirty Years' War, already in a state of stagnation if not decline.[17] Later sixteenth-century progress, however, was remarkable in what today would be called secondary education, and what also was to be considered preparatory training for higher learning. It was the time of the secular schools sponsored by the Estates, with still an inordinate stress on Latin and little, if any, attention given to history, geography, mathematics, and science. On the other hand, in some of these schools the vernacular was taught rather thoroughly according to then existing standards. Any graduate from such a school could be considered at least well grounded in reading, writing, and simple arithmetic.

As much as these rather dreary schools left to be desired, they gradually improved toward a broader, more modern curriculum. Yet even at their worst they all had one positive asset: this instruction definitely stressed development of skills, and though the transmitted knowledge was on the whole rather elementary, instruction was at least not concerned with ideological indoctrination. Neither was it focused on intellectual uniformity.

All this changed radically when, with the success of the Counter Reformation in Habsburg lands, the religious schools, those run by the Jesuits foremost among them, superseded the earlier system almost completely. Before the reign of Ferdinand II these Jesuit institutions were one of several types of schools; now they were *the* schools of higher learning. The Jesuits now controlled university education almost entirely.

As far as the actual transmission of knowledge went, the Jesuit schools were certainly not inferior to the secular ones. They taught the classic languages as the secular institutions had done, though with much greater restrictions on the interpretation of ancient literature. Like the secular schools, they paid little attention to history, except for that of the biblical age. In mathematics, science, and the vernacular language they were in practice neither better nor worse than the secular schools, though on principle they were more strongly opposed to teaching the vernacular than the Estates schools had been. Yet in their stress on dialectics, in their whole interpretation of knowledge, they subordinated the objectives of education strictly to their militant religious philosophy. No student was to leave these schools merely as the recipient of useful knowledge and training for better citizenship; he was to become first and foremost an obedient adherent or, even better, an active and militant champion of the philosophy of the Order in its attitude toward the Church and its interpretation of the objectives of Catholic restoration.

It would be wrong to assume, however, that graduates of monastic preparatory schools in general, and of the Jesuit schools in particular, were uniformly crusaders, ascetics, and zealots. It would also be wrong to conclude that the monastic school was concerned primarily with the furthering of the careers of the socially select few. In some ways almost the contrary is true. Monastic, particularly Jesuit, education was on the whole less puritan, more favorably disposed toward the formative arts, dramatic literature, and music than the Protestant schools were. It would be too much to say that these institutions did away with class privilege in higher education; but they at least began to change it, and certainly they were not more backward in this respect than the Estates schools. Monastic education did not and could not change the social composition of the rising Austrian high bureaucracy. Yet it should be readily admitted that—apart from the professional men called from abroad, who stood outside the rigid administrative hierarchy in Austria—the cleric, the artist, and in some respects the scholar of low birth each had his chance within the monastic educational system.

But he had this chance only if, when, and as soon as he was indoctrinated with the spirit of the established religious and social philosophy. Accordingly, Austrian intellectual culture at the time can never be measured in terms of the tremendous philosophical and scientific evolution in the West. The basic ideas of Descartes, Spinoza, Hobbes, Locke, Newton, Bossuet, Pascal, Leibniz, Bodin, Althusius, and Pufendorf simply did not exist in Austria—not for the intellectual elite, let alone for the body of those interested in or drafted for higher learning. Only within this limited framework is it possible to perceive intellectual achievements in late-seventeenth-century Austria.

n. *Literature*

Despite the limitations, those achievements are quite respectable. The late seventeenth century is not generally considered an outstanding period in German literature. Its lyric poetry does not compare well with the religious poetry of the first half of the century, as represented by the Protestant poets Simon Dach, Paul Fleming, and Paul Gerhard and the Catholics Friedrich von Spee and Angelus Silesius in the North. The secular Baroque lyric poetry of the era between early-seventeenth-century Martin Opitz and early-eighteenth-century Johann Christian Günther is not particularly distinguished. The Baroque drama of the North, the drama of Gryphius and Weise, is rightly forgotten today. The same can be said of the sensual school of Silesian novelists Hofmannswaldau, Lohenstein, and others of their kind. The one truly great German novelist, Grimmelshausen, the reporter of the horrors of the Thirty Years' War, had died in 1676. In view of the in many ways less stringent cultural separatism of the German North and West, it would be almost absurd to expect a more fertile development in German Austria. The exception is Abraham a Sancta Clara, but he was able to make an outstanding contribution only because the true source of his strength and appeal lay not primarily in his unquestionable literary abilities but in his ecclesiastical status and his philosophy.

The same holds true for most other major German-Austrian literary achievements of the period. They are to be rated and respected as professional contributions to the advancement of applied arts and sciences; in general they cannot claim to possess any philosophical and aesthetic distinction. Particularly noteworthy is the fact that this period abounds in the production of studies on institutions and geographical and socio-economic conditions of the various Habsburg lands. Valvasor's and Francisci's studies on Carniola, in their way works of unprecedented thoroughness, deserve very honorable mention in this connection. Brandis' more modest study on the Tyrol and similar treatises on Styria, Lower Austria, and Pessina's survey of the war devastations in Moravia belong in the same category. So to a certain extent does Count Revay's work on Hungary, which already claims Magyar supremacy over a multinational empire of ten national groups.[18]

While none of these and similar works can match the high standards of Valvasor's thoroughness and visual clarity, they all attempt honestly to furnish information; and in view of the manifest restrictions of time and place, the non-analytical, purely descriptive character of these writings cannot be held against their authors. This applies also to strictly historical literature, though here these limitations naturally impair the character of Austrian historiography in a more serious way. Nevertheless, in some instances the interpretation is not entirely cut-and-dried. The histories of the reign of Leopold I by the Italians Priorato and Comazzi extol the supranational, anti-Mohammedan, Christian mission of the Habsburg power with the specific intention of defending it against anti-Habsburg currents in the Holy Roman Empire. On the other hand, some Austro-German historians like Burkhard, Rink, Mencke, Franz Wagner, and above all Hans Jakob Wagner von Wagenfels in his *Ehrenruff Deutschlands* look upon the rising Habsburg power, particularly in regard to its oriental policy, as the standard-bearer of the Holy Roman Empire's imperial mission. Nicolaus Isthuanffi's rather well written history of Hungary from the death of Matthias Corvinus to the coronation of the Emperor Matthias, as seen from the standpoint of Magyar Catholicism, belongs in this class. So do the writings of Johann Constantin Feigin on the Turkish wars, which glorify the Austrian imperial mission. These and similar works are rather poorly balanced and simple in their argument, yet they do not lack a central idea. The same cannot be said for the numerous popular historical calendars, but even their informative value is considerable. This holds true to an even greater degree of the new projects of collecting sources of Austrian history by Paul Lambeck, Raimund Duellius, and Philibert Hueber.[19]

The work of none of these writers can compare in historical significance with the earlier contributions of the Humanist historians, Celtes, Cuspinian, and others of their school at the court of Maximilian I. Yet consciousness not so much of Austria as such—though we find that name referred to increasingly—but of the rising Habsburg power and its political and ideological ties is substantially strengthened through these activities.

The Crisis of the Baroque Era

Now the concept of the Holy Roman Empire of the German nation merges gradually with that of the rising Habsburg Austrian Great Power. It is easy to see that the means to that ideological union lie in the widely proclaimed Christian mission of the liberation of eastern Central Europe from the Mohammedans. The idea, declining in force but by no means dead, is the medieval imperial-crusade scheme, sponsored by the Pope and led by the emperor. The means employed for partly rationalized imperialist, partly sincere missionary, aims are primarily those of the lands of the House of Austria. The future design—not of a rejuvenated empire but of a newborn imperial Austria—derives largely from this synthesis. It is already traceable in the historical literature of the period.

The outstanding literary work of the period is, however, far removed from history and politics, though still in a way within the realm of the social sciences. It is Wolf Helmhard von Hohberg's *Georgica curiosa*, or *Adeliges Landleben*, of 1691, the rich picture of the life of the lesser nobility on their estates. It deals with domestic economy, family life, and agriculture in the widest sense, as well as industry in the era of the beginning entrepreneur system. But Hohberg's encyclopedic work is of even farther-reaching significance. It presents a survey of social relations from the point of view of a Protestant member of the rural lower nobility, but the author definitely transcends the boundaries of the feudal system. Within its limits—limits not of literary ability but of social perspective—it is a unique historical contribution to the understanding of the early transition period from the noble's world to one socially, though not yet politically, increasingly penetrated by the burgher and the bureaucrat.[20]

Thus the relative richness and the respectable standards of Austrian historical, socio-geographic, and descriptive economic literature balances to some extent the lack of significant contributions to belles-lettres. They cannot make up, however, for almost complete stagnation in the natural sciences. This serious deficiency can be explained only partly by the obvious restrictions imposed by political conditions. After all, some generations before, Tycho de Brahe and Kepler had greatly extended the realm of human cognition under conditions in many ways even less favorable. Obviously it will never be possible to link the existence or absence of true genius in a fully satisfactory way to social and political conditions. This much can be said with some assurance: the late-seventeenth-century failure in Austrian scientific development is probably due to a large extent not so much to specific restrictions as to the longstanding isolation from the great philosophical revolution in the West, which, with the partial exception of Leibniz, could not penetrate the barriers of the Habsburg realms. Thus is confirmed again the fact that progress in the natural sciences is far more conspicuously connected with new ideas in philosophy, and thus in a wider sense with international cultural relationships in general, than any achievements in the social field.

o. Music

This sort of interrelationship was wholesomely unrestricted in music and in the formative arts, though here native genius played at least as important a part as foreign influence.

In a way, music in later Baroque Austria is very intimately connected with architecture, painting, and sculpture. Its development at that time received a powerful stimulus from the same source: the visual, more correctly perhaps the visual-emotional, factor so characteristic of the Baroque period. Just as in literature it was drama, in particular the Jesuit plays, that attracted public interest, so in music it was opera and ballet in the Italian style. Perhaps at no other time has there been so much agreement between the taste of court and society and that of the general public. Operas such as *Pomo d'Oro,* composed for the wedding of the emperor, were performed three times weekly for a full year without admission charges. The stage management of the theatrical architect the famous Burnacini was considered sensational. Not only grand opera and ballet, of which several hundred were performed in Vienna in the high Baroque era, but oratorios and serenades and even respectable treatises on musical theory, such as the one by J. J. Fux, were produced as well.[21]

As is well known, Leopold I, a true connoisseur of music and a composer of no mean ability, took a distinguished part in this development. Indeed without him, or without his son Charles VI, the two most musical rulers of a house generally renowned for its musical interests, the Baroque musical culture in the Habsburg lands would not have been what it was. Yet it is precisely this factor that also limited music as a cultural factor in the Austria of that time.

The Crisis of the Baroque Era

Neither opera, ballet, nor the great Italian oratorios could have been produced and promoted by anybody who lacked the space and the wealth that was at the disposal of the imperial court, the estates of the greatest nobles, and the proudest and wealthiest monasteries. This fact by no means detracts from the value of the activities of these small circles, but it restricted considerably the range of cultural penetration of Baroque music. Its influence on the development of music of wider popular appeal, while not negligible, is limited. On the other hand, seen in wider perspective, the musical interests of the top class of society could not fail to influence the entire development of classical music in Austria and beyond as far as Haydn, Mozart, and Beethoven. Yet the uncontestable fact that the interests and achievements of the past, developing within narrow but not isolated strata of society, had their effect on the future is not to say that they determined the course of the future. The tremendous developments that took place in music in the late Baroque and the Rococo, under Classicism and Romanticism, would have been inconceivable without a broadening of the basis of active musical interests. Such a broadening was again unthinkable without profound changes in the intellectual and social climate brought about by the Enlightenment and, in the case of Austria, by industrial evolution rather than revolution.

Did the earlier Baroque music in the Habsburg lands herald an unhealthy development? Yes and no. The social factor involved in the evolution of music of a less pompous, decorous, and extravagant character was the widening as well as the deepening of interests in the body politic. And here the strong escapist element in the appeal of courtly Baroque music must not be overlooked. It offered impressive *circenses* for the eye as well as for the ear, and the standards were respectable. With some highly important exceptions, however, Austrian Baroque music did not as yet open the road to new ideological developments. It did not, on the whole, inspire and foster new lines of thought and deeper vistas of feeling and vision. In fact, this kind of music helped to stabilize existing conditions—as seen through rosy spectacles. Even this controversial effect is no mean achievement, but it was not—not yet—that produced by truly great art.

p. Formative Arts

The qualifications pertinent to Baroque music apply in a sense also to the even more spectacular achievements of the formative arts during that era. Architecture, equally outstanding in its monumental character, sense of color, originality of composition, and graciousness, is of a very high order. Sculpture and painting and many aspects of interior decoration and formal landscaping, while aesthetically pleasing and attractive, do not quite come up to this extremely high standard. Yet this is not a specific feature of the Austrian Baroque but of Baroque in general. Even here the wonderful harmony that links these more modest achievements of Baroque art with its sterling architectural accomplishment is worthy of admiration. The whole rich period of creative artistic development had not quite reached its peak in Leopold's reign; this was not attained until the two decades after his death. Yet in history as in nature, the very brief period preceding full bloom, the period of high and well justified anticipation, is the most attractive.

This applies to that period of the late seventeenth century between early and high Baroque. It applies to the work of the great Italian architects in Bohemia and Moravia, the churches and palaces built by Orsini, Loragho, and Da Porta in Prague. It applies equally to the palaces of Dal Pozzo, Martinelli, and Carlone in Vienna, to Solari's cathedrals in Salzburg and St. Pölten, and to Sciassa's monasteries and churches in Styria and Upper Austria. But it was above all the time of the great Austro-German builders, the time of Prandauer's magnificent monastery castles in St. Florian, Melk, and Herzogenburg, the era of the earlier works of the older Fischer von Erlach and the young Lukas von Hildebrandt in German Austria and of Diezenhofer in Bohemia. The fresco-painters Gran, Schmidt from Krems, Rottmayr, and the older Altomonte are associated with the interior decoration of an impressive series of churches, monasteries, and palaces. While in their achievements they are not quite the equals of the great architects, they share their exquisite taste and noble sense of perspective. The work of the greatest Baroque sculptor in Austria, and one of the very greatest of the Baroque period generally, Rafael Donner (1692-1741), lies just outside Leopold's era. Also the sculptural work of Mattielli, Steinl, Paul Strudel, and Caspar is much more than mere decorative art.

Leopoldus I. Romanorum Imperator Semper Augustus
Germaniæ Hungariæ Bohemiæ Rex etc

Emperor Leopold I

Johann Bernhard Fischer von Erlach

The Crisis of the Baroque Era

In sculpture, one of the less conspicuous fields of Austrian Baroque art, Italian influence is less prevalent than it is in architecture and painting. But even those arts in which southern influence was dominant well into the latter part of the seventeenth century are unmistakably Austrian in character. Despite the facts that foreign influence was strong in these grandiose building programs and that they most certainly imposed heavy financial burdens on the country, it is inconceivable that artistic development of such scope, topical range, and grandeur could have developed without the active response, support, and contribution of the people.[22] Thus in a broad sense, formative Baroque art in Austria is representative of the abilities, the gifts, and the desires of the Austrian people. While all this applies to music as well, formative art manifests sooner and more clearly a characteristic Austrian style.

Certain important qualifications, however, must not be forgotten; they are pertinent to the intellectual as well as to the social sphere. Baroque art in Austria represents only one facet, though a highly important one, of the culture of the age. Baroque in general, as has been pointed out previously, does not express merely passion and emotion, organization of space, harmony of architecture, rich colors and dramatic sculpture, religious ecstasy and voluptous sensuality: it is also the period of the great deductive systems in philosophy, of the union between cosmological speculation and mathematical reasoning, of the endeavor to bridge the gap between reason and faith in political science by the still-axiomatic logic of the contract theory. As has been pointed out previously, little of all this is traceable in contemporary Austrian culture. As far as the Habsburg lands are concerned, Bruno, Descartes and Pascal, Galileo, Spinoza, and on the whole even Leibniz, Huygens and Newton, Althusius and Pufendorf, Bossuet, Hobbes, and Locke were still unknown. The reasons for these stark facts do not require re-examination at this point. Nevertheless, it is still a question whether the fundamental intellectual changes in the West could fail to exercise at least an indirect influence on Austrian artistic development. Is it possible to assume that countries cut off from the intellectual development of the West could have the same artistic development? Obviously an isolated analysis of the arts in intellectual and social history is as outdated as it is unsound. Yet within the complex framework of the synthetized history of the period it is obvious that contemporary developments in France, in England, and to a lesser extent in Italy accentuate to a much higher degree the background of the high Renaissance and indirectly the Classical tradition. Baroque, there, is to a point a revised and relaxed Classicism; Baroque in the Habsburg lands is, or rather tends to become, not a revision but a denial and a reversal of the humanist tradition and its ideological offspring.[23]

Thus in a way the Austrian Baroque is what the French Rococo tended to become half a century later. At the time of Louis XVI, when France was still under the influence of this change from (in Friedell's terms) "Cartesian Baroque" to Rococo disintegration, Austria under Joseph II was groping for a new Classicism which in some respects is the ideological expression of what was inherent in French high Baroque culture a century earlier. Thus in a very real sense the last becomes the first. The brief Austrian Rococo period does not compare in ideological significance with the similar French style. In a way Austrian formative arts skip a stage of Western development. Rising new forms of Classicism in Austria still represent ideas of the French high Baroque; yet chronologically in its external manifestations Austrian art headed the parade. The Empire style, or rather Biedermeier in its unpretentious Austrian form, and early Romanticism were again, if no longer ahead, at least fully abreast of Western development in the formative arts.

It should be noted that in these reflections, particularly with regard to Austrian artistic Baroque achievements, no aesthetic evaluation is implied. What they are meant to convey is that aesthetic interpretation is only one aspect of art analysis and, further, that the (in many ways) backward ideological conditions as they still existed in Leopold's Habsburg realms do not completely reflect the *Zeitgeist* as represented by the Baroque style across Western and Central Europe.

It may well be argued, however, that while Baroque in Austria is only halfway representative of the European spirit of the age, it may still be entirely representative of the spirit in Habsburg lands. According to this view, it is precisely the partial lack of a link with the Western world which makes Baroque in Austria fully true to the character of her culture of the time.

Here another question must be raised. While the character of Austrian Baroque art does not collide with the intellectual limitations then imposed on the Habsburg realms, does it also conform to the social character of the imperial domains?

The fact that Baroque art precisely in its highest achievements represents predominantly, though not exclusively, a courtly and religious style is by no means confined to the Austrian area. There, however, it is particularly conspicuous. The one great exception to the general rule is the contemporary Protestant Dutch city culture in the age of Hals, Rembrandt, and Vermeer van Delft, with its very different social stratification. The religious factor itself is here of secondary importance. To be sure, Puritanism is unquestionably a supporting factor in the development of bourgeois Baroque culture. Yet the grand Baroque art, with good reason associated primarily with the Catholic Church and the Catholic courts, was adopted by the Protestant courts and to a certain extent by the Anglican High Church and was introduced even into the Lutheran ecclesiastic atmosphere. Thus the courtly character is the primary, the Catholic ecclesiastic the secondary, factor in the rise of grand Baroque art.

Things were not always that way. Gothic art was to an even higher degree than Baroque dominated by the ecclesiastical idea, but in the Gothic age, particularly in German craft and merchant cities, it was decidedly also under the influence of city-guild culture. This second sphere was of less significance in late medieval Austria. But the still dominant ecclesiastical factor helped to secure Austria its immortal share of Gothic art. The Renaissance art that succeeded it was of course universally far more strongly governed by secular bourgeois elements, though the ecclesiastical factor was by no means negligible. Yet north of the Alps, including Austria, it was diverted from its course by the Reformation. Consequently, not excepting the pre-Gothic feudal, religious, Romanesque culture, the Renaissance was the period that has least influenced German-Austrian artistic development. This does not hold true for the different social and religious conditions in Bohemia. German Austria, however, during this transition period in the Alpine lands from the old to the new and, in a way, back to the old again, lost much of its style of artistic expression. It seemingly regained it at the time of the Catholic Counter Reformation, the suppression of the peasant wars associated with Stephan Fadinger, the national revolts in Hungary and Bohemia, the time of the new strengthening of the old order.

Seemingly, but not actually. Restoration is of course never

identical with and frequently is only superficially similar to the order it wants to re-establish. The economic order produced by the slowly rising industrialization of the period was largely different from the feudal and guild economy. The noble society in its gradual affirmation of a more centralized bureaucratic state was equally different from the late-medieval Estates system.[24] Even the newly fortified Church was in many external aspects never to regain the homogeneity of the scholastic and mystic late-medieval atmosphere. Renaissance, Humanism, Reformation, and peasant wars may have been seemingly superseded; their ideological impact could not be wiped out. All this adds up to the simple fact that the ideology and social order of Lepoldian Baroque did not have so strong a hold on great masses of the people as had the Gothic era, with its Church and its feudal and Estates order as well as its guild organization.

This consideration applies to the sphere of arts as well. While Austrian Baroque culture could easily supersede the Renaissance, with its relatively narrow basis in the Alpine lands, its impact never penetrated to any appreciable extent the full range of the social order, as Gothic art had done.

Yet Baroque—and not entirely without justification—is called the typical Austrian style. As noted before, its proud achievements would never have been conceivable without the active response of the people, though this response was not the same as that of the Gothic world. To a great extent it was determined by new political conditions. Baroque, it is true, represented the more recent victories of the *ecclesia militans,* but even more clearly it reflected the rise of Austria as a great power. This helps also to explain why high Baroque becomes increasingly a secular style, though by no means a bourgeois one. Jesuit ecclesiastic architecture, the great monastic architecture in Austria, was more and more replaced by secular palace architecture, the Belvedere of Eugene of Savoy, Charles VI's *Reichskanzlei* tract of the Hofburg, the Schönbrunn of Maria Theresa. They represent the surface but not the core of Austrian feeling; they represent the creative, imaginative abilities of Habsburg subjects; they do not express their very being, as did the village church of the Gothic age, the spire of St. Stephen braving the Turkish onslaught. Baroque is the style of the period and, as such, a true expression of its political, artistic, and economic conditions. As such it is genuine and sincere, but it is only a partial emanation and symbol of the Austrian heritage.

It could not be otherwise. The homogeneity of the medieval world could never be reconstructed either in that era or in succeding ages of social and ideological conflict. Austrian Baroque art is representative of Austrian culture insofar as that is possible in a world which, since the Renaissance, has become ever increasingly less homogeneous, both spiritually and socially. Its small share of modest but respectable and pleasing bourgeois features will be strengthened and enhanced only by the new style of the late eighteenth century.

Now the princely palaces of a proud aristocracy still represent wealth, social prestige, and feudal tradition, but they no longer stand for genuine political power. As in many other ways, the splendid Baroque façades merely pretend that a bygone sovereign power had been preserved. The modest style of the coming age would drop even this false pretense. Majestic monasteries like Melk, Göttweig, St. Florian, Klosterneuburg, symbols of the rejuvenated power of the first Estate, would never be erected again. The polychrome symphony of magnificent churches would yield to a new austerity. But all these changes and those still to come would attempt only to revise and correct the artistic reflection of the social order. They would neither balance nor harmonize it so long as the social and ideological conflict, camouflaged but not resolved by the Baroque era, continued.

q. *Baroque Times and Men*

This conflict explains not only the ambivalent and contradictory character of Baroque art and science but that of Baroque man as well. It would be rather superficial to conclude that the struggle existed only in the West, where new science and philosophy, an ideological harbinger of the Enlightenment, came into conflict with the Counter Reformation and the problems of absolutist state capitalism. Austria, as has been pointed out before, except in the sphere of economic theory had hardly been touched by the great intellectual controversy of the West. The problems of new cognition, however, are only one aspect of a much more comprehensive problem, which is man in the era of transition between Baroque and Enlightenment, man overwhelmed by the new experience of Renaissance, Humanism, Reformation, Counter Reformation and religious wars. This means that man faced with a political and ideological restoration, which in all of its manifestations—the rise of Great Powers, imperialism, state absolutism, and state capitalism—carries the seeds of truly revolutionary development. In this sense the striking contrast between the comparatively stagnant state of literature in Central Europe and of almost all branches of the humanities and the highly dramatic development of the formative arts is part of the same problem. The specific characteristics of the Austrian people, what might be termed their specific genius, gave it its peculiar character. Art is certainly an outlet for repressed feeling and thought, and that this sort of frustration existed can hardly be denied. But art is much more than that: it is also an entirely valid mode of expression for significant ideas, independent of any vicarious connotation. In this case it is the convincing manifestation of an era essentially not of restoration but of transition. The transition, it is true, was severely restricted by social conditions and barriers that seem ideologically almost insurmountable. As a result, art still filtered down from above through well-established channels and its full ideological effect was felt only at a time when the style of the period had been superseded by less spectacular productions of a new era. Its effect was not lost, however; rather, it contributed to a broader and deeper stream of spiritual development and increasing cultural interaction.

The period with which this discussion begins is described in a very general way by Franz Borkenau, an intellectual historian of wide perception, as follows: The seventeenth century is,

> . . . I don't hesitate to state it, one of the gloomiest periods in the history of mankind. Religion still rules unquestionably the great majority of minds. Yet it has lost its mild and conciliatory features, and has preserved only the terrifying ones. . . . The fraternity of co-operative associations of past times had disappeared. Nothing has been left of the organized order of life of the Middle Ages but its pressure. The realm of beauty, glorified by the great of the Renaissance, is gone. Only a mystical, unearthly light announces in Rembrandt's paintings in the midst of darkness the groping faith in redemption. The proud consciousness of heroic feelings, as glorified

by Shakespeare, has vanished: to Racine, passion leads only into the abyss of irrevocable damnation. Even death, according to the testimony of sources in this terrible century, is, it seems to me, harder than in other times. Dying is not yet alleviated by faith in the bright day which humanity is approaching. It is not alleviated by the natural self-evidence of a homogeneous order of life. The light of Enlightenment does not yet mitigate the terrors of hell; no gleam of paradise radiates any longer from the lost sweetness of naïvely religious times. In the earthly hell of these terrible times there rose those powerful thinkers who asked for the possible meaning of a philosophy of life.[25]

This statement is subject to strong qualification in the religious and artistic spheres. It ignores the political altogether. Nevertheless—and this is, after all, the main issue—it brings out clearly the unrelieved and ever-increasing pressure and tension of a deceptive "restoration" period. In this period, in "these terrible times," the ray of light bringing promise of a brighter future does not come from the great thinkers of the West and their deductive systems. Their achievements on the whole tend rather to accentuate the vast loneliness of the human intellect, focused as it is not on the earth but on the universe. Only a small, artificial bridge, constructed *post factum,* connects its findings with the Enlightenment. The only solution will lie in the realization that depth and breadth of cognition will open the vista to new horizons. Signs of such a fusion are not lacking in the Austrian Baroque period, which, despite its narrow intellectual confines, possesses broad ideological, social, and aesthetic potentialities.

II

ABRAHAM A SANCTA CLARA[1]

1646-1709

1. *Of Pulpit and Public*

a. *Background and Career*

By friends and foes alike Abraham a Sancta Clara is considered the most eminent preacher as well as the finest prose writer of his time in Catholic Germany. Even as adverse a critic of his work and influence as the distinguished liberal literary historian Wilhelm Scherer admits that "Abraham a Sancta Clara succeeded where every other writer of the outgoing seventeenth and early eighteenth centuries failed. He alone at that time knew how to permeate some of his writings with such dash and verve, he alone knew how to put them in such a vigorous spiritual setting, that even today we feel their attracting and compelling force."[2] On the other hand, N. Scheid, who might be expected to extol the famous preacher and writer, refers in the *Catholic Encyclopedia* to many of his works as a "confused mixture" and concludes: "Even up to the most recent times Abraham's influence is chiefly noticeable in the literature of the pulpit, though but little to its advantage."[3]

Surely the man whose work is characterized in so contradictory a fashion occupies a strange ideological position. And it is a prominent position as well. This great satirist and critic of manners, mores, and social institutions is an outstanding figure not only in the history of Austrian and German literature but in the general cultural history of Austria as well. Of even greater significance, however, is Abraham's spiritual influence on Austrian

50

posterity, an influence far more powerful and far more controversial than is generally realized.

To understand this influence and the fascinating problem
that it presents it is necessary first to review Abraham's life, which
offers ample material for the study of social conditions in the
Austria of his time.

Abraham a Sancta Clara, whose real name was Ulrich Megerlin, was probably born in 1644 at Kreeheinstetten in Swabia,
then technically Bavarian territory. He did not come to live in
Vienna until 1662. His childhood was spent in his native village,
and he received his education at the preparatory "Latin" school
of Mösskirch, at the Jesuit convent school at Ingolstadt, and
for three years at the Benedictine *Gymnasium* in Salzburg. Yet
in later years he was to exemplify many of the characteristic
features of the Viennese and of the German Austrian, though
perhaps not always the best of those features. He thus provides
an example of that almost complete process of assimilation that
took place more often in the cosmopolitan city on the Danube
than in any other major German capital. To be sure, this kind
of assimilation can be and has been successful only when it is
based on a distinct cultural and psychological affinity between
the place and the immigrant. Psychologically and ethnically the
relationship may well have been strengthened by Abraham's
Swabian imaginativeness. From the cultural point of view, as
Scherer correctly points out, he is the product of the two chief
details of Austrian and German ecclesiastical education at that
time: the minute, thorough, yet frequently pedantic and impractical scholarship of the Benedictines; and Jesuit instruction,
with its powerful effect on imagination and emotion.[4]

Benedictine and Jesuit education and activities provided in
southern Germany and Austria more than the clerical framework for higher education toward parochial, missionary, academic, administrative, and diplomatic work. The teaching of the
two famous Orders also offered what was considered then
almost the best kind of higher education in Austria. It strongly
influenced the cultural activities and general philosophy of the
aristocracy and of a new secular "top" bureaucracy at the imperial court in Vienna. These in turn exercised a powerful influence on the intellectual and spiritual standards and ambitions
of the next-highest stratum of society, the provincial squirarchy.
Thus all of these groups, either directly or by a process of ideo-

logical penetration, were under the influence of the still-effective fervor of the outgoing Catholic Reformation. As to the cultural development of the urban middle classes, it was not so strongly affected by those factors; but then the cultural influence of free urban commoners did not compare in strength with that of the groups mentioned.

Abraham a Sancta Clara was by birthright neither an urban nor a free commoner. Nor did he belong to the large and still oppressed peasant class. Of rural origin but not of rural occupational background, he belonged rather to a semi-urban, semi-rural, semi-free group somewhat between two main social bodies, the free, urban lower-middle-class commoners and the unfree peasants. Scherer rather dramatically perceives in Abraham's humble and technically still-unfree rural parentage a powerful factor in his development; as he puts it, ". . . we see him with true delight passing merciless judgment on the mighty of this earth, he the son of the unfortunate, despised, and for centuries mistreated, downtrodden, and tortured Estate, he the serf of Kreeheinstetten."[5]

Actually, this interpretation is correct only in a technical sense. Abraham's parents, it is true, were not legally free; but his father, though a bondsman, was a comparatively well-to-do innkeeper. Thus the social understanding that Abraham certainly possessed to some degree is derived from other—primarily religious—sources, rather than from his humble but by no means abjectly miserable origins. In fact, his rise in social status to the rank of imperial-court preacher, and later of prior of his monastery and even provincial administrator within his Augustine Order, would never have been possible, despite all his superior abilities, without a solid academic ecclesiastical education. It is a very plausible assumption that his father's respected brother, the widely known composer of ecclesiastic music, court conductor of the archbishop of Salzburg, and eventually canon, Abraham Megerlin (ennobled as von Mühlfeld), may have helped his nephew to obtain the desired education.[6] Thus Scherer's statement is contradicted by the facts, and Abraham a Sancta Clara's family, far from being "downtrodden," appear to have been relatively well placed.

Scherer's interpretation of another aspect of Abraham's upbringing is at least controversial: his contention that the distinct aversion and hostility toward women that seems to be expressed in Abraham's sermons and writings [7] (and this in itself is open to question) can be traced to his childhood. There is evidence that Abraham's mother was an unusually cantankerous and quarrelsome woman.[8] But here again, as Scherer himself admits, the monkish upbringing of the period would offer sufficient explanation for Abraham's attitude toward the female sex.

As a monk, he obviously adopted the first name of Abraham in honor of his uncle when he entered the novitiate in 1662 at the monastery of the Barefoot Friars of St. Augustine in Vienna. Under the added designation "Sancta Clara" he remained a faithful and distinguished member of that strict Order all his life. Irrespective of the connections and influences that may have paved the way for his ecclesiastic career at the outset, there can be no doubt that he owes his success primarily to sincere devotion to his cause as well as to his outstanding though in some ways extravagant abilities.

The external milestones in his career are the following. Ordained as priest in 1666, Abraham, in accordance with the rules of his Order, spent a few years as a simple parish priest in Taxa near Augsburg. Nearly twenty years later he was to write the story of the miracle of Taxa, *Gack, Gack, Gack a Ga!* which tells of the discovery of a newly laid egg adorned with the picture of the Holy Virgin. This tale, highly characteristic of Abraham's interests and style of writing, became within a short time a genuine "best seller." Recalled to the monastery of St. Augustine in 1668 or 1669, he began to perfect himself as a preacher. So great was his talent and proficiency that in 1677 Emperor Leopold I appointed the young cleric, who meanwhile had already obtained the degree Doctor of Divinity, as court preacher. According to Richard von Kralik, Abraham owed this appointment to the fact that he made a very favorable impression on the emperor with a "prophetic welcome" sermon, predicting the glorious events that were supposedly to result from Leopold's third marriage to Eleonore von Neuenburg. There is no doubt, however, that Abraham's outstanding abilities played a part in his selection as court preacher.[9] It should be noted that this important position, which gave the incumbent almost unrestricted access to the imperial majesty, was one of the few of distinguished noble rank in Baroque Austria in which non-noble or even unfree ancestors were not considered an impediment but were, to a certain point, perhaps even an asset, since the appointment of such a man proved that the emperor in his relationship to the divine paid no heed to worldly titles and honors.

The next decisive event in Abraham's life, an event that was also momentous for his Viennese contemporaries, was the great plague of 1679. This tragic experience inspired him to set down what is the first major account of that great trauma of late-seventeenth-century Vienna. The directness of his impressions and his sensitivity of mind and feeling easily explain why *Mercks Wien,* in which he recounted the experiences of the plague year and reflected upon their meaning and the lessons to be derived from them, appears to the reader today to be perhaps the least controversial of his writings. His next major work, *Auf, auf Ihr Christen,* is likewise based on a great historic experience, the siege of Vienna by the Turks in 1683. The fact that here (though to a lesser extent than in his later works) the trite conclusions tend to make one lose sight of the original observations does much to scare away the modern reader.*

In the following years the pater, now famous near and far as court and visiting preacher, became an ever more prolific writer, with nearly twenty full-length volumes to his credit.[10] In addition, he was made prior of his monastery in 1680 and provincial of his Order in 1690. Unquestionably he was a man of extraordinary vitality, energy, and industry. He died in 1709, at the height of his activity though by no means of his ideological influence. This influence declined somewhat during the reign of the young Emperor Joseph I, who was only moderately interested in religious matters. As will be shown below, this fact did not in the least affect Abraham's long-range appeal.

A proper evaluation of his sermons and writings will require a study of certain excerpts from his work and preliminary information on the following topics: (1) the scope of Abraham a Sancta Clara's knowledge; (2) the peculiarities of his style; (3) his general attitudes; and (4) the extent and limitations of his life work as a source of information on Austrian history. In his

*Abraham had actually observed at least the beginning and the end of the great plague in Vienna, though at the height of its horror he was confined as chaplain in the palace of the land marshal for five months, a factor that possibly saved his life. The year of the great siege and the following years, however, Abraham spent far from Vienna, at the filial house of his Order at Graz. (See Th. von Karajan, *Abraham a Sancta Clara,* 265 ff., 277 ff.) There is not the slightest evidence that absence in either case was due to overcaution on Abraham's part.

books and pamphlets as well as in his sermons, he dealt with the entire field of mores and morals as reflected in human actions and social institutions within his own areas of observation—Austria, particularly Vienna. Obviously, in order to judge the qualifications of any writer of so ambitious an enterprise, his educational standards and knowledge must be carefully considered.

A linguist of rare talent, he certainly read and spoke Latin fluently. He had also at least a smattering of Greek and Hebrew, both of which were necessary for his further theological training and certainly for acquisition of the degree Doctor of Divinity. We know that in later life, particularly as guest preacher, he also delivered sermons occasionally in Italian, which in all probability he learned as an adult. There is no evidence that he studied his native German systematically, not even at his first school, the "Latin" preparatory school of Mösskirch. There exists ample and obvious proof that, through no fault of his own, this linguist of outstanding natural ability did not have complete command of the written High German of his time: his grammar and spelling remained faulty all his life. His literary acrobatics are therefore all the more impressive.

We possess information on the extent of his training in rhetoric, that important Jesuit discipline, and of his knowledge in his other central field of action, moral theology. As far as homiletics are concerned, the basic structure of his sermons follows established patterns;[11] they do not owe their priceless originality of language to any new kind of rhetorical architecture.[12]

The erudition of a polyhistor, "poly"-preacher and, above all, "poly"-talker like Abraham cannot be gauged by his casual references. He can be credited with real learning only in cases where he at least attempts to check on the all too frequently obscure sources of his information. Thus it is hardly a serious exhibition of knowledge and learning when, for instance, he enumerates the catastrophes that occurred in the year 79 of every century from the creation of the world to 1679. One might be impressed more by his loquacity than by his veracity when he lists all the dishes pleasing to the Roman emperor Vitellus in order to bring out a certain point in his discussion of the great penitent St. Magdalen. Similar examples, which could be supplied by the hundreds, need not be taken as evidence of erudition.[13]

Thus while the vast conglomeration of names and alleged facts paraded by Abraham a Sancta Clara must be accepted (if at all) only with great caution as evidence of genuine learning, it is also appropriate to mention certain facts that do not appear in his writings. Scherer has pointed out that in the age of Bacon, Descartes, Leibniz, and Spinoza, Abraham says absolutely nothing about these men and their ideas.[14] Obviously a casual reference to a writer by a loquacious and often bombastic preacher who wishes to exhibit his wide knowledge is scarcely proof of his acquaintance with the works of that writer. On the other hand, failure to mention famous writers and works, some of which in all probability he would otherwise have violently attacked, makes it highly probable that he had no knowledge of them. Furthermore, why should we assume that Abraham was acquainted with the ideas of a Descartes, Leibniz, or Bacon even to the extent of a crossword-puzzle solver in a tabloid paper today, when he says practically nothing about a subject much closer to him—scholastic philosophy? In a sermon in praise of Thomas Aquinas (published in *Geistlicher Kramladen*) he discourses about the astrological significance of the date of Thomas's birth and various important dates in his later career, yet in forty-one pages of such reflections he does not give the slightest indication that he grasped or even knew the most elementary facts about the great scholastic's life work.[15] His ignorance of Western seventeenth-century intellectual progress may, of course, be laid to the limitations of his environment. The far more amazing lack of understanding of the foundations of scholasticism becomes comprehensible only after acquaintance with the major aspects of the life of this strange personality.

b. Medieval Means—Baroque Ends: The Problem of Superstition

While in principle Abraham a Sancta Clara violently denounces superstition, he uses the term in a peculiar way. To him "superstition" means not simply blind and irrational belief in allegedly supranatural phenomena, but rather a belief that conflicts with his own. If, however, he agrees with the interpretation of certain phenomena, he speaks not of superstition but of "revelation."

The preacher repeatedly begins his biographical eulogies or condemnations with an analysis of the horoscope of his human

subjects. At the same time he inveighs not only against dishonest astrologers but against astrology itself. Superstitions, as
Abraham asserted with an obvious feeling of intellectual superiority, are cultivated with particular intensity by women and
should be rejected. As examples he cites such things as signs in
the sky that precede fateful events, premonitory dreams, and
fear of ghosts. Even Abraham's most loyal admirers, however,
cannot avoid comparing these statements with others in which
he affirmed his faith in astrology, signs in the sky representing
armed men, fiery swords, battle arrows, comets, and so forth.
He speaks in all seriousness of lamentations heard in the air,
oracles, etc. He believed, and his thousands of listeners were
advised to share his belief, in werewolves, corpses that can blush,
bells that ring by themselves. His parishioners were warned to
beware of the magical power of sorcerers, who among other
things are able to control tempests. Responsibility for the plague,
however, is not laid at the door of magicians but is attributed
to witches, the Jews, and gravediggers. Their evil deeds are of
the same order as those of the "wild hunt" and all kinds of
ghosts, some of whom Abraham had seen himself. As a matter
of "fact," he had seen them quite as clearly as the devil, whom
of course he met frequently.[16]

These and similar notions are considered not as residues of
medieval superstition preserved by the common people but as
doctrines pronounced, revised, and reasserted *ex cathedra*
by the most renowned German-speaking preacher of his
time, the imperial-court chaplain. It is obvious, as we know
from other sources, that there was little if anything in the principles of Abraham's education to combat these superstitions.
Therefore what is surprising is not the fact that a man of his
standing should subscribe to them but that in almost the same
breath in which he proclaimed his own superstitious beliefs he
denounced as fallacies others that are quite similar.

The reasons for these strange inconsistencies provide an important key to the understanding of Abraham and his "school"
of thought. His intellectual equipment was dominated by glorification of irrationalism, but this does not mean that he himself
was either simple-minded or insincere. Contrary to appearances,
it would be erroneous to attribute either of these qualities to
him. His approach to his mission was pragmatic, and was based
on similar methods that were successfully employed in the mis-

sionary campaign of the Counter Reformation. It is extremely practical in the sense that the goal of desired salvation precedes in importance the question of the means employed to achieve it. The assumption that he was following the doctrine often attributed to the Jesuits, that the end justifies the means, may be discarded at once. The demagogic effect of Abraham's contradictory statements is in part deliberate, and in part it may be explained by auto-suggestion, which made him believe in signs and apparitions that suited his purpose and reject those that did not.[17]

Accordingly, superstitions are affirmed or denounced in numerous passages of Abraham's writings in order to prove or disprove certain moral doctrines. The innumerable followers of this way of "thinking" in every generation may well acclaim Abraham a Sancta Clara as one of their leaders. Both intention and auto-suggestion are impressively intermingled in the prefaces to *Judas der Ertzschelm* and *Hui und Pfui,* where he makes the following statement, which, while it does not speak for his lucidity, can certainly not be described as naïve: "I have interspersed various stories and songs, which a serious Cato and Plato would frown upon. . . ." After reference to St. Gregory in support of the use of fables, which term obviously is understood here in the wide sense of fairy tales in general, he continues: "My God, who knows my mind exactly, is aware that I have used such things to no other end and goal than to bait the present predominantly shameless and tameless world for its own good."

c. Style Is Content, Content Is Style

Important as this subjectivity is for the understanding of Abraham a Sancta Clara's work, it would be of no further interest if he had not made use of it very effectively in his literary style.[18] It is a weapon which he handled with consummate mastery in the service of his cause; it is also a key to understanding his personality and appeal.

If one agrees with the theory that the most effective way to write is to write as one talks (in Abraham's case as one preaches), then the famous Augustine monk was a very effective writer indeed. Further, if one is willing to discount the tendency to bias and demagogy that is often present in this kind of writing, one can readily admit that Abraham was one of the most effective writers and speakers of all time—effective in language, and effective in the service of his cause. According to stricter standards, however, to write as one talks does not in itself make for effectiveness. Genuine effectiveness does not demand real identity of written and spoken word; it requires naturalness and poise of speech and writing, but above all it must convey an impression of sincerity. As evidenced by very many of his sermons transmitted to posterity, Abraham met these stricter standards as well.

These qualities, important as they are, serve merely to explain his appeal and have very little to do with his unique technique itself. This technique, which makes use of jest, of satire—frequently on the level of farcical buffoonery, evoking a puckish glee at the supposed villain's misgiving—was not new. It had been widely employed by preachers in France, Italy, the Low Countries, and Germany from the fifteenth to the seventeenth centuries; it was indeed one of the chief propaganda techniques of the era of Reformation and Counter Reformation. It is besides the technique employed in the so-called "fools' literature," in which a humorous attack is made on human frailties. The chief examples of this are Sebastian Brant's widely imitated *Narrenschiff* of the late fifteenth century and, on a higher level, Erasmus of Rotterdam's *Praise of Folly*.

In spite of the vogue of this "fool" style, it should be noted that the Church very soon became aware that the technique might impair the dignity of the preaching of the Word. Thus already a century before Abraham, the Jesuit Georg Scherer, himself a sardonic and witty preacher and missionary, observed in his *Lutherischer Bettlermantel*: "Scolding and slandering is not difficult, yet it is difficult to preach genuinely and simply the Word of God. . . . Preachers should not be jesters, storytellers, and fabulists; they should treat the word of God with proper dignity and majesty." And yet Georg Scherer was no Puritan: "From time to time to entertain and invigorate the tired audience with an amusing story or saying that fits the subject is all right. But to concentrate on ridiculous and stale ribald jests and foolishness is improper, and such spitting [*sic*] does not belong in the pulpit but in some other place."[19]

In spite of this sensible attitude, a century later (for reasons to be discussed at the conclusion of this essay) all these dubious literary techniques reach a new culmination in Abraham a Sancta Clara's writings and preachings. One element of that propagandistic style in particular was developed by him to an unprecedented degree—the play on words, the pun, in hundreds of variations, which he employed to drive home every point. These parallel and supplement his other technical devices—the sometimes tedious enumeration of all kinds of ill-assorted data and names, with its numbing effect on the critical faculties of the audience.

It must be admitted that Abraham is an unexcelled virtuoso in that field. Only a man of innate wit with great feeling for his native language could master this instrument. However, as with his other techniques, predilections, and prejudices, he exploited this one, which can be entertaining and refreshing at certain points and in moderate doses, to the limit of toleration and often far beyond it. In view of the constant nerve-racking repetition of the stratagem, it is surprising that one fairly obvious point has never been brought out: Abraham's technique —by force of habit, natural disposition, or both—becomes a kind of compulsive mannerism characteristic of many men of letters, particularly satirists with neurotic tendencies. His gay antics notwithstanding, such a disposition can hardly be overlooked in the hectic and violent manner in which his views are usually expressed. As he put it himself, "the high office of a preacher requires that he bark well if he observes that the wolves attack the shepherd dogs of Christ."[20]

There is a difference between the fanaticism of medieval preachers who campaigned for the cause of the Crusades and the farcical antics of Abraham a Sancta Clara. Yet the basic difference lies neither in the supreme cause for which they stand nor in their emotional appeal, though in Abraham's case he gained his appeal largely by stirring up cheap prejudices. In short, it is a difference not in substance but *in modo;* it is the difference between the intense spirit of ideological communication of the Gothic and the ambivalence of the Baroque, oscillating between ecstasy and rationalism.

d. Critic of Austrian Society?

A superficial observer might assume that comprehensive criticism of mores and manners of all classes of society by a social critic like Abraham a Sancta Clara is in itself an invaluable source of cultural history.[21] This is true only with reservations.

The vices which Abraham castigates, the virtues which he extols, are not Austrian or Viennese but are those that he regarded as standard virtues and vices. To be sure they are dressed up in Austrian costume; Austrian events, mores, and customs have obviously influenced the manner in which they are presented. On the whole it can be said that he tried sincerely to give the general character of his subject precedence over the local character and to make use of the local chiefly to illustrate his point. In this he was successful. But if his writings and sermons are viewed in a broader perspective, it can be seen that, consciously and perhaps to an even greater extent subconsciously, he offers valuable information on Austrian cultural history of a different kind.[22]

Scherer, perhaps in an attempt to compensate for his otherwise all too harsh and severe judgment of Abraham a Sancta Clara, sees in him the son of and spokesman for the exploited serfs, and exclaims: "With heart and head Abraham always remained a complete and true plebeian."[23] This interpretation is hardly borne out by the facts. Abraham undoubtedly had a warm spot in his heart for the afflicted, provided they were of the right faith, and occasionally he sharply censures the excessive exploitation and cruelty of the lords as manifestations of more frequently condemned prodigality and luxury in general. Yet at least as frequently he castigated the poor for their laziness and exaggerated pretense of misery, and he always tried to trace the cause of human tribulation to ungodly conduct. In short, he was primarily concerned with the question of how far people measured up to the heavenly order as he saw it, not with the terrestrial social order, in the reform of which he was not primarily interested. Thus he had very little comprehension of the merely mundane aspects of social problems of his time.

In the same way his interest in politics, in the great issues of his day, was limited—with the single exception of the Turkish onslaught (to him exclusively a religious issue). His knowledge was distorted by his education. In his encyclopedic diatribes against society and its activities, no reference is ever made to the beginnings of Austrian mercantilism in his time. There is no evidence that the names of the foremost Austrian mercantilist writers, Johann Becher, Wilhelm von Schröder, and Wilhelm von Hörnigk, were known to him. It is indeed likely that, had he known the Austrian mercantilists, he would have assailed them, if only for their German-Protestant connections. On the other hand, he had a large though inaccurate store of anecdotes and legends of Austrian history from the Babenbergs to his day, the presentation of which served the selfsame purpose as his other tales did.

Abraham might rightly claim a certain awareness of the specific national character of Austria as compared to that of the Reich, though by clear implication he perceived Austrian culture as purely German.[24] His references to other nations are varied and frequently contradictory. They are consistently negative only in regard to heretics and heathens—the Protestants, the Jews, and the Turks. As a typical comment on the various national vices the following passage will serve as an example:

> *Einen Österreicher vom Sauffen, einen Reutter vom Rauffen, einen Juden vom Betriegen, einen Böhmen vom Lügen, einen Granner (from Carniola) vom Klauben, einen Polacken vom Rauben, einen Walschen von der Buhlerey, einen Frantzosen von der Untreu, einen Spanier von Stoltzheit, einen Francken von Grobheit, einen Schlesier vom Schreien, einen Sachsen von Schelmereyen, einen Bayer vom Kaudern, einen Schwaben vom Plaudern zu bekehren, den lass ich seyn ein Bidermann, Der solche Leut bekehren kann.**

The passage is a typical example not so much of Abraham's prejudices as of his irrationalism, of the way in which heart and mind served tongue. Obviously the various vices denounced are not at all commensurate. The robbery of the Pole, French promiscuity, and Italian adultery are lumped together with the shouting of the Silesian or the small talk of Abraham's own countryman, the Swabian, for whom he shows an understandable preference. The alliterations, such as *Reuter-Rauffen, Schlesier-Schreien, Sachsen-Schelmereyen,* were presumably chosen because they are pleasing to the ear. On the basis of abundant evidence in many of Abraham's writings, it seems suggestive that the

---

*"The one is truly honorable who can dissuade an Austrian from drinking, a horseman from fighting, a Jew from cheating, a Bohemian from lying, a reaper (from Carniola) from picking grains, a Pole from robbery, an Italian from adultery, a Frenchman from infidelity, a Spaniard from pride, a Franconian from roughness, a Silesian from shouting, a Saxonian from rougish tricks, a Bavarian from gabbling, a Suebian from chatting." (*Lauberhütte* [1721-23], I, 72, quoted from Karajan, *Abraham a Sancta Clara,* 212.)

association of specific attributive qualities with a given subject was quite frequently dictated by acoustic-aesthetic rather than critical considerations. Only a reader unfamiliar with the range and character of Abraham's genuine prejudices and with Baroque literary vagaries in general will be shocked by the idea that the evaluation expressed in the quoted excursion into international relations may have been dictated not only by the social critic but by the stylist as well.[25]

e. Abraham a Sancta Clara and Vienna

While this relatively well-traveled preacher's knowledge of European nations* was rather sketchy and even his impressions of Austria spotty, he had an intimate and warm relationship with Vienna, the city of the main activities of his manhood. The deepest impressions of his life, the plague of 1679 and the Turkish siege of 1683, were linked with the imperial capital. The two most natural, least farcical of his writings, *Mercks Wien* and *Auf, auf Ihr Christen,* were products of this warm affection. Yet even here it is unmistakably Abraham who is speaking. In all seriousness he reports as true the story that Vienna had been founded eight hundred years after the great flood by a certain Abraham—a fairy tale which Aeneas Silvius and others had repudiated more than two centuries before him.

The basic theme of his reflections on the Viennese is that people in general, the Viennese in particular, were better in the old days. Employing generalization, a popular device of homiletics, he reflects "that the first century [after Christ] was curious, the second victorious, the third lonely, the fourth erudite, the fifth barbarian, the sixth contradictory, the seventh ignorant, the eighth pernicious, the ninth licentious, the tenth political, the eleventh envious, the twelfth poor, the thirteenth cantankerous, the fourteenth cruel, the fifteenth schismatic, the sixteenth apostatic, the seventeenth suspicious, and this eighteenth century, in which we live today, may rightly be called deceitful and hypocritical."[26] If for argument's sake somebody had questioned the authoritative imperial-court preacher as to why, for instance, the third century should be considered lonely, the tenth political, or the eleventh envious, he might have met with the answer,

---

*It is certain that he knew Bavaria, Suebia, Lower and Upper Austria, Styria, Salzburg, Carniola. He also visited Rome twice.

Why not? In all likelihood the asker would have been shouted down as a heretic. And upon some reflection it can be admitted that the line of reasoning that Abraham represents has to this very day found no more effective arguments than these two: Why should anything not be true that serves the given purpose? Who but a sinister person of devilish motives could doubt it?

Contrary to appearances, these reflections do not represent digressions in Abraham's discourse on the Viennese. On the contrary, they form an intrinsic part of it, since even in his best writings Abraham's "philosophy" is dominated by reflections of this sort. He is not taking a new road but is following an already well-trodden path when he associates the curse of the great plague with certain characteristics of the Viennese, which had also been criticized, though not necessarily justly, by others. Extravagant luxury in food, drink, and attire, particularly on the part of women, are pictured and characterized in great detail, and not without some obviously well-observed and equally well-presented evidence. A certain snobbism, a tendency to high living, superficiality, mockery, and flippant criticism,[27] may likewise have been correctly noted, but on the whole Abraham's clerical zeal for comprehensiveness, his effort to subsume every vice under the decalogue, goes too far to remain within the bonds of personal observation. Yet the plague to Abraham was to be connected not only with the morals of the people but with a mythical background. It was announced by comets, certain weeds, animals, shells from the stars, mysterious nocturnal lamentations—in short, forces neither recognized by the Church nor legitimately to be brought into any moral consideration.[28]

As Abraham returns from the aberrations of his confused ego to actual experience, the level of his reflections rises. He gives a vivid picture of how the first victims of the plague were found in the poor Jewish quarters across the branch of the Danube. He tells how the plague spread from there to the suburbs, how it hit first vagrant beggars, the poor in the crowded quarters, the scum of the city. Then he saw how the rich and well-to-do believed, or made themselves believe, that "it could not happen to them" and how anarchic conditions began to develop as soon as the radically egalitarian character of the plague was recognized. Even the reader today is moved by his description of this ravaging death, which did not spare even those people who had looked for refuge in the churches, which struck them down in the streets and at home, which caused parents and children to look with suspicion at each other as potential sources of contagion, so that fear poisoned all human relations and the stricken were deprived of help, solace, and the company of their fellow mortals, despite all the efforts of a courageous clergy. But even in the midst of this tale of misery, the inveterate clown in Abraham cannot resist brandishing his wooden sword, describing in a series of queer alliterations how *In der Herrengassen hat der Tod geherrschet; in der Klugerstrasse ist der Tod nicht klug gewest, sondern verschwenderisch; in der Bognergasse hat der Tod ziemlich seinen Bogen abgeschossen; in der Singerstrasse hat der Tod vielen das Requiem gesungen; in der Schulerstrasse hat der Tod keine Vakanz gesetzt; in der Riemerstrasse hat der Tod aus fremden Hauten Riemen geschnitten . . .** and so on and on for pages.[29]

The same moral line, the same confused mystical and neurotic linguistic aberrations, are to be found in the moving narrative of *Auf, auf Ihr Christen,* the reflections on the Turkish siege of 1683—otherwise one of the most attractive of Abraham's writings (a fact splendidly made use of by Schiller in the Capucine sermon in *Wallensteins Lager*).† Yet the striking feature of *Auf, auf ihr Christen* is not the account of the siege itself but the evaluation of the enemy conducting that siege, a point to be appreciated better if it follows a further review of Abraham's criticism of society.[30]

f. Emperor and Clergy

In Abrahams' social hierarchy the emperor naturally holds the highest position; as wearer of the crown of the Holy Roman-German Empire, he is the only secular force absolutely above

---

*"In Herrengasse [Noblemen's Street] death has ruled; in Klugerstrasse [Wise Men's Street] death was not wise; in Bognergasse [Archers' Street] death has shot his arrows; in Singerstrasse [Minstrels' Street] death has sung a requiem for man; in Schulerstrasse [School Street] death has not allowed for any vacation; in Riemergasse [Strapmakers' Street] death has cut straps from the skin of many people. . . ." (*Mercks Wien,* 32-33.) Abraham a Sancta Clara refers here to actual street names in Vienna.

†As is well known, Goethe drew Schiller's attention to *Auf, auf Ihr Christen,* and Schiller has not only faithfully copied the style of Abraham a Sancta Clara but borrowed a number of puns. The better a reader becomes acquainted with the writings of Abraham, the more he will admire Schiller's success in molding the farcical features of *Auf, auf Ihr Christen* into one of the most brilliant episodes of his dramatic work. (See letter of Goethe to Schiller of October 5, 1798, and letters of Schiller to Goethe of the same date and of October 9, 1798, in any edition of the correspondence between Goethe and Schiller.)

criticism. Adverse critics of the Augustinian prior might perceive evidence of a good deal of servility in the three decades of intimate relationship between the shy and introverted Leopold I and his flamboyant court preacher, as for instance in the welcome sermon on the occasion of the third marriage of the emperor. On the basis of prophecies revealed by the well-known method of opening the Bible at random, the entire history of the Holy Scriptures was made to serve as a build-up for the glorious career of Leopold I and his spouse.[31] Yet obedience to the rules of etiquette in his relationship to imperial majesty certainly did not make a fawning hypocrite of Abraham, as is evidenced by his frank criticism of court life.[32]

Naturally the only social system that Abraham really understood was that which existed under absolute monarchy. Consequently some of its features, such as its intolerance, were not only respected but admired by an Augustinian prior of similar tendencies. It is obvious that he revered an emperor who granted him a rare, indeed for that time almost unique, freedom of expression. To be sure, it was a freedom partly confined to the religious-spiritual realm and partly (as we may fathom even from contemporary criticism) a fool's freedom.[33] It carried little social significance and was never effectively put to use by Abraham in the service of social reform.

As to the various Estates of society, naturally the one most respected by him was the clergy; he defended his own sacred profession strongly against attacks on its way of life. Here he followed the line of stating that in certain respects members of the clergy are human beings too and that occasional vices must never lead to unjust generalizations. Among such occasional vices he criticizes particularly a tendency to good and indeed luxurious living. Yet in general "if a cleric is taller and bigger than other people this is due to the fact that he thrives better on a scanty diet because he lives the right way."[34]

Thus while the lives of the clergy in general, and foremost among them those of members of the Holy Orders (especially the most distinguished group, the Jesuits),[35] are on the whole exemplary, there are certain unwholesome features particularly characteristic of ecclesiastics. Among these are a certain vanity that can occasionally be seen and, even more frequently than among laymen, envy—concentrated here on spiritual powers, greater abilities, greater knowledge, and above all greater public appeal. Abraham concluded that envy of this sort was the chief driving force behind Luther's apostasy.[36]

A further charge, curious to hear from this source, is that preachers should not antagonize their audience by too much scolding and that confessors must not be too strict and relentless.[37] The inconsistency in these remarks at variance with many others and with his homiletic style in general is quite characteristic and gives an insight into his way of thinking. Abraham was a contradictory and in some ways a confused man, but he was by no means one who always followed blind intuition or was wholly unconscious of the motives and the consequences of his actions.

What is most characteristic of Abraham's views not only of the clergy but of professional men in general is his intense dislike of intellectualism. For the cleric it is not his knowledge of scholasticism but his faith that is important, for the doctor not his success in healing but his personal experience of suffering, and so on through all the professions.[38] Science is useful, worthy of protection and appreciation, but only if coupled with virtue: *Sonst isst die Scienz ohne Conscienz wie ein Pferd ohne Zaum, ein Spiel ohne Rahm, ein Kleid ohne Brahm, und ein Markt ohne Kram.** And he concludes with the impressive picture of Isidorus, on earth a Spanish peasant, sitting in heaven as a saint while the doctors Plato and Cato (the second added probably for the sake of rhyme) are still burning in hell.[39]

The schools of thought that have maintained this attitude toward science in full vigor from the Middle Ages to our day owe much to Abraham.

g. *The Nobles*

As to the Second Estate, the nobles, Abraham frequently refers to the merits of the great noble families, some of whom ranked among his and his monastery's personal benefactors.[40] It testifies to his warm heart and spirit, however, that occasionally he denounces the cruel abuse of power on the part of the nobility, particularly in regard to the serf peasants, the obnoxious methods of *Bauern schinden*. Referring to the basic equality of all men, he goes so far as to quote several times in his writings the revolutionary song of the peasant wars:

*"Otherwise science is without conscience like a horse without bridle, and heath cock without cream in the gravy, a dress without fur lining, and a market without merchandise." (*Mercks Wien*, 116 ff.)

67

Als Adam drasch und Eva spann,
Wo war denn da der Edelmann?

and he asserts: *Es stinckt der königliche Prinz so Kraeftig als des schlechten Mistbauerns neugebohrener Hansel. Warum? Sie sind beide aus einem Teiche gebacken....* However, references of this kind apply strictly to equality before God and do not imply any necessity for social reform.[41]

His main charge against the nobility, however, is the familiar one of sumptuous display, luxury, and high living, together with the absence of any genuine piety. Some of his reflections in this respect are genuinely entertaining and offer a good picture of noble life in contemporary Baroque Vienna. Thus he characterizes the life of a noble lady:

> A lady of high nobility comes home from a party Saturday at midnight. Since she has eaten quite a lot of the delicacies at dinner she retires, sleeps Sunday until ten o'clock in the morning, and then sits down at her dressing table in front of the mirror. She combs her hair with the generous help of lotion, dresses and clips her hair, adorns and anoints herself, and puts on valuable hairpins. Everything glitters with jewels, gold, and silver. Finally like the star-spangled sky she enters church at noon, sits down in the big front pew so that she may look at everybody and everybody may look at her. The footman carries a book bag of red velvet richly gilded at the edges. He lays out half a library of prayerbooks. Meanwhile the chaplain has been informed that he should say Mass quickly. . . . Meanwhile she turns over the leaves of her books a little, but thinks more of how to while away the Sunday. Where to go to a party? What comedy will be performed today? Whom should one visit in the afternoon? . . . Meanwhile Mass is over. The dignitaries and statesmen stand around in powdered wigs, turn their backs to the altar, offer each other a pinch of snuff, read letters, and exchange intelligences. One or the other is leaning against a pillar, is reviewing the new fashions, is looking at a pretty woman, winking

---

* "The royal prince stinks like the humble peasant's newborn baby boy. Why? They are both baked from the same dough." (*Todten-Capelle* [1710], 101, 254, quoted from Karajan, 167 f.)

at her ... so that she may understand his enamored look
soon enough. .... This is morning service with Christians,
with nobles.

From thence Abraham passes to the joys of the afternoon, the
lascivious talk, the long nap, and includes the pleasures of the
common people who play ninepins, eat, and drink. "The parents
drink, the children drink, the servant and the servant girl, the
master and the journeyman, the judge and the juryman." And
at night after such a day, there is quarreling, scuffling, and fighting.[42]

Yet one cannot help thinking that, through no fault of his
own, the imperial-court preacher in his later life had a much
better, a more direct and intimate knowledge of the life of the
rich than of the middle classes and the poor. As to the rich,
Abraham, following a familiar homiletic pattern, frequently
castigates the tempting power of money, avarice, covetousness,
and insufficient charity. On the whole his repeated discourses on
the effect of money convey the notion that inordinate display
and expenditures are vulgar, but are at least partly excused by
noble rank, which is entitled to a certain luxury.[43]

This again can be easily understood. The Baroque cultural
environment in which Abraham lived was one in which (unlike
that in some German lands to the West and the North) the
court and high nobility almost exclusively set the pattern of living. To Abraham and to his contemporaries, Austrian Baroque
culture was a noble, ecclesiastic culture. Gradually rising bourgeois wealth still copied those ways of life faithfully or, as often
happens, crudely. In Baroque feudal Austria, which lacked the
autonomous city economy and culture of the European North
and West, the burghers had not yet developed full confidence
in their own cultural values and achievements. Their evolution
was not yet presaged even by men of far wider vision than
Abraham a Sancta Clara's.

h. The Free Professions

These factors, added to Abraham's traditional anti-intellectualism, help explain why he held the professional classes generally
in rather low esteem. Physicians and surgeons, dentists and
pharmacists, it is true, were denounced by Abraham merely for
their crass ignorance—in his time not without justification—

while he respected their professions as such.[44] The same cannot be said for lawyers, judges, and magistrates, whom the preacher castigated consistently for avarice, corruption, and procrastination. A particularly amusing illustration is the story of the old lawyer who, after his son's graduation from law school and his subsequent marriage, entrusted him with the independent handling of two lawsuits. When the son after three months triumphantly reported that he had won both cases, the father declared that young people should never be lawyers: within three months the son had brought to an end cases that had supplied the father with a livelihood for twenty years.[45]

Crude and erratic as Abraham's discourses frequently are, once he gets down to the facts of real life he can be charged with gross exaggeration but never with poverty of invention. Indeed, his estimate of the lawyer follows a tradition still very much alive at least since the sixteenth century, since the popular carnival comedies (*Fastnachtsspiele*) and fools' literature—in other words, from the time of the acceptance (*Rezeption*) of Roman law in German-speaking lands onward. For centuries, because it was very abstract and highly technical, its qualities notwithstanding, that legal system appeared as alien to the people as its servants appeared suspect. While the popular attitude is reflected in Abraham a Sancta Clara's writings, it is further intensified by his own aversion to rational abstraction.

i. Trades and Crafts: Abraham and the "Little Man"

Artisans, tradesmen, innkeepers, and merchants belonged in Abraham's social philosophy to that middle class that had even less excuse than their noble "betters" for deviating from the path of thrift, industry, and piety—the first two qualities being substituted for those chiefly required of the nobles, valor and generosity.

Abraham definitely talked down to the lower middle class, whose members he censured primarily for laziness, for unreliability in keeping their promises to do their jobs in time, for petty dishonesties in their work, and for crooked dealings in business. Particularly in *Etwas für alle,* a highly detailed register of the little man's sins, he talks with an impressive knowledge of technical affairs about the hooper who used old hoops, the baker who wet the dough too much to make it heavier, the butcher who sold too many bones or sold beef for veal, the tailor who allegedly lost the measurements he had taken, and so on and so on. He is particularly strict with that class of apprentices, journeymen, and helpers who drank and danced on Sunday and spent more than they ought to—which in Sancta Clara's eyes left them open to the suspicion of thievery.[46]

His attitude toward the class that might be called "the petty bourgeoisie" of the Baroque era was on the whole decidedly benevolent in a strictly paternalistic sense. As will be shown at the conclusion of this essay, he has exercised on no other group an influence even remotely as strong. But toward these favored recipients of his ecclesiastic censure his whole outlook was still definitely dominated by the medieval concept that everybody should stay within the class to which he was born and to which he supposedly had been assigned by divine Providence. Thus in addition to anti-intellectualism that perceived the scientific approach as sinful, he upheld another equally powerful tradition of *quieta non moveri,* which, linked to the first, helped to separate Austria still further from the evolution of urban culture in the West.

j. The Peasant

The well-defined boundaries within which the Third Estate was supposed to live were even more strict and rigid in regard to what may be called a kind of Fourth Estate, the peasants, the servants, and the large numbers of dispossessed beggars. Unquestionably there was strong sympathy for the peasants, that is, the serf-tenants, in the warm heart of the Augustinian. But as with artisans and tradesmen, it was upon those he loved that he applied the rod of censure most generously. He castigates the peasants for their grumpiness, avidity, cunning, and frequently also their laziness. In his characterization of these vices, however, the human touch of personal observation, which is evident in his censure of nobles, lawyers, and many groups of artisans, is entirely lacking. Laziness, too much interest in earthly comfort, gluttony, and drunkenness on their rare holidays were to Abraham the typical vices which he was forever denouncing in those non-privileged peasants, whose earthly lot, sweat and toil, should be accepted without a murmur. There is on the other hand a strong emphasis, based undoubtedly on deep personal conviction, on the dignity of rural labor and on the cruel injustice of excessive *robota.* Revolutionary self-help was, of course, ruled out. He expressly denounced the *Jacquerie* in France, the great early-sixteenth-century Swabian peasant uprisings, and Fadinger's still well-remembered revolt in Upper Austria during the Thirty Years' War. Even without reference to the issue of Protestant heresy, which frequently existed among the revolting peasants, these insurrections were condemned just as vehemently as were the uprisings of peasants almost two centuries before denounced by Luther, their Protestant affiliation notwithstanding. Thus the religious abyss between the two most powerful preachers of their respective ages in German-speaking lands is solidly bridged in more than one way by the similarity of their social philosophies.[47]

k. Servants, Keep Your Place!

The servant to Abraham was not in the same class even with the serf-peasant. From him not only contentment with his humble state in society but unqualified subordination in the patriarchic relationship to the master were required. The master, it is true, should in turn not rob the faithful servant of his livelihood. Yet to Abraham faithful servants were rare, an opinion that according to him was shared by Paul of Tharsus and Thomas Aquinas. Many servants were dishonest, lied, slandered, were consistently lazy, and had a most deplorable fondness for entertainment. Abraham had little tolerance for Ursula, the servant girl "with a green taffeta skirt," a fur coat, and laced underwear. Her conduct was under strong suspicion. He frowned upon the shop helper Theodor, "who on Sundays acts like a cavalier, eats, drinks, dances, and *wann der Kopf schwer, so wollen die Füss leicht sein, man singt und springt, man winkt und* [for the sake of rhyme] *stinkt.*"* The honesty of Theodor the swain with his meager income is again questioned.[48] "What indeed are these wicked times coming to? Formerly women used to wear beautiful dresses only in royal palaces; now one can find them even in ordinary houses. Many a servant girl [*Stubenmensch*] . . . parades in taffeta, the silken ribbons floating around her head . . . her hair curled like snails. All this is evidence that she is a snotty scab hussy [*rotziger Grindschippel*]. She wears Italian gloves on

---

*"When the head is heavy, one wants to be light-footed, and one sings, jumps, winks, and stinks." (*Etwas für alle,* 467 ff.; 95, 410. Karajan, *Abraham a Sancta Clara,* 185.)

her hands; nobody must say paws . . ." as Abraham adds sarcastically.[49]

While Ursula and Theodor and their kind were sharply censured because in Abraham's view they wanted to snatch from another social order some earthly pleasure that did not rightly belong to them, he showed greater indulgence toward the class of habitual beggars still enjoying their medieval status. Although he solemnly warned his audience to beware of their false pretenses of sickness and inability to work, and of their dishonesty, he conceived the beggar class as a permanent institution ordained by God. God wills this, according to that strange interpreter of divine Providence, Abraham, for the twofold purpose of enabling the poor man to gain heaven through his sufferings just as surely as the rich man through his charity, for which the poor man serves as a welcome object.[50] A new powerful reason was added for not fighting a social evil allegedly willed by God.

l. *The Soldiers*

An Estate in itself, a most important one in Abraham's world, was that of the military. His views were dominated by his concept of war, which in turn was wholly conditioned by a stale, pragmatic, and deterministic philosophy, very different from the tenets of Natural Law, which was the subject of lively discussion among the intellectual elite of his time. The great Catholic Spanish pioneers of international law from Victoria and Las Casas to Suárez had opened a vista to absolute standards of international conduct. Abraham, some one hundred fifty years later, two generations after Grotius and in the age of Pufendorf, still strictly maintained the double standard of morals in the war against the infidels, the kind of *bellum justum* in which the end indeed justifies any means.[51]

To be sure, Abraham chided and scolded the soldier: *Ein mancher prangt mehr mit der Plumaschi als mit der Courage: Ein mancher versteht sich besser auf die Pasteten als auf die Pasteien: Ein mancher befleisst sich mehrer auf das Haar-Pulver als auf das Schiess-Pulver: Ein mancher steckt ofter in der Schlaf-hauben als Beckel-hauben: Ein mancher hört lieber die Flöten und Flauten, als er sicht die Flinten: Ein mancher liebt mehr die Sabindel als den Sabel. . . .** Yet this does not apply to the soldier in general but specifically to the Christian soldier who is lukewarm in the cause of those "who have fought for the protection and advantage of Christianity, for the preservation of the fatherland, and for the glory of the sovereign."[52] These are unusually solemn words for Abraham, and while frequently in even sharper words he castigated the horrors of war and the concomitant crimes of murder, debauchery, rape, and pillage, such condemnation applied only to war between Christian nations: Abraham's in several ways distorted Christian ethics stop short of applying such standards to wars against the infidels.

m.   The Enemy: Moslem, Jew, Protestant

The devil, in his various incarnations frequently pictured by Abraham, had in that age two principal forces at his disposal: the external foe, the Ottoman Turk, and the internal infidel, the Jew and to a lesser degree (or rather, not so strongly denounced) the Protestant heretic. Whoever is shocked by the violence of Abraham's moral censure should reflect that the preacher thus far had berated only his own friendly environment, not those whom he considered enemies of his faith and country.

"What is the Turk? You Christians, don't answer before you are informed! He is a replica of the antichrist; he is a vain piece of a tyrant; he is an insatiable tiger; he is a damned world-stormer; he is a cruel 'never-enough'; he is a vengeful beast, he is a thief of crowns without conscience; he is a murderous falcon, a dissatisfied, damned bag of a wretch; he is oriental dragon poison; he is the chainless hell hound; he is an epicurean piece of excrement; he is a tyrannic monster"—he is God's whip.[53]

Who is Mohammed? What is Moslemism? Abraham obligingly informs us: "This Mahomet was such a stinking kind of buck that he kept forty women, and in addition to these, by falsely claiming divine privileges and liberties, he had other women at his disposal according to his beastly concupiscence."[54]

What do Moslems believe? "The Moslems believe that their Mohammed on Judgment Day will be changed into a ram, and

*"Quite a few shine more by feathers (on their hats) than by their courage. Some know more about pastry than about bastions; some are more interested in hair powder than gunpowder. Some put on more often the nightcap than the helmet. Some prefer the flute and lute to the flint. Some like Sabine better than the saber." (*Etwas für alle,* 59 ff.)

Abraham a Sancta Clara

Der Dienstbott.
Wer Fein seyn kan, nehm dienst nicht an.

Domestic Servant

Der Schulmeister.
Mischt der Artzney, vom Gifft nicht bey.

Schoolmaster

they themselves all into fleas. After they have settled down in his soft wool, he will take them to heaven, where they will change back into their former appearance. . . . Mahomet is a devil's cook who from various religions, Old and New Testaments, Arianism and Nestorianism, cut off some slices and roasted them in a pan so that the Turks lick their finger for that mixed dish."[55]

While obviously no rules of ethics could ever deter him from his laudable purpose of wiping that Moslem vermin off the face of the earth, Abraham's readers and even more so his hearers must have been surprised to learn that he had actually many more good than bad features to report of these Moslem hell hounds.

In the very work in which the Turks had been so characterized he discoursed at some length upon the fact that those same Turks paid much greater respect to the name of God and his sanctuary than Christians did. He went so far as to say that the loss of Jerusalem to the Christian world had been due to lack of respect for God's Church and a lack of religious zeal in the sanctuary. Yet on this supremely important point of proper reverence to the holy the Turks were exemplary.[56]

Furthermore, "we Christians could very well learn from these infidels charity to the poor and pity for those in need."[57] Christians could also learn from the Turks military discipline. They had executed soldiers for as small an offense as grazing a rider's horse on a peasant's pasture or having uninvited taken a drink of milk from a farm. "The peasants in Turkey never lock up their chicken or geese, even if the whole Turkish army marches through. They are well aware that by threat of the most severe punishment nobody is permitted to expropriate so much as an apple. . . . If such commendable military and soldierly discipline existed here, not so many poor people would cry to heaven and complain to God the Lord about their misery and the unbearable license of the soldiers. . . ."[58]

The Turks were further exemplary in the strictness and the impartiality with which they meted out justice. The cruelty of the bastonade held a great appeal for Father Abraham as a good way to castigate the mortal flesh. Moderation in food and drink, strict observance of fasting, and nonexistence of gambling were all aspects in which the Turks were superior to the Christians.[59]

The educational purpose of these strange eulogies of the

archenemy of Christendom is clear. It is part of a development from the Crusades to our day, with its world-dividing issues. It has been one of the problems of applied moral theology that —as the Church sees it—the dangerously seductive procedures of the antichrist are often aimed at imitating Christian teachings, the better to forestall their realization on earth. To be sure, the whole question presents no problem to basic Christian philosophy, which includes the faithful and the infidels, heretics and apostates, all under the broad mantle of Christian charity. Yet from the standpoint of earthly politics, growing realization of the subjective feeling of righteousness in the infidel and the morally unspoiled ways of life of the savages in the Americas have decisively influenced the growth of international law. Precisely because of its comprehensive validity beyond the Christian world, this law is one of the most noble fruits of Christian culture evolved by clerics in Catholic sixteenth-century Spain.

For Abraham however, a blind representative of an exalted cause, it did not exist. To him enumeration of Christian virtues in the un-Christian Turks was merely a crude way of shaming the Christian world. Not for a moment did he waver in exhortations to wipe them out without mercy; not for a moment did he reflect that those Moslems would be a worthy object for the application of Christian virtues. In view of the ecclesiastical origin of international law, Abraham might well have known about the trend toward the conversion rather than the destruction of heathens. Even if he did not, he like others might well have felt at least a moral dilemma when confronted with well-intended behavior of abstract ethics. In contemplating such a problem he would not have in any way gone beyond the realm of ecclesiastical discipline. Neither his cantankerousness, his frequently uncouth manners and ways, nor the ignorance of his sometimes warped mind absolves him entirely on this point. In more than a score of volumes on morals he injected hardly a single original reflection on Christian ethics. On the contrary, often enough he fought as bitterly, as blindly, the moral principles that were advanced and courageously defended by other, greater champions of the Church.

Abraham a Sancta Clara's approach to the problem of the inner enemy, the Jew, was of a different nature. Here he proceeded in a spirit of highly personal animosity, fomented by centuries-old prejudices. The history of the Austrian, in particular the Viennese Jews, from their first expulsion in 1421 to the second of 1669-70, and even throughout the eighteenth century to the time of Joseph II, is indeed somber and depressing. Yet within that complex history of intermittent persecutions and their problematic causation, there are important variations in the actions of secular and ecclesiastic authorities. Strange as it may seem, the Jewish position in German-speaking Austria was less oppressive under the rule of the most zealous secular representative of the Counter Reformation, Ferdinand II, who in the Jewish question was largely advised by his Spanish Jesuit confessor, Lamormain. It should be noted also that Ferdinand II's attitude toward the Jews was determined far less by need for financial support through war years than by the moral distinction that this adamant foe of Protestantism made between the revolutionary Protestant heretic and the inveterate infidel —the conservative Jew who did not know any better. To a certain extent this was true also of the reign of Ferdinand III and the first part of the rule of Leopold I up to the expulsion of 1669-70, which in large part was due to the continuous economic crises of that uninspired reign.[60]

It is important to bear this in mind in evaluating Abraham's anti-Jewish attitude. A sane (though of course in modern terms by no means just) Jewish policy was not without precedent in Austria. Even after the expulsion of 1670 such a course had some support in the administration. On the other hand, a violent kind of anti-Semitism could count on the fervid acclaim of wide segments of the urban masses. While it required no extraordinary courage to endorse a moderate policy, enthusiastic popular support could be expected only by maintaining the radical point of view.

Here, where it would have required vision and a certain independence of thought to take a stand in support of a somewhat unorthodox policy, Abraham a Sancta Clara sided with the broad and turbid stream of medieval prejudice. What is even worse, he became in this case one of the chief carriers to spread social disease in his century. From his description of "the godless, wretched, virtueless, faithless," and even "reasonless Hebrews," we can perceive that the Jew was a determined foe of the Christian. "These knaves have committed so many misdeeds by this time that one could fill big volumes with them.... O knaves,

knaves!"[61] He furthermore refers again and again to the Jews as envious, vicious, crooked, sinful, and without conscience.[62] In *Mercks Wien,* published in 1679, the year of the great plague, the most popular preacher of Vienna solemnly charges them, along with witches and gravediggers, of having intentionally brought about that disaster—an accusation which at that time naturally had a tremendous effect. He also repeated the medieval charge, most pernicious in its influence on the masses, that the Jews had attempted to get hold of a consecrated host for sinister purposes.[63]

He considered it just that these vicious Jewish scoundrels should be persecuted everywhere since, next to Satan, Christians have no worse enemy than the Jews.[64]

Employing the same technique as that applied to Moslem virtues, he meant to shame Christianity by references to the strictness with which the Jews observed their Sabbath and to the justice of the Mosaic Law as laid down and applied by Moses.[65] This contradiction between at least partly laudable conduct and a damnable fate would, according to Abraham's contemporary David Fassmann, have been resolved by Abraham as follows: "Even though many Jews, in view of their conduct of life, would not deserve to adorn the gallows, I [Abraham] still believe that in view of their religion they merit not only the gallows but the pyre, though the former would do in many cases." However he personally "consoles" a Jew who is afraid of drowning on a Danube boat: "He would not drown, because what should swing on the gallows won't find burial in the Danube." And to quote Abraham directly: "Nowhere among all the people does one find such stubborn and faithless persons as the miserable Jews; they are the scum of the godless and faithless."[66]

In his anti-Jewish diatribes, which could be multiplied almost ad libitum, the question of good faith is noteworthy. In contradiction to much nineteenth- and twentieth-century anti-Semitism there is no reason to assume that an inveterately superstitious, prejudiced, and bigoted man like Abraham acted and talked, talked, talked against his better knowledge. He undoubtedly meant what he said, but just as undoubtedly he could have acquired some information (as quite a few of his contemporary betters did) on the subjects on which he poured out his irresponsible tirades. Here again he did not follow the narrow but not impenetrable path of reason, but responded to the pressure of the masses.

Abraham a Sancta Clara

It should be carefully noted that Abraham a Sancta Clara's anti-Jewish campaign did not precede but followed the great expulsion of the Jews of 1669-70, which had taken place against the advice of several of the emperor's responsible political councilors. Abraham's violent diatribes against the Jews were spoken in a city without a single permanent Jewish inhabitant. Perhaps they may be regarded as a belated justification of a policy which, at least from the economic viewpoint, was soon enough to be recognized as grossly mistaken. From a psychological point of view one might see here the subconscious fight against a feeling of guilt on the part of the masses as well as that of the preacher himself. These are mere conjectures. This much, however, is certain: that the violence of Abraham's anti-Judaism is an important argument against the oversimplified opinion held even in our day that persecutions paralyze, exhaust, and satisfy the aggressive urge.

In a personality such as Abraham's the hate and contempt in which he held beliefs and actions opposed to his own must be measured qualitatively by the character as well as quantitatively by the number of his attacks. Obviously his standards (and in fairness it must be added, the standards of his time) of personal responsibility for his accusations were very different from ours. Many of his invectives against the Moslems are as strident and crude as those against the Jews, but they are counterbalanced by a far greater number of commendable citations.

As to the Protestant heretics there is likewise no lack of references to their damnable heresy and wickedness. Luther is denounced as vain and envious; Calvin and Melanchthon are censured. On the other hand, since in German-speaking lands as a whole certain aspects of the problem of majority-minority interrelations obviously did not come up, this issue was treated by Abraham in a manner very different from the Jewish question. Thus in the second generation after the Thirty Years' War, attacks against the Protestants are on the whole confined to the religious sphere and are not, as in the case of the Jews, directed against their conduct of life as well. Occasionally Abraham was even willing to concede that the baptismal font represents a bond between Catholicism and Protestantism.[67] In view of the spirit of the last phase of the Austrian Counter Reformation and of Abraham's own temperament, one must regard his attitude toward Protestantism as one of the saner aspects of his philosophy. It is difficult to ascertain how far this is due to understanding, to a changed political atmosphere in court circles, and to the feeling that a systematic crusade against the politically recognized and psychologically and socially accepted power of Protestantism would meet with an unfavorable reaction. Possibly all of these factors influenced Abraham's attitude to some extent. But in any event, conscious political opportunism was never a controlling factor with him when he chose to vent his prejudices.

n. Of Women and Marriage

As to feminine influence in human society, Abraham might with complete conviction have reversed Goethe by asserting: *Das ewig Weibliche zieht uns hinab.* Abraham's continuous storming and inveighing against all kinds of luxury is particularly applicable to dresses, cosmetics, and imported foreign luxury goods in general. Likewise sermons attacking dances, comedies, serenades, as potential threats to feminine chastity and virginal innocence are common topics in contemporary sermons.[68]

It is clear also that the Baroque court culture of Austria, with its extravagance, which was entirely out of line with the economic condition of the Habsburg realms (and seems even more out of place in a city undergoing the double ordeal of plague and siege), aroused Abraham's indignation. Obviously he was neither the first nor the last to link primarily feminine shortcomings and infatuation with extravagant standards of living. Yet in view of his often rather witty attack not only on women's venial sins but on the feminine character in general, such an explanation is too simple. There is something more than mere philosophy behind his reaction to the mores of Baroque society.

In one of his most important though by no means unique reflections on the female character, Discourse XII of *Gehab dich wohl*, "On the Malice of Women," he asserts, substantiating his remarks with a number of illustrative stories, that apart from the outstanding malice of women, apart from their stubbornness, "those bad women show a more than beastly temper and an implacable thirst for vengeance. A woman's hatred and anger are far stronger than her love, because her love is not permanent, but her hatred and ire are irreconcilable." Quotations from Scripture and other, even minor literary sources in support of his theory are numerous, as for instance the statement of the noble poet Phocyllidis "that, as it were, women have inherited and taken over qualities from four unreasonable animals. They took filthiness from the pig, biting ire from the dog, the sting from the hedgehog, and vanity from the peacock, which vanity, as the first chief and deadly sin, is innate in women from childhood on, grows with them, and does not cease before death." The accusations of vanity are illustrated by amusing references to quarrels over rank among the wives of the judge, the teacher, the choir conductor, and the town clerk, such as may well have occurred in Austrian small-town life. Yet on the whole, as is not usually the case in Abraham's moral criticism, there is little of the farcical in his denunciation of female vice.[69]

Neither can his attitude toward the female sex be accurately described as hostile. Rather, he was firmly convinced that women are inferior in every respect, above all morally, and he rationalizes his conviction accordingly. This becomes particularly clear in his views on marriage, where he advocates a relationship based on the patient and moderate leadership of the husband, who ought to be fully cognizant of the frailty of the weaker sex. The wife, on the other hand, should keep her place and should not make herself in any way conspicuous, even through laudable activities. "Nothing is more reasonable for a woman than to keep quiet, nothing more foolish than to talk foreign languages." . . . *Auch tragen sie gleichförmig den Titel Frauenzimmer, wodurch sattsam erwiesen wird, dass sie auf Schnecken-Art sollen zu Haus bleiben: widrigen fall müsse man den Nahmen ändern, und an statt Frauen-Zimmer, Frauen-Gassen setzen. . . .**

The wife confined strictly to the notorious three K's, *Kirche, Kinder und Küche,* will be worthy of the full, indulgent, and lenient protection and guidance of a husband whose task is not easy and whose conduct may not be in general blameless, but who ought anyway to be the morally superior and intellectually responsible pilot in the marriage relationship. And this relationship will be blessed only if the husband selects his wife not for the transitory and seductive quality of beauty but solely for her

---

*"Also they uniformly bear the name *Frauenzimmer,* which proves that they ought to stay at home like snails; otherwise one should change the name and call them *Frauen-Gassen* instead of *Frauenzimmer.*" (*Narrennest* [ed. 1753], 2, 108, quoted from Karajan, 211. *Judas der Ertzschelm,* 44.) The German word *Frauenzimmer*—literally "women's room"—is a term used for women. Hence the pun on *Frauenzimmer* (women's room) and *Frauen-Gassen* (women's street).

virtue. Beauty may be present as well only if male desire is directed exclusively toward the nobler purposes of marriage— though unfortunately in actual life *Es ist freylich weit beliebter ein purpurfarbener Mund bey einer Jungen als eine alte Runkgunkel, wann sie ein Maul hat wie ein rostiges Schlüsselloch an einer alten Kellertür. Es ist weit ergötzlicher eine wohl proportionierte Nasen einer herzigen Rosimunda, als ein trifender Destillirkolben einer garstigen Schmutzibunda. Es ist weit erfreulicher anzusehen eine solche Docken, welcher die Zähne in dem Kund stehen wie die Orientalische Perlen, als ein alter Meerwolf, der da ein Gebiss hat wie die ausgefaulte Pallisaden.**

Thus the problem of self-denial and inhibition is raised in the context of the husband-wife relation. It is the leitmotiv of Abraham's philosophy on this key issue. First and last, woman means to him the object of sinful masculine desire, the instrument of hellish temptation. All conscious efforts to defend the virtuous spouse and her honorable position in society cannot drown out the underlying theme.† To be sure, it is an old one in the clerical tradition and the mores of Abraham's time; he certainly cannot be blamed for playing it. Yet it is neither the basic idea expressed in the Scriptures nor the one that has been more and more clearly understood by the Church in modern times. Again, with an unfailing instinct Abraham espoused the cause of medieval error and took the involved and cramped notions of temporary clerical misinterpretation for the broad and clear religious idea itself.

o. Of Dangerous Pleasures

The temptations of the world were for Abraham largely indentified with carnal sensations. Women are pictured as all too suscep-

---

* "To be sure the red mouth of a young girl is more attractive than the snout of an old hag that looks like the rusty keyhole at the old cellar door. The well-shaped nose of lovely Rosamonde is far more attractive than the dripping still of ugly Schmutzi[dirty]bunda. It is far more pleasing to look at a girl whose teeth seem to be oriental pearls than at an old shark with teeth like a rotten fence." (*Gehab dich wohl*, 290, in Discourse XVI, "Nützliche Haus-Regul vor die Ehe-Leute," 283-300, 367. On the marriage problem see also above all *Judas der Ertzschelm*, part L, "Der unglückseelig Ehestand," 24-64; *Mercks Wien*, the discourse on "Markt's Eheleut!" 117-38; *Hui und Pfui*, 101 ff.)

† Wilhelm Scherer, in *Vorträge und Aufsätze*, 171, regards the reminiscences of Abraham's youth concerning his mother, a notoriously cantankerous woman, as a chief reason for his views on the issue. Considering the broad tradition on which Abraham's attitude is based, such an interpretation seems rather too narrow.

tible to the insidious lure of dancing and the theater. They are
also accused of being partial to sumptuous dresses, food and
drink, and all kinds of foreign luxuries.[70] In this array of sins,
dancing, obviously invented by the devil himself, ranks as the
most serious one; indulgence in lavish food and drink—the
favorite pleasure of Abraham's little man—is treated with greater forbearance. Thus the most hated group of evildoers, the
Jews, are blamed again and again, though indirectly, for having
too little appreciation of these least-dangerous pleasures. Abraham even castigates the Jews for their dislike of manna in the
desert, though it tasted like the favorite dishes of the Austrian
cuisine:

> Besides other very great proofs of divine grace, this too
> was given them by God, that he fed them with the best
> manna or heavenly bread, and this manna had every
> kind of desired taste: Westphalian ham, Austrian lark,
> Tyrolian goose leg, Swabian pie, Bohemian cake . . .
> Spanish chocolate, Turkish sherbet. . . . All the most
> tasty dishes were included in this manna or heavenly
> bread, and yet they hated it and they grumbled against
> their leader Moses. They also wished they were still sit-
> ting by their Egyptian onions and garlic. O ye nasty,
> stinksnouts, do you like the musty vegetables better than
> heavenly bread? Yes, yes; the reason was this and no
> other, that the Jews had been used to onions and garlic
> for many years and what one is used to is hard to leave.[71]

This comic passage gives much information about Abraham,
the Jews, anti-Judaism, and incidentally Austrian cooking of the
day. Obviously the attack on the Jews regarding manna is, to
say the least, somewhat farfetched and certainly at variance with
the Scriptures (Exodus 16). As a matter of fact, from quite another standpoint the censured Jews might well have been held
up as examples of moderation. Yet to Abraham the Jewish garlic-
and-onion diet—their diet in his day—like their likes and dis-
likes in many another field, was completely out of step with
those of the Austrian people. What Abraham really censured
was their arrogant presumption, as he saw it, that they are entitled to be different from others. It was the foreigner's disin-
clination to share that one harmless and venial sin that Abraham perhaps might have consciously committed himself. The

dilemma posed by the conflict between asceticism and Baroque culture was very real to him in its influence on all spheres of carnal physical sensations. He commended self-denial but he did not appreciate what he regarded as indifference to the temptations of daily life in infidels living outside the pale of Austrian Baroque civilization.

p. Education

It is to Abraham's credit that within that civilization he comprehended the full significance of the key issue in human attitudes and relations, the problem of education. He dealt with it amply (in his case that always means repetitiously) but also with unusual seriousness. That his intentions were noble, again, is beyond doubt, but here the positive evaluation of his views on the subject comes to an abrupt end.

Abraham, in his peculiar way a friend of humanity insofar as it professed the Catholic faith, was certainly no enemy of youth; yet he was a determined opponent of juvenile behavior and psychology. This is evident in the following sentence (in style one of the finest ever written by him): "Free, alert, fresh, gay and friendly is youth, and thus youth and virtue are rarely connected."* Thus, *"zu vil, zu vil, zu vil werden die Kinder geliebt.* [Too much, too much, too much are children being loved.] Daily we see the none-too-small misery of parents who, not from hunger but from confused love, want to eat up their children. . . . *Destwegen all dero dichten, schlichten, sorgen, borgen, lauffen, schnauffen, schauen, bauen, gehen, stehen, schreiben, treiben, dahin zilt, dass den Kindern wohl gehe.* [Therefore all their thinking, planning, worrying, borrowing, rushing, panting, looking, building, walking, standing and writing is exclusively focused on their children's welfare.] But unfortunately they think only of the body, not of the soul; they think only of the temporary and not of the eternal welfare of the children."

What is to be done about it? One and one thing alone: don't spare the rod;[72] mortify the flesh but save the soul. The rod applied to the child in time will save the adult from the hangman's noose in time to come. This idea is repeated cease-

---

"Frei, frisch, frech, fröhlich und freundlich ist die Jugend, wessenthalben Jugend und Tugend selten beisammen." (Hui und Pfui, 479.) This is one of the passages in Abraham's writings where the conciseness and vigor of the thesis, allied with his here moderately used technique of alliteration, produces a grandiose artistic effect.

lessly in all the Baroque vagaries of Abraham a Sancta Clara's language and thinking. Which ought to be king among the trees? The birch, naturally. What does Clementinus Alexandrinus call children? He calls them *flores matrimonii,* "flowers of matrimony." Well, there must be a fence of rods and sticks around the flowers, or any sow can get in.

What does the Holy Father Augustinus call children? He calls them *naviculas fluctuentes,* "little floating boats." Well, for these boats one needs paddles that the broom-maker sells.

What does the holy Gregorius Nazanzius call children? *Oculos suorem parentum,* "eyeballs of their parents." Well, nature has linked those eyeballs to eyebrows shaped like rods.[73]

And now a tougher question: Who is the angel for whom Abraham has no great liking? It is the angel "who checked the sword of the obedient patriarch Abraham and shouted: *Non extendes manum tuam super puerum.* Don't stretch out your hand over the boy, and don't hurt him. I know very well that such was the command of the supreme God, and thus no blame can be voiced. Yet I am assured that if a father or a mother wants to strike a boy, no angel will prompt them with serious words: *Extende manum tuam super puerum.* Stretch out your hand over the boy."[74] It should be remembered that Moses' rod remained a rod only so long as he held it in his hand; when he dropped it, it changed into a serpent. The moral application is clear: he who does not whip his children poisons them.[75]

Yet the rod, wholesome as it is, cannot do everything. Ceaseless efforts to follow the right path on the part of both youth and elders are necessary. Abraham's teaching abounds in warnings to elders to keep children away from evil company and pleasures—that is, by implication, from any company and any social activities that are non-religious in character. In the same spirit he issued a warning to youth, particularly the gay youth of Vienna, with their deplorable interest in French and Italian manners, entertainments, and finery.[76]

In putting that philosophy into effect, the role of the teacher, next to that of the parents, is obviously of the greatest importance.[77] In view of what has been said, it is noteworthy and indicative of the sad state of German elementary education after the Thirty Years' War that Abraham had to warn the teacher to beware of too much ire and cruelty, though the demand for strict rod discipline is of course strongly reiterated. So is the obvious but probably necessary demand for exemplary conduct on the part of the teacher. What is lacking, most characteristically lacking, in Abraham's admonitions is any demand for training in specific aptitudes and knowledge, for any intellectual advancement in the strict meaning of the word.

It might be presumptuous to measure Abraham's educational philosophy according to the traditions and standards of his elders—and betters—Erasmus, Comenius, and Locke. However, it is certainly fair to Abraham to point out that the educational product of Jesuit culture, so much admired by Abraham, was very different from the ignorant, beaten-up, de-personalized object to whom he addressed his instructions. Again, not only in the Western world at large but within his own system he had with unfailing instinct taken the wrong road.

It was a broad road, to be sure. Yet within the framework of a supreme religion that allows for wide horizons of peace, love, and joy, was it natural for a basically warmhearted man, with both feet firmly on the ground of seventeenth-century life, even on this point to preach exclusively a gospel of mortification and self-denial? The answer goes straight back to the central position of his philosophy. Its basic tenet may be clearly illustrated in a final reflection of his on the educational problem. In the discourse *Die billige Sünder- und Kinderstraf* ("The Just Punishment of Sinners and Children") he discusses the tough theological problem presented in the well-known narration of the travels of the prophet Elisha: "And he [Elisha] went up from thence unto Beth-el: and as he was going up by the way, there came forth little children out of the city, and mocked him, and said unto him, Go up, thou bald head; go up, thou bald head. And he turned back, and looked on them, and cursed them in the name of the Lord. And there came forth two she-bears out of the wood, and tore forty and two children of them." (II Kings 2: 23-24, A.V.)

Why were small children punished so severely for an offense that in the eyes of many of Abraham's parishioners and readers was obviously excused by the insignificance of the offense and the juvenile irresponsibility of its perpetrators? First, according to Abraham, the offense was not small. Yet the chief reason for this terrific punishment was the fact that the children had been brought up badly by their parents. Why then, asks Abraham, were not the parents punished instead of the small children? "Because," he exclaims solemnly and impressively, "it is far harder and more painful for the parents if they have to see that to their own children will be meted out all kind of punishments, sadness, even death itself, than if these parents themselves had to suffer." He dwells further on this thought:

> My God, how the parents of these children will have cried and lamented when they found their beloved children so cruelly mangled in their blood on the ground. What a piercing stab in the hearts of these fathers and mothers will it have been to see their own sons so pitiably murdered.... Remember this chapter, O parents, and be perfectly sure that God will punish in your sons all the unjust property that you, your ancestors, and great ancestors have acquired unjustly.... God, to be sure, could punish some parents on their body or property; he could spoil the fruits of the field; he could destroy arable land and meadows by fire; but this punishment would be far too small. *Ego Dominus fortis Zelotes*, God, the strong zealous Lord [*Eiferer (sic)*], will avenge the sins of the parents upon the children so that while the parents still live, the children will suffer all kinds of ignomy and derision, even the gallows and the wheel.[78]

This horrid line of reasoning was not unique in Abraham's thinking. The same idea of the punishment of parents for the sins of their children is just as drastically brought home in the story of the destruction of the high priest Heliogabalus for the crimes of his sons and his own insufficient correction of their misdeeds. It is even surpassed in his terrible distortion of Christ's teaching for the purpose of proving that God is strong and sharp in his justice. "When Peter cut off the ear of Malchus, our Lord reproved him. How so? Why? He was an ecclesiastic who should not wear saber or sword: if somebody else had done so, the Lord would inevitably have approved of it and commended it."[79]

Thus the issue of education was brought home to the world in general, which should tremble before the eyes and under the rod of a stern, unrelenting, and zealous God. In linking parental correction to the divine correction of society as a whole, Abraham was enraptured by the vision: "Those parents, sovereigns, governors, rulers, and magistrates are and will be fortunate who in front of their children, subordinates, and servants always have watered the stern rods of punishment and correction and who will be always ready and quick to punish their wrongs and correct them. . . ."[80]

These are not *gemütliche* paternal reprimands, nor is there anything farcical or clownish about them. Indeed, humor intentional or unintentional, exemplification by means of ample, pointed, well-characterized references to the venial sins of the Austrian people in regard to food, drink, dancing, and play, do not give the complete picture of Abraham a Sancta Clara. More correctly, they give a picture only of the "superstructure" of his personality, the thin veneer that gives color to the portrait of the Baroque moralist. These impressions do not reveal the character of the zealot behind it, a character of far sterner stuff, who shapes the image of a revengeful God after his own frustrated and aggressive personality. At the core of that personality, of that man's views and demands upon society, lay an overpowering feeling of guilt for the impurity of deeds and even more so of thoughts. Carrying the Augustinian doctrine of original sin to the extreme, he conceived human life as a constant, tragic, and unsuccessful struggle to free oneself from that guilt. Yet in his attempt to achieve earthly happiness, man is dragged ever more deeply into the toils of sin.

q. *Abraham a Sancta Clara Behind the Mask*

Abraham's prescription for freeing oneself from that vicious circle is as follows:

Prescription

Take, O man, take, O Christian soul,
　　this which I prescribe for you:
First, take from the memory of your birth,
　　from the pity of your nothingness,
　　from the bitter pain of sadness,
　　from the myrrhs of mortality,
Take a big handful of each,
　　grind it in the mortar of a repentant heart,
Wet it with the water of your tears of repentance,
　　boil it on the fire of fervent worship,
　　blow on it with the sighs of your repentance and pain,
　　cook it well by means of reflection.

Abraham a Sancta Clara

A full spoon of it, taken every day with pure, clear conscience, is an excellent drug against every kind of sin.

Here the Baroque form, sustained even in the supreme reflection, can still distort but can no longer hide the ascetic and ecstatic core of that strangely repellent and even more strangely attractive character whose conscious thoughts are centered around the sacred warning: *Memento homo, quia pulvis es et in pulverem revertis!* [81]

That this man, with an uncanny subconscious directive, put on foolscap and clown's mask must be charged to the account of Austria, which he regarded as his adopted fatherland, where as he (rightly) believed he could teach most effectively. Thus the clown's mask is not the key to his personality; it is merely the key to his tremendous effect on contemporary and subsequent developments.

2. Abraham a Sancta Clara: History of an Influence

a. Abraham in Literary History

In evaluating the ultimate significance of a writer, the influence of his own ideas or of his promotion of the ideas of others is only one important factor among several. In viewing him as a link in the chain of historical development, however, this single factor assumes an overwhelming importance. It also raises a problem of extraordinary difficulty, that of gauging the extent and the nature of his influence on public opinion. That is difficult enough to determine in the case of a contemporary figure; in the past it can be a matter only of surmise.

Concerning the contradictory hero of this study, there of course exist a number of important and illuminating evaluations. With the single exception of Scherer, virtually all of them deal primarily with criticism and analysis of his personality and work. The influence of a writer in the judgment of literary criticism is determined primarily by the question whether or not his writings are still alive—that is, whether they are worth being read today. This, however, is largely an aesthetic problem with which this study is not directly concerned.

The question why Abraham a Sancta Clara's writings have been largely forgotten will not be taken up here. Whether this oblivion is deserved or undeserved—and in the case of Abraham's in many ways fascinating personality, it is probably not entirely deserved—is not the issue at stake. It is sufficient to recognize the fact that neither the artistic values, the specific intellectual range, nor even the wide range of topical problems of late-seventeenth-century homiletic literature appeals to the aesthetic standards of the literary reader in our day.

Yet acceptance of this simple fact by no means disposes of the question of the influence of a writer. His work may have, may still exercise, a powerful influence not on "literature" but on the chief medium of ideological communication, public opinion. This kind of influence obviously diverges from the literary field and enters the broad sphere on social relations in general. Yet inasmuch as there is a direct though sometimes seemingly tenuous connection between social and literary evaluation and criticism, it is advisable to survey briefly the history of this literary tradition in regard to Abraham a Sancta Clara. Once this literary insight is gained, it should be easier to go into the wider historical aspects of the problem.

Changes in literary taste notwithstanding, the opinion that in language and in the service of his cause Abraham a Sancta Clara was one of the most effective writers and speakers of all time is fully upheld here. This is not contradicted by the fact that his style with some notable exceptions is marred by excessive use of faulty syllogisms, forced alliterations and rhymes, and excessive play on words. As were few before and perhaps even fewer after him, he was capable of forging his own tools, of shaping language to his purpose—of putting his views across.[82] By reason of this, he was a truly eminent personality. Yet eminence merely conveys the notion of an outstanding position with relation to others; it does not imply the presence of true greatness in an absolute sense.

Abraham's own contemporaries realized this point rather clearly. In a literary sense he may have been the most outstanding late follower and leading innovator of that important social-satirical school of fools' literature, which, beginning with the *Narrenschiff* of Sebastian Brant, dominated the outgoing fifteenth and early sixteenth centuries. Other literary trends left their imprint on Abraham's writings as well. As an ecclasiastic literary writer he in a sense resumed the tradition of the early-sixteenth-century Franciscan monk Thomas Murner and his own contemporary, the Capucin frater Martin von Cochem. He also possessed in some of his works the urban social appeal of the

Abraham a Sancta Clara

outstanding sixteenth-century plays of Hans Sachs,[83] and as stylist and writer of prose he is closely related to the great late-sixteenth-century satirist Johannes Fischart. Abraham is in a way one of the last major writers whose work combines definite features of late Gothic, Renaissance secularism, and Baroque passion. Yet in spite of his very genuine feeling, all this cannot compensate for his failure to make a deep emotional appeal because of his constant brandishing of the harlequin's wooden sword. Broad, far-reaching, and lasting, yet not deep, is the work of the man characterized by a late anonymous contemporary as follows:

Ertz-Vatter Abraham', es lachet deine Sara,
Statt dass sie Gott dem Herrn aus wahrem Hertzen danckt;
So lacht auch jedermann bey Abraham a Clara,
Wann er ein Predigt macht bey Augustinus Sanct! [84]

That poem, published at the beginning of the second quarter of the eighteenth century, marks the initiation of the literary period that rejects Abraham most categorically. To the early and even later Enlightenment a man like Abraham a Sancta Clara was an opponent whose work was to be attacked rather than measured aesthetically. Thus it is only natural that the chief German representative of that era, Lessing, should reject Abraham outright.* However, the incontestable fact that in the realm of belles-lettres in Austria the era of the Enlightenment was the truly dark age, far more so than the Baroque, greatly diminishes the effectiveness of that enlightened renunciation. Classicism, with its greater composure and intellectual detachment, could take a more objective view of Abraham. Goethe, though fully aware of Abraham's mannerism and irrational-demagogic tendencies,[85] called Schiller's attention to *Auf, auf ihr Christen.* He saw in that work "a rich treasure, very full of atmosphere [*Stimmung*]," by which he is obviously referring to the genuine and sincere setting of the Baroque and the Counter Reformation. This, of course, is a purely aesthetic view, and Schiller accepted a basically similar interpretation. The masterfully drawn Capuchin pater in *Wallensteins Lager* is one of those none-too-numerous characters drawn

---

*See the second letter in Lessing's treatise *Anti-Goeze* (the polemic against Pastor Goeze; Braunschweig, 1778). "The one who lacks [logics] in a sermon could never manage to write a tolerable comedy, even if he was the most inexhaustible jester under the sun. Do you think Father Abraham could have written good comedies? Certainly not. His sermons are all too miserable."

by Schiller who speak exclusively for themselves and the historical idea they represent, and neither for nor against Schiller's own viewpoint. It is again exclusively the artist in Schiller who states in a letter to Goethe: "This Father Abraham is a man of wonderful originality whom we must respect, and it would be an interesting though not at all an easy task to approach or surpass him in mad cleverness."[86]

It is understandable that the irrationalism of Abraham a Sancta Clara, though perhaps only as a reaction to still-prevalent ideas of the Enlightenment, should on the whole have been given a friendly reception by Romanticism. This may be due not so much to Abraham's ideas as to the atmosphere of his writings. They have been acclaimed by the devout Catholic Eichendorff, and Jean Paul, a subtle literary critic, said of them: "His gift of creation and verbiage suffers from nothing but the century and the threefold stage: Germany, Vienna, and the pulpit."[87] Of these factors Scherer, commenting on this observation, rejects "Germany" and "the century," which are to him the period of a rationally oriented philosophy of Natural Law, Protestant-Puritan church literature, and dawning Enlightenment. He adds, however, in speaking of the influence of "Vienna" and "the pulpit" that "this is the reason why Abraham's picture oscillates in our imagination as between that of a punishing prophet and a court jester and harlequin."[88]

This last remark is an oversimplified criticism of a technique that in its ultimate effect was far more than mere buffoonery. Yet its impression on authoritative liberal literary historians like Karl Goedeke, and somewhat later on Georg G. Gervinus[89] and Scherer himself, may have greatly contributed to the mid-nineteenth-century rejection of Abraham. Literary developments since that time have not been influenced to the same extent by dominant doctrinaire literary theories of the day such as those of the Scherer school. To Austrian literary historians with clerical leanings, as represented by the analysis in standard works on German-Austrian literary history, Nagl and Zeidler (first edition) and Richard von Kralik, Abraham appears by implication as the possessor of greater literary merit than Walter von der Vogelweide and as an "intellectual giant among dwarfs."[90] A very distinguished historian, Hugo Hantsch, in line with Joseph Nadler's glorification of Abraham's ideas has only recently referred to Abraham a Sancta Clara as the most ingenious master of language between Luther and Goethe [91]—Grimmelshausen, Winckelmann, Wieland, and Herder in the realm of prose notwithstanding.

Remarkably different in this respect is a non-German evaluation of Abraham, approved by ecclesiastic authorities—that by N. Scheid in the *Catholic Encyclopedia*. After paying due respect to his ability to arouse the interest of his hearers and readers, Scheid frankly condemns the confused writings and stylistic harlequinades. He concludes (as quoted at the beginning of this study) that "even up to the most recent times Abraham's influence is chiefly noticeable in the literature of the pulpit, though but little to its advantage."[92] The character of this evaluation is all the more significant when compared with the routine comments in the standard German Catholic encyclopedia, the *Grosse Herder*, and with Scherer's far too categorically expressed negative views in *Allgemeine deutsche Biographie*.[93]

Extreme nationalism, at least in the National Socialist era, naturally could not be expected to extol the extreme but sincere clerical views of Abraham a Sancta Clara, notwithstanding the fact that his approach to the Jewish question and the violence, the rudeness, and the intolerance of his attacks against opponents or imagined opponents of his doctrine had much to recommend it to that movement.[94] There is, however, a pre-National-Socialist, so-called German-Christian ideology (with the accent on the first word) which praised Abraham's language for its snappy, pithy simplicity and—of all things—"conciseness which nevertheless is full of poetic art. It is bound to captivate the part of the German-speaking people which has not been spoiled by aestheticism or the importation of a foreign language spirit. This language must captivate those German-speaking people who have not apostatized from the Christian moral views which have been passed down from our fathers, so that they will not reject their strong ally [Abraham] a priori. The deeper reason for the fact that the work of Abraham a Sancta Clara has remained alive is the same which in his times was the basic explanation of his tremendous success: genuineness, purity, personality, character."[95]

And Herbert Cysarz, a writer of even more pronounced nationalist leanings, complements this praise with a eulogy of Abraham's literary form: "The noblest *Wortkunst* of the declining seventeenth century is the creation of Abraham a Sancta Clara, perhaps the only poetic personality in his Austro-Bavarian environment."[96]

It is significant indeed that Abraham has been praised far more uncritically by semi-Radical-Nationalists and pseudo-clerical-nationalist writers than by those who adhere to the rigid standards of clerical doctrines. Indeed the uncalled-for support of camouflaged integral nationalism, with its flair for scenting related ideas or techniques, does much more serious damage to Abraham's standing than criticism of the liberal Scherer type.

Nevertheless, taking a cross section of the literary estimates of Abraham from his own time to the present day we find that— wide differences of opinion on his serious shortcomings notwithstanding—there is general agreement in regard to these positive qualifications: In the main he is considered a man of broad though badly disorganized knowledge. Irrespective of the aesthetic and logical merits or demerits of his style, he is generally recognized as one of the most effective, if not the most effective, German prose-writer of his time. It is further widely acknowledged that as such he was able in German-speaking Austria and Catholic southern and western Germany to maintain an eminent position for nearly a century. That this was possible only because of the long period of literary stagnation undoubtedly detracts somewhat from the achievement, but it does not alter the fact.

b. History and Evaluation of Abraham's Appeal

Richard von Kralik asserted, and rightly in many ways, that Abraham represented "the strongest personification of the Viennese spirit of the seventeenth century."[97] Scherer pointed out the fact that just a year before Abraham's death Joseph Stranitzky, the buffoon, opened the first show of the Punch and Judy type in Vienna. According to him Stranitzky, in his popular harlequinades, is the true and legitimate successor of Abraham.[98] It is indeed quite true that the harlequin inherited an audience that had responded to the farcical and truly popular elements in Abraham. There is much more to this relationship, however, than Scherer himself may have been aware of and than is realized by the superficial observer.

First of all, the *Hanswurst* Stranitzky (possibly unknown to Scherer) actually quoted or, rather, as it was termed in that age of literary freebooting, "borrowed" freely from Abraham a Sancta Clara.[99] Even more important, the *Hanswurst,* the harlequin, as introduced by Stranitzky and developed by his more subtle successor Joseph von Kurz (Bernardon) in the Rococo period, assumed the important task of critic of society. To be able to do so with impunity he must don the foolscap and thus he gained *Narrenfreiheit*, the fool's freedom. Because he stressed the farcical, he was forgiven by the authorities and by society for alluding to the serious. Even when and where Abraham's seemingly passionate social criticism is not on the right side of the fence for the absolutist regime, his clownish antics made his intemperate attacks acceptable to the authorities. The curious concoction of thrill, fear, awe, and merriment appealed to the public. The fool's freedom was readily granted him by the authorities. This was not much due to the fact that the clownish and the puckish are always assumed to be politically innocent, not much even to a respect for the clerical garb. Above all, its wearer was understood (in principle rightly understood) to be a defender and an ally of the established order. Subjectively his rantings and ravings were of course perfectly sincere. Viewed objectively, what they actually covered behind the clown's mask of attack was a defense of the existing social order. By and large, criticism is not directed toward social action but is shifted to the kingdom to come. It does not call for reforming action; apart from its unchallenged spiritual obligations, this criticism diverted social dissatisfaction into the fields of mirth, fun—and hatred of dissenters. The social critic in his foolscap thus performed a highly welcome conservative function; and his personal honesty made the fool's services all the more valuable.

To be sure, comparison with the harlequin of the coming generation falls down in certain respects. Obviously Abraham's life work can by no means be conceived solely within the framework of buffoonery. Only a segment of the habitual activities of a clown of Stranitzky's stamp is devoted to a criticism of society. But after all, the quantitative differences are certainly no greater than the disparity in social prestige between the imperial-court preacher of admittedly lofty intentions and the vagrant jester with his necessarily camouflaged social opposition. Yet no differences can blot out the weird similarity of their popular appeal and its consequences.[100]

The frantic efforts of the Austrian Enlightenment notwithstanding, this harlequin was not entirely superseded until more than a century later by the truly great comic-satiric art of Raimund and Nestroy.[101] While the *Hanswurst* was extremely popular in Vienna and urban Austria in general, the generation after Abraham was constantly being told by the enlightened reformers and, from the time of the young Joseph II on, by government authorities that this kind of humor was rude, crude, undignified, and not in keeping either with the laws of decency or with national cultural pride.

The effectiveness of this enlightened propaganda is a rather controversial issue to be discussed more fully in the essay on Sonnenfels. This much, however, may be anticipated here: it is more than likely that, from the second half of the eighteenth century onwards, the educated, and in the course of time the other classes, did not enjoy the *Hanswurst* without a perceptible feeling of shame—which is to say guilt. The same does not apply where this type of entertainment could be "sublimated" by the noble purpose of the pulpit. Vulgar taste, opposition to the dreary instructions of enlightened reformers, and obviously more deeply rooted desires thus became elevated by the lofty purpose. The success of a pulpit style that combined and rationalized all these complex factors, endowing them for the masses with the aura of a truly genuine religious feeling, is easily comprehensible. This technique has been followed through the centuries far beyond, in fact, primarily beyond, the religious sphere.

It is of course true that the specific technique introduced by Abraham in his sermons changed in the course of time, though the spectacular devices of the Baroque style were employed almost continuously in this field long after Abraham. Yet the basic idea—that of enjoying the farcical criticism of human weakness, primarily the weakness of others as it appears to individual members of the audience—remained attractive when it seemed to be justified by the noble purpose.*

Perhaps even more effective is the sublimation of aggression in attacks not merely upon sin but upon social groups of sinners—the Jews, to a lesser degree in the eighteenth century the Turks and the Protestants, and nonconformists on social and moral issues generally. The unwholesome and unholy effect of the aggressive intolerance of group convictions sheds at times an un-

*An excellent example of the sublimated thrill experienced by the audience, produced and used to advantage by the brilliant convert preacher Zacharias Werner at the time of the Congress of Vienna in the Stephanskirche, is given by K. A. Varnhagen von Ense, *Denkwürdigkeiten des eigenen Lebens* (Leipzig, 1888). See also A. de la Garde, *Gemälde des Wiener Kongresses* (Munich, 1914), II, 346 ff.

pleasant light upon Austria's history. In short, a key to the strength of Abraham's influence seems to be the fact that he offered his audience and readers a means of sublimating their emotions.

The most important objective yardsticks for measuring this influence are contemporary evaluations of his appeal.[102] The ample and undeniable evidence of the success of the man who in his day was Catholic Germany's and Austria's most popular preacher can of course never be supplanted by analytical studies of his personality written after his death. Yet his specific effect on public opinion in later times can be gauged by several facts: first, the widespread and persistent imitation of Abraham's style in the pulpit. As Abraham's admirer Herbert Cysarz puts it in a sincerely meant but actually rather dubious compliment, "wit, gaiety, entertainment, dominate the Bavarian and Austrian pulpits in the next decades."[103]

Of further significance is the strong indirect effect on those literary polemics of a popular and dialectic character that were widely introduced in the era of Enlightenment.* Finally, in itself not too important a point yet valuable as an indication of his continuing appeal, is the widespread plagiarization of Abraham's work, which would of course never have taken place had his style not remained in public vogue throughout the best part of the eighteenth century.[104]

The most valid proof, though an indirect one, of this widespread influence on public opinion is the vitality and the popular appeal of Abraham's ideas themselves. This can be seen not only in the eighteenth but to an even greater extent in the nineteenth century, though the direct connection between Abraham and his successors and imitators in the later period could hardly have been consciously perceived. His influence had merged with that of the great cause that he and his later followers stood for and misunderstood. The spiritual force that had the most powerful effect of all time on public opinion obviously cannot easily be broken up into its individual components. Yet the deeply and widely recognized purity of that cause focuses attention all the more sharply on those not too numerous but all too influential agents of the Church in the field of public communication who

---

*Such can be observed in a way even in the journalistic controversies of the late Enlightenment, wherever they touch upon popular issues, as for example the attacks against Sonnenfels' anti-harlequin campaign.

impaired the dignity of the Church and distorted her message. There cannot be the shadow of a doubt that Abraham a Sancta Clara—this man full of medieval superstitions and aggressions in which he half believed and which he propagated far and wide—did not do this intentionally. It was done in good faith, though not in pure faith. Yet this merely adds a tragic overtone to the problem of his in many respects unwholesome influence. It does not alter the problem itself.

c. Abraham a Sancta Clara and the Problem of Cultural Lag

In one of his exaggerated reflections, which however often contain an important element of truth, Scherer observes: "The characteristic feature is that in his relationship with the imperial court and the educated public of the Catholic capital Abraham was permitted to keep to the lowest kind of joke and to perfect it. At that time it [i.e., this type of the comic] dared present itself in Protesant Germany only at the lowest level of education. Thus the factor of delay is the characteristic one. Abraham is the contemporary of Bossuet. The court of Vienna in the seventeenth century is no farther developed than the court of Paris in the fifteenth. The dirty brook, which elsewhere is drying up, here with Abraham once more grows into a river."[105]

And Ferdinand Kürnberger, one of Austria's most brilliant literary essayists in Scherer's time, expresses ideas of amazing similarity in a more general setting: "We are writing among a people whose claim to two centuries of German culture has been suppressed for two centuries by Spanish Jesuit tyranny. In these two centuries in which the cultural education of the German people was accomplished, in those two centuries from Luther to Kant in which Germany did everything, what did Austria do? While the immense literature of Germany developed, Austria wrote tickets of confession, dream books, and cookbooks after the fashion of Linz. Everybody on his own and for himself had to start cultural education from the beginning; no river from which everybody could draw flowed through the country...."[106]

There are obvious exaggerations and distortions in these remarks by a rigid academician and a more flexible essayist. The approach in both cases is unhistorical. Neither writer shows much understanding and appreciation of the spirit from which popular humor developed in Western Europe in the two centuries before

Abraham a Sancta Clara

Abraham a Sancta Clara. Here and in other observations by Scherer* and Kürnberger the transitory intellectual superiority of northern and central German over southern German and Austrian intellectual achievements and standards in the eighteenth century is being far too little evaluated on historical grounds and far too closely linked to the ecclesiastical issue. It is difficult, on the other hand, to contradict the assertion that Abraham's farcical campaign style revived an at least two-century-old tradition that had its *raison d'être* in its time but was ill-suited to the era of tremendous intellectual and social-economic transformation of the late seventeenth century. There is at least a possibility that, without Abraham, an intellectual life that obscured problems of morals, prejudice, and aggression under the mask of the harlequin might have come to an earlier end in the southeastern German cultural orbit.

At this point it might well be argued that an enlightened era, more receptive and adaptable to the taste and the intellectual requirements and abilities of the masses, should have been able to check the confusing and irrational element in the Baroque spirit. Such an argument, based on the flagrant psychological weakness of the Enlightenment, is not unjustified in itself. Yet while the fact that the enlightened opponents of a Baroque cause put up a weak fight may reflect unfavorably on this opposition, it does not necessarily strengthen the case of the cause under attack. Its popular appeal, so powerfully voiced by Abraham, might indeed have helped delay the progress of Enlightenment. In any event, except for her outstanding achievements in the field of the formative arts and music, Austria seemed to be for a long time after her transition to Classicism and Romanticism out of step with the intellectual development of Western Europe. Max Michel formulates this line of thought succinctly:

> This seems to be the essence of Abraham's creative work. Two elements determine Abraham, the Church and society. He starts from the Church toward society in the in-

*See for example the following question posed by Wilhelm Scherer: "How was it possible that at the very time in which Spener gave Protestantism reform and purification, in Catholic Germany the most gifted preacher lowered himself to the character of a clown? How could he think that he would administer the sacred function of moral education of the people best by addressing his sermons of reprimands to the desire for laughter of a capital that always wanted to be entertained?" (*Vorträge und Aufsätze*, 154.)

terests of the Church. . . . It is the fate of Abraham to
have lived in a period of intellectual transformation in
which he could not participate but of which he felt the
full impact. He could not bring himself to make concessions of a spiritual character. On the contrary, his own
conviction forced him to oppose a new growing spiritual
development and to confront it with his own direct
ecclesiastical mentality. Thus the work of Abraham appears to us as a grandiose attempt to give a declining
spiritual attitude a new garment by means of language
and therewith new opportunities of action.[107]

At least indirectly, these penetrating remarks dispose of another argument that could be advanced to meet the charges
against Abraham's detrimental influence. If his life work was
devoted in the main to the propagation of doctrines that were
frequently promoted in the medieval Church, why then should
he, whose ideas are certainly not original, be charged with so
far-reaching an influence? The obvious answer is again Abraham's style, which was used as a means not only of promoting
doctrines but of strengthening and arousing certain emotions.
Its effect may well be compared in a twofold way to that of a
loud-speaker: first, it amplifies the sound so that it reaches its
audience more effectively than any other means of direct communication; second, the imperfection of the apparatus distorts
and vulgarizes the clear, harmonious tune still traceable in the
original message. In this sense, misinterpretations of the medieval
Church found a loud-speaker in Abraham, who at the same time
amplified her errors and drowned out with his noise the pure
underlying melody of the Gospel.

This function is not an insignificant one in intellectual history. Along with the landmarks representing the formulation of
new ideas are those others that stand for wide propagation and
revision of old ones. They mark a less conspicuous but not necessarily less important achievement in the history of thought. Men
who are able to discharge this sometimes dubious function are
not always of great intellectual or moral stature, yet they command rare skills that they exercise at rare historical opportunities.
At the crossroads where the Baroque with its still-vigorous medieval tradition meets the Enlightenment, Abraham found and
seized upon such an opportunity. Instead of new ideas, he

managed to offer old wine in a new bottle—and a bottle of enduring quality at that. Whether his ideas are old or new, he stood at the crossroads of historical action, and his work may have been a co-determining factor in setting the further course of ideological history in Austria toward lasting cultural delay.

Before this diagnosis can be finally accepted, however, it is necessary to enquire further into the nature of the specific social-political doctrines that were determinedly maintained by Abraham in contradiction to the dynamic idea of progress.

d. *Abraham a Sancta Clara and the Concept of Social Change*

As shown in the first part of this essay, Abraham's social doctrines express an entirely static view of the character of social evil. They embody roughly three concepts or beliefs: (1) the deterministic, medieval concept that everybody should live in and remain true to the Estate in which he was born; (2) the concept of the sinfulness of good living and above all (closely related to concept 1 but not identical to it) of the sinfulness of active desire for improved standards of living; and (3) the belief that intellectual interests should be renounced, except in a strictly teleological religious sense. Yet even in the last, religious expression based on emotion is distinctly preferred to religious utterances based on intellectual reasoning.

Abraham, to be sure, was not a logician. His theses are axiomatic and are "elucidated" and illustrated by an abundance of examples. He never even attempted to define his principles: their character must be evaluated simply by the quantity and the intensity of arguments presented in defense of implied principles. This method adapted to the peculiar problem of Abraham's semantics gives the three listed principles the following specific meaning: the idea that the existence of evil is willed under God is interpreted in such a broad way that it outrules the desirability of social reform. Thus the social evil of poverty is sanctioned by the fact that it offers opportunity for charity. In a more general form, social evil does not exist without divine reason; it ought to be checked in any individual case, but it is not up to men to interfere with the general order of creation.

This is the idea behind the continuous fight that Abraham waged against the laziness and yearning for pleasure of the lower working class—i.e., against their interference with the first principle, that it is not up to man to change by his own volition and effort the Estate into which he was born. In contrast to this, the extravagances of the nobles and the wealthy are censured merely as deviations from the path of faith to that of worldly dissolution and temptation. These classes, however, are not rebellious against the divinely willed social order.

Again closely connected to this concept is that of the sinfulness of good living in general, which may be tolerated as mere venial sin but never accepted or approved. There is no idea of social discrimination in the proclamation of these tenets, as there is none consciously propagated in any of Abraham's works. The consequence and effect of these doctrines, however, is clear: general, planned endeavors to improve the standard of living can never be considered as an acceptable social goal.

The last principle, renunciation of free play of the intellect in the service of what can be called today non-predetermined research, permeates all of his writings and has something to do also with the slight respect in which he holds the free professions. There is abundant evidence in his writings that (by implication) he prefers religious experience based exclusively on intuition, miracles, and emotions to faith supported by logical reasoning, even though it be of a strictly scholastic character.

It could well be argued, however, that Abraham himself by education and profession, though perhaps not by preference, belonged to the type of the ecclesiastical intellectual. In fact, the rhetorical and the literary techniques employed by him do not deny the value of knowledge in itself. On the contrary, his own method overwhelms and drowns the reader with floods of illustrative, allegedly true, historical evidence.[108] There is no need to go into the vast difference between medieval bookishness and the lavish Baroque display of alleged knowledge on the one hand, and the true spirit of independent thinking on the other. Abraham's whole life work clung to the first and denied the second; he thereby implicitly denied the principle on which all evolutionary social progress is based.

Again it may well be held that in subscribing to these principles Abraham did only what had been done by many others throughout more than a millennium. This is exactly the point. Abraham followed the pattern of those who had not fully understood the social application of Christian teaching: he had misinterpreted the true meaning of Christian social doctrine as set forth clearly through the entire history of the Church. He had, moreover (again like some of his confreres), little inkling of the significance of the social reorientation injected into the Church by the ideas of the Catholic Reformation.[109] The answer to the question why his particular teachings should be singled out is found again in his peculiarly effective manner of presentation. It secures his personal philosophy, related to but by no means identical with that of the Church, an otherwise incomprehensible influence.

e. Style, Method of Thought, and Posterity

It is necessary at this point to consider how far Abraham's technique, the form of his writing, determined its content and therewith its social-cultural influence.

To put it in a nutshell: By sugar-coating the bitter pill of frustration, inhibition, and public censure with harlequin antics, he made his drug acceptable, even to a certain point popular. In the end, inhibitions and self-denials can be accepted only by complete insight into the problem and truly voluntary acquiescence to sacrifice. To obtain acceptance of a rigid standard of living by the injection of a mixture of terror, superstition, ridicule, and aggression into the mind and emotions of man does not make for true insight but for deception, which more often than not can lead to a subconscious resistance to the demands of the spiritual authority. Thus a neurotic attitude is produced in others by Abraham, who, as revealed in various features of his style, was himself neurotic.

Such a neurotic attitude can of course be further transmitted by threat, intimidation, particularly by the sinister though subconscious exploitation of superstition. Yet it stands to reason that a constant display of ridicule and satirical contempt by means of farcical antics can create the same result. The artisan and the worker who had enjoyed an ample meal and a drink on Sunday would not be really convinced by Abraham's tirades against gluttony; neither would the agricultural worker see the light as a result of the preacher's castigation of his laziness, nor the servant girl as a result of the censure of her love of pleasure and millinery. None of them would be really convinced, but all of them might desist from the further enjoyment of their pleasures if intimidated by the preacher's mockery, which was cruelly shared and heeded by those who did not happen at that moment to be targets of his attack—an attack that sets class against class and, by its unwise severity, husband against wife, parents against children, majority against minority.

To be sure, all this except the attack against the permanent minorities, above all Jews and heretics, is not done consciously. But it does not alter the corrosive and divisive effect of the attack itself. Abraham does not dishonor human attitudes *in abstracto;* he gets right down to cases in his censure, but that censure is not directed against humanity as such, not even against his community, but against "the butcher, the baker, the candlestick maker"—in short, against the attitude of social, but also of ethnic and occupational, groups. It is directed against the cocksureness of the intellectual as personified by the lawyer, the usury of the Jew, the frailties of woman. The moral conclusion that was supposed to be drawn by Abraham's audience and readers is that, just as no individual is free from weakness and vice, no group is without these failings either. Yet apart from the fact that Abraham used very different yardsticks in the evaluation of human shortcomings, the conclusion presumably accepted by his audience is that everybody turns against the group that happens to be under attack. And it must never be forgotten that the majority's approval of this attack might have been spiced with malicious glee over other people's misgiving, a false feeling of moral superiority, and the rationalization of aggression, because all these seemed to be authorized by a sacred though badly abused cause.

Nor is this all. The special, perhaps the principal, attraction of this attack lies in the fact that it is based on complete irrationalism. Abraham's arguments were to be accepted on faith, but also, more often than not, out of fear and because of their appeal to the emotions. Whatever evidence he presents is usually to be judged by the sheer quantity of the illustrative material, hardly ever on the basis of logical arguments. In many cases his evidence creates a kind of pleonastic irrationalism, in that it attempts to support an irrational thesis with even more irrational evidence.* That such a technique is either consciously

*For one of many cases in point, see *Mercks Wien,* 112 ff., where the assertion that Jews, witches, and sextons create the plague is "supported" by the expert opinion of a scholar stating that by means of a mirror these malefactors could poison the moon. The rays of the poisoned moon received by the mirror could be directed to good advantage at the wax image of the person selected by these Jews, witches, or sextons as a victim of the plague.

or subconsciously aimed at the broadest possible target of mass credulity, aggression, and hysteria is obvious.

f. Inhibition and Appeal

How could a spiritual program win mass consent if it imposed severe inhibitions both on individuals and on groups? The provision of safety valves for dubious desires offers at best a partial explanation. Above all, one must not forget that behind Abraham's moral censure stood the full authority of the Church, whose faithful though often erring servant he was. This does not mean that the authority of the Church can in any essential way be weakened by the failings of ecclesiastics, however renowned. Yet it does mean that people could reasonably assume that the teachings of Abraham were fully in line with the doctrines of the Church and her official interpretation. In this sense the strictness of Abraham's demands imposed no new burden on the public; he merely reinterpreted already accepted restrictions. By his buffoonery and the channeling of aggression he made them in fact more acceptable.

Here is the fundamental difference between Abraham and the great preachers of penitential sermons and censors of morals of the type of Savonarola or the mighty missionaries like Loyola or St. Francis Xavier: they were not the servants but the leaders of their cause. Undeterred by majority opposition, they went to dangerous extremes in the social application of their doctrines. In the ecclesiastical realm they accentuated rather than camouflaged the serious implications of their message. Abraham, playing a role rather like that of a jester, always on safe grounds as to his relationship with secular authorities, did the contrary. This also helps explain his wide, lasting, but shallow success and the cheap laurels that he gained. At this point one must agree entirely with Scherer: "Abraham does not dominate his audience; he serves it. . . . He cultivates success. He puts up gladly with the unconscious influence which the mood and the tastes of the public exert upon everybody who in his activities and their effects is dependent on the public. . . ."[110]

g. Abraham and Class Appeal

While Abraham's success in relation to this public was wide and lasting, it was socially by no means all-inclusive. Max Michel rightly challenges Abraham's right to the title "the people's preacher." In an analysis focused primarily on Abraham's style, but which actually has much wider implications, he observes:

> One talks so much about the people's preacher and people's writer Abraham a Sancta Clara and one forgets that he himself neither wanted to be a people's writer and preacher, nor was he one. Abraham is primarily a court preacher. He has worked with an eye toward an intellectually higher class, taking the imperial court into account as well. . . . Abraham does not even think of using a generally understandable language; on the contrary, he considers a public which is supposed to understand his often very pointed play on words and their meanings. . . . Abraham certainly created his chief work, *Judas der Ertzschelm*, for an intellectually higher class. Also his *Etwas für alle* cannot in all aspects of its linguistic structure be understood by the simple peasant or burgher. It is the intellectually alert stratum of the urban population and the ecclesiastics, as Abraham knew them at Graz and particularly in Vienna, to whom he dedicated his work. We are faced by an exclusively urban milieu in his works. . . . The specific means of language as used by Abraham for his purpose is determined by the conscious appeal of his work [*Adressierung*] to the educated part of the urban population.

While Michel further strongly emphasizes the thesis that Abraham's work was primarily directed at what can be called the urban population from the lower middle classes upward, he rightly admits that not only the more simple-minded urban dweller but also the peasant in Abraham's time could, to a point, absorb his teachings. They could at least grasp his countless crude, realistic jests if not his more subtle puns and chaotic erudition. All in all, "the necessary link between Abraham and the medieval ecclesiastical milieu must not deceive; the treatment of this topic has influenced Viennese society decisively."[111]

These remarks, much to the point in some respects, must be modified in others. First of all, the fact that Abraham was imperial-court preacher does not in any way indicate a spirit of servility. As noted before, in accordance with the concept of

the humbleness of exalted secular authority before the Church
in matters of conscience, rather the contrary might have been
true as a determining factor in his appointment. Abraham a
Sancta Clara's status as court preacher does mean, however,
that he stood for and had to stand for a basic though not unqualified endorsement of secular authority. While in his social criticism he does not refrain from questioning the habits of life
of the upper classes, he never applies censure to the body politic.
In this sense his position as court preacher influenced directly
the content of his work; but because of this, his sermons were
quite acceptable to the ruling classes, unlike those of the great
fighting ecclesiastics of the late Renaissance and the early Baroque.

His upper-class listeners could make themselves believe in
true contrition without having to fear that the preacher's teaching would lead to any dangerous social conclusions. This again
is an important factor in establishing a well-known political
technique: that of expressing an inherently conservative social
philosophy in a form that is modified or spiced by radical antics,
thus making it an apparent outlet for social dissatisfaction.

Michel is perfectly correct in his statement that the court
and urban element determined Abraham's style. Yet the environmental factor probably does not have quite the restrictive
influence that Michel claims for it. In the first place, Austrian
society received at court was not the "intellectually elevated
class" referred to by Michel. The Austrian aristocracy and
some members of the gentry of that time were certainly more
sophisticated, more artistic, more well versed in superficial
aspects of French and Italian manners than the burghers; yet
at the same time they were decidedly anti-intellectual and never
pretended to be otherwise.

Austrian intellectual activities of the period were fed from
three main sources: monastic education, in particular that of
the Jesuits; southern German urban culture; and the Protestant
influx from the North, representing partly cities and towns,
partly a rural gentry.[112] None of the groups molded by these
sources was strong in numbers in German-speaking Austria or,
except for the Jesuits, strong in cultural influence. While their
influence on Abraham a Sancta Clara is certainly indisputable,
it is equally certain that secular intellectualism was negligible in
Abraham's audience. His puns, some of his alliterations, and the

ostentatiously displayed treasures of his pseudo-historical knowledge may well have been selected with an eye to the few more sophisticated members of his audience. Yet it stands to reason that his antics made a hardly less marked impression on the most simple-minded of his hearers and readers.

The point is that Abraham's deductions, the structure of his work, though not necessarily his "documentation," could be easily understood by everybody. The Baroque paraphernalia—the plays on words, the images, parables, metaphors, historical allusions—may have had a bewildering and intellectually stunning effect on Abraham's contemporary audience and future readers. In all probability they were, however, not detrimental to his cause.

All these antics conveyed the impression of scholarship. Though actually simple in dialectics, they intended to appear impressively erudite and cultured. This means that it was probably quite to the taste of the petty burghers, who at all times comprised a substantial portion of Abraham's audience. This burgher may have been annoyed by the presentation of Abraham's moral lectures; he may have been merely entertained by his jests, but the admixture of ill-understood scholarship made them irresistible. Cheap entertainment, sublimated aggression, and pseudo-scholarly authority produced the brew that has always had widespread and powerful attraction for certain sections of the urban lower middle class.

That formula, however, did not retain its influence on the feudal strata of society, whose interest in Abraham's style waxed and waned with fashion. Though pleased by the negativism of his social doctrine, these groups, whose influence was in any event on the decline, became repelled by some of the vulgarities of his style and by the character of the bourgeois part of his audience. It is clear that, although in Abraham's time and setting no strictly crystallized major social groups of entirely free men existed below the level of the petty burghers, even in later times the current of thought connected with his social conservatism and resulting caste pride held no attraction for the workers. For different reasons this was true of the peasants as well. Abraham's connection with agriculture and peasant life became increasingly tenuous. His whole life and activities were directed to the goal of influencing large audiences and potential readers in the city. His examples were drawn mainly from the vocationally highly stratified urban population, which was also the principal target of his censure. Undoubtedly the mere technical difficulty of communication in rural areas also made their contact with Abraham's ideas difficult. The chief reason for the failure of Abraham's ideology in this respect, however, goes deeper.

Relations between serf-tenant and overlords, both groups divided well into the middle of the nineteenth century by the entire breadth of the social order, were too strained: the recollections of the peasant uprisings in the sixteenth century and particularly the seventeenth century in Austria were still too much alive. The shadow of the revolt of the peasant leader Stephan Fadinger hardly a generation before Abraham began to preach helps to explain the lasting failure of his appeal in rural areas. Beyond this it is obvious that the simple agricultural social order did not offer the bondsmen the psychological enticement that existed for the lower urban burghers—that of identifying themselves with the interests, prejudices, and style of life of the next-higher class. For a hundred fifty years after Abraham the social gap was too wide and deep for anyone even to attempt to bridge it by appealing to the potential ambitions and prejudices of that class.

Thus with the negative factors eliminated, the chief field of Abraham's influence, based upon positive affinity, was and remained that of the urban petty burgher. Quite obviously this is not to imply that a seventeenth-century authority had a direct and specific impact on the nineteenth-century social process. It suggests, however, that the social philosophy of the rising urban lower middle class reveals a close affinity to Abraham's way of thinking.

h. Abraham's Appeal to the Lower Middle Class

It is easy to follow the path of this kind of thought; it is apparent in the opposition of local authorities and the lower Estates to many of the reforms of Maria Theresa and Joseph II. The narrowness of this opposition emasculated some of the truly constructive reforms of the Enlightenment at the very outset. In the following generation ideological apathy changed the meaning of the Napoleonic wars from wars fought for the sake of liberty to wars waged merely for the purpose of liberation from Napoleon's imperialism.

Within another three decades a deeply entrenched political quietism—out of line with the state of affairs in North, West, and South—sustained the pre-March period and helped wreck the positive aspects of the revolution of 1848.[113] This was not much due to the fact that Austria lacked the type of intellectuals who in other countries promoted the idea of national unification, constitutional government, freedom of expression, and social reforms; the chief reason seems to have been that there was no adequate response to the ideas of an enlightened elite.

Responsibility for this state of inertia cannot be laid at the door of the socially isolated and not fully free peasants, and certainly not at that of a politically scarcely existent industrial working class. However, certain segments of the lower middle class in the cities, which had far better means of communication and a somewhat better education, cannot be fully absolved in this respect. Their smug satisfaction in the economic sphere, their aversion to new ideas of a social-intellectual nature, and the fact that their chief form of diversion was a kind of spectacle in which fun was poked at minority groups produced in them a negative attitude toward change comparable to that of Abraham and his kind. Final judgment as to whether this is more than mere parallelism, however, will have to be reserved until a later point.

In one respect the introduction of permanent representative government in 1867—or, more precisely, the various ensuing electoral reforms starting in 1868 and ending with the final introduction of general equal franchise in 1906-07—changed matters substantially. During that period the lowering of property qualifications in regard to franchise (still short, however, of their complete elimination)[114] gave the lower middle class an increasing and increasingly vociferous influence on public affairs, and even more so on public opinion. From the 1880's onward, this process took place chiefly within the framework of two political ideologies—that of the Christian Social movement, and the German nationalist associations of various brands—while the power of the German Liberals declined abruptly and the influence of the Socialists before the introduction of general equal franchise was strictly limited.

The socio-economic interests of the first two of these political camps were somewhat similar. So were many of their political techniques. However, the nationalists' claims of German racial superiority and a decidedly negative attitude toward the Austrian state and even more toward the Roman Catholic Church place this ideology in a category that has no connection with the thinking of Abraham a Sancta Clara or with the history of his influence.

As to the Christian Socialists, since 1907 the largest single non-socialist party in Austria, the situation has been entirely different. Deeply loyal to the Habsburg monarchy and to the Catholic faith, this party exercised a strong influence on the lower clergy at the parish level and was in turn influenced by it, although in its early stages it was frequently in conflict with the conservative, nonpartisan Austrian episcopate. Conscious of the German traits in Austrian culture, however, the party was not entirely oblivious of the multinational imperial tradition. In social questions—and this is of decisive importance in its earlier history—the party proclaimed itself the champion of "the little man." Later this also included the peasant. In the earlier, formative phase, however, party program and practice were primarily geared to the interests of the small artisan, the craftsman, the retail merchant, and the lower segments of the white-collar workers—in short, the bulk of what was the lower urban middle class. All these groups were to be protected from the alleged usurious and exploitative influx of big business within the framework of Jewish-dominated high finance. They also had to be guarded against the openly hostile anti-clericalism of the nationalists as well as against the allegedly more insidious atheism of Liberalism in the cultural field. Liberal intellectualism and scientific pursuits, without regard for religious principles, were again linked to Jewish influence. This Jewish spirit appears lastly in the guise of Socialism, though in the rejection of it as well as of German nationalism, criticism was also based on more substantive grounds.

In its adolescent phase the movement with which we are concerned here, in contradistinction to the party in a strictly parliamentary sense, was strongly influenced by its radical fringe. At least officially it was hardly ever repudiated by the political leadership. Here we find a social radicalism that spoke in warning tones of the time when the rich may be strung up along the roads, while at the same time it frequently opposed even moderate social legislation. In its extreme anti-Semitism the movement did not hesitate to wage a concerted campaign against modern infidels and even to revive the ritual-murder legend. Allegedly

A Study in Austrian Intellectual History

atheistic medical science is suspected of sinister motives in its experiments. Invectives are showered on highbrow snobbery, the so-called *Bildungsprotzentum*.* It could well be said that the bite in these diatribes was not nearly so bad as their bark.† No discriminatory minority legislation was put into effect, though minorities were unquestionably harassed. The radical criticism of the capitalistic system left it untouched, and this included the matter of Jewish personnel

*See in the standard work on Austrian parliamentarism Gustav Kolmer, *Parlament und Verfassung in Österreich* (8 vols.; Leipzig, 1902-14), VIII, reference to a speech by the party leader and mayor of Vienna, Dr. Karl Lueger, in the Lower Austrian Diet of 1903, in which scientists are declared to be bunglers as long as they cannot produce grass that a cow can eat; see further, 306, on a drastic speech by Monsignor Scheicher concerning the low level of parliamentary debates on the part of opponents of the party. The editor calls attention here to the amazing similarity in style between Scheicher and Abraham a Sancta Clara.

A similar analogy is apparent between Abraham and the colorful Viennese parish priest and eventual prelate Sebastian Brunner (1849-93). Endowed with a strong sense of humor, Brunner was a skillful writer of popular religious-political and strongly anti-liberal, anti-Semitic literature. See at this point also J. W. Nagl and J. Zeidler, *Deutsch-österreichische Literaturgeschichte* (ed. 1914), II, 846-48, and 317. The relationship between Abraham a Sancta Clara and the Jewish convert-priest and preacher at St. Stephan in Vienna, Dr. Johann Emanuel Veith (1787-1876), on the other hand seems far more controversial.

See further Kolmer, *op. cit.*, IV, 142 ff., on the absurd ritual-murder charges in the Rohling-Bloch trial in 1885; similar charges in the Deckert trial, 1893-95 (V, 414 ff.); Scheicher's warning of possible mob violence against the rich in 1891 (315); attacks against snobbery of the educated in the Lower Austrian Diet, 1892 (318); Deputies Vergani, Gregorig, and Schneider on the poor as victims of vaccination and of the Jewish doctors who want to dissect them (318 ff.); see also the debate on vaccination in 1898 (VII, 256); experiments on animals in 1903 (VIII, 486 ff.).

See further the motion of Deputy Schneider in the same body in 1898 on bounties to be paid for the shooting of Jews as amendment to the law for the killings of birds of prey (VI, 408), and the same motion repeated in 1899; also the motion by Deputy Gregorig on the expulsion of the Jews from Austria (VII, 246 ff.), and on snobbery of the educated (250); Schneider in 1898 against Judaized university extension courses (VI, 408). See also in 1898 Deputy Bielohlavek against the quotations from scholarly books and their "silly theories," which he was "fed up with" (VII, 32). On the discriminatory disciplinary action and dismissal proceedings against progressive teachers see VIII, 213 ff.

†The remark of the right-wing Socialist, the deputy Engelbert Pernerstorfer, to the effect that "anti-Semitism is the socialism of the stupid fellow" is very like that expressed in private by the leader of the Christian Social party, Dr. Karl Lueger: "Anti-Semitism is an excellent means of propaganda and of getting ahead in politics, but after one has arrived, one cannot use it any longer; it is the sport of the rabble." (A. Spitzmüller, "... Und hat auch Ursach es zu lieben" [Vienna, 1955], 74.)

on the higher echelons of banking and industry. The pursuit of scholarly activities was in many ways hampered but not suppressed. Was this due to lack of opportunity or serious intent? A clear-cut answer is of course impossible. It is, however, possible to state that the brown and red totalitarian heirs to these political techniques, who had the opportunity to translate their atrocious words into worse deeds, did not hesitate to do so in the very fields in which their predecessors had merely indulged in thunderous verbiage.

In no way is it suggested here that these predecessors consciously prepared the ground for the evil developments that were to follow. In fact, the Christian Socials, the last German-Austrian party of broad popular appeal to support unconditionally the idea of the multinational empire in the Danube area, could in many ways rightly lay claim to laudable intentions. They attempted to uphold a free economy but to inject into it some notions of protective social measures on behalf of the economically threatened urban and rural lower middle class. Particularly, achievements in the field of municipal administration under the mayoralty of the leader of the party, Dr. Karl Lueger, deserve respect.

It is not the purpose of these observations to reopen a discussion of the age-old argument whether or not laudable intentions and, to a point, constructive results can ever justify the means of bellicose irrationalism, cheap incitement to prejudice, and the promotion of make-believe social radicalism. Nor is there any need to elaborate further on the fact that all these serious failings illustrated in the analysis of Abraham's life work show up again in the new movement. To be sure, neither the activities of Abraham nor those of his political successors can be identified in full with these policies. Both can point to laudable intentions. And here in the interrelationship between questionable means and noble purpose the analogy becomes most obvious.

i. *Parallelism or Influence?*

This leads to the final question: Are we confronted here only with an analogy, mere parallelism between Abraham's line of thought and the late-nineteenth- and early-twentieth-century champions of the little man, or can we speak of a direct influence? Neither answer would be correct. Obviously specific nineteenth-

or twentieth-century policies cannot be traced back to the ideas of a man who died in the early eighteenth century, quite apart from the fact that it was not his task to develop programs of social action but merely their underlying principles.

As to the promotion of these principles, the analogy is striking indeed. It might be argued, however, that Abraham was the child of his time and that his ideas merely reflect its system of values, which happened to run parallel to that of future generations.

An attempt has been made to show in this, as well as in the preceding essay, that even from the point of strictly immanent criticism, Abraham's system of values and above all the manner in which they were presented were not entirely in line with prevailing contemporary opinions. Even within the strict framework of his ecclesiastical status, he did not lack opportunity to be better informed, to be more moderate in his judgment, to be more enlightened and sane in his method of appealing to the masses. In some respects his life work is typical of his time and place, but in others it is strikingly individualistic. Accordingly, if there is an influence, even though not a direct one, as far as specific programs of social action are concerned, such influence would be specific. It evolved from a personality who was the spokesman not merely of the thought and methods of communications of his time but very much of his own as well.

But even if for argument's sake it were granted that Abraham's life work was entirely typical, this could explain only why he thought as he did—never why others followed suit two centuries later. In this respect some facts stand out clearly. Nobody in the intervening period between the early eighteenth and the late nineteenth centuries in German-Austrian history handled the complex instrument of mass appeal with the mastery of Abraham a Sancta Clara and Karl Lueger and some of his lieutenants. Though there is an obvious difference between communications made from the pulpit and those from the dais of a smoke-filled assembly hall, it can be stated further that nobody in the intervening period came even remotely as close as these men to the position of spokesman of the feelings of an urban lower middle class faithful to their religious and political traditions and disturbed by symptoms of a social crisis. In this sense there exists no barrier of time between Abraham and later generations; there is only a vacuum. In this sense we feel entitled to recognize here a social phenomenon of more than mere parallelism.

At this point the concept of the intellectual image that bridges the pillars of historical continuity and social action is helpful. "The image of the mighty is part of their story, like their work, the picture(s) which they impress on a turbulent period . . . are forms of their own energy. Creatively they manifest themselves in every new womb, radiating from ever-changing eyes; their full being cannot express itself until it has been influenced by the centuries."[115]

III

FROM LATE BAROQUE
THROUGH ENLIGHTENMENT

a. Creative Transition and Beginnings (1711-40)

The century from the death of Abraham a Sancta Clara in 1709 to that of Joseph von Sonnenfels in 1817 covers such significant hills and dales of cultural history as the late Baroque, the short-lived Austrian Rococo, the revival of Classicism, and the impressive Empire style, which in its unassuming Austrian form was soon transformed into Biedermeier. In the history of political ideas, the developments in this period, almost to the year, can be described far more succinctly as ranging from conservatism through the full course of the Enlightenment to the establishment of a renewed though strangely altered conservatism. The long middle period of rising, ruling, and declining Enlightenment as exemplified (though by no means fully represented) by the life work of Sonnenfels, and its reflection in nineteenth- and twentieth-century history, is the subject here. But before embarking on the task it will be necessary to give a brief survey of the setting of the Austrian Enlightenment similar to the preliminary study of the Baroque setting of Abraham a Sancta Clara's activities.

Two facets of the Enlightenment are glaringly conspicuous in the body politic. One is the injection of would-be-rational, would-be-scientific principles into the basic philosophy of authoritarian government; the other is the penetration of the spirit of humanitarianism accompanied by authoritarian administrative actions. By and large in continental Europe, rather in contrast to British developments, the evolution of the first of these elements distinctly preceded the second. It must be added further that from the city of Paris to the St. Petersburg of Peter the Great there was practically no region in the first quarter of the eighteenth century in which the basic philosophical objectives of the Enlightenment were developed as cautiously as in Habsburg lands. On the other hand, it is also true that practical application of the humanitarian tendencies—which is so very different from their theoretical foundations—was in many ways recognized sooner in Austria than in eastern and even western continental Europe. Yet it should be noted that an at least partial victory for enlightened humanitarianism in the second half of the eighteenth century became possible only because at that time authoritarian principles and practice had become very strongly entrenched.

It will be clearly understood that the rational authoritarianism of the Enlightenment is not to be regarded as the antithesis of absolutism. It is, in fact, a more integral form of absolutism, which now in growing opposition to feudalism was able to exert itself more fully and in many more branches of government. Semifeudal despotism just because of its crudeness was not able to exercise that rigid, comprehensive, and legally rationalized control that could be assumed by enlightened *étatisme*.

This was not the case in the early phases of the new system that was gradually emerging. A review of the reign of the last male Habsburg in Austria, Charles VI (1711-40), confirms this fact. Just how far the mediocre personal qualifications of that pompous ruler are responsible for the lack of bold and efficient leadership is difficult to ascertain. It can hardly be doubted, however, that the emperor's activities, or, more often, inactivities, determined the course of the Austrian regime for the next generations. Charles VI combined in his character such contradictory qualities as stubbornness, inability to follow a steadfast course, artistic imagination, and a deplorable lack of political vision. He was imbued with a deep, almost mystical feeling for the grandeur of his House. Yet when he became the transplanted king of Spain and was rudely awakened from this dream, he showed a profound disregard for Austria's potential Central European mission. In spirit Charles is indeed the true heir of his father Leopold I, not of his ambitious, tolerant, and reform-ready older brother Joseph I, whose short, promising reign of six years (1705-11) was squeezed between the two long ones of the benefactor of Abraham a Sancta Clara and the patron, often the tool, of the emigrant court camarilla from Madrid.[1]

Thus Austria, rather by force of circumstances than as a result of determined leadership, stumbled and frequently blundered into a new era. The necessity of maintaining herself economically during the long-drawn-out wars in East and West against the French and the Ottoman Turks acted as a strong incentive. So did the ideological influence of friend and foe, British, Dutch, and French mercantile practice as well as political theory. Gradually in the course of two generations at least the surface structure of the Habsburg lands was completely changed. Even in the Austria of Charles VI there was a marked increase in the authority of the imperial government in Vienna as far as the German-Bohemian territories are concerned—though not to the same degree in the Hungarian, Belgian, and Italian possessions. The power of the Secret Conference and of the state chancellery was on the increase; the position of first Court Chancellor gradually developed to that of a kind of imperial Prime Minister and Minister of Foreign Affairs, thus preparing the ground for the future functions of a Kaunitz and a Metternich.

In financial administration, such measures as organization of the government-sponsored *Stadtbank* of Vienna and permanent establishment of the tobacco monopoly, henceforward a chief source of income for the Austrian state complex, were steps in the direction of advanced mercantilistic financial reform. In trade and industry one of the chief stumbling blocks to economic expansion—the guild autonomy and its *numerus clausus* policy, already shaken in the seventeenth century—was now definitely on the way out. While a beneficial economic effect of such belated policies was not immediately apparent, their impact on the establishment of stronger governmental power became obvious. Outside of Bohemia, state-subsidized industry, particularly textiles, glass, and china, was still on rather a small scale; but the products, especially in Vienna and Linz, were of remarkable quality. Here (as noted previously) the early enlightened cameralists Becher, Schröder, and Hörnigk can claim a good deal of credit. The plans of Charles VI—the only ones in which to a point he followed the pattern of his abler brother Joseph for building up Austrian export trade, foreign markets, and in the end colonies—were, however, doomed to failure. This fiasco, contrary to widely held notions, was due not so much to English, Venetian, and Dutch opposition as to the limited volume of Austrian exports and inability to build a navy, owing to insufficient resources. Yet while the Merchant Company with its seat in Ostende which bid for trade with the East Indies proved a brief and unsuccessful experiment, the establishment of Trieste and Fiume as free ports were first steps in a promising development. If other reforms like the planned inland-waterway communication system had not been abandoned, they might have changed the economic and social character of Austria profoundly.

These, however, were not the worst deficiencies of the regime's economic policy. In no other field did the Carolinian reign fail as glaringly as in the "heart area" of economic and social reform, that of overlord–serf-tenant relations. The unendurable burden of the *robota* system was not alleviated by the government's feeble legislative attempts to reform it. The imperial Robot Patents of Leopold I and Charles VI, after cumbersome restrictive stipulations as to purpose and extent of legalized *robota,* consistently obviated any limitations of the peasants' load by an insidious *clausula generalis.* It sanctioned additional services, provided the lord based his further request simply on a true or alleged emergency situation. The drafting of that kind of legislation in so deceptive and sterile a manner was of course largely due to feudal opposition, but lack of skill in handling new and serious legislative problems in an appropriate form may also have played a part. Still, the point must not be overlooked that even unsuccessful attempts at agricultural reforms represented a significant step in advance. The authorities of that time at least clearly recognized the connection between the unsatisfactorily meager tax returns and agricultural mismanagement—i.e., exploitation by the feudal *robota* system that killed the goose that had to keep laying golden eggs. Equal credit for this is due to the doctrines of the mercantilists and of the physiocrats.[2] Altogether, the failure of the reform attempts under Charles VI at least prepared the ground for more successful agricultural reforms under Maria Theresa and Joseph II.

An even more unfavorable example of the strict pursuit of an anachronistic tradition from Leopold I to his granddaughter Maria Theresa is apparent in the government's religious policy, which under the bigot Charles VI remained strong and rigid in the denial of tolerance to heretics. The exclusiveness of the state religion was strongly asserted. Protestant activities in Bohemia were punished by forced labor and finally expatriation. Heretic agitators were even threatened with capital punishment. Large-scale expulsions took place in the Alpine lands and Austrian peasant "pilgrims" were driven to Prussia, Lithuania, and some indeed as far as the American colony of Georgia. Not entirely lost to the Habsburg fortunes were Protestants forced to settle in Transylvania, but the German-Protestant peasants forcibly recruited to Italian regiments had to sacrifice their national and religious status. The question as to how far these renewed counterreformatory drives were directed against enlightened rationalist influences from the North rather than against Protestantism is difficult to decide; undoubtedly both motives played a vital role in determining Austrian ecclesiastic policy.

Yet there were marked changes in the status of the Church in Austria. While her hold on the strictly religious sphere remained firm, a tendency to exert governmental authority in other areas where the Church claimed jurisdiction was equally marked. This, to be sure, was merely the continuation of a development that had been going on for at least two generations. Now, however, it was accelerated. In the realm of practical politics this change in pace marked one of the most visible differences between the Baroque and enlightened absolutism.

Secular officials prevailed increasingly in the imperial councils. Efforts to cut down clerical taxation, not for the purpose of easing the load of the peasants but of leaving more unharvested ground to government revenues, became apparent. Even more obvious was the change toward secularization in cultural affairs. The Jesuit drama gradually yielded to the Italian *commedia dell' arte* and the German *Hanswurst*. Artistically this was not necessarily a change for the better, but it was a change of great cultural significance. True, in Austrian literature no work of major importance was yet connected with the new philosophies of Western Europe; there was no counterpart to achievements in the formative arts as represented by the late Baroque glory of the works of Fischer von Erlach, Hildebrandt, Prandauer and Carlone, Donner, Altomonte, and Daniel Gran. Yet signs of coming change in the intellectual atmosphere were not lacking. As mentioned above, the fight against Protestant infiltration into Bohemia and the German-Austrian Alpine lands from the North and the West was actually directed to some extent against rationalist, enlightened literature. Complaints were raised that half of the bookdealers in Vienna were not true Catholics; the foremost soldier-statesman of the empire, Eugene of Savoy, while no reformer, at least did not hesitate to establish intimate intellectual relations with Leibniz, Rousseau, and Montesquieu. Others followed suit.

Still, these changes did not as yet form a general pattern. In the sphere of practical politics they were more than offset by the conservative, intolerant spirit entrenched at the court of Charles VI. And for a time that spirit was even considerably strengthened by the influence of the notorious Spanish camarilla injected by the emperor into Austrian political and cultural life. Faltering progress in the direction of greater centralization in Vienna notwithstanding, comprehensive progress in government was still blocked not only by the imperial cabinet but, more fervently and effectively, by the Estates of the Habsburg lands. In these bodies in German-Bohemian territories (to a lesser extent in Hungary) the influence of the great ecclesiastic and secular liege lords was still prevalent. Hopes for reform still rested exclusively with the greater or lesser degree of rational humanitarianism injected and to be injected into the ruling absolutism. The idea that there existed a continuous evolutionary development from the Estates system to that of truly representative government was indeed a naïve one. While the Austrian Estates and the future Austrian democracy are, it is true, connected in a complex, roundabout, above all technical way with eighteenth-century Enlightenment, at least on the surface they represent not historically contiguous but opposing forces. Such progress as is worth mentioning in the generations from Charles VI to Leopold II would still come from above.

Concerning the people themselves, insofar as they could exert any ideological influence at all, Wilhelm von Schröder (1640-88) wrote as follows: "They are so religious that they don't want to tinker with God's work. They want to keep things as it had pleased God to give them. This is the great ignorance which makes them sullen and negligent when it comes to work for their own good."[3] This statement was made somewhat before the Carolinian era; it may be colored also by the writer's Protestant background, yet it strikes the leitmotiv of the first, the fumbling stage of the Austrian Enlightenment.

b. *Pragmatic Progress (1740-80)*

The first and fumbling stage was followed by the second, the pragmatic. This empirical feature of the Austrian Enlightenment—i.e., reform based on recognized need and expediency but not on an assumed "social contract," let alone a rationalized popular will—is most characteristic of Maria Theresa's era. Thus in theory this period was far more clearly separated in spirit from the following doctrinaire period of Joseph II than from the preceding Carolinian regime, which had stumbled along, trying to patch up isolated cracks in the governmental system, with no thought of overhauling the whole building according to definite principles. In practice, however, this lack of comprehensive outlook in the reign of Maria Theresa's predecessor makes her own regime of widely initiated and largely completed reforms appear by comparison much more similar to that of her successor, major ideological differences notwithstanding.

The specifically constructive features of this long and respectable reign appeared far more clearly in its first part from 1740 to roughly 1765—that is, the beginning of the co-regency of Joseph. Thereafter, at first slowly and cautiously, then with increasing speed, the ideas and actions of the concentrated Josephine Enlightenment were injected into the Maria Theresan era, and finally after taking a radical turn, they prevailed in 1780, after the death of the empress. While it is true that the Josephine influence up to 1780 in terms of action remained rather limited, it was strong enough to change completely the spirit of the later years of Maria Theresa's reign. A steadily though haltingly developing reform movement was converted into a defensive apparatus with the chief purpose of checking the impact of the new dogmatic Josephine ideas. As for total results of the reforms, they may have differed little from those of the previous era, yet within the regime the split into a conservative and a radical trend could now be clearly discerned. Ultimately, of course, a compromise between them had to be found; but friction between the previous, rather smoothly operating middle-of-the-road policy and the impatient doctrinarianism under Joseph was inevitable.

After all, Maria Theresa inherited her philosophy of government from her father. And Charles VI and many of his advisers were arch-conservative and (by no means necessarily a *sequitur*) highly intolerant. Maria Theresa, unquestionably far superior in achievements, would of course by modern standards be called strictly conservative in her outlook as well. This is due not so much to the comparative moderateness of her reforms and their cautious administration as to her obvious aversion to considering evolutionary administrative changes within the framework of accompanying ideological transformation. Yet important reforms were introduced after all. Thus (though with important reservations) the term "moderate conservatism" can adequately describe the spirit of the regime. One of the most important reservations to the term concerns the question of tolerance. Maria Theresa was in some ways just as intolerant as her father and grandfather had been—in view of the different spirit of her times, perhaps even more so. How, then, is it justifiable to connect the spirit of the Enlightenment in the first two-thirds of the eighteenth century with the then-existing regime in Austria?

Beyond and apart from the individual will of the ruler and his advisers, social conditions forced Austria to take up many measures that in several other countries were inspired and initiated by the philosophy of the Enlightenment. The connection between Enlightenment and reform was thus transferred to the Habsburg lands, though in a reversed sense, owing to the prevalent religious atmosphere and still largely semi-feudal conditions. It was not primarily philosophy that called attention to reform; philosophy could be brought in only as the argumentative rearguard of successfully initiated reforms. However, its persuasive force was so little needed and at the same time so greatly feared that this philosophy, which had its short day under Joseph II, was again given its walking papers under his successors—something which, at least in so abrupt a fashion, did not happen to reformism itself. Thus while enlightened philosophy had only a tenuous connection with the Austrian theory of government—except during the stormy decade of Joseph II's reign and in the case of a few men before that time—it was closely linked with enlightened practice. The pragmatic reformism of the first, longer, more significant part of Maria Theresa's reign ranked with the previous rational imperialism of the expanding national empires of the generation of Louis XIV, Peter the Great, and Wilhelm III. Mercantilist measures in trade, industry, and agriculture, educational reforms, revised State-Church relations, in substance somewhat similar to the above-mentioned eastern and western pattern, differed from them in that their foundation was on the whole non-imperialist, and in many ways genuinely humanitarian. And this last factor, an issue worth pondering, appears more clearly in that non-intellectual, unphilosophic reign of Maria Theresa than in those of the two contemporary rulers who were deeply imbued with enlightened philosophy, Frederick II of Prussia and Catherine II of Russia.

Intellectually the equal of neither of them, Maria Theresa also cannot be held personally accountable to the same extent for the actions initiated by her advisers. But since it was she who was responsible for the approval, if not for the initiation, of her reform policy and its objectives, she deserves no mean share of the credit. This applies especially to the great centralistic reforms of her reign, in the military as well as in the civilian sphere—the only ones executed according to consistent principles. The objective of these far-reaching measures, designed primarily to strengthen the monarchy defensively, is obvious. Less obvious is the progressive consequence of these measures, which may not have been foreseen. The chief example of this is Haugwitz's comprehensive military reorganization, which in effect wrested recruiting, military financing, and equipment and supply systems from Estates' control. Thus major steps were taken toward the destruction of the feudal system. By comparison, the far more widely acclaimed centralization of the supreme government agencies in Vienna, the organization of the state chancellery as a definite Ministry of Foreign Affairs, the clear separation of internal from external and more gradually of financial from general administration, the establishment of the commerce directory, etc., pale in importance. Of far greater significance in the long run was the separation of the judicial from the administrative functions of government, one of the few issues in which the direct influence of Montesquieu's theories on the pragmatic phase of the Enlightenment cannot be denied.*

The most important issue in which Austrian reforms, in practice though not in theory, were in some respects ahead of Continental enlightened reforms from Spain to Russia was that of serfdom. This problem in particular demonstrates clearly the frequent conflict between the actual humanitarian and potential egalitarian objectives of the Enlightenment. Austria represents here a significant case study of a general European ideological crisis in this question. Maria Theresa, from the beginning to the end of her reign, in principle as well as in practice was op-

---

*The censorship commission admitted *L'esprit de loi* for unrestricted distribution in 1752.

posed to the abolition of the authority-subject relationship between liege lord and tenant. As she put it succinctly as early as 1742, "to abolish the subject status [*die Untertänigkeit*] completely can never be considered advisable. There is no country where there is no distinction between overlords and subjects. To free the peasant from his obligations to the overlord would make the first irresponsible, the second dissatisfied. From every angle it would collide with justice."[4]

Limited as is the political philosophy expressed in this statement, it must be judged in the light of a threefold consideration. First, as much as the empress and her chief advisers were opposed to Rousseau's and later Sieyes' and Mirabeau's pattern of a free and equal Third Estate, she was equally averse to the idea of an only thinly veiled property relationship between overlord-master and serf-tenant, which though not legally valid was socially ineradicably connected with the concept of serfdom. Second, even if the empress had wanted (as she most certainly did not want) to establish a kind of "rights of man" doctrine in Austria, she could never have done so against the opposition of the great territorial aristocracy, without at least the partial support of which her system of government would have lost its *raison d'être*. And yet, as the third and most important point, the government, prompted by strong economic and social considerations, went to far greater lengths to attain its limited objectives on this issue than did the Russia of Catherine II and the Prussia of Frederick II, with their allegedly far broader and loftier aims.

As to imperial Austria, it must be recognized that the more important though less conspicuous part of the Maria Theresan administrative reforms—those on the lower administrative level —were introduced with the chief objective of making possible an amelioration of the peasant status. The organization of gubernia and *Kreisämter,* firmly entrusted with provincial and district administrative power wrested from the Estates, were only indirect yet in the long run decisive steps in the attack on feudalism's still-strong power. It is a characteristic feature of the Maria Theresan reforms and of the rising Austrian bureaucratic state as a whole that the administrative organization set up to introduce ameliorations was in practice far more important than the limited direct reforms concerning various issues themselves. Thus the liege-lord–peasant legislation in the times of Maria

Theresa, including the Robot Patent of 1775, amounted mainly to partial and gradual transfer of patrimonial jurisdiction and administration to the government and to definite regulation, but only indirect to alleviation of *robota* services and peasant taxes. These limited but not contemptible results do not, however, justify the reproaches frequently heaped upon the new bureaucracy. In the first place, legally restricted hardship was definitely preferable to arbitrarily imposed and unlimited obligations. In principle, moreover, it was reasonable to work first toward setting up a government organization equal to the task of the proposed reforms. It was sound logic to assume that in the long run the tools were basically as important as the job itself.

Apart from the peasant question and the closely connected administrative reforms, the new order of State-Church relations rather than the often exaggerated effect of revised criminal procedure should take definite precedence in an evaluation of the Maria Theresan reform era. In view of the rigid attitude of the empress on any question that involved the problem of religious freedom, this fact might appear paradoxical. Actually it must not be forgotten that Austrian developments in this area, as in many others, in spirit as well as in political action were at least one generation behind those in Western Europe at the beginning of Maria Theresa's reign. The ecclesiastical battles of the reign of Louis XIV were not fought by his Austrian contemporaries, her grandfather and father, but had to be tackled by Maria Theresa. It must be emphasized further at this point that the Austrian Enlightenment on the whole combined in one phase developments that in Western Europe, and on the surface even in Russia, had occurred in two distinct periods: those of despotic and enlightened absolutism. The era of centralization of the new national state under a controlled mercantilist economy, the subsequent gradual transfer of economic benefits to the middle class, and greater protection of civil security, though by no means the establishment of the political rights of the individual, are rather clearly separated in French, Prussian, and even Spanish and Russian eighteenth-century history. The reigns of Philip V, and Charles III, Frederick William I, and Frederick II, Peter the Great and Catherine II, and to a lesser degree Louis XIV and Louis XV mark this difference.

The situation was different in Austria. For a variety of reasons —foremost among them the multinational composition of her territories even at that period—the Habsburg power had not kept up with general European developments. This applies of course to the West, but at points even to Eastern endeavors to overcome feudalism in the authoritarian centralized state in the late seventeenth and early eighteenth centuries. The uncertain groping of Charles VI's regime in this direction notwithstanding, it was Maria Theresa's reign that first overcame political and, though not to the same degree, economic feudalism in Austria. Political and economic conditions of strict absolutism were established which had been secured half a century before in France and in Prussia.

Apart from the issue of feudalism, an intrinsic part of this struggle for state power in the technical sense was of course the battle against the political power of the Church. This was a battle that had to be fought through, although it was waged against the empress's volition. The struggle had little to do with the conflict between the Enlightenment and the dogmatism of the Church. On the other hand, it will be remembered that this great contest took place in an intellectual atmosphere different from that of the high Baroque at the beginning of the century. Even a ruler as unwilling as Maria Theresa to link the issue of political church power to that of freedom of conscience was forced to take cognizance of a new intellectual atmosphere. What is more important, she had to accept the support of the enlightened rationalist forces, whose political intentions were very different from her own. Without this uncalled-for but skillfully used intellectual help she could hardly have fought to the finish this fight against secular interference by the Church. Thus a ruler upholding unconditionally the exclusive rights of the Church's pastoral functions became an equally determined opponent of her political claims. As a result, a mighty step was taken in the progress from the feudal to the centralized, bureaucratic authoritarian state. But it could be taken only with the help of those rational forces that alone were able to master the problems of the new administrative policy. *Nolens volens,* the new course had to draw on men of a new spirit. It mattered relatively little that these men, to be acceptable, had in their turn to compromise everywhere with traditions and rationalizations of the old regime.

Thus while the empress fully upheld State versus Church power, she only reluctantly made inevitable concessions in the cultural field in response to the advice of intellectual guides like Kaunitz, Van Swieten, Sonnenfels, Felbiger, and, above all, the prodding of Joseph. It is interesting to see how this conflict of conscience with clearly evolving political interests caused her even to overrule the decision of the president of the censorship commission, the trusted Van Swieten. Thus she ordered the destruction of Febronius' famous *Von dem Zustande der Kirche und die gesetzliche Macht des römischen Papstes* of 1763, but permitted, or rather felt bound to admit, its restricted distribution among scholars five years later.[5]

Yet Febronianism in many ways—though not in regard to the conciliar theory and episcopal power—was close to the ecclesiastical policy of the new, modernized authoritarian and gradually de-feudalized state. The opposition of the empress in this matter was merely a last protest before finally yielding to the demands of the absolute state. In the same way she complained a great deal about the dire necessity of dissolving the Province of the Jesuit Order in Austria, yet she eagerly insisted on the public administration of the expropriated funds.[6] A similar pattern of policy can be observed all through the wide range of the Maria Theresan ecclesiastical reforms. Once qualms of conscience were either overcome or (as was more often the case) temporarily assuaged, the empress with firm determination insisted on Caesar's dominant share of political and economic power. As to this second aspect, the number of free church holidays was restricted and the amount of working time increased correspondingly. Fees and dues for establishment and maintenance of ecclesiastic authorities were strictly regulated, administration of church property supervised by the state, purchase of land by religious institutions made dependent on government approval. The political authority of the state in regard to clerics was asserted in questions of the admission of novices to monasteries and of the founding of new cloisters. Ecclesiastical authority over clerics in disciplinary matters and the question of legacies and estates left by clerics to the Church were to be considered as within the judicial authority of the state. The Church, to put it succinctly, had ceased to be in any but purely religious matters an autonomous body within the state. And even there the empress in the very last years of her reign saw the exclusive religious power of the Church, as she perceived and upheld this religious power, in retreat. With the year 1774 the expulsion of Protestants from the Alpine lands, still quite frequent in the 1750's, ceased forever at the insistence of the co-regent. Four years later academic degrees were conferred on Protestants at the University of Vienna. Thus even before the Tolerance Edict of 1781 at the beginning of Joseph's exclusive reign, reforms in regard to religious minorities entered Austrian public life as a natural corollary of secularization. The importance of such facts transcends by far their limited practical effect. They introduced cautiously and gradually a transformation from the traditional Church-State conflict (confined by no means to the enlightened era) to one of supra-denominational state policy. Thus *nolens volens,* another gap between Austrian and Western conditions was bridged.

While the reform of State-Church relations under Maria Theresa followed an established though retarded pattern in Austria, new developments in many other fields not only were delayed there but were handled in a basically different way. This applies above all to commerce and industry and, in a wide sense, to issues of intellectual life. Belated Austrian mercantilism and agricultural policies based on physiocratic doctrines produced results differing in many ways from earlier French, Dutch, and British achievements in these fields. There new political doctrines to a large extent influenced new economic policies. In an Austria stagnant in the field of political theory, we observe a reverse situation. Not only did the leading industrial and commercial nations establish strong ties with the Central European markets, but in spite of economic and political restrictions, they influenced Austrian-German ways of life and ideas increasingly. In the course of time this by-product of Western mercantilism became, to a point, more important even in the economic field than the active trade balance itself. Though only one of several important factors in the sphere of cultural interchange, Western trade left its mark on Austrian relations with the West far beyond the economic sphere.

As to Austrian industrial development and export trade, endeavors that were on the whole merely experimental and small-scale in the half century before Maria Theresa's accession were broadly systematized during her reign under the Universal Commerce Directory of 1746. Particularly on the industrial side, the new policy had only limited success. The textile industry in Bohemia developed at a very satisfactory pace; a new one in

Vorarlberg in the Alpine Hereditary Lands was set up. China-manufacturing in Vienna, the dye industry in Carinthia, and sugar refineries in the Littoral are further cases in point. Since, however, these and other industrial enterprises were not adequate to serve even the domestic market, a large-scale export policy of Austrian manufactured goods was completely out of the question. Yet this industrial development was considered substantial enough to promote a radically altered Austrian commercial policy. In a crude and elementary way high tariffs were imposed on foreign merchandise in general. In 1749 the import of luxury goods (defined in a very loose fashion) was altogether forbidden. These general prohibitions were only modified in 1775 in favor of a high tariff fence, the results of which in practice were not too different from absolute import prohibitions. Only Joseph II, who followed in general the protectionist course of the empress's regime, qualified this policy at least on one important point: he established the principle that the most rigidly enforced import prohibitions and other protectionist measures should be applied only to goods available in sufficient supply on the domestic market.

Obviously the impact of such a policy on a domestic industry not yet sufficiently developed ruled out competition and had rather harmful effects on standards of quality. More serious were inadvertent hardships imposed on consumers in need of industrial goods. Least recognized was the fact that, since the products of Austrian mercantilism because of their quantitative limitation could not enter Western markets on a large scale, import restrictions (all the more rigidly enforced for this reason) might actually have cut Austria off from direct economic relations with the West altogether. Newly established cultural relations were thus endangered as well.

To sum up: The economic policies of the mercantilist latecomer, Austria, had quite naturally a rather unfavorable influence on her economic and political relations with the West. Whether the over-all effect of belated mercantilism on Austria, however, was purely negative is a quite different and very complex question that is essentially academic in character. By the very nature of mercantilist doctrine, the one who is the last to adopt mercantilist policies fares worst in the end and has to pay the bill. Yet before Austria was forced into such a situation, political mercantilism all over Europe was on the way out as a result of the revolutionary and Napoleonic wars. Austria for all her trials was thus spared from footing the ultimate bills for her trade policy.

Culturally, as stated before, the new economic policy brought Austria closer to the West, though by no means so close as would have been possible under a more moderate economic course. But again, the indirect character of this influence must be emphasized. Austria's ideological ties with the West became more intimate not through stronger commercial contacts but, as a by-product, through a more thorough acquaintance with Western ideas. Dimly, however, a new factor appeared on the horizon of the declining Enlightenment. The new ideological ties with the West no longer worked clearly in support of governmental policies. Gradually they changed in content and quite frequently began to express opposition. These phenomena of not generally realized importance might have become more obvious if the French Revolution and its political aftermath had not placed East-West relations on a very different footing. Even so, these facts must be considered carefully in evaluating the social-economic and intellectual developments of the period of Maria Theresa and Joseph II.

To be sure, intellectual development was greatly handicapped by several factors. There was Abraham a Sancta Clara's and his "school's" ideological inheritance. In the empress's time and in the empress's entourage its spirit appeared still vigorous and little impaired by the considerations of high politics that then governed State-Church relations. There is further, during the great Silesian-war period, the natural strain on cultural relations with the Protestant North. There was also the strangely unfavorable effect of the "reversal of the alliances," particularly in regard to the political marriage with France. This relationship was so distinctly the product of circumstances and of political expediency that it led to a cooling-off rather than to an intensification of French-Austrian cultural relations. While England was now in (or almost in) the enemy camp, Austria was being drawn increasingly into the orbit of Russia, whose ostentatious reform spirit under Catherine II barely scratched the surface of domestic development. Above all, individual noble *frondeurs* notwithstanding, there was the feudal ecclesiastic and secular opposition to a firm course of cultural reforms in Austria. It would have been exceedingly difficult for the empress to overcome this resistance, even if she had had her heart set on a program of that kind. How could such a policy be expected from a ruler who believed that intellectual activities could be justified or even excused only (1) if they were strictly incorporated into and controlled by the new bureaucratic system, and (2) if they led to profits for the state—profits to be measured in terms of a money economy? Independent intellectual activities beyond these strictly limited fields not only were suspect but were frequently resented and suppressed as anti-religious and, by implication, disloyal as well.[7] It will be very necessary to remember this point in the subsequent discussion of the work 'of that rare enlightened theorist in Austria, Sonnenfels, whose bureaucratic activities excused and protected his work as a free-lance writer.

In view of these facts, Maria Theresa's successful endeavors to introduce general elementary education in Austria deserve all the more credit. Yet even here one cannot help comparing the reforms accomplished with those projected, and one must realize that those accomplished represent only a diluted and feeble version of a program that even in its day was considered very moderate.[8] This applies least to the organization of elementary or "trivial" schools, the district schools, precursors of the future burgher schools, and normal schools, a kind of teachers' colleges. But even here, according to the Pergen plan,* instruction in the elementary kind of grade schools was to be confined to the essential requirements necessary for the work of the lowest social Estate. Attention was called to the danger that more education would create more dissatisfaction. The curriculum and textbooks drafted by the able Silesian canon Johann Ignaz Felbiger could not disregard these ideas entirely. The new elementary school was not a state school in the modern sense; organized by a distinguished and capable priest, the parish schools remained in practice under the direction of the local minister, though under fairly strict government control. Plans to extend these reforms beyond the German-Bohemian lands met with failure. Yet even within the western parts of the Habsburg empire the idea of extending benefits to the poorest among the poor, the soldiers' children who spent their childhood in the desperate atmosphere of army camps, was largely wrecked by

---

*Count Anton Pergen, Minister of State.

the opposition of Joseph. The co-regent feared that such benefits might interfere with military order and discipline.

More serious flaws pertained to the reform of secondary education, or, rather, of the secondary higher education preparatory to graduate training as given in the universities. Here the empress turned down the Perger-Hess* reform ideas, which would have definitely dispensed with instructions by monastics —i.e., after the dissolution of the Jesuit Order in Austria, primarily by the Piarists. With the rejection of complete secularization went also the plan to give teaching of history priority over instruction in Latin. With it went the idea of stressing physics, mathematics, and geography and the notion of introducing an altogether more individualistic and interesting method of instruction by "Socratic" discussion rather than mere recitation. While some of these concepts were not entirely rejected, all of them were at least diluted. Completely abandoned was the idea of calling for enlightened reformers from Germany, since, as Joseph II with the complete endorsement of the empress put it, "We know or ought to know our countries, our statutes, our deficiencies, our funds, better than any foreign scholar, however understanding, who is appointed here. What would come of it but expenses? . . ."[9] As will be shown later, this is a by no means unique example of the way in which the emperor's enlightened philosophy, making a kind of intellectual somersault, reverses its direction completely. Here, however, he was only the mouthpiece of his mother, who emasculated the spirit of the reform of the *Gymnasium*, an advanced kind of secondary school. By connecting it administratively and in the curriculum with the burgher or normal school, she reintroduced or, rather, preserved a good deal of the old spirit there as well.[10] There was some definite planning for specialized schools, such as the Oriental Academy, which ultimately became a first-rate training school for diplomats, the Commercial Academy, and Maria Theresa's Military Academy, which in its social composition was still a semi-feudal institution.

Yet as to the most important objective, general university education, there simply did not exist any comprehensive reform plan. As in other fields of learning, this applied to the theory

* Matthias Ignaz von Hess, educational reformer and professor of literary history at the University of Vienna.

of education, but in this case it was true of administrative practice as well. Reform was confined to individual schools, or, rather, to individual scholars in such schools. In the field of law this applied to the representatives of secular-versus-ecclesiastical power, Paul Joseph Riegger and Karl Anton Martini, the pioneer of the coming Austrian civil legislation, and in a different sense to the leader in the field of developing political science, Joseph von Sonnenfels. In the medical schools, it is true, the influence of Gerhart van Swieten was overwhelming and lasting. Indeed, there is hardly any other field of intellectual activities where progress from the superstitions of the seventeenth century to the proclaimed scientific spirit of the eighteenth was as startling as here. Van Swieten's tactful, and therefore in Austria doubly effective, influence reached even farther, though his success as president of the imperial censorship commission, as a leader in the attempt to remove matters academic from Jesuit control, was not quite so spectacular.[11]

The high regard in which as enlightened, sane, wise, and courageous a personality as Van Swieten was held by an empress, who was in some ways a prejudiced woman, may of course be due partly to the confidential relationship between patient and personal physician. This does not detract from the credit the ruler deserves here for underwriting objectives and results of a cultural policy the underlying philosophy of which she steadfastly and sometimes violently disapproved. Yet in a wider sense this relationship is representative of the whole reform spirit of the Maria Theresan era in the cultural field. It illustrates well the pragmatic, individualistic approach that scored successes in specific issues as the result of an almost intuitively lucky personnel policy, but often failed abjectly in regard to long-range objectives. A case in point is the partial failure of Felbiger's educational reform plans, and beyond this Sonnenfels', Gebler's,* and Van Swieten's largely frustrated attempts at an intellectual transformation of Austria in general. In this sense the elementary-school and medical-training-school reform and the systematic indoctrination of the new bureaucracy with the ideas of political science of the day are practically isolated islands of enlightened progress in a vast sea of ignorance.

On the other hand, the rise of a reformed theater, which

---

*Tobias Philipp von Gebler, Councilor of State.

fortunately did not break as completely with the tradition of the old as was originally intended by the prosaic Sonnenfels, court support of the noble architecture of Austrian late Baroque, Rococo, and early Classicism, and progress in the natural sciences as exemplified by the names of Jacquin, Scopoli, and Hell* stand again as examples of a successful personnel policy. A system can be found here only in two aspects, however. In a positive sense it is the compilation and codification of civil laws from Martini through Riegger and Sonnenfels to Zeiller.† Yet not only were these reforms not even halfway completed in the Maria Theresan period, but reform itself had to be smuggled in by the back door as a kind of by-product of codification and clarification of already-existing statutes. It is this limited objective that on the whole dominates the legal reform plans under the empress's rule.

Equally characteristic of Maria Theresa's reign is the fact that, within the cultural life of the period, literature and philosophy occupied a safe place at the bottom of the scale. This ties in with an only slowly changing state of affairs in the German-speaking South that has already been touched upon in connection with the discussion of Abraham a Sancta Clara's activities. Indeed, the whole reign of Maria Theresa, beyond the realm of those cultural interests limited to applied science, music, and formative arts, did little to encourage independent intellectual activity and a good deal to hamper and even to endanger it. It is futile to ask whether truly great thinkers and creative artists could not have braved the restrictions of the regime, as in the course of history they have done in other countries and under far worse external conditions. The point is that a long, unbroken, rigid tradition in Austria prevented the rise of independent thinkers, or at least slowed it down for a longer time than in other countries of comparable standards. To be sure, no government on earth could have created such thinkers and writers. The amazing results of an even transitory break in that tradition, as soon as its heaviest fetters were loosened, suggest, however, that the Austrian atmosphere, including Maria Theresa's court and administration, was a contributing factor in literary stagnation.

* Nicolaus J. Jacquin, eminent professor of botany; Johann Anton Scopoli, professor of chemistry; Maximilian Hell, professor of mathematics and astronomy.

†Franz von Zeiller, chief author of the famous code of civil law of 1811.

Reluctantly one cannot entirely reject Erich Schmidt's contention that "basically the clown [the *Hanswurst*] is the most gifted, indeed the only vital, phenomenon in the Austrian literature of the eighteenth century."[12]

Thus the emotional roots of what should not be referred to as the first major period of the German-Austrian Enlightenment, but more correctly as the period within which the Austrian Enlightenment developed, were still deeply embedded in the Baroque-Jesuit era of Leopold I, with its intellectual pitfalls and the great emotional-artistic potentialities of the spirit of Abraham a Sancta Clara.

c. Systematic Cultivation

The difference between the reign of Maria Theresa and the era of Joseph II is so great that it cannot be fully explained either by the legal transformation of the Austrian realms or by the popular reaction to it. After all, it should never be forgotten that chronologically the better part of Joseph's era, from the beginning of Joseph's co-regency in 1765 until his mother's death in 1780, coincided with the reign of Maria Theresa. The influence of the co-regent was substantial but, except in affairs of military organization, still by no means predominant. Yet the basic changes put through in the following ten years of unrestricted Josephine absolutism amounted in many ways to no more than a revised and systematized continuation of projects laid out, initiated, and checked under the previous regime. In legislative matters the ten hectic years from 1780 to 1790 of course witnessed the injection of many new schemes and ideas. The bulk of the planned legislation, however, still represented an inheritance from the preceding era that had not been put into effect at the time of the empress's death. As to administrative problems, that decade was far too short a period to train a bureaucracy basically different from that of the previous regime. The Josephine reforms had to be executed or, rather, attempted by officials who were for the most part the same as those of the previous regime. Only an entirely different body could have been independent of the inheritance of the old era and completely amenable to the spirit of the new one. On the basis of the legislative record, the following conclusions must be drawn: Important as the reforms of Josephinism were, fundamentally they were not different enough from those of Maria Theresa's regime to have made Joseph's reign a radically new chapter in Austrian history. Yet, though this chapter obviously had strong roots in the past, it stimulated even stronger ideological currents and emotional reactions that have remained alive into modern times.

Thus very clearly Josephinism in Austria gains its rightful significance less through its actions than through its ideological effects, through the profound change in the spiritual climate of civilization in Austria.

The word "spiritual" in this context should be weighed carefully insofar as it includes an ideological as well as an emotional element, the second being often too easily overlooked in the concept of Josephinism. On the strength of its ideology alone, Josephinism could never had secured its lasting influence; inseparably connected with it is the intellectual and far more important ideological reaction to it. Again, the word "reaction," as used here, must be carefully weighed. It means not just the responsive counteraction to the Josephine reforms; above all it means very specifically the emotional opposition to it. This violent ferment very naturally deflected the course of reforms under Joseph; but what is more important, it amplified its appeal: it created rightly or wrongly the standard associations Josephinism, liberalism, radicalism, anti-clericalism, and so forth. In other words, this response, which identified a late-eighteenth-century reform movement with a standard ideological pattern of the future, released the subconscious "chain reaction" that kept Josephinism alive.

After a brief review of the major trends of the era, it will be the main objective of the analysis of Sonnenfels to study the effect of these highly charged eighteenth-century currents on the following generations of Austrian cultural development.

These, very roughly, are the main reform trends of "exclusive" Josephine absolutism from 1780 to 1790. First is the revision of Church-State relations, the reorganization of the ecclesiastical organization within the Habsburg lands, and a new approach to the problem of religious minorities. Within the first group falls the prohibition of appeals from Austrian church and state jurisdiction to decisions by the Roman Curia in the question of marriage legislation, as well as the strong assertion of imperial rights as to episcopal appointments. To the second, more important group belongs the major issue of monastic reforms with the dissolution of a large number of cloisters not engaged in charitable or pastoral work. Here it is necessary to mention the establishment of the *Religionsfond,* which, henceforward under secular control, had to meet the financial demands of pastoral obligations. It should be stressed that this reform did not intend to bring about a weakening but, on the contrary, the numerical increase and financial stabilization of parish districts. Here belongs also the introduction of state-supervised clerical training.

Finally, as to the question of religious minorities, the new legislation began with the *Toleranzpatent* of 1781, which sanctioned private religious services for recognized denominations. The reforms opened civil service, academic education, and ultimately teaching positions to Protestants, although these measures were by no means sufficient to ensure establishment of full legal equality, let alone full social and religious equality.

It would appear from a review of more than one hundred fifty years of Austria's ecclesiastical policy preceding the reforms under Joseph that it is not the historically quite comprehensible intolerance of a time-honored policy, but its psychological shortsightedness, that is to be most severely criticized. This became increasingly evident now. The reforms did not lead to any appreciable increase in Protestant conversions or Protestant immigration into Austria. Thus despite the obvious complexity of the problem, the earlier harshness of the Counter Reformation in Austria—with the dire concomitant consequences of a cultural and social "Iron Curtain" policy toward the West and the North—appears difficult to justify not merely in the light of a liberal historical interpretation but from the viewpoint of an over-all Austrian ideology itself.

Finally, the beginning of the emancipation of the Jews—of great significance for future Austrian development—must be mentioned in this connection. Until the era of Joseph II Jewish emancipation, unlike Protestant recognition, was not primarily a political move based on an acceptance of the inevitable; neither was it a straightforward act of tolerance. It was above all a social measure for the purpose of raising the status of the non-privileged and wiping out the entity of a separate social group whose pitiable plight was in direct contrast to the leveling objectives of rational absolutism.

Proper evaluation of these reforms shows that the new regulation of State and Church relations was well on the way in the era of Maria Theresa even before Joseph's co-regency. Within

Jannissar

Christian Soldier

Emperor Charles VI

the empress's regime fell also the beginnings of monastic reforms, a new approach to the question of episcopal appointments, and (very much against personal wishes of Maria Theresa) a gradual improvement of the Protestant position. Thus the originality of the Josephine ecclesiastical reforms in Austria is confined to a few, though important issues—the financial question of church organization, parish relocation, and Jewish emancipation foremost among them. Equally significant problems in these and related fields had been raised before in Austria, and not always in an ultramontane spirit. A more liberal approach to these problems was applied in the half century following Joseph's regime, otherwise reactionary tendencies notwithstanding. Yet the question of relations of Church and State, more correctly of church control and administration of church agenda by the state, has always been connected in Austrian ideology with Josephinism. To a point the same applies to the logically hazy but politically distinct concept of what is commonly referred to as "anti-clericalism," and also to the pseudo-liberal notion of mere lip service to tolerance, mere economic emancipation of the Jews, not excluding the anti-Semitic reaction that was thereby aroused.[13]

It is not the Josephine reforms but the Josephine ideology as the first emanation of a not merely pragmatic but abstract rationalism in Austria that explains the reaction to that spirit—explains the social and psychological phenomenon that the intent of the reforms outdistanced in significance the issues involved.

To be sure, in the realm of serf-tenant–manorial-lord relations —that is, within the social core of the waning feudal order—the permanent effect of the reforms is of far greater technical significance. On the other hand, the connection with Maria Theresan legislation appears here even more obvious. The completion of the change from *Leibeigenschaft* to *Untertänigkeit,* in eighteenth-century terms from half serfdom to a permanent tenantship entailing certain personal services, was a major step leading to the disintegration of economic feudalism. Its salutary consequences were impaired but not obviated by the fact that a qualified *robota* system still remained in force. The termination of the major functions of patrimonial jurisdiction and the new tax laws, however, regularize peasant obligations in favor not so much of the tenant as of the government. They are in some ways complementary steps in a scheme aiming at entrenchment of bureaucratic absolutism in place of what may be called a crude administrative rural semi-feudalism. These reforms appear far more organic than those in the religious sphere, insofar as they were the belated but inevitable consequences of economic change. Yet the issue they represent did not remain as alive as the problems that arose in the course of the bitter struggle between faith and rationalism. Still, the emotional atmosphere of the era of Joseph has set its mark on these trends as well. The bugbear of bureaucratic omnipotence has been widely but not necessarily fairly connected with these reforms.

In the same context belong the problems involved in increasing bureaucratization in general and in particular the "professionalization" of municipal government. Related to them is the question of the new law codes, the Allgemeine Gerichtsordnung (Order of Civil Procedure) of 1781, the first part of the famous Austrian code of civil law of 1811 dealing with the personal status of the individual, and the penal code of 1787. The various codifications, as for instance the civil secular jurisdiction in the question of marriages or the unrestricted transmission of feudal landed property, exemplify again the victory of the bureaucratic over the semi-feudal state. In other points, however—as in the modification of sanctions in regard to offenses against the state and religion and in the milder usury laws—significant liberal trends otherwise not too frequent in the Josephine era become apparent, though as usual they were directed chiefly by a utilitarian economic rather than an outright humanitarian philosophy. There were still harsh features, such as the substitution in criminal law of lifetime hard labor accompanied by chaining and flogging for capital punishment. Here may be seen typical totalitarian features, such as the cruel exploitation of human life, instead of the brutal but less "rational" destruction of human beings that characterized the high Middle Ages.

In a wider sense, this totalitarian atmosphere could be perceived throughout the entire realm of education, which from another point of view was just as unfree as had been the bitterly denounced setup of ecclesiastical control. Indeed one might carry the point farther and argue that clericalism had merely disapproved of the pursuit of research not based on fundamentalist premises, whereas radical enlightened absolutism under Joseph II categorically rejected non-applied research and renounced academic education for any other purpose than training civil servants and professional men.

Yet legal codification and education under Joseph has again been regarded by five generations of public opinion as primarily "liberal," and this because the struggle of secularism versus clericalism has generally been understood as a conflict in intellectual history and, as such, as a "liberal" revolution. A salient fact has seldom been understood: that in political history this conflict is not so much a battle between clericalism and an in fact nonexistent Josephine liberalism as it is an early stage in the evolution of the pattern of modern nationalism. From the vantage point of today, the nationalist aspect of late-eighteenth-century Enlightenment appears stronger than was generally assumed in nineteenth-century historiography. And while this disquieting facet of enlightened ideology is not yet the paramount issue in the decade preceding the Jacobin Revolution, it is already of wide and increasing significance in Josephine Austria.

Indeed, the endeavors of Joseph's regime to impose German as the official language of his realms—in Hungary, according to the Edict of 1784, within not more than three years—appear now in a new light. Such Germanism has been frequently pictured as a mere design of rational expediency on the part of enlightened absolutism to streamline governmental functions. As to its objectives, it has been regarded as a straight furthering of the enlightened philosophy. As to its apparatus, a German-trained bureaucracy, these measures were comprehended as the allegedly supranational forerunner of the German-directed centralism of the reigns from Francis I to Charles the Last. Up to a point the wording of the legislation under Joseph supports such an interpretation.[14]

On the other hand, the gradual evolution of this Germanism, the political ambitions of literary, government-sponsored endeavors in the Josephine era, imply deeper-lying motives. One should not fail to see Josephine Germanism in conjunction with the beginnings of the Slavonic cultural Renaissance and of the early Magyar-Hungarian reform period as a stage of cultural nationalism. In this sense the bureaucratic justification of this Germanization drive was to a large extent a mere rationalization of a national ideology. That this nationalism, unlike the parallel Slavonic and Magyar developments, was sponsored but not invented from above does not alter this fact.

Frequent misinterpretations notwithstanding, Josephinism

was not a lifeless though reckless government-inspired paper structure but an organic and dynamic link in a chain of ideas and events. Nevertheless, there of course are significant differences between Josephinism, the preceding era of Maria Theresa, and the coming Franciscan antithesis of the reform spirit. Thus at the beginning of this analysis the question often raised, where Josephinism should be placed ideologically, must be asked.

One salient aspect of that controversial and stormy era, its unfettered absolutist tendency, has hardly ever been contested. Yet there has been a wide divergence in the historical thinking from Joseph's time to the present as to the interpretation of that absolutism. Unquestionably the following regimes of Leopold II and Francis I by no means looked upon Josephinism as a sudden and abrupt break with the Austrian tradition. Their strictly modified but none the less implied approval of Joseph's bureaucratic, essentially anti-feudal, administrative course cannot be explained simply as a cautious bow to its supposed popularity. There is little doubt that this popularity is an intentional (though in the end even believed-in) fabrication of Austrian liberalism dating from the middle of the nineteenth century. That there was violent and widespread opposition from Joseph's contemporaries, even among large strata of German Austrians, may be considered today an established fact. Thus the link between Josephinism and the reigns of Leopold II and Francis I is based not on an understandable craving for popular appeal but on a rather shrewd recognition of the fact that the centralist bureaucratic mechanics of Josephinism—i.e., its superstructure—were to succeeding conservative regimes more important than its content, its spirit. Similarly, it was clear that Josephine governmental structure was adapted far better than semi-feudalism to deal with an era of political emancipation of the Third Estate in the West, incipient nationalism, and growing industrialization with all their political consequences.

It is quite understandable also that the new Austrian liberalism of the middle period of the nineteenth century was not and could not be satisfied with as distorted an image of Josephinism as that conjured up by the neo-absolutists Kübeck, Schwarzenberg, and Bach. Early Austrian liberals, in their desire to link an Austrian liberal program as well as its gradually evolving national tendencies to some vital chapter of the country's historical tradition, alighted naturally enough upon Joseph's reign and placed upon it their own interpretation. Less natural, however, was the fact that they overlooked the inherent despotic aspects of the regime on the one hand and confounded its loud rationalism with an alleged liberal, pseudo-democratic ideology. Yet from 1848 to the 1880's the image of Joseph II and his program lived on this myth of a short-lived Austrian liberalism.[15]

Actually this identification of Josephine trends of thought with liberalism is a clear distortion of historical truth, however unintentional. Neither its deeds nor, what is more important, its objectives show any major trends in Josephinism indicating a greater concern with the interests of the individual as such or with even very modest steps in the direction of self-government. Quite the reverse. Josephine reforms, with their glorification of the state, its power, and its expansion, implicitly exclude respect for individual interests as a primary objective of government. In Joseph's own time, it is true, Josephinism further stands for the destruction of selfish Estates' interests in favor of a centralized state that is to act as a protector of the rights of the non-privileged. In other words, even more clearly than Maria Theresa's regime, genuine Josephinism stood for unlimited absolutism and against the very poor kind of existing representative institutions. It is, of course, very much open to question whether the Estates could ever have been changed into an even imperfect form of popular representation. Such a possibility may well be doubted. The point is that no step in that direction was ever taken by Joseph's regime: in other words, if there had been a genuine streak of liberalism in Josephinism it would not have ignored the idea of reforming existing pseudo-representative institutions in the direction of possible representative democracy. It was the intention of Josephinism, however, to stand for strictest absolutism, as champion of the little man against powerful group interests.

Thus it is indeed no wonder that modern totalitarianism from both the right and the left has claimed a deeply rooted relationship with Josephinism. While the Communist left cautiously praises Joseph as a kind of forerunner of the idea of "people's democracy," National Socialism is far more outspoken in this respect 'and considers Joseph as a veritable party member.[16]

No other German prince [it is claimed] has done so

much pioneer work for the National Socialist People's
Law as the "revolutionary," the "socialist on the
throne," the "peasant emperor" Joseph the German.
Absolutely totalitarian in his state concept, he attempted
to clean up everything rotten and shaky from the past
of the German people. By force of his own sterling
example he represented the idealistic demand that common welfare should precede individual welfare. He declared war on the alien Roman spirit, on political
Catholicism. In all his thinking he considered himself
part of the people without distinction of classes. Last
but not least, he belonged to the peasantry, the blood-
spring of the German people, which he tried to preserve
on his soil.

After a bow to Joseph as champion of German culture and
German national feeling in the fight against French and Italian
influences, Joseph's national glorification is thus concluded by
Victor Bibl: "Particularly in these days, when, even beyond the
Great German people's empire, leading statesmen consider
authoritarian leadership social-welfare work as fundamental to
the coming new order in Europe, the character of the emperor
Joseph II appears more than ever vivid and timely to us."[17] He
thus represents (in totalitarian terms, to be sure) not merely
government for the people as he saw it but, as a mystical *Führer*,
government by the people themselves.

Viewing Bibl's crude and trite observations in conjunction
with basic concepts of Josephine reformism, one might easily be
misled into admitting that Josephinism does indeed seem closer
to totalitarianism, particularly of the National Socialist brand,
than to political liberalism. Almost solely on the basis of the
noble purpose common to both Josephinism and liberalism,
liberals in the nineteenth century built a parliamentarianism in
the spirit of a largely fictitious Josephine model. Totalitarianism may at least claim a genuine similarity as to methods
and, in quite a few points, as to *alleged* objectives as well. Its
transgressions, of course, are another matter.

Here, however, is a salient point of difference. The Josephine
reforms, with all their technical and psychological shortcomings
and their dubious methods, stand for phases in the struggle
against decaying feudalism and semi-mystical irrationalism. They

are not, like their alleged totalitarian left- and right-wing relatives of the future, partly dodges in the fight for a missionary program of world domination, partly tools for domestic group repression. Josephinism wanted to control Austria, not the world. It is true that it attempted to obtain control over the people, who were to be leveled, in an exaggerated equalitarian zeal, by compulsion. Yet the aim of genuine Josephinism is not to impose the rule of totalitarian violence, not to unleash aggression of group versus group; it is not to appeal to the emotions but to reason. The idea of imposing the rule of reason by force, however, is in itself irrational, and this indeed is the tragic breach and contradiction in the Josephine system.

Yet this profound error, which was to have such far-reaching and tragic consequences, does not establish the totalitarian character of true Josephinism any more than humanitarian objectives justify the liberal aura of the pseudo-Josephinism of later generations. Commonplace as the statement seems, it none the less badly needs to be repeated in a time of ideological collision and distortion: genuine Josephinism must be understood and judged exclusively in its own terms of historical reference—enlightened absolutism. The fatal error around which the curious appeal and revulsion of the Josephine image has revolved in later times makes this system human—as is every fault based on noble purpose but imperfect reasoning. Thus its history is a human story, based both in its strength and in its weakness on the tragic dilemmas, the half-success and half-failure of the Austrian Enlightenment.

IV

JOSEPH VON SONNENFELS

1732-1817

a. *Background and Career*

In the introduction of this study it has been asserted that the major trends of a period and their repercussions in the realm of ideas may be reflected in one distinctive character. In the essay on Abraham a Sancta Clara we tried to prove this contention in regard to the late Austrian Baroque period. In the present essay on Sonnenfels evidence will be offered in regard to the Austrian Enlightenment. Only the final conclusions of this chapter will show how far this plan has succeeded.

Yet long before arrival at any conclusions, even before going into the biography of Sonnenfels, it will become clear that in this present chapter there are greater odds to be overcome than in the one on Abraham a Sancta Clara. The colorful and brilliant personality of Abraham, as is indeed the case with other outstanding characters in history, is of course only partly representative of the spirit of his period, though all major trends of that period may be reflected in his life work. Yet there is hardly a feature in the complex character of the eminent preacher, hardly a facet in his comprehensive writings, that contradicts the main ideas and tradition of his era. This does not hold true of Sonnenfels to the same degree. There are major aspects of his life that appear to be at variance with the spirit of the Austrian Enlightenment. Only their reflection in the character and the extent of his ideological influence long after his death should show why these particular contradictory factors may help to give the ultimate effect of his work a greater reality than that of many other major figures of his time.

What are these unorthodox features? Above all the foreign, northern German background of Sonnenfels' family and, related to it, his early childhood association with the Jewish faith and community. Since the relationship of the world of Sonnenfels' family to the Protestant culture of Brandenburg-Prussia was only tenuous, the influence of this first factor may be considered as primarily negative. The ideological link between the Catholic peasant and clerical world of southern Germany and Austria, so conspicuous in Abraham a Sancta Clara's upbringing, was lacking; yet it was not replaced by a correspondingly strong Protestant tradition influencing Sonnenfels from the North. It is different with the second, the Jewish factor. Here a distinct, at that time alien, atmosphere collided with the basic conditions under which the peculiar character of the Austrian Enlightenment evolved.

Not too much material pertinent to this discussion is available concerning Sonnenfels' ancestry and early upbringing. His grandfather, Rabbi Michael the Pious, was chief rabbi of Brandenburg. He held office in Berlin from 1713 to 1725—that is, at the time of the soldier-king Frederick William I. Distinguished as this position certainly was within the Jewish community, it scarcely contributed to the establishment of any intimate cultural relationship with the gentile world under existing Prussian conditions. The son, Sonnenfels' father, Lipman Perlin (meaning "from Berlin") for reasons unknown emigrated to the Habsburg realms, first to Eisenstadt in what was then German western Hungary, today the Austrian Burgenland. From there he moved to Nikolsburg in German southern Moravia. Both Eisenstadt and Nikolsburg were old and famous Jewish communities; both were under the feudal lordship of eminent peers of the realms, the Princes Esterhazy (well-known benefactors of Joseph Haydn) in Eisenstadt, the Princes Dietrichstein in Nikolsburg. Lipman, already a Hebrew scholar of some reputation, became friendly with members of the Piarist order in Nikolsburg, who were interested in his learning as an orientalist. Through the Piarists Lipman was presented to Prince Dietrichstein, who proved helpful in furthering the family's fortunes.

In itself the career of the father, who came directly from the ghetto, is far more startling than that of his famous son. To start on his way Lipman, in the words of Henrich Heine, paid his "admission ticket" to the Western world of his day: he became converted to Catholicism some time between 1736 and 1739. We do not know whether Lipman, who then began to write under his new Christian name of Alois Wiener, accepted conversion out of religious conviction.

Two factors would seem to indicate the contrary, though neither of them is entirely convincing. For one thing, his wife did not follow him in this decisive step. In fact, Sonnenfels' parents separated at that time, and the mother is never mentioned again in Sonnenfels' voluminous writings. It is rather likely that Lipman-Wiener, endowed with the traditional authority of the head of the Jewish family, might have won his wife over to the new faith, had he truly seen a new light. Psychologically perhaps more salient is the point that the genuine and sincere convert would not have put his new opportunity to such quick use. Wiener promptly proceeded to write a treatise on the reality of the Holy Communion. He also published a Hebrew grammar in German and in Latin. In 1745 he was appointed professor of oriental languages at the University of Vienna, where he taught Hebrew, Samaritan, Chaldean, and Syrian, and served also as interpreter in Hebrew. In the following year, 1746, he was ennobled under the name von Sonnenfels. Possibly the government, in view of Lipman-Alois' early life in Berlin, had employed the versatile man as consultant on some aspects of life in Prussia. In fact, this may have been a main reason for his amazing rise. Yet there is no proof for such an assumption.[1]

Considering the spirit of the times, however, it is rather difficult to believe that the merits of the older Sonnenfels' teachings alone sufficed to give him the spectacular advantage of nobility. In any case, this was the culmination of the elder Sonnenfels' career. He held his chair at the University of Vienna until 1759, then bought a printing office, and died in the second half of the 1770's as an only reasonably well-to-do businessman.

Both of his sons, Joseph and Franz, were born in the Nikolsburg period, in 1732 and 1735, respectively. The younger, Franz, spent the best part of his life there as administrator of the Dietrichstein estates, with the respectable title Aulic Councilor. Later, under Joseph II, he held a position in the Commerce Department, and died in Troppau, Austrian Silesia, in 1805. Not much is known about Joseph's relation with his younger brother in later life. Both Joseph and Franz were baptized in early childhood, in the older brother's case between the ages of four and seven. Thus he could never really have been indoctrinated in the Jewish faith. This, however, means only that Joseph never had to face the moral problem of conversion; it does not mean that he did not have to struggle with the issue of change in spiritual and social environment. Perlin-Wiener the father, had been converted before the beginning of the emancipation of Austrian Jewry, at a time when the concept of the assimilated westernized Jew did not exist in German lands. One lived either in the orthodox atmosphere of the ghetto or in gentile surroundings; no intermediate position was possible. Lipman, without any transitional stage, jumped from one world into the other. Joseph was thus brought up by a father whose intimate acquaintance with the gentile world dated only from his manhood. His sons were to experience the full impact of this sudden break with his environment, with all its implications.

Young Joseph probably received his early elementary education from his father. He studied afterwards at the Piarist college in Nikolsburg, a kind of not yet reformed secondary school that laid considerable stress on Latin and religion and little, if any, on world history and science. From 1745 to 1749 his education was continued in Vienna, a kind of irregular university training with some philosophy and a somewhat better linguistic schooling, particularly in German. As Sonnenfels wrote later, he did not rate very high this kind of schooling in the transitional period between the decline of the humanist pedagogic tradition and the enlightened educational reforms of the coming generation. With a fair knowledge of classical languages, with only an indifferent command of literary German, and with a complete ignorance of the French parlance of society, he appeared not too well equipped for a higher vocation.[2]

Thus limited in his choice of occupation, he still managed to choose a career that could offer him one of the most important formative experiences of his life. In 1749 he joined the army as ordinary long-serving private in the famous *Deutschmeister* infantry regiment. Had he taken to the colors in the most famous army of his time, the Prussian, his new letter of nobility would have secured him at once the position of a *Junker* ensign, and soon enough he would have obtained a commission. Not so in

A Study in Austrian Intellectual History

Austria, where (contrary to widely held notions) nobility then counted less in the army, except in a number of cavalry, particularly guard, regiments and among the graduates of the new Theresan Military Academy of 1752. This, however, did not necessarily mean that service in the Austrian forces was based on more democratic foundations, to use what in this context is an unhistorical term. It simply implies, for one thing, that nobility of letters counted less in the feudal Habsburg realms than in Prussia and, for another, that service in provincial garrison regiments did not carry the unquestionable social prestige generally enjoyed by the Prussian officer caste. Thus while a qualified commoner might well have secured a commission in Austria, an otherwise unqualified member of the new nobility of letters had not sufficient social prestige to make up for his lack of qualifications.[3]

On the other hand, it should be noted that in Sonnenfels' case the whole issue of a commission on the basis of elevation to nobility could have come up in neither the Prussia of Frederick Wilhelm I nor that of Frederick II, where tradition and prejudice would have barred the sudden social rise of a recent convert family. Still, the new nobility of letters implied so much social ambiguity in Austria that the young recruit resolved to drop a title embarrassing to him as a common soldier. He served under the simple name Joseph Wiener.

He served well. During the five years of his military life he was stationed in Styria, Carinthia, Hungary, and Bohemia. Thus on the basis of a very practical and strenuous experience he got firsthand information on conditions in a fair part of the Habsburg lands. He obtained this knowledge particularly through command of the languages that this gifted young man had acquired with great rapidity. As he put it, "I learned French from French deserters who arrived as recruits, Italian from deserters from Italian regiments, Czech from the girls at Jungbunzlau and Sobotka. I read what I could get hold of, and worked out a style of writing from it. I thus wrote French in the manner of Lepais, I wrote German prose following the pattern of Lohenstein and Klipphausen. I made verses which Hofmannswaldau could not have made more bombastic and fuller of metaphors."[4]

According to a credible source, Wenzel Lustkandl, Sonnenfels could speak nine languages, or had at least a smattering of them at the time he left the service in 1754.[5] Obviously such knowledge could not simply have been picked up by a quick intellect: it must have been, at least in part, the result of the well-planned endeavors of a highly ambitious and persevering mind. Sonnenfels once observed that it went against his principles and abilities to make a career by humbling himself before the mighty. "Since you are not in a position to look out for yourself," he said, "you have to educate yourself so that others will look for you."[6]

As to the premise of this resolution there may well be room for doubt. Sonnenfels, by nature certainly not cringing and humble but rather of stubborn and at times cantankerous disposition, was quite capable of pushing himself to the fore if necessary. Yet in his conclusions he stated nothing but the pure truth. Primarily he wanted to make himself useful on the basis of merit rather than connections, and whoever might avail himself of his services could be sure that he had made no bad bargain.

Presently, however, his connections came in handy. He felt that the army had done for him all it could do. Through the good services of Princes Dietrichstein and Trautson, he obtained his honorable discharge as corporal in 1754, to make a career in civilian life. Neither the main trends of his time nor his own inclinations were toward the search for knowledge for its own sake. He wanted to study the institutions of the body politic so as to be able to serve it eventually. Thus he decided now to study law at the University of Vienna. In this second period of his studies, 1754 to 1756, he heard the usual lectures on institutions and the history of Roman law as well as canon law. He attended also the course given by his father in oriental languages. His main and most rewarding experience, however, was his acquaintance with the famous professors of natural and ecclesiastic law, the ancestors of the rightly celebrated Austrian code of civil law of 1811, Karl A. von Martini and J. P. von Riegger, the second being the man who "had really taught him to think."[7]

The second decisive step taken at this time was the successful effort to improve his German to a point that would enable him not only to master the literary language but to become an unchallenged pioneer in its use in Austrian public service and political writing. He resolved upon this at a time when the court language was French, the language of higher learning was Latin, and the people conversed in a dialect, charming in many ways but lacking in clarity because it frequently was not based on knowledge of the written language. It is said that Friedrich Nicolai, that traveling salesman of the literary German Enlightenment, challenged Sonnenfels' efforts in this respect in a passage of his treatise on German literature. Nicolai charged that Austria had not yet produced a writer worthy of the attention of Germany. Her literature had not even reached the stage at which Saxony and Prussia had arrived a generation before. The dreary formalism of a Gottsched and his school, ridiculed in the literary Germany of the 1750's and '60's, was still the idol of Austrian intellectuals, who even in that category could hardly point to a distinguished native writer.[8]

Thus Nicolai. Unquestionably this evaluation was correct, if Austrian literary development was to be measured by the standards of the early phases of German Classicism; yet it was woefully wrong in its disregard of Austrian achievements in the domain of popular literature in the form of plays and poetry. That Sonnenfels shared the haughty prejudices of Nicolai and the Enlightenment in this respect is a fact that will have to be discussed more thoroughly at a later point. Yet this common weakness of the intellectual trends of his time in no way detracts from his endeavors to improve the standards of the literary language. Sonnenfels was not an artist but a public servant who succeeded in his life work chiefly through the medium of the written language. Even the fact that in his zeal he unduly trespassed upon the literary freedom of the artist cannot obscure this.

Sonnenfels' ambition, in any case, hardly needed the prompting of Nicolai's criticism. All of his endeavors were directed toward linking Austria to the reform ideas of the Enlightenment on the basis of the common but in Austria not fully developed possession of the German literary language. In 1761 he became chairman of the one notable cultural association in Vienna, the Deutsche Gesellschaft. At that time he tried hard, though unsuccessfully, to obtain an appointment to the chair of German literature at the University of Vienna. In his writings he strove incessantly and, to a point, even creatively for furthering the potentialities inherent in the language of his time.[9] There are few facts in Sonnenfels' life work that honor him, his later sovereign Joseph II, and Austrian culture in general more than the assignment to write a manual on style in affairs of government and in particular his appointment as member, later vice-chairman, of the Hofkommission in Gesetzessachen, the legislative-reform commission for the creation of new Austrian law codes. In this capacity he had the specific and unique task of seeing that those famous codifications should be written in clear, simple, and pure German. The Austrian code of criminal law of 1805 and the code of civil law of 1811 still bear testimony to the success of Sonnenfels' linguistic-legal reform task. Though associated only with preliminary work on those great codifications, he was able to establish a long (though alas not permanent) judicial tradition of verbal lucidity, conciseness, and unpretentious clarity.[10] One can go even further and admit that the renaissance of German prose in Austria was the one major cultural achievement of the Franciscan period (1792-1835) that to some extent was accomplished not independent of the government's spirit or even in spite of its influence, but largely as a result of endeavors of the regime. And these achievements were largely due to the efforts of a man who started from premeditated linguistic concepts rather than from the idiomatic tradition of the Alpine lands.

Was this accidental? Was Sonnenfels' limited connection with the tradition of German-speaking Austria—an obvious weakness in many respects—a source of strength in this particular field, where he started from the abstractions of Latin syntax rather than from the melodious ease of the Austro-Bavarian dialect? The question goes to the core of Sonnenfels' peculiar position in the Austrian Enlightenment and its ideological repercussions. Only a full evaluation of the reformer's life work will provide a possible answer.

The most pertinent external factors of his further career are the following.[11] After finishing his studies he practiced law for several years. At that time he began to make his reputation as journalist and writer, was active in freemasonic activities and in the German literary society, but he was still without fixed income. To make the best of a precarious situation he applied for the modest position of bookkeeper of the imperial Arcière guards, which he obtained through the good offices of a general, formerly his military superior. While his endeavors in 1762 to obtain appointment to the academic chair of German literature had failed, he succeeded in the following year in becoming the first professor of *Polizei- und Kammeralwissenschaften* (i.e., applied political science) at the University of Vienna. At approximately the same time he was made instructor at the Theresianum, the famous college founded by Maria Theresa primarily for the training of nobles in government service.[12] The duties of his position were varied and cumbersome. He was to give prescribed courses in an all too wide field of academic teaching; he had to write textbooks on order; and he had to hold examinations for candidates for government office. All of this work was under strictest supervision by the authorities, and all the services were rendered for an inadequate remuneration.[13] The fact that he was refused the distinguished chair of German literature and obtained the new and obscure chair of political science is only one indication that in the beginning his new office carried little prestige. It was due to his creative efforts and teaching ability, as much as to the trends of the immediate future, that his reputation and largely those of his academic successors were established. This academic chair was to become a key position in regard to political reforms.

Strained as his external circumstances still were, he was able to set up a household in 1764 and to marry the daughter of a provincial government official, Therese Hay, sister of a future bishop in Bohemia. Though the couple had no children, the marriage proved a very happy one, a fact to which Sonnenfels more than once attested. Doubtless it also increased his social prestige, an advantage to which he never was blind.

The following years were busy ones. The most arduous of Sonnenfels' tasks remained that of writing textbooks on various aspects of political science. In addition to other duties, he engaged more and more in unsolicited writing of his own on all kinds of public questions. He established his reputation as Austria's first journalist; he engaged in a voluminous correspondence with the outstanding champions of the German Enlightenment. This was not all. More and more frequently his services as government consultant were called for in the fields of judicial and economic reforms, commerce, literary censorship, and on numerous other questions. For a brief period in 1770 literary censorship of the theater is assigned to him with practically unlimited power. In 1779 he was finally appointed Aulic Councilor, member and rapporteur of the Studien und Zensur Hofkommission (Commission on Studies and Censorship). He also became a member, and soon vice-president, of the Commission of Judicial Reforms. He was furthermore councilor on police problems. He had reached the summit of his career; but his influence even exceeded the technical limits of his government position.

With the death of the empress in 1780 the strength of this position declined markedly. Joseph II was not overly fond of him. Sonnenfels continued his academic work and was further employed where his assets appeared least controversial, in the field of purification of language in government documents. Yet as to the basic reforms of that hectic period, his services were now seldom requested. And with the untimely death of the emperor in 1790 the heyday of reform had definitely passed. Thus under Leopold II (1790-92), the aging and disillusioned Sonnenfels was glad to be relieved of his academic activities, though he was called to the rectorship (presidency) of the university for the customary annual tenure in 1794 and again in 1796. In 1791 he again became a member of a fashionable new commission, that on the compilation of administrative laws, a function less important, however, than his previous assignments. The same is true of the chairmanship of the commission for the purification of the Talmud, his participation in the final codification of the code of criminal law in 1805, and the vice-presidency and finally the presidency of the Academy of Formative Arts, which he obtained in the last decade of his life under Francis I. While the Franciscan era had little use for the old man "who with other stragglers of the Viennese Enlightenment fought rear-guard actions against the advancing Romanticism,"[14] the authorities treated him kindly, in a superficial way even generously.

In reverse proportion to his vanishing influence, he was now showered with external distinctions. The high Order of St. Stephen, elevation to the rank of baronet, honorary citizenship of Vienna, foreign decorations, and honorary membership in academics were conferred on the by now anachronistic reformer. Could all this compensate him for the gradual abolition of much he had stood and fought for, overtly and covertly, by intrigue, complaint, petition, remonstrance, often by courageous action, but always stubbornly though in the end only halfway successfully? We do not know. His last public action was refusal to deliver a precensored oration at a celebration of the academy in 1814, three years before his death at the age of eighty-

five. Sonnenfels' own evaluation of his lasting tie to the Enlightenment can perhaps be deduced from this incident. It appears perhaps even more clearly in his reaction to the news that
the patriotic poet Collin was to be honored by the erection of
a monument. Deeply moved, his eyes full of tears, the octoge-
narian Sonnenfels cried, "If they erect a monument to Collin,
what will they erect for me?"[15]

Was he merely childishly vain at that time? Was he pleased
by the expected post-mortem honors? Did he feel that empty
ceremonies could not make up for the paralysis of the very essence
of so much of his life work? Did he see still farther ahead to a
possible rejuvenation and reconversion of his ideas in a distant
future? Again we do not know.* Yet we might acquire better
insight from the following as to whether his "great expectations"
regarding the durability of his fame were justified.

This much is certain. The character of Sonnenfels' position
in history was not decided by the empty honors given him at
the time when he and his ideas were in their decline. Yet neither
was the relatively modest external position that he held, primarily
as consultant of executives under Maria Theresa and Joseph, in
any way indicative of his ideological influence. It can be gauged
only from the discussion of his work as shaped to a large extent
by the influence of general and specific environmental factors.
The general obviously are the forces that determined the broad
course of the Austrian Enlightenment. As to the specific environmental factors, hardly any element is more significant than
the one that separates Sonnenfels' life from the Austrian tradition of his time—that is, his Jewish background.

b. "The Alien Corn"†

The few more-detailed studies on Sonnenfels have been written
from a liberal viewpoint, since he has been considered, not entirely correctly, as a pioneer of Austrian Liberalism. All of them,
as is to be expected, minimize the significance of the Jewish
factor in his life; that greatly impairs the value of the studies.‡

*Sonnenfels' letter of March 19, 1817 (about a month before his death),
addressed to a lady whose identity could not be ascertained, indicates however that he was then still in full possession of his mental faculties.

†A title borrowed from one of the finest short stories of Somerset Maugham.

‡Representative of that kind of analysis are the studies of Müller and
Kopetzky cited in the bibliographical notes to this essay at the back of the
book.

To be sure, it would be just as grave a mistake to regard Sonnenfels, like Disraeli a century later, as an emancipated Jew and to interpret his life and work accordingly. In view of the early age at which both were christened, neither is even a "convert" in any but a strictly technical sense. But no English historian would deny that early environmental factors, psychological frustrations, social traditions, and prejudices are connected with the British statesman's background. All this in spite of the fact that in Disraeli's time England had gone through a centuries-old constitutional liberal evolution, so that conditions there cannot be compared with those existing in Austria in the Enlightenment. How much more relevant is such a discussion in regard to a country where, in the lifetime of the hero of this study, the property and even the security of people from whom he originated were not yet legally fully protected. The Jews themselves, not entirely against their own volition, were completely segregated from the gentile world. Still the direct impact of persecution and discrimination is of only secondary importance here in any but a psychological sense. Since technically Sonnenfels could not be considered a Jew, he was not directly affected by the tragic impact of the Jewish fate. Whether, had his background been different, his career would have been smoother, his character better poised, his work less hectic, are questions certainly worth pondering. The problem will have to be touched upon in the following, but it does not affect the basic issue of this analysis, which is how Sonnenfels' association with the Jewish problem affected his image in the future and the ideas for which he stands in history. This is a question deeply connected with the whole issue of Enlightenment, Josephinism, and liberalism in Austria.

From the time of the expulsion of the Jews from Vienna under Leopold I in 1669-70 and the unofficial and limited repeal of this measure a few years later, their position had improved very little in Austrian lands. True, during the War of the Spanish Succession and under the later reign of Charles VI the emotional tension that, particularly from the 1660's to the 1680's, had caused people to link Jewry with the heathen Moslem danger of the East had somewhat diminished. Admittedly also, compelling economic reasons at a time of continued financial crises forbade suppressions by force, which had failed so lamentably in Leopold I's reign. Yet restriction as to domicile, humiliating and oppressive special taxation, even the infamous yellow badge and the permanent threat of renewed expulsion, still continued. Fluctuating economic prosperity led to increased enmity on the part of the guilds, the commercial and industrial class. Enforced as well as self-imposed segregation was instrumental in increasing the irrational fear of the alleged enemy in the dark.[16]

In fact, the situation of Jewry in Austria at that period was, in an economic sense, far inferior to the by no means easy lot of Jews in northern Germany, whose position in Prussia, relatively tolerable under the Great Elector and Frederick I, had deteriorated under the Soldier-King. Still the emigration of Sonnenfels' father to Austria, into a land of inferior opportunities where his people were treated much less well, can be understood only if one assumes that he was already contemplating conversion at the time he migrated.

Maria Theresa fully subscribed to the partly Spanish, partly home-bred tradition that had determined her father's prejudiced attitude in the Jewish question. In fact, far more emotional and frank in character than the pseudo-Spanish last Habsburg emperor, she looked upon any modifications of the anti-Jewish course for the sake of economic-political expediency as positively immoral. As she saw it, such compromises meant the sacrifice of religious principles for worldly profit. The fact that in her later reign she could not dispense with the necessity of dealing with Jewish financiers did not shake these convictions but probably even increased her resentment against them. Possibly her belief that the ill treatment of the Jews was pleasing to God and should therefore be pursued with an uncompromising firmness was more honest than the opinion of Charles VI's economic advisers. Certainly it was also harsher and more cruel in its effect on the oppressed minority.

Within the first five years of Maria Theresa's reign the Jews were driven out of Bohemia (1745), and less than three years before her death, less than five years before Joseph II issued the famous *Toleranzpatent,* in 1777 she wrote these words: "In the future no Jew shall be allowed to remain in Vienna without my special permission. I know of no greater plague than this race, which on account of its deceit, usury, and hoarding of money is driving my subjects to beggary. Therefore, as far as possible, the Jews are to be kept away and avoided."[17]

It is not within the scope of this study to discuss the historical situation that gave rise to those sentiments. Though in any case unjustified, the empress's attitude certainly was more understandable or, rather, less incomprehensible at the height of the Silesian-war crisis than in 1777.

This prejudice is only one and by no means the decisive factor in the evaluation of Maria Theresa. Yet it is as obvious as it is important to realize at this point that that inveterate imperial enemy of the Jews—who used to receive Jewish businessmen, her so-called "court factors," behind a screen so as not to be sullied by their physical proximity—could never have considered Sonnenfels a Jew. Guglia goes so far as to assume, though not to prove, that the obvious benevolence shown by the empress to the reformer had a good deal to do with the pleasure derived from the conversion of an infidel.[18] There is little doubt that her own anti-Jewish feelings and those of her day were inspired by strictly religious and not by racial considerations. But did it mean that the Jewish descendant would encounter no feelings of hostility whatever in court and government circles?

Obviously other factors quite apart from that of subconscious reaction enter here. Time and time again the empress shielded Sonnenfels from attacks made upon him by the powerful archbishop of Vienna, Count Migazzi, and the supreme chancellor Count Chotek in matters of the reform of criminal law, the controversial population theories, questions of censorship, and other public matters. By tradition and philosophy basically on the other side of the enlightened fence, Maria Theresa nevertheless frequently upheld Sonnenfels, though with many modifications, restrictions, and reprimands. She probably considered him a kind of brilliant *enfant terrible* whose limited fool's freedom of criticism might serve a useful purpose so long as the problem child had no actual power of decision. In this context it is important to remember that Sonnenfels the academic teacher, writer, and member of various government commissions never possessed any actual executive power, except in literary matters and related questions of censorship, under either the empress or her successors. In particular, Joseph II, probably because he was so much closer to Sonnenfels' ideas, was far less in need of an enlightened monitor and far more sensitive to the man's frequently criticized faults, his disagreeable loquaciousness, irritability, tactlessness, and vanity. The qualities in the reformer which in the empress's eyes largely made up for these faults, his indisputably sincere zeal and originality, did not count much with a ruler who himself was amply endowed with these traits.[19] Sonnenfels' unswerving loyalty to the whole imperial house is uncontested. His whole career is focused on the empress, the object of his pathetic and touching, at times ridiculous, devotion. Unquestionably the fact that this exalted woman, who was worlds apart from him in rank, tradition, and sympathies, upheld him so frequently is a major psychological key to their relationship. Twice he expressed these feelings publicly, once in the birthday eulogy of May, 1762, delivered in the Deutsche Gesellschaft, again in the necrology given in his first academic lecture after her death in 1780. The first oration is notable for its queer and slightly comic dialectics. After a glorification of enlightened absolutism in general and of the empress in particular, he exclaims: "She may learn by her own experience the unlimited liberty which we enjoy under her! She may learn that we are at liberty not to obey her!"[20] In what way? With his habitual lack of humor and irony he explains that her subjects are at liberty to praise her, even though the empress prefers complete privacy to public homage. Is this Byzantinism? Not necessarily in the sense of the still-absolutist eighteenth-century relations between sovereign and subjects. Yet this is the language neither of the people nor of the government but of an alien and intellectually ambiguous sophistication. Much warmer, though hardly less bombastic, is the necrology of 1780.[21] Yet here too, where Sonnenfels' feelings of affection and admiration break through the thick veneer of pathos, his praise is spoiled by his exaggerated language—the slender bridge that connects Sonnenfels with the spirit of the Baroque.

Imperial sympathy on the one side, reverence and sincere love on the other, were not sufficient to keep Sonnenfels' character and image out of the welter of ambivalent environmental antipathy inspired by his background. The strength of this opposition, in spite of Sonnenfels' backing by Maria Theresa, probably the most popular ruler in Austrian history, may well serve as a yardstick to measure the intensity of this antipathy. Arneth is one of the few outstanding historians of Austria's early liberal period who, quite out of line with prevailing liberal sentiments, do not "tactfully" ignore the issue. He admits (his wording at this point is very careful) that anti-Jewish feelings played their part in the attitude of Sonnenfels' most powerful opponents, Cardinal Archbishop Count Migazzi and the supreme chancellor

Count Chotek.[22] Kopetzky relates in this context that Sonnenfels was frequently and certainly not in a complimentary sense referred to as "the Nikolsburg Jew."[23] Literature of the Enlightenment and its aftermath, which praises Sonnenfels as an intellectual hero, indirectly supports this evidence by stressing the fact that Sonnenfels was able to accomplish what he did—i.e., by implication, despite the handicap of his Jewish background.[24]

To be sure, it can be maintained that the opposition to Sonnenfels was chiefly based on honest ideological disagreement. Furthermore, it is undeniable that a certain arrogance and vanity in his character, not directly connected with the question of bias, played its part. Yet all things considered, the ethnic issue served as an aggravating factor. Sonnenfels had to meet a stiffer opposition than such reformers as Van Swieten, Gebler, Sperges, Born,* and others. The underlying implication was probably that a man of his ancestry had better not mix in controversial issues. He ought to have every reason to keep quiet and leave reform, if there had to be reform, to others.

The point would be less obvious if Sonnenfels had not met with the same kind of emotional antipathy from his ideological allies. A case in point is the notorious Lessing controversy (to be discussed later), in which the great man was and remained infuriated at what was after all a minor lapse on Sonnenfels' part. Most suggestive is the idea that Lessing felt that, if someone had been liberal enough to accept a Sonnenfels as an ideological ally, he might be entitled to demand stricter rules of conduct from him than from others. This holds true as well of Sonnenfels' co-reformer Gebler and his criticism of Sonnenfels.† Even more illuminating is the fact that the two great champions and sponsors of Sonnenfels' ideas in Austria, Prince Kaunitz, the architect of foreign policy, and Van Swieten, the scientist who was equally distinguished as physician and as reformer of higher education and State-Church relations, also basically disliked him. Anti-Jewish feeling is more definite in the case of Van Swieten than of the prince, for whom the issue is somewhat obscured by disagreements in matters of literary taste and the vast difference in social background. Though it cannot be asserted that either

*Aulic Councilor Joseph von Sperges; Ignaz von Born, scientist and writer.
†Significantly enough, however, Sonnenfels, who refers to Gebler as his friend, overlooked this entirely. (Sonnenfels in Ignaz de Luca, *Das gelehrte Österreich*, 168 ff. See also bibliographical note 173 to Chapter IV, at the back of the book.)

Kaunitz or Van Swieten deviated from their ideological policy, the fact that they considered Sonnenfels as an essential but undesirable ally can hardly be contested.[25]

Nobody even faintly conversant with the history of Jewish emancipation in Central Europe will be startled by these facts. On the contrary, it would be surprising indeed if they had not played the important part in Sonnenfels' life that they did. Yet in view of the foregoing reflections on the evolution of the image of Sonnenfels' personality and ideas they are of extraordinary importance for three specific reasons.

The Austrian Enlightenment, particularly in its later form of Josephinism, is clearly—though far more psychologically than logically—connected with the development of Liberalism.[26]

This ideological link accentuates the significance of the tradition that Sonnenfels helped to establish.

Finally, the Pan-German and Christian Social idology that rose very rapidly in the last quarter of the nineteenth century and effectively blighted the tender flower of Austrian Liberalism put an inordinate stress on the connection between Jewish character and the liberal tradition. It is here, in this anti-Semitic climate, that a distorted but at the same time exaggerated conception of the historical role of Sonnenfels comes into prominence. For better, and equally for worse, he is perceived as a keystone in Austrian ideological development.[27]

All these factors will have to be properly considered after an evaluation of Sonnenfels' work.

c. The Personality

No evaluation of this work and of its influence could be complete without a proper analysis of Sonnenfels' character. This would be true even if his personality were less controversial, less irritating to many, less appealing to some.

In discussing the many facets of this fascinating character, one might be tempted to lay too much emphasis on the environmental factor and on psychological insecurity deriving from the break in tradition, which manifested itself in his lifetime in such "overcompensated" features as stubbornness, arrogance, and vanity. While these elements certainly played their part in the biography of this unusual man, his character was too colorful, too peculiar and original, to justify the assumption that his environmental heritage and his reaction to it can explain everything. For one thing, Sonnenfels was brought up in a family that was moving away from its Jewish background, though it did not become hostile to it. The older Sonnenfels in word and print was and remained a steadfast fighter against the medieval superstitions of the ritual-murder legend and other hostile beliefs in Jewish magic.[28] There certainly was nothing in the father of the odious "convert" type, such as Pfefferkorn, that sixteenth-century character of ill repute who befouled his former nest. Neither was there any trace of that tendency in the son, who after all had some specific share in the emancipatory legislation of Joseph II.[29] In spite of the fact that Sonnenfels' own approach to Jewish problems was always a detached one,[30] as was natural enough from a psychological standpoint, his influence on the ideological groundwork that made the tolerance legislation under Joseph II possible is tremendous. The fact that his influence was on the whole far more indirect than direct of course makes an evaluation of his character rather difficult. Yet if one sifts the evidence of contemporary accounts and of later historical presentations based on them, several features appear conspicuous.

Sonnenfels emerges as a man of tremendous industry and ambition. Except for the declining years of his life, when his authority was on the wane, this ambition was focused far more upon wielding influence in drafting legislation than on securing the prestige of high executive power.

This, however, does not mean that Sonnenfels liked to work behind the scenes. It merely indicates that he wanted to be primarily a legislator and, within the limits of what was then possible, a free writer rather than an administrator. His often criticized interference in the reform of the Austrian theater is an exception. Yet certainly he was not inclined to "hide his light under a bushel." He obviously liked public controversies and, even more, recognition. Gräffer, who gives Sonnenfels full credit for his achievements, relates two anecdotes that illustrate this. When Sonnenfels had to interview a young man applying for a government position, he lectured incessantly. The candidate had no chance to utter a single word. Afterwards Sonnenfels said: "I enjoyed my conversation with that young man very much. He is gifted." At another time Sonnenfels drove home late at night with a foreign scholar whom he had taken on a sight-seeing expedition.

The moon rose. "What glorious illumination!" the stranger exclaimed. "I installed it," Sonnenfels answered, assuming that the stranger was referring to a system of improved street-lighting in Vienna, which he had initiated.[31] These two stories, if not true, are certainly good inventions. Sonnenfels was by no means a wallflower and was probably all too convinced of his own importance. On the other hand, it must be admitted that without considerable self-assurance and publicity he could not have accomplished what he did. Yet by and large he conveys the impression of a fighter, not of a fool. He certainly was cantankerous and vain, and he was not noted for his tact. But all things considered, these were merely the reverse side of his virtues. He did fight courageously for his convictions and (as will be shown), at least in one instance in regard to the abolition of torture, at considerable risk to himself. After all, while a more amenable man might have met less opposition, he undoubtedly would also have achieved less. In view of this basic fact, the issue of Sonnenfels' vanity is a trivial one.

More serious is the charge that Sonnenfels had complete disregard for tradition and environmental factors.[32] This kind of criticism can of course be directed not only against Sonnenfels but against the Enlightenment in general. Of the two great contemporaries who criticized Sonnenfels in this respect, the young Goethe and Lessing, only Goethe can be considered free of this common error. Certainly their criticism, as well as that of others, was correct to a point. Again this question can be properly understood only in a far wider context. Could the Enlightenment have left its mark on Western civilization, could it have accomplished what it did, if it had proceeded more cautiously, if it had been less ruthless toward the established cultural setting? Obviously this question is highly debatable. Eighteenth-century reform trends might have failed altogether if they had been more respectful for tradition. On the other hand, they conceivably might have been more successful if the reformers had shown greater psychological understanding of the past. It is easy to make this criticism after the event. Only the greatest among friends or one-time adherents of the movement, such as Lessing and the young Goethe, were really able to perceive this dilemma as early as the 1770's. Yet would it be fair to take their vision as the yardstick by which the errors of a Voltaire, a Rousseau, a Bentham, or a Sonnenfels should be measured? This question will of course come up again in regard to specific problems. It is, however, necessary to make the point here that the issue revolves around a comprehensive ideological problem and has little to do with a specific disregard for tradition deriving from Sonnenfels' radical break with his Jewish background.[33] All things considered, Sonnenfels' personality, irrespective of the reflection of his life work in the future, emerges as far less ambiguous, as far more human, than it seemed to many of his critics and admirers. The course of his life, the intellectual platform on which he fought, are clear and are little obscured or distorted by the peculiarity and difficulties of his position. His obvious human frailties do not compromise the value of his intentions and achievements.

d. Man and Work

Two trends can be rather clearly seen in the political reformism of the Enlightenment. One is strictly bound up with the concept of enlightened absolutism; the other is the direct forerunner of representative democracy in the modern sense and led straight to the American and French revolutions. No strict chronological sequence in these two currents is discernible; they are issues and patterns not so much of gradual evolution as of ideological climate. Even the work of Locke in the seventeenth century is much closer to the development of democracy than that of most of the late-eighteenth-century reformers in Central Europe. The influence of the historical setting of English constitutional life on British political philosophy is obvious. This applies in a way to France as well, though political conditions under Louis XIV, the Regency, and Louis XV were certainly not more propitious for the development of representative institutions than conditions in Austria or in Prussia. Yet there the social basis of intellectual life was broader. The economic foundations of a rising non-feudal economy were stronger, the cultural interchange with England far more intimate, than in Germanic lands. Montesquieu and Rousseau, one Sonnenfels' senior by forty-three years, the other by twenty, started under far more favorable conditions than a Lessing, a Justus Möser, a Nicolai, a Van Swieten, or Sonnenfels himself.

This should help to explain why Austro-German Enlightenment well into the era of the French Revolution did not move out of the framework of enlightened absolutism. To be sure, within that setting there was a continuous series of far-reaching social, political, and cultural reform programs that parallel those in the West, and at some points were even in advance of them. The general Central European frame, however, was different. Sonnenfels in his life and work kept strictly within its limits.

The almost immediate intellectual heirs of Sonnenfels and his confreres were neither Reform Liberals of the British type nor Jacobins of the French variety, but conservative Romantics. The middle link in the ideological development of Western Europe is lacking. Thus the direct, though not eventual, effect of Central European reformers on the later nineteenth century was not as strong as it might have been in a less-restricted political climate. These specific limitations in the German-speaking intellectual orbit must be kept in mind in gauging the life work of the champions of enlightened absolutism there.

This work can be roughly divided into two main streams of action and thought, reform in regard to the body politic and to cultural-literary matters. Obviously while the fields to some extent overlap, a rough distinction on intellectual grounds is defensible. In the cultural field Sonnenfels worked to a considerable degree as a free agent, partly as executive with some limited power of decision, partly as a free-lance writer. His work as a political scientist, including his functions as academic teacher, was far more strictly supervised. The specific reforms that are credited to him are the result of the actions of commissions of which he was a member or a consultant. It is more difficult to establish his individual share there.

Partly for this reason, but also because his cultural activities have seemed far more controversial to later generations, they have received much greater attention. Neither of these considerations will be accepted here as sufficient grounds for putting the cart before the horse and discussing the less important activities before examining those that are more weighty, though less conspicuous and less colorful. The following analysis will thus start with a discussion of Sonnenfels' broad activities in the realm of administrative and judicial reform, economics, social welfare, and education for good citizenship.

e. Sonnenfels' Political Philosophy

The fact that the philosophy of Sonnenfels and that of his Austrian fellow reformers was entirely subordinated to a governmental concept of enlightened absolutism does not mean that they were ignorant of or deaf to the teachings of Rousseau and his intellectual forefathers Hobbes, Locke, and Montesquieu. It does mean, however, that they tried within strict limits and with questionable success to incorporate Rousseau's basic ideas of social structure into their own concept of the enlightened monarchy. This concept differed very much from that of the enlightened classics, according to the modern interpretation. In particular they realized the significance neither of the social contract nor of Locke's "right to revolt" or Montesquieu's separation-of-power concepts in the evolution of modern democracy. The implications of Rousseau's doctrine of national self-determination and the cultivation of national institutions were likewise alien to them.[34] While the model of the reformed society (the model of Sonnenfels) was certainly not that of Rousseau, it was not that of the Austria of Maria Theresa or, in fact, of Joseph II either. In other words, actual Austrian institutions corresponded only very roughly to the social structure that Sonnenfels wanted to see realized.

The term "realized" should be stressed. Sonnenfels was anything but a Utopian. Though his approach to the body politic was certainly not merely pragmatic, he was a theorist only in an eclectic sense.

This has been clearly pointed out by Wilhelm Roscher, who in his classic *Geschichte der Nationalökonomik in Deutschland* observes with specific reference to economics: "Before the system of Adam Smith was accepted, all German economists, with the exception of the physiocrats and the historical-conservative opponents of modern times, may be divided into two principal groups: absolutist and liberal eclectics. The first lean toward the two German Great Powers, chiefly Austria, the second toward the middle-sized and small states of northern Germany, above all the Hansa cities."[35] In a way this distinction does not apply only to economics; yet even when it is applied to Sonnenfels' whole life work, Roscher's views gauge the man only from a short-range viewpoint, within the historical setting of evolving enlightened absolutism in Austria. They are not concerned with the image of Sonnenfels as perceived and developed in the course of future generations. It is a liberal image of a not yet liberal man.

Within the limitations of the Austrian reality of his day Sonnenfels took the intellectual concepts of the great political philosophers of his and his elders' times as he saw them and adjusted them to the reality of feasible reform. This reality paid little heed to the force of prevailing Austrian tradition, yet it was even more blind to the full evolutionary implications of enlightened political philosophy. The effect of the first point has generally been overstressed, that of the second underrated. Dominant Austrian conservatism, even in the Maria Theresan reform period, was quite willing and able to defend the Austrian tradition. The task of representing it was not Sonnenfels' but that of his superiors and opponents. If he had not gone as far as he did, not even a meager compromise between enlightened reformism and stable conservatism could have been achieved. It was perfectly natural that in the Austrian play of politics the principal parts were divided among different actors.

What was less natural was that Sonnenfels did not quite comprehend the full significance of his own part. Rousseau's doctrines meant to him basically this: The state should be penetrated by the *Gesellschaftsgeist*. This social spirit, enhanced by general education, strives for public welfare.[36] It ought to operate within the frame of constitutional government. Yet Montesquieu's concept of constitutional government is just as far removed from Sonnenfels' interpretation of this concept as is his social spirit *(Gesellschaftsgeist)* from Rousseau's social contract. Social spirit in the service of public welfare is a goal, not a method, that can feasibly be pursued by the system of enlightened absolutism. Constitutional government is connected neither with democracy in general nor with its specific form of separation of powers. It simply means government by law. Law—according to Sonnenfels Natural Law[37] —is decreed by the ruler in the spirit of public welfare. His power to impose and to change it according to his lights remains unchallenged. Thus everything hinges on the interpretation of this concept of public welfare as directed by a lawgiver of absolute power.

The state is divided into four classes. First the nobility, whose *raison d'être* is taken for granted. The second class is made up of merchants, manufacturers, artisans, and "useful artists," i.e., all those who give to the state what it needs for its preservation. Third are those who serve the state directly—clergy, courtiers, soldiers, scholars, entertaining artists, and domestic servants. The fourth class likewise receive their livelihood from the state, without however doing any work for their maintenance; this odd incongruous group, harmful to the public welfare, consists of those who live on their private incomes, the unemployed, and beggars.

It is the government's obligation to see to it that the wealth of the state, the aggregate of the property and income of all citizens, is channeled into all social groups that earn their livelihood. Inordinate discrepancies in standards of living between the groups should be adjusted by the state. Yet basically, inequality between the various Estates should be maintained as an essential principle of the social order, which is to be perceived as a pyramid rising up from the lowest class of citizens to the ruler.[38]

This curious system, which employs rather superficial similarities as a basis of classification and therefore lumps together the most heterogeneous groups, is characteristic of the spirit of enlightened political science *(Polizeiwissenschaft)* of that time. Typical of Sonnenfels in particular is the queer utilitarianism that perceives art, for instance, only in the light of its practical use and entertainment value. Significant is also the strong neo-mercantilistic tendency that considers "manufacturing" as the decisive economic contribution to public welfare—the frequently acclaimed virtue, industry, and social value of the peasant notwithstanding. This guiding principle admits state intervention in all kinds of economic activities. This social philosophy, which was advanced a full generation after the publication of *The Wealth of Nations,* is typically "enlightened" and, in particular, typically Sonnenfels indeed.[39]

Sonnenfels, however, is a child not only of the Enlightenment but as well of ancient classical philosophy, as perceived by the Enlightenment. In a discussion of what is essentially the Aristotelian analysis of governmental systems, he comes out in favor of a certain relativism. Republicanism and democracy may well be preferable to despotism. Yet can an outvoted minority ever be assuaged? Not according to Sonnenfels. Thus democracy may be pleasing to the many, but how about the few, to whom equality means the surrender of long-established privileges?

Yet the Sonnenfels who poses this question is not blind to the injustice involved in the rule of a privileged aristocracy. He frequently criticizes the evils inherent in entailed property, exemptions from general jurisdiction, tenure of office based on birth rather than on merits. There is, he states, danger of abuse and injustice here and there. At one point—and this is perhaps the decisive one in this evaluation—democracy comes out on top: inequality through the rule of aristocracy weakens above all the effect of the most noble virtue, patriotism; democracy, on the other hand, furthers it decisively. Still, Sonnenfels seriously questions whether democracy can be sustained, whether it can act effectively under the harsh requirements of war. According to the experiences of history (to him still chiefly Roman history, the vade mecum of political pragmatism from Machiavelli to Vico) he answers that question in the negative. On the other hand, Sonnenfels is able to conceive an aristocratic regime with self-imposed restrictions upon its privileges. "Aristocracy makes the people love this form of government because of the secure life offered to them. The people, conversely, endear themselves to aristocracy by the honor and respect rendered to it."[40] Indeed a strange contract theory!

Is this the final solution? Certainly not explicitly. "For forms of government, I say with Pope, let fools contest! Whichever is best administered is best."[41] It is only in theory, and even then by no means consistently, that Sonnenfels carries relativism to such extremes. His work as a whole conveys the idea that while the best-administered form of government may be the best, on a pragmatic basis one type of government tends to be best administered—the monarchic form in the frame of enlightened absolutism. It is quite obviously the only form compatible with his position as Austrian civil servant, professor of political science, and enlightened reformer in the absolutist state. There may have been a good deal of subconscious expediency in this philosophy, but above all one has to recognize that, considering Sonnenfels' Austrian setting, no other frame of reference would have given his doctrines so firm a *raison d'être*.

Enlightened monarchy . . . It is thus to be! "We perceive society, we perceive ourselves as part of it in the sovereign, in this permanent oracle of general intelligence—of which he is the symbol, the mirror, the awe-commanding image. In the monarchy the burgher perceives the center of power, concentrated in one, as the center of welfare."[42] The noble keeps his rank as well. The prerogatives of each social sphere are secured and at the same time restricted by the sublime power of the crown. It preserves the amenities of social stratification for the higher classes and at the same time protects the lower ones from license. Extraordinary merits and abilities may even open to the burgher the way to

MARIA THERESIA   ROM. IMPERATRIX
VIDVA. HVNGARIAE.   BOHEMIAE. ETC. REGINA.
ARCHIDVX AVSTRIAE.   DVX BVRG. ETC. M. PRINC.
TRANSYLVANIAE.   COMES TYROLIS. ETC.

Empress Maria Theresa

Joseph von Sonnenfels

those exalted offices which by right of tradition belong to the noble. No constitutional guarantees but the character of the monarch, his enlightened and benevolent objectives which he will transmit to his successor (read: Maria Theresa to Joseph), will secure this most nearly perfect form of government.[43]

While the state depends upon production, in particular industrial production, for its support and prosperity, its social structure is still based on the political dominance of the noble class. Sonnenfels has so frequently criticized the evils of aristocratic prerogative that in making the following proposal he is attempting to come to terms with the intangibles of Austrian reality rather than to express a personal conviction. The young feudal aristocrats (Sonnenfels is hardly concerned with the mere nobility of letters) should be educated in state institutions according to enlightened principles. Thus they will be trained to become the leading class not merely by right of birth but by virtue of achievement as well. Time and time again he elaborates this theme that special rights—privileges, at that—entail special duties.

As professor of *Polizei- und Kameralwissenchaften,* as commissioned author of textbooks on political science in 1765, economics in 1768, and public finance in 1776, he has indeed as one of his chief functions that of converting young dandies into conscientious bureaucrats. In his honest endeavor to convince them that noble birth alone is a very unreliable basis for a future career, he does not shrink from advancing what, in his case, is a specious argument: that claims to exalted office based exclusively on birthright are comparable to the (by implication) unjustified pride of the Jews in their ancient history.[44]

Here as in other cases Sonnenfels shows poor taste. To a certain extent he betrays naïveté as well.[45] And surely, in view of his difficult position, without this ostrich-like naïveté he could not have managed to maintain the poise necessary to proclaim many of his constructive ideas. Yet in his specific task of training the young nobility entrusted to him by reason of their compulsory attendance at the Theresian Academy, the over-all results of his work were meager. In the light of the fact that a very large percentage of the higher bureaucracy during the last part of Maria Theresa's reign and an even larger proportion of Joseph's, Leopold's, and Francis's administrators went through Sonnenfels' school, the result is particularly disappointing. None of his students, with the possible exception of Ignaz de Luca, rose above the level of well-trained efficiency to standards of independent thinking and action. None of them even tried to withstand the pressure of advancing reaction. Surely this was not so much the fault of Sonnenfels as that of the circumstances of his times; yet he must take part of the blame for having failed to comprehend that the bureaucratic system, supported and reformed by him with so much sincere zeal, was outdated in a far deeper sense than he ever realized.

Still two ideas, that of respect for the law as a system of contemporary social thought and that of subordination of social activities to the public welfare, though already antiquated in their specific frame of reference and application, had been brought closer to the public conscience through Sonnenfels' incessant work. His was the only half-satisfactory task of expounding these ideas; it was for others to understand them, and for a still-later generation to infuse them with reality.

f. The Church

In the Austrian system of government under Maria Theresa it was inconceivable that a man like Sonnenfels should be entrusted with a major part of the work of settling the crisis in State-Church relations. Under Joseph II such a participation might have been possible if by that time the influence of Sonnenfels had not been already on the wane. Under Joseph's successors it was out of the question again.* Yet so basic was and remained the factor of State-Church relations, and indeed the general issue of religion in eighteenth-century Austria, that on various levels this problem plays a vital part in Sonnenfels' work.

His stand on this issue is clear and unequivocal. He believes

---

*The authors of two recent major works dealing with State-Church relations under Maria Theresa and Joseph II—Eduard Winter, *Der Josefinismus und seine Geschichte* (Brünn, 1945), and Ferdinand Maass, *Der Josephinismus* (Vienna, 1951), I-IV—thus feel entitled to ignore Sonnenfels' standpoint in this context altogether. The same holds true for Fritz Valjavec, *Der Josefinismus* (Vienna, 1945), though he like Winter refers to Sonnenfels' work in a different connection.

Maas notes, however, that Aulic Councilor Heinke referred the complaints of the Austrian episcopate of 1790 "in the first place" to his colleague Sonnenfels. He assumes that this clause refers to Franz von Sonnenfels (see Maass, *op. cit.*, III, 121, 466, 495). Though the first name is not given in the document, there can be little doubt that Joseph and not his brother Franz, administrator of the Dietrichstein estates at Nikolsburg, is the person indicated by Heinke.

that without moral-religious foundations the rule of law would collapse. Therefore in his syllabus of 1767, made up of 65 theses which constitute an introduction to political science, he states: "THESIS 24: Religion is the most effective instrument to further moral conditions. Secular legislation will be insufficient on several points if not supported by the bond of religion and its 'punishments.' "

Accordingly, the police must pay attention to it, not as an end in itself but as means to an end. "THESIS 25: Therefrom it follows that libertinism must be punished as a political crime, since it invalidates one of the state's most powerful restraining powers. Therefrom it follows that it is the concern of the sovereign as secular authority that his subjects should be well instructed in religious matters. . . . Therefrom it follows that even as secular regent he [the sovereign] is entitled to demand from the citizens evidence which, as it were, must prove that they are religious. From Catholics, for instance, he may ask the certificates of confession. . . ."[46] In other words, religion—in Austria naturally Roman Catholicism—is an instrument of government that must be upheld and supported insofar as it strengthens the authority of the state.[47]

The implication, then, is that religion has no other *raison d'être*. And this being the case, it is only logical from his point of view that Sonnenfels should oppose the Church whenever he fears that her influence on religious matters might encroach upon the power of the state. This view, deriving from the doctrines of the French Enlightenment but shaped in the climate of the rigid Austrian Catholic faith, is the ideological basis of State-Church relations. It was the position which Maria Theresa had to accept, which Joseph adopted, and which was asumed by Kaunitz and Van Swieten in their conduct of affairs.

In his *Über die Ankunft Pius VI. in Wein* (fragment of a letter, published in 1782)[48] Sonnenfels discusses the question of whether the purpose of the Pope's famous visit to Vienna, that of persuading Joseph to undo or modify his religious legislation, may be considered as a Canossa in reverse. While dissociating the policy of the diplomat Pius VI from the sweeping aspirations of a Gregory VII and a Boniface VIII, he impresses on the crown the need to stand firm on every item of Joseph's church reform— that is, above all on the curtailment of episcopal jurisdiction, state curtailment of marriage legislation and church finances.

ecclesiastic education, monastic organization, etc. He believed that such a policy protects not only the interests of the state but, in the long run, those of the Church herself.

This line of thought is surely consistent with the whole tenor of Sonnenfels' writing. He had welcomed the new church policy when it was initiated hesitatingly, halfheartedly, and grudgingly under the empress, and he fully endorsed it under Joseph. Sonnenfels quite naturally got little credit from the emperor for his support of what by that time was the obvious course,[49] but the empress did not take his religious indifference very much amiss either—numerous reprimands and relatively minor restrictions as to Sonnenfels' writings on specific reform issues notwithstanding.[50] Maria Theresa's thoroughly respectable reign exemplifies the difference between moderately enlightened absolutism and morally inferior totalitarianism.

g. *Political Economy and Social Welfare*

The core of Sonnenfels' social doctrines and actions is to be found in his works on economics. The endeavors of the Central European "cameralists" of the eighteenth century largely overlap those of the political scientists of the West. Both lines of thought are basically far less concerned with specific reforms than with the desire to set up a whole new body politic, though the stress in the West was on political rights, in Austria and the Germanies on economic prosperity. This difference alone does not make for a clear demarcation in scientific spheres. More important is the difference in the political climate. In the relatively greater intellectual freedom of the West, publication of Utopian political doctrines was permitted, but any attempts to realize them were frequently blocked. In Central Europe even literary activities of Utopian brand were generally considered taboo. Enlightenment could proceed not in the garments of ideal freedom but merely in those of reform, and it was most active there, in the relatively least-controversial sphere of economics, in the service of the prosperity and power of the state.

Physiocratic theories, the neo-mercantilism of the later eighteenth century, the doctrines of Adam Smith, were no longer studied and applied in the early mercantilist spirit of the despotic absolutism of Louis XIV and the soldier-king Frederick William I. They were of course still considered instruments of state and of royal power, but they were also perceived as tools for creating a new middle class, tools with which to limit if not to destroy the forces of feudalism. In the sense of economic reform as a means to realize political aims, the economic doctrines of the Austrian Enlightenment are pervaded with a much stronger sense of political realism than contemporary Central European reflections on the best-possible form of government. If one considers further that the endeavors of these cameralists were based directly or indirectly upon the work of the great theorists Quesnay, Turgot, Smith, and others, the significance of their potential achievements becomes obvious.

Thus Sonnenfels, though by training no more an economist than a political scientist, a lawyer, and a literary critic, is shown here as in other fields to be merely a well educated, highly gifted dilettante with strong reformist zeal. Yet as was pointed out, he could feel less inhibited in the sphere of political economy than in others and here he was working not with tedious and artificial reinterpretations of ancient political philosophy but with new findings of his century.

Though still deeply involved in the contradiction between an octroyed absolutism and its partly liberal aims that is very characteristic of the enlightened century, the economist Sonnenfels followed a straight course. He started from the premise of the so-called populationist theory as developed before him by Johann Heinrich von Justi and as implied in a far more subtle way in Adam Smith's doctrines. As was characteristic of the intellectual sources of the Austrian Enlightenment, Sonnenfels was far better acquainted with the work of the long-forgotten German than with that of the foreign giant.[51]

According to Sonnenfels, whom Roscher considers the most eminent populationist in German lands, the people are the basic asset of the state. Increase in population means increase in power, security, wealth, and cultural progress. Thus the simple populationist doctrine, based on the notion that Providence would never create more human beings than could be fed, is more than a mere economic thesis; it is a principle of social philosophy. To examine Sonnenfels' reform proposals in detail lies beyond the scope of this study. For our present purposes it will be sufficient to keep rather closely to the unequivocal spirit of Sonnenfels' economic ideas, ignoring for the most part the outmoded dialectic exercises and the imperfectly reasoned explanations and deductions of his theory.

Some of these deductions, however, shed considerable light

on his social philosophy. Sonnenfels believed, as is evident elsewhere in his writings, that change must not be left to the free play of economic forces. It ought to be initiated and supervised by the state. Thus the promotion of population increase should go hand in hand with an economic policy that guarantees an adequate standard of living to the masses. This necessitates a fight against increase in prices. Prices will increase, particularly where large masses of people are concentrated—that is, in big cities. As early as 1769 Sonnenfels called attention to the major problem of later and earlier generations, flight from the land. He advocated decentralization of the administration, establishment of institutions of higher learning in small towns, distribution of industry over the entire country.

Only if and when the state has consolidated the economic foundations for the maintenance of the masses—and that includes the obligation to care for those unable to work—can the government proceed to further population increase by means of direct regulations. Marriages should be forbidden between elderly matrons and young men, because they would prevent the men from giving the state its richest asset, children. The same applies to marriages between sick people. The state may even go so far as to invalidate the vows of celibacy of monastics in the interests of the common welfare. Society should fight to prevent the stain of illegimate birth. Children born out of wedlock should be cared for in foundling homes. The mothers also should be supported; strictly enforced secrecy should be maintained and any attempt to search out the father prohibited. Thus the neglect and quite frequently even the murder of illegitimate children could be prevented. As is well known, these last ideas formulated by Sonnenfels and others found their way into the Austrian social legislation of Maria Theresa and Joseph II, as well as into the Code Napoléon in a more concise way.[52]

The functions of "populationism" are confined however neither to general protection of the consumer nor to social-welfare legislation. They impose stern duties on the individual citizen. Every able-bodied person is obliged to work; idleness is to be punished; migration as a loss to the state is to be forbidden. The number of Catholic holidays, through which the state loses valuable working time, is to be severely restricted. The question is even raised, from the point of view of populationism, as to whether capital punishment should be eliminated, since it deprives the state of the benefits of penal labor.

There is nothing in the basic objectives of the populationist theory to which the Church would have to take exception on principle. In fact, in later times populationist arguments could be considered as valuable refutations of Malthusian and neo-Malthusian theories. They differ only in specific matters. Yet Sonnenfels had to face the violent opposition of the Cardinal Archbishop Count Migazzi[53] not only on such understandable and obvious points as control of the vow of celibacy and abolition of holidays. In fact, in the holiday question Sonnenfels was fully sustained by the devout empress and his proposals actually became law. The reasons for the archbishop's protest went deeper; he perceived populationism as an over-all utilitarian concept according to which religion, like people, was a mere means in the service of a new doctrine of public welfare. As Migazzi put it, "Already the basic principle of Sonnenfels' doctrine, that the wealth of the state is based on population, violates the doctrines of Christianity, the evangelic counsels," and lastly "the celibacy of priests."[54]

This opposition came to the fore particularly as the result of the publication of Sonnenfels' treatise *Über die vermindernde Bevölkerung der Residenzstadt Wien,* of 1767, in which he proposes that part of the population of big cities should be settled in the country. Largely, but again probably not exclusively, at Migazzi's instigations this treatise had to be withdrawn from sale, and preventive censorship was imposed on Sonnenfels' further writings.

At this critical moment in Sonnenfels' relations with the empress, he stood his ground steadfastly. As a result of his representations, Maria Theresa issued instructions to the effect that Sonnenfels, the enactment of advanced censorship notwithstanding, should be permitted to continue to write according to his principles. He might do so even if he promoted ideas that challenged existing institutions. He was thus permitted to criticize valid Austrian legislation and was entitled to draw on government authorities for information. "While," as Maria Theresa put it, "the freedom of teaching is an issue here, the teacher must always act with reasonable moderation."[55] Indeed, this truly Austrian compromise does credit both to the empress and to the reformer. And since Sonnenfels had retrieved his right to work, he made a conciliatory gesture to the archbishop in the form of the dedication of the third part of his *Der Mann ohne Vorurteil* in the very same year, 1767.[56]

The whole incident might be considered a tempest in a teapot if it were not for the underlying implications. The fact that Sonnenfels presumed by rational means to influence conditions that should be left to divine Providence was considered basically far more objectionable than any specific reform proposals. It was not an economic doctrine that was being challenged here but the *étatisme* of the Enlightenment and its rationalist foundations. Reforms were frequently condoned on a purely technical level. But as soon as they touched upon the realm of faith—however indirectly—they were to be rejected, irrespective of their specific merits. This conflict, though often circumvented by means of enlightened interpretation on the part of ecclesiastical authorities, has been bridged at times but it has not been settled even to this day.

In this case the cause of reform at least held its ground. There now arose ideological conflict between physiocratic and neo-mercantilistic principles. Sonnenfels as a thoroughgoing neo-mercantilist wished to avoid giving the impression of being oblivious of the significance of agriculture. He glorified the Estate of the peasant as the most ancient and venerable. He abounds in proposals to give land to the peasants in the interest of population increase. He promoted the idea of export premiums for grain. Yet by and large these proposals were prompted not by economic utilitarianism but by humanitarian concern for the poorest class in the realm. On the whole he rejected the belief of the physiocrats that the chief emphasis should be on agricultural problems. This is as obvious in his writings as in his over-all influence on the Josephinian civilian legislation.[57] Contradictions in Sonnenfels' writings on this point may thus be explained by a certain shift in his standard of judgments. His promotion of physiocratic ideas is primarily based on ideas of enlightened humanitarianism, his mercantilist doctrines far more on the concepts of enlightened rationalism.

Sonnenfels' stress on the overwhelming importance of industrial manufacturing for the expansion and prosperity of the economic order does not conform entirely to the conventional mercantilistic doctrine, however. Again social considerations play a major role. This becomes particularly clear in his fight against price rises and usury. Here his chief aim was to establish some kind of compromise between the need of the industrial working class for a tolerable standard of living and that of the agricultural class. He wanted to secure it without endangering economic initiative and a reasonably free play of economic forces by all too stringent legislation.[58]

This aversion to ordinances that threaten to paralyze the free play of economic forces comes out further in his no longer particularly original campaign against the guild system and its intolerable restrictions. Again the social angle of his attack is notable. Thus he states: "Society should demand only that every citizen ought to work! The permission to work is dependent on guilds; whoever is not a member of the guild is forced to become a scoundrel. The roads to support oneself honorably are blocked. You whose function it is to punish crime, do you wonder that the prisons are crowded with criminals? Do you wonder that examples of severity have to be set so often and yet all are in vain? Stop being unjust and indicting human nature! There are only two roads open to make one's livelihood if one does not have an inherited fortune: work or crime. The man who is denied the one path is forced to walk the other!"[59] These were unusual and certainly not mean-spirited words in eighteenth-century Austria!

Sonnenfels regarded the occupation of a skilled, economically unrestricted artisan not only as most useful but also as relatively easy and pleasant. Consequently, in order not to draw too many people from the strenuous toil of agriculture to the less arduous crafts, he proposed to modify the attraction of the crafts by means of strict requirements for apprenticeship and vocational training. Thereby a double purpose would be served: a sound proportion between the various occupations could be established and at the same time the level of craftsmanship would be raised. Many potential artisans might thus prefer to continue with agricultural work, provided standards of living in the country were raised. Conversely it would be necessary to keep a great number of prospective intellectuals within the crafts. Sonnenfels strongly warned of the danger of an influx of lazy, snobbish people of mediocre talent into the free professions, government, and academic positions. Stricter requirements should help to keep only an intellectual elite within the professional class.[60]

In its economic effect this means that small tradesmen and skilled craftsmen, who were not yet strictly separated, should comprise the middle class of the state. Ideologically, the implied notion that neither economic profit nor ability should be the sole yardstick applied in the government's occupational policy is a rather original thought. Important also is the stress laid on the psychological factor in the suggestion that the convenience of working conditions and the question of social prestige should be given major consideration in channeling people into work and finally also in evaluating their compensation. Some hundred fifty years later in the early history of the Austrian republic this problem stated by Sonnenfels provoked an acrimonious discussion as to who should be entitled to higher pay, the research assistant at the university with his interesting work, pleasant working conditions, and social prestige or the toiling laundrywoman. To pose this question is not to answer to it, but to raise it is a service to the community.

As to trade, Sonnenfels' prolific writings are typical of the revised mercantilism of the second half of the eighteenth century, which at that time was modeled after the English rather than the French pattern. While he did not show much originality here, his discrimination and self-taught learning in this sphere are impressive. The demand for a favorable trade balance is qualified by the concept of lasting advantages to the national economy, which cannot be expressed simply in terms of the surplus value of export over import. All this was fairly well known even in Sonnenfels' time. Yet it was characteristic of him that he perceived this advantage chiefly in human terms, employment for increasing numbers of people. Thus populationist considerations lead again to an expression of enlightened humanitarian principles.[61]

To this must be added a reference to Sonnenfels' ceaseless fight against serfdom.

> Despotism of oppressive princes over people is a horror. Yet the most obnoxious, the most intolerable despotism is the one which citizens exercise over their fellow citizens. This was serfdom—that stain on the constitution where it is tolerated, that stain on an alleged jurisprudence which reasoned man down to matter and fabricated faked evidence. Never has defenseless weakness wanted to entrust its rights to the stronger but for its protection . . . never has confidence been more shamefully abused, than when protection was converted into the right of the lord, when people, endowed by nature with equal rights of body and soul, were degraded to

property of their fellow human beings. How, by every aspect of reason, could people even for the sake of protection of their life ever have wanted to sell what is the greatest, the only value of life? . . .[62]

Along with these words, which for once are neither bombastic nor loquacious but truly noble, mention should be made of Sonnenfels' fight against tax exemption on the basis of social and historical privileges. One may add to this his fight for the *portio sacra,* a tax-exempted minimum to maintain the livelihood of the poor. From all of this one can see the true picture, the genuine line of thought, of the economist Sonnenfels. With Van Swieten he represents here and elsewhere, in spite of his various shortcomings, the most advanced reformer of the Maria Theresan age.[63]

h. Judicial Reforms

One of the most paradoxical problems in the evaluation of Sonnenfels is his contribution to judicial reform. Unquestionably the image of Sonnenfels, as shaped by early Austrian Liberalism and transmitted to posterity, is chiefly that of a champion in this field. While the significance of every other aspect of his life work has been questioned, even his most vehement opponents agree that in this area his achievements were memorable.

This would be rationally defensible, though not correct, if the entire range of Sonnenfels' contribution to judicial-reform legislation were taken into account. Though not quite comparable to his efforts in other fields, his record here remains impressive enough. Yet those who shaped the image of Sonnenfels were not interested in his contribution to civil legislation but exclusively in his ideas on the reform of criminal law. Even within criminal law their attention remained focused only on one aspect of his work, his efforts to bring about the abolition of torture. It was just this aspect of his work that was far less broad and radical than that of some of his contemporaries. While his outstanding contributions in many another field are entirely forgotten, his fame rests on an achievement that was only partly his own.

The underlying reasons for this strange phenomenon go far beyond the specific aspects of the Sonnenfels case. That penal justice, particularly in its more cruel forms, has always held a weird appeal for the general public is common knowledge and is easily explicable. More complex is the reaction of the person of higher moral and intellectual standards who feels ashamed of this morbid but compelling curiosity concerning an area of human experience that is shocking and abhorrent. Such a person then is only too glad to have the curiosity and shame converted into indignation and to sublimate them psychologically by fighting against barbarian justice. Thus the campaign against torture at the same time satisfies and assuages sinister emotions. If this were not so, the emotion aroused by specific problems of torture and the spate of literature that it produced throughout eighteenth-century Europe could scarcely be understood. This is not, of course, to deny the barbarian character of torture, though its use in times that did not recognize circumstantial evidence could be rationalized to a point. Yet torture, even in the eighteenth century, was only one conspicuous rock on a mountain of injustice and cruelty—social injustice and cruelty, it should be added, that hurt far more victims than did the anachronistic system of criminal law. The specific psychological reasons outlined above help to explain why this particular residue of barbarism more than any other was singled out for enlightened attack.

There are, of course, still other factors involved, among them (as has been demonstrated all too clearly in our time) the inability of the human mind to grasp emotionally the impact of mass horror and mass injustice. Identification with the sufferings of others is far easier in the case of the specific prisoner, the single defendant in the clutches of a system of deadly "justice."

There is furthermore the fact that in many ways the fight against torture hit what had become emotionally the least controversial of the abuses of feudalism and despotic absolutism. Not all the anachronistic institutions of that period, appearances notwithstanding, have been completely superseded. Official torture, however, is morally dead. Here the line of thought leading from enlightened absolutism to Liberalism has been consistently maintained. However widely and brutally practiced even in our own times behind the barbed wire of concentration camps and the thick-walled tombs of the secret police of many a totalitarian country, torture has never since the eighteenth century dared to raise its ghastly head in public. Thus it is small wonder that this almost uniquely successful battle waged by the Enlightenment has attracted such wide attention.

Joseph von Sonnenfels

There is a final aspect of the problem. The human mind is inclined to perceive history in terms that it can most easily comprehend both emotionally and intellectually. It tends to regard history as a passionate struggle between such forces as justice and injustice, civilization and barbarism, freedom and servitude, good and evil. The prototype of this is the trial in which two forces oppose each other and the judge (in a way the symbol of history) pronounces judgment. This symbolical approach to history, which appears to make the issues quite clear-cut, helps to explain the repercussions produced in every age by cases such as that of Jean Calas, of Dreyfus, or by the Nürnberg trials. In this chain, torture is only a small link, but the very fact that it is a link suffices to give it symbolic value. Accordingly the fight against torture and its protagonists has assumed a prominent place in history.

As mentioned before, Sonnenfels' action and writings on the torture question form only a fraction of his endeavors in behalf of judicial reform. It should be remembered first that Sonnenfels was the student of those outstanding teachers of Natural Law at the University of Vienna, Riegger and Martini. To these men, of whom particularly Martini left a decisive mark on that sublime piece of legislation, the Austrian civil code of 1811, Natural Law is rooted in reason. This reason, however, is co-determined by the forces of mores and ethics as formed by social tradition. This basically is the philosophy of Sonnenfels, expressed succinctly in the words "It is unnecessary to refer to written law, show me first the repeal of Natural Law! Law is as old as human nature; it is imbedded in your feelings. . . ."[64] Thus to Sonnenfels' practical mind, reason represented the guiding principle of legislation, tradition the necessary and, in view of the Austrian setting of his work, the imperative link with the past. A compromise between the two forces is required; but it is a compromise dictated by necessity rather than by conviction.

Sonnenfels' over-all influence on Austrian reform legislation rested chiefly on an indirect though highly important contribution, his membership and later vice-chairmanship in the reform commission for legal agenda, with the specific assignment of editing the new codifications in clear and succinct German. As a member of that commission, which between 1801 and 1806 alone held not fewer than 132 meetings, at least in a formal sense he actually drafted a major part of the Austrian code of criminal law of 1803; and as the minutes of the reform work on the civil code of 1811 prove, he jointly with others had a considerable share in that work as well.[65]

Still the influence of this part of Sonnenfels' activities, important as they were, must not be overrated. The editor of a law code can exercise only an indirect influence on legislation itself, if his work is confined to the literary aspects, though that influence may be substantial. The exact extent of such a contribution to the content of the civil code is difficult to ascertain. Yet it is certain that Sonnenfels, though not one of the chief architects of the civilian and criminal legislation of the Austrian empire and the future republic, injected into the civil legislation of 1811 the ideas of populationism. This can be seen in several provisions of marital settlements and in the evaluation of personal services as commodities of intrinsic values.[66]

His specific contribution as to the substance (not the form) of the code of criminal law of 1803 is even more difficult to gauge. As in other fields, Sonnenfels' chief contribution was that of the introduction of ideas into Austrian legislation. These ideas had not matured at the time when his influence was at its height, in the later Maria Theresan era and only to some extent under Joseph's regime. Under Leopold II and Francis I his ideological influence was negligible. Thus to establish the real significance of Sonnenfels' work in the judicial field it is necessary to look primarily into his work as free-lance writer and its indirect influence on legislation under Maria Theresa and particularly Joseph. These efforts helped pave the way for the great codifications of today. The Maria Theresan Peinliche Halsgerichtsordnung of 1768 (revised in 1786), the torso of the Josephinian civil code of 1786, the code of criminal law of 1787 (in this context of lesser significance), and the order of general procedure of 1781 are the legislative works in question.[67] Yet only two of them, the Josephinian statutes of 1786 and 1787, actually prepare the ground for the major codifications of lasting value, the codes of criminal and civil law of 1803 and 1811, respectively.

As to Josephinian civil legislation, the great impact of the Enlightenment is obvious in regard to limitation of privileges of the First and Second Estates, restriction of personal services, state control in ecclesiastic matters, etc. Through his writings Sonnenfels can claim a fair share of credit for the injection of these principles into the new Josephinian code, though his influence was limited by his basic disagreement with Joseph

II's essentially physiocratic economic philosophy. The part of
the code dealing with contracts, however, where Sonnenfels' neo-
mercantilist populationist ideas would have made a more specific
contribution, was not completed in the emperor's lifetime.

Far more conspicuous, though not quite rightly so, is Sonnenfels' work on penal legislation. He started his campaign against
the Constitutio Criminalis Theresiana of 1768-69 just as soon
as it was issued, both by writing on it and on the lecture platform. This campaign was directed not only against the still-
surviving institution of torture but against the barbarous forms
of capital punishment (breaking on the wheel, impalement,
quartering, maiming, etc.), various methods of corporal chastise-
ment, and the lack of distinction between prison sentences and
imprisonment on remand.[68]

Sonnenfels' basic views on capital punishment are set forth
in his famous treatise on the abolition of torture of 1775.[69]
The peculiar background of this treatise, actually a defense
against the empress's censure of Sonnenfels' criticism of the
Theresan penal code, helps to explain his curious line of reasoning. Assailed by his old opponent Cardinal Migazzi as a revolutionary because of the alleged anti-absolutist and irreligious
character of his reform ideas,[70] Sonnenfels took great pains to
prove that he was guided not by libertine, radical humanitarian
motives but exclusively by considerations of state welfare. He
points out that, contrary to the fundamental reform ideas of
Beccaria, he is not opposed to capital punishment on principle
but only where public security does not necessitate its application. He goes further and explains that lifetime penal labor
is actually a stiffer punishment than execution and a more
effective deterrent.[71] In taking this line of defense Sonnenfels
was sure to win the support of the co-regent Joseph, who disliked the parading of humanitarian feelings and who in his
future penal reform actually abolished capital punishment as
too mild an expiation for the most serious crimes as well as a
useless squandering of human labor.[72]

It is not the task of this study to analyze the strange character
of Joseph, in which benign and humanitarian impulses were
curiously and frequently offset by the harshness of his words
and actions. Certainly Joseph's character cannot be judged
solely by some of his almost inconceivably cruel directives in
this field.

Yet it is even more certain that the true Sonnenfels is not

to be identified with the belief that the chief purpose of reform is to introduce more reliable methods of detecting the culprit and punishments that are more effectively deterrent. His whole literary and administrative work in the field of political science bears convincing testimony to the fact that such motivations were offered and stressed by him as a matter of expediency to cover a humanitarianism that had, by necessity, to be smuggled in by the back door. Where he could promote genuine humanitarianism without endangering his cause he did so manfully. Where to base his arguments on humanitarian considerations would have meant to court defeat, he took the tragic course of fighting for a program of questionable motivation that promised success. The blame for this doubtful method of reform does not rest with Sonnenfels but with the *imponderabilia* of a tradition that was still too strong to be defeated in outright frontal attack.

This will become even clearer if one looks at the focal point of the reform controversy, the torture question itself.[73] Only such aspects of the history of this dramatic struggle are given here as involve Sonnenfels, and only in their broadest outlines. In 1767, before the promulgation of the Theresan criminal code, Sonnenfels had already attacked the draft of the new codification in the first part of his textbook on political science. His criticism was directed primarily against the all too frequent sanction of capital punishment for numerous crimes, the barbarous forms of execution, and above all the institution of torture. At that time the ground for Sonnenfels' action had been well prepared by Voltaire, Beccaria, and Justus Möser and by the fact that torture had already been abolished in Denmark, Prussia, Saxony, and several smaller German states. Catherine II of Russia, the leading actress of the Enlightenment stage, was known to frown upon it. Even in Austria, Sonnenfels' own revered and, also in court circles, highly respected teacher Martini had denounced torture, though with certain reservations, in his *De juri civitatis.**

It is notable that Sonnenfels did not support the unqualified abolition of the cruel institution. He declared it reasonable to

*In his continuation of Sonnenfels' autobiography Ignaz de Luca claims that Sonnenfels had taken up the torture question two years before Beccaria (*Das gelehrte Österreich*, 177). Actually, the famous philosopher of law, Christian Thomasius (1655-1728), had already taken a stand against torture. (See also S. Brunner, "Joseph von Sonnenfels," in *Die Mysterien der Aufklärung in Österreich, 1770-1800* [Mayence, 1869], 59 f.)

continue the use of torture in the case of the convicted criminal who refused to reveal the names of his accomplices to the authorities. It is not likely that he did so for reasons of expediency, since he maintained that viewpoint even at a time when the government had swung round to the decision to abolish torture entirely. Sonnenfels, however, with that mixture of formalism and stubbornness so characteristic of him, continued to insist on this point even in the 1804 edition of his textbook—that is, a generation after the abolition of the rack in Austria.

While this qualification would have been pertinent only in rare cases, it represents a flaw in Sonnenfels' noble record in regard to the general issue. Yet it does not reflect either on his sincerity or on his courage, nor does it diminish his share in the reform movement. In any case, his reservation remained for several years a merely academic issue. His inveterate opponents Vice-chancellor Count Kolowrat, Court Chancellor Count Chotek, and Cardinal Count Migazzi opposed him for some time on much broader grounds. They attacked him not because he believed in the continued use of torture under certain conditions but because he sought to abolish it as a general practice.

Kolowrat, Chotek, and Migazzi denounced Sonnenfels to the empress not merely as a critic of judicial procedure but as a determined foe of the God-willed order itself. As discussed previously, Sonnenfels' promotion of populationist theories played a major part in this protest.* The empress was obviously caught in a conflict between rational demands, the justice of which she could not help but see, and a fear of the ultimate objectives of a reformism that in general ran counter to many of her deepest convictions. As usual in such a dilemma, she resorted to the kind of compromise discussed in connection with the populationist issue; Sonnenfels was admonished to exercise greater caution and moderation, but his right to continue to promote his ideas remained essentially intact.

A compromise between the forces of a declining past and a

*As to penal legislation on only one point—the demand for abolition of the right of ecclesiastical institutions to grant asylum to fugitives from justice—did Sonnenfels at that time directly challenge established ecclesiastical rights. (See the memoranda by Count Chotek and Cardinal Count Migazzi of 1767 in Österreichisches Staatsarchiv, Allgemeines Verwaltungsarchiv, Polizei- und Cameralwissenschaffen, Fascicle 10; also [*ibid.*] the rescripts of the empress of February, June, August, and September, 1767, and of 1772. See also Arneth, *Geschichte Maria Theresias*, IX, 202; S. Brunner in *Die Mysterien* ... 75.)

stormy future inevitably results in the victory of the future. Sonnenfels continued to promote his economic ideas for the most part unmolested, and as to judicial questions he launched a fresh attack immediately after the promulgation of the Constitutio Criminalis on December 31, 1768. For a time he could be sure of the direct support of Kaunitz and an at least tacit protection by the supreme chancellor Count Blümegen and the co-regent, Emperor Joseph himself. Yet once again his opponents were successful. In August, 1772, the empress directed him in an official missive to refrain from further discussion of the question of torture and capital punishment.[74]

This action was due only in part to clerical pressure. In most of his writings Sonnenfels had promoted theories and had assailed principles. In the penal-reform question he had challenged the wisdom of specific statutes—statutes moreover that had been issued after long deliberations only a few years before. This meant in effect almost a frontal attack on conservative absolutism—in a field, what is more, that was to become a focal center of public interest.

Sonnenfels immediately responded with a countermove that at this critical juncture, as Arneth puts it, "will always greatly honor him, whatever one may otherwise here and there and perhaps not entirely without justification hold against him."[75] Even if Sonnenfels had at that time desisted from pursuing his aims further, it is unlikely that the abolition of torture could have been delayed for long. Public faith in the wisdom of the institution had been too much shaken already. Yet it is certain that the man who at that point resolved to continue his struggle risked, if not his personal freedom, certainly his career, and perhaps also his livelihood in Austria.

Sonnenfels' second presentation of the issue was again based chiefly on rational arguments, but it concluded with a passionate appeal to the kind, charitable, and humane feelings of the empress. These feelings had not as yet fully prevailed. Blümegen, asked by the empress for his advice in the matter, expressed the opinion that the authority of the law made a revision of the new code after so short a time inadvisable; that while Sonnenfels' arguments were unquestionably sound, the order not to pursue the matter further should remain in force, but that no *sacrificium intellectus*, not even the suppression of his previous writings in the matter, should be demanded of Sonnenfels.[76]

Maria Theresa heeded this advice. Thus again a compromise was reached and again it portended victory for reform. As early as 1773 the government reopened official deliberations on the question. The majority of the provincial administrations and of the state council supported abolition at least with qualifications. Once again Sonnenfels aroused imperial displeasure because his official report, a government document, was published without imperial authorization in Leipzig in 1775. This is, in substance, the famous treatise *Über die Abschaffung der Folter*. Though Sonnenfels in a rather lukewarm way denied that he had arranged publication of the treatise himself, he was officially reprimanded for indiscretion. While technically the government had a good case, it is obvious that publication pressed the matter further.

The empress resolved now to turn the matter over to Joseph, a decision that is the most humane of her actions in the whole affair. "I ask the emperor, who has studied law and, what is more, whose sense of justice, reason, and love of humanity I trust, to decide this matter without my advice. I do not understand it at all and could act only by majority decision. . . ."[77] One cannot help but find here and elsewhere that Maria Theresa's modesty, the frank recognition of her intellectual limitations, is certainly among her most attractive features.

After further careful consultations, the emperor and Blümegen recommended abolition of torture, and with the decree of January 2, 1776, Maria Theresa ordered its elimination, except in the lands of the Hungarian crown. Joseph's further recommendations to restrict capital punishment but to increase the hardship of imprisonment by frequent public whippings, chaining, and hard labor were put into force only after the empress's death.

Sonnenfels had little share in the last stage of the reform. Here as elsewhere his role was that of promoting ideas the acceptance of which still hung in the balance, rather than that of putting into effect principles that eventually met with little opposition. Though it can be assumed that the abolition of torture would have come about in any event without Sonnenfels' efforts, it probably would have come about several years later, certainly not before the death of the empress in 1780. These five years, however, must not be measured in terms of time but of human misery. This is the yardstick according to which Sonnenfels' achievements in this field should be evaluated.

A Study in Austrian Intellectual History

i. Sonnenfels and Education

It is logical to round out a survey of the views of a reformer of the body politic with a discussion of his ideas on the education of the future generation that was supposed to put these reforms into practice. The chief problem that interested Sonnenfels in this field is the issue of public versus private education. His views are not what might be anticipated from many of his other writings. Education, which to him meant compulsory education, is and should obviously be a matter of intense public interest and concern. He perceived various methods of rearing good citizens. There is first the method of public education, according to Rousseau the surest means to establish brotherly love as the foundation of society. According to Sonnenfels, Rousseau wrote as a mere theorist; the state schooling of youth had not been put into practice in his Geneva but in the Sparta of Lycurgus. Sonnenfels was quite impressed by Sparta's achievements, but he pointed out that the requirements of the small warrior and slave state with its emphasis on military discipline were not the same as those of the large, highly stratified state organization of his own time. Sparta, apart from the helots, the state serfs who did not enjoy the right of citizenship, was a one-class state with one type of education. The modern state is based on the diversity of classes. The same type of education does not fit the noble, the cleric, the professional man and the artisan, the peasant and the worker, of his day. The Spartan type of education thus would reduce society to the Spartan structure. "As long as the diversity of Estates and property lasts, it will be impossible to have public education."[78] Since we need this diversity, the lower classes must not be spoiled by a type of training suitable only for the upper classes, whose standings and ambitions at the same time must not be infringed upon. Equality of thought, furthered by this type of education, is dangerous to our society. "It is not to be expected that the children of common people can ever think like princes; one may fear that princes will be taught to think like the crowd!"[79]

According to Sonnenfels, public education therefore would not necessarily have to be equal education. Yet, he asks, are there not advantages in the fact that training in public boarding schools makes for greater discipline, diminution if not eradication of prejudice, moderation for privileged ones, greater poise for the poorer student? Cannot a simple, sober, industrious way of living best be taught in such schools? Sonnenfels answered the question in the affirmative, but he felt that disadvantages would still outweigh advantages. Public education makes for uniformity; it is anti-individualistic; it destroys the possibility of developing individual abilities and increases the danger of spreading the faults of one student to the whole body. It promotes mechanical, blind obedience on the basis of "theirs not to reason why," since the level of instruction must be that of the lowest common intellectual and moral denominator of the whole student body. It promotes routine rather than ingenuity. It has its place only where the opportunity for sound family education does not exist. In short, the orphan asylum is the only institution where the boarding school is fully justified.[80]

Home education should proceed according to elaborate principles. Parents should consider it as their own high responsibility and must not leave it to unqualified servants. The choice of special training and ultimately of vocations should be influenced not by their own predilections and ambitions but by the children's abilities and the requirements of the state. As a member of the court commission on higher studies, Sonnenfels also demanded that corporal punishment, equally humiliating to the one who administers it and to the recipient, should be banned, at least from higher education.[81]

Sonnenfels is critical not only of the arbitrary way in which parents decide on the future vocations of their children. Even more dangerous may be their power to select their future mates, particularly in the case of girls who have gone through the unrealistic "ivory tower" education of the convents. He outlines the institution of a board of wise elders from all walks of life before which adolescents of both sexes would appear and which should guide them in the selection of their future consorts.[82]

More than a century after Sonnenfels published the last part of his *Mann ohne Vorurteil* another Austrian writer, Anzengruber, came out with the drama *The Fourth Commandment,* considered sensational in his time.[83] Here a young murderer, the son of depraved parents, says to the priest who visits him before the execution: "If you teach the children in school to 'honor thy father and mother,' tell the parents from the pulpit also that they should act accordingly." These sentences, the core of the play, were cut out by the censor as being revolutionary in character. Yet in 1767 Sonnenfels developed exactly the same noble thought at very great length[84]—alas, at too great length.

Sonnenfels' dialectics, with their constant allusions to ancient mythology and alleged ethnology, are tedious. His finest thoughts are often buried beneath a landslide of hollow phrases. A good deal of the effect of his writings is spoiled simply as a result of the unfortunate loquaciousness typical not only of him personally but of much of the enlightened literature in general. Still, many of his thoughts are fine.

Appointment to public office even of the lowest rank should be made only on a competitive basis.[85] He demands that the education of women should be equal to that of men, and his reasons for this follow a line very reminiscent of that of Ibsen's *A Doll's House*.[86] In a way he went even farther than Ibsen did a century after him, since he was concerned not only with the treatment of married women as "living dolls"—he actually uses those words[87]—but of unmarried girls as well. Yet again, though Sonnenfels anticipated Ibsen's thought as he did Anzengruber's, he was not their equal in literary ability; indeed, so antidiluvian is the form in which he couched his thoughts that even his most refreshing ideas can scarcely be saved from oblivion.

j. Noble Youth and Public Service

As indicated by his concern with the problems of the "misunderstood woman" and those of the *jeunesse d'orée*, the young men of noble birth, he was primarily interested in higher education. Naturally, as a supporter of the Maria Theresan school reform of elementary public education,[88] Sonnenfels followed a course determined by his membership on the Commission of Higher Studies and by his position as professor of political science, which entrusted him with the training of prospective government officials. That his general social philosophy called for reform only within the narrowly circumscribed conditions of the Habsburg empire is obvious from the foregoing.

Here he was particularly concerned with the rise of a generation of pseudo-intellectual snobs, who though only partially educated were thoroughly arrogant. He demanded higher standards of learning in universities, and suggested that these institutions should be moved to small places far removed from the hustle and bustle of the big city.[89]

The most important aim of university reform, in his opinion, was to provide for the proper training of young aristocrats as future bureaucratic leaders of the state. It should be remembered again that Sonnenfels was acting here strictly under orders. It was not for him to determine whether this class was best-fitted to run the state. Since it was chosen for leadership by higher authorities, his function was merely to see to it that these young men were adequately prepared for their future task of achieving the end for which he labored with frankness and courage. Thus in his introductory lecture at the Savoyan Academy in 1768 he states that "the dark times have passed in which the fame of ancestors and their privileges were defended only by birthright, by deep-seated ignorance and a brave fist . . . on the contrary, one demands from the scion of noble descent that culture and learning distinguish him from the people." And after a severe castigation of the arrogance, prejudice, and ignorance of very many of the highborn, he continues: "I don't hesitate to state that it would be better for bourgeois society to leave aristocracy entirely to its ignorance rather than to lead it to learning at the expense of general concord."[90]

Sonnenfels goes in fact one important step further:

Family pride may have presented it to you gentlemen differently. But the kind of burgher whom you call the common man is no less a member of the state because chance has denied him wealth, which is the opportunity for unlimited extravagances, because fortune has denied him a family tree, which very frequently is the invention of an avaricious genealogist. The qualities of the burgher give him an undeniable claim to every kind of equality. This applies to people who live under the same social order, who hold the same rights and share the same obligations and burdens. Not without aversion can the burgher see the rule of an inequality, which may perhaps be necessary because of the disparity in property . . . activities, emoluments, and . . . advantages but which is displeasing to him. However, since the burgher by his education and through all his life . . . is used [to this] he will in view of the unchangeable nature of conditions . . . modestly take the place assigned to him. . . . Yet if the class so much favored by inequality of fortune and social advantages shows its contempt openly, then this inequality of fortune, opportunities, and the social differences in society will hurt and the heart of the burgher will be filled with bitterness. Then he will perceive his barely sufficient livelihood as distress, his obedience as suppression. He will not perceive society as a bond the separate links of which are held together by common welfare, but as oppressive, insupportable shackles which chain him like the condemned galley slave eternally to the state.[91]

These passages more clearly than most of Sonnenfels' other writings show the intrinsic weakness of his position. The conditions laid down here mean something more than *noblesse oblige.* Amazingly frank in his criticism of the abuse of aristocratic privileges, he has actually nothing to say in defense of birthright except that society must put up with these established though unjust privileges, provided they are exercised with restraint. The logical conclusion of Sonnenfels' reflections, if carried only one small though decisive step further, would lead to the proclamation of the rights of man, of the true equality of all citizens. The limitations of his time and, even more, those of his milieu did not permit him to take this step. He went far enough to displease the authorities, but not far enough to offer a solution acceptable to the non-privileged majority of society. With the best of intentions he tried to assuage dissatisfaction, but he did not quite dare to think, let alone to act, in line with the exigencies of a future that was already on the threshold. Thus when some twenty years later, in 1789, European society received a decisive jolt, history bestowed its credit on those who took the final step. The men who had merely prepared the ground for the new institutions were conveniently but quite naturally forgotten.

k. *The Man of Letters: A General Estimate*

Sonnenfels the political-scientist–reformer, except for his role in the torture campaign, is an almost forgotten man. As controversial as the over-all picture of the man and his work appears to posterity, his specific proposals are either no longer contested or no longer associated with him. His ideas were either accepted in a form very different from that submitted by their author or were discarded altogether. It is different with his activities in the field of letters. Secondary in importance to his contribution to political science, they have remained associated with his name far longer. Posterity on the whole has either revised them or, more often, rejected them outright.

In a way this is natural. Sonnenfels' political ideas, though in several respects highly controversial in his time, belong on the whole to a cultural inheritance that has not been expressly accepted by later generations but has been incorporated into their cultural evolution. The political philosophy of Sonnenfels and his confreres was in line with the trend of the period. Sonnenfels' literary endeavors, on the other hand, represented the philosophy of a particular time and place: they were the literary views of the Austrian Enlightenment. They had little in common with the ideas of rising German Classicism. They ran counter to the Romantic views of the coming generation and the political literature of the era of 1848. They had no connection with the poetic realism of the third quarter of the nineteenth century. They were ridiculed if not ignored with the advent of Naturalism.

If one takes a short-range view, however, the situation appears somewhat different. Then it should become clear that Sonnenfels' work gave a mighty impetus to a change long overdue: the change from the outgoing Baroque period to the preclassical Enlightenment. From this angle the chief criticism directed at Sonnenfels in this sphere actually boils down to one point: he believed to be worthless and dead what was only outdated in the setting of his time. He believed further that the literary ideals that he promoted were of lasting validity, but they expressed only the demands of a specific period. Yet this misconception not only is typical of reformism in general; it is also the result of a subjectivism that is in fact a basic premise of reform. Reform is based on the conviction that it eliminates something definitely wrong and replaces it with something else definitely good. Without this strong inner conviction reform would accomplish little indeed. It is up to the more detached judgment of later generations to correct and modify the conclusions of reformist zeal. Yet for an innovator, relativistic considerations of the future are no substitute for a burning energy.

After all this has been said in defense of Sonnenfels, it should be added, in order to put the following analysis in the right perspective, that such a defense would be far less necessary if he had been a different man. His views, as judged by adherents and opponents of his literary concepts and taste, might still be controversial, but he would be more respected and would appear more attractive in this field if he had been a man of greater artistic talents and had possessed a better sense of literary originality. While he was a critic of no mean ability, perspicacity, and erudition, he was merely a critic, not an artist. And the authority of the self-appointed literary critic without creative literary credentials always has been and always will be challenged—a fact that on the whole may be all to the good.

l. *The Journalist*

A further difference between Sonnenfels the political scientist and Sonnenfels the man of letters lies in the fact that in the first capacity he acted chiefly as servant of the state, whether as academic teacher or in various bureaucratic functions. The literary man, again within the limitations of his Austrian setting, was chiefly a free-lance writer. Chiefly, but not entirely.

As member of various government commissions, particularly those on higher studies and censorship, as professor of political science, Sonnenfels had many opportunities to express himself in an official capacity on literary matters. These functions, however, except in the question of censorship of the court theater in 1770 (to be discussed below), carried with them scarcely any executive power.

As to censorship, there is no doubt that Sonnenfels accepted this institution clearly and unequivocally. In his *Grundsätze der Polizeiwissenschaft* he stated "in regard to the mores as well as the religion and the political opinions of the citizen, nothing is more apt to check vice than the curtailment of the freedom to write and to read writings of a kind that run counter to religion, state, mores, and righteous ways of thinking. It is the function of censorship to prevent the spread of erroneous, obnoxious, and dangerous opinions."[92]

These are harsh words and opinions. True, the censorship entrusted to Sonnenfels in practice was confined strictly to literary matters, and its specific objective was a controversial "purification" of public taste rather than political control. And yet it may appear startling to many that the same man who had felt the oppressive power of that institution in his fight for judicial reforms and populationist theories should voluntarily have made himself a tool of the very force that threatened to paralyze his life work. This conduct seems surprising, however, only if it is judged according to present-day standards, not if it is viewed within the context of "enlightened absolutism."

To reiterate at this point: It would be erroneous to regard this enlightened absolutism as a pre-liberal movement because many of its final objectives as to judicial reforms, public education, and Church-State relations were to be taken up by the Liberalism of the future. The great dividing lines in the political philosophies of Western civilization are not these ultimate objectives. It would be easy to comprehend most of them under the broad general principle of the greatest good for the greatest number. To distinguish properly, it is necessary to shift the emphasis to the method employed and promoted by a system. And by that very token the pre-revolutionary Enlightenment represents an integral, because increasingly efficient, type of absolutism entirely alien to the spirit of Liberalism. Possibly the revolutionary break at the end of the eighteenth century in Western Europe may have been due almost as much to opposition to the traditional methods of an absolutism that had already changed in its content as to demands for specific social reforms.

This is not to disparage reform itself, or the highly creditable efforts of its promoters. They were not only consciously champions of new objectives but unconsciously heralds of new political methods as well. Yet within the political structure of the pre-revolutionary Enlightenment, its standard-bearers were acting in accordance with the spirit of the age when they used the oppressive methods of the system to gain their objectives instead of fighting these methods and thereby risking failure. Sonnenfels the advocate of censorship is not an anachronistic figure but the typical product of an age of conflicting ideological means and ends.

Sonnenfels' activities in matters of literary censorship pertained primarily to those connected with the stage. He himself was, of course, subject to censorship in his double capacity of government official and man of letters—to a far lesser degree, however, in the second function than in the first. As a journalist concerned either with general ideas or with causeries in the field of belles-lettres, he felt relatively little of its impact.

As free-lance journalist of this kind he was considered one of the foremost Austrian writers of his time. *Der Mann ohne*

Vorurteil, published as a weekly from 1765 on, was the only Austrian journal that managed to remain in circulation for several years.[93] Sonnenfels' energy and initiative in starting this literary project is all the more impressive because a previous attempt with another journal, *Der Vertraute,* had to be abandoned after the publication of only seven issues. Also a journal (one might be tempted to call it a magazine) *Theresie und Eleonore,* written and edited by him primarily for ladies of intellectual and artistic interests, had not survived its first year of circulation.[94] Neither did other journals, such as *Welt und Patriot* (composed after the pattern of Addison's *Spectator*), to which Sonnenfels occasionally contributed,[95] meet with any more success. Their failure was not primarily due to any political difficulties with the authorities. The plain fact was that the number of people interested in an Austrian literary journal was far too small to support it. To be sure, if these journals had been less sophisticated, if they had catered to the taste of a larger public, their fate might have been different. But then they could not have promoted the specific spirit of the rising Austrian Enlightenment. They would merely have been mouthpieces of the popular burlesque form of the waning Baroque spirit. Whether this would have been for the better or the worse from the standpoint of literary value is a moot question. Since Sonnenfels and his literary friends were firmly opposed to that kind of ideology, they could not possibly make a concession diametrically opposed to all they stood for. They could not escape the vicious circle of public taste and wider circulation in which they were caught.

For an appraisal of Sonnenfels' journalistic merits, one can refer here to the opinion of one of his most learned and most severe critics, the well-known literary historian Erich Schmidt. He calls the *Mann ohne Vorurteil* ("the man without prejudice" —a pseudonym of Sonnenfels himself) "a skillful and courageous journalist who appealed to the ambition of the Viennese, asked them to compare themselves to other people, and dared to criticize aristocracy and clergy."[96] This is indeed true. Many of Sonnenfels' ideas were discussed in one form or the other not only in learned or semi-learned treatises and official reports but in his weekly literary articles as well. Much of the new Western thought, though often diluted, was transmitted thereby to the Austrian public, and thus the ground for subsequent reforms was laid. Literary criticism and interpretation, new standards of taste, were put before the reader. Sonnenfels, except in strictly political matters, certainly fulfilled one of the foremost requirements for a journalist—that he be a transmitter and a stimulator of new ideas—for he acted as a connecting link between the West and the later phase of the Austrian Enlightenment.

This task, though important enough, was not one-sided. As a result of his initiative and energy Sonnenfels not only brought the West closer to Austria; he attracted the respectful attention of at least the German North to the new Austrian activities. No less a witness than Lessing refers to this in connection with Sonnenfels' journalistic work in a letter to Friedrich Nicolai of Hamburg, August, 1769: "Let it be attempted once to write as freely in Berlin . . . as Sonnenfels has done in Vienna. Let it be attempted there to tell the truth to the noble court rabble as he has done [in Vienna]. Let somebody in Berlin stand up who will raise his voice for the rights of the subjects against exploitation and despotism, and you will learn soon enough which country up to this day is the most slavish in Europe."[97] Surely this letter is chiefly meant to compare Austrian conditions favorably with those in Prussia, but by implication it is also no mean compliment to Sonnenfels' journalistic daring and achievements.

Was he a great journalist then? In a technical sense this question cannot be answered, since in his Austria no journalism existed of a type that would enable the reviewer of the day to set up definite standards of comparison. From a long-range point of view, the scope and objective of Sonnenfels' journalistic work, which covered a wide sector of reform activities, was of a high quality and, within the limitations of the given historical situation, very successful as well. It may be added further that in this sphere Sonnenfels did much to raise the standards of German literary prose.

And yet the reverse side of the medal must not be overlooked. Sonnenfels did not have the ability to be brief and succinct if he could manage to be long-winded and verbose. His style does not lack clarity, but it certainly lacks simplicity. Attempting to be dignified, he managed only to be pompous. Unable to resist any opportunity to show his learning, his tirades are apt to bore the reader whose interest might have been aroused by the incisiveness of a Lessing. Irony certainly was not a weapon in Sonnenfels' intellectual armory, though this may appear stranger to the reader of today than to Sonnenfels' contemporaries, since this characteristic feature of Austrian journalism is a somewhat controversial product of its maturity rather than of its beginnings. There is also a personal question involved. Irony is closely connected with a certain kind of humor, and of a sense of humor Sonnenfels was utterly devoid. He took himself extremely seriously and he was serious in the treatment of matters of even the slightest significance.

How much more effective, how much more human, he would have been in his literary feuds without this glaring deficiency will become apparent in the following discussion of literary, particularly theatrical, matters. There the deadly seriousness of his ire against the charming superficialities of popular vogue and tradition frequently borders on the obnoxious, and his manner of writing in this field has frequently been described as such. Yet it would be unjust to connect this manner primarily with Sonnenfels' vanity and his undoubtedly inflated ego. He was serious mainly because he took seriously the issues he stood for as well as those he fought. And he did so largely as a protest against the easygoing light-mindedness that he regarded as frivolity and that appeared to him a chief stumbling block in the way of progress. He did not approach things with the serene detachment of a future student of mores, but with the zeal of a fighter—though unfortunately he claimed the authority of an incontrovertible judge for his most controversial views.

No doubt, had he been a man of different temper, a man of less obvious frustrations and aggressions and of even greater abilities, he would have spoken and written differently. He would have had to be a much better-balanced personality in order to be a greater writer and journalist. In short, in his time he would have had to have been a Lessing. Yet as Muncker rightly points out—and this is indeed part of Sonnenfels' tragedy —this man, torn between the imperfect understanding of the new literary style and the oversaturated sterility of the old one, was bound to combine the roles of a Lessing and a Gottsched.[98]

m. The Cycle of the Spirit

The Gottsched-Lessing antithesis from the modern standpoint

is not so much a matter of controversy as an index of attitudes. The superiority of the *tragédie classique* to Shakespeare—or, vice versa, the preservation of the Aristotelian unities of time, place, and person—and the cultivation of the high dramatic style as against the use of local tradition and folklore are no longer burning questions today. The formal Aristotelian French tradition of Gottsched* is not as universally condemned as it was by that era of genius from Lessing to Goethe, which revolted against Gottsched, the literary pope at Leipzig. In fact, it has become increasingly obvious today that the literary feuds of the enlightened century in Germany represent in a way cyclical patterns of thought that appear again and again in intellectual history. Literary historians all too often commit the error of confounding issues and men. Late Enlightenment and Classicism in German literature were represented by far greater men than were Baroque, Rococo, and early Enlightenment. Yet this does not necessarily settle the question of the validity of the ideas of either era. Thus the basic issues that divided a decaying Baroque tradition from what turned out to be the dawn of a glorious age actually remain in essence controversial.[99]

They remain controversial, however, only to a limited degree. The literary issues of the nineteenth and twentieth centuries were largely by-products of political and social tensions and conflict. The great literary feuds of the Enlightenment, on the other hand, were far more directly the outgrowth of an intellectual revolution. From this it follows that they loomed as much weightier and more fundamental problems in the minds of the educated men of that era than did similar questions at a later time. To those men shut off from political activities literature was as serious a business as are politics to men of a later age. It touched the very core of their being. This factor is important in evaluating the significance of the literary battles of Sonnenfels and his contemporaries.

There is another point to be considered. The dice in this contest were loaded. If one accepts the cyclical premise in many ideological conflicts, then it becomes clear that at times certain trends are in eclipse which, a generation later, may be in the ascendant again. The question why a trend at a given time is on the decline rather than in the ascendant, or vice versa, can

---

*Johann Christoph Gottsched (1700-1766), extremely doctrinaire critic and playwright of great literary influence in the mid-eighteenth century.

of course be explained only as part of a comprehensive analysis of synthetic history as undertaken in a limited sense, for instance, in Toynbee's concept of "withdrawal and return." Yet this much is certain: a cyclic change could never take place if at the time the outgoing era had not become more or less sterile in its accomplishments, if the new one did not show the seeds of original thought. This does not mean that the spirit of the declining era is dead; it is merely forced to leave the stage for a time, to have another day in the future. Thus in accepting here the cyclical terminology of Heinrich Wölfflin, which conceives not of the Gothic, the Renaissance, the Baroque, but of the recurring phenomenon of a Gothic, a Renaissance, a Baroque period, it is clear that the Baroque spirit, challenged by the Enlightenment, was not dead but that a temporary incarnation of that spirit had merely been arrested in its further development.

And here we come to the core of the Gottsched-Lessing antithesis—to the Lessinguian as well as Gottschedian soul of Sonnenfels. A Gottsched, a Nicolai, and it must be added a Sonnenfels were incapable of feeling, let alone of accepting, this cyclical approach to intellectual history. In the case of Sonnenfels, this does not mean that he was unable to see that there are two sides to every issue. Yet as soon as he had decided upon one on the basis of rational deliberation, the other was dead for him. He and those like him acted as judges, not as attorneys for a cause. After weighing the arguments of both sides they decided in favor of one, and the case was then settled for them for good. All future endeavors were focused entirely upon the task of embodying their findings in rules of law, of codifying their views, and of forcing their acceptance upon others. This is the reason for the dreary and pedantic attempt to impose on literature a rigid set of rules.

The spirit of Lessing is different, but different in its approach rather than its results. As to results, Lessing's views also were generally perceived as aesthetic laws; yet unlike those of Sonnenfels, they were regarded as such to a far greater extent by others than by Lessing himself. He pleaded where Sonnenfels judged. Lessing, with his incisive reasoning and passionate argument, weighed his ideas on the merits of each specific case. He did not claim to be the mouthpiece of eternal truth. As he put it himself, he considered the fight for truth as he saw it more important than the truth or, rather, infallibility that others claimed for their views.

Gerhard van Swieten

Wenzel Anton, Prince Kaunitz-Rietberg

Joseph von Sonnenfels

The famous sentence of Lessing, "If God were to hold in His right hand all the truth and in His left the ceaseless desire for truth, though with the qualification to err continuously, if He were to say to me then: Choose!—with humility I would take His left and say: Give, Father! Pure truth is for Thee alone," even in a less clear-cut form could never have been written by Sonnenfels. Not primarily because Lessing was a greater writer, but because, though often harsh and sometimes unjust, he was the true herald of a democratic age of discussion of ideas, the true Liberal who knew how to combine the enlightened objective with a corresponding liberal method. Sonnenfels, his zeal, courage, and intelligence notwithstanding, is the perennial bureaucrat, the typical product of enlightened absolutism, with its heteronomy—a man with a humanitarian goal and an autocratic method.

Why should it be right to attribute to Sonnenfels not merely the doctrinaire mind of a Gottsched but to some extent at least the spirit of a Lessing? For one thing, there is a similarity, though by no means an identity, in their ideological objectives. True, Sonnenfels was a tool of enlightened absolutism. He was not an obedient tool, however. In his zeal for reform he showed in fact much of the spirit of a dissenter. The notion of imposing the conclusions derived from this dissent on his contemporaries links him to enlightened absolutism; the belief that they could be embodied in law in the field of literature just as much as in politics links him with Gottsched, the outstanding transition figure between German Baroque and Enlightenment.[100] Yet the inner urge that aroused the dissent itself and made Sonnenfels stand and fight for it is the inseparable bond between him and that early pioneer of German Liberalism, Lessing.

n. Sonnenfels' Literary Standards

In order to comprehend Sonnenfels' position in the passionate literary feuds of the 1760's and '70's it is necessary first to form an estimate of his literary taste and critical competence. Undoubtedly he had an early and genuine interest in literary questions. His resolve to become a writer, with the purpose of raising Austrian literary standards to the level of those of the German North, can be traced back to the time of his military service and the subsequent period of his academic studies and his service as accountant of the imperial guards. As early as 1761 he was elected chairman of the German Literary Society in Vienna. In the following year he tried without success to obtain the chair of German language and literature at the University of Vienna. His appointment as professor of political science in 1763 thus represented a second choice. Yet this was by no means the end of his interest in literary matters. Indeed, his academic as well as his bureaucratic activities bordered and quite frequently encroached upon the literary field. It is a moot question whether Sonnenfels' life work centering on a professorship of German literature might have led to entirely different results, whether in that capacity he might have achieved more or less. On the whole it seems likely that his broad ambitions and interests would not have kept him away from the social sciences. Thus the difference, had he been able to choose a different career, might not have been a basic one. It might merely have meant a shift in emphasis in his life work. In any event, he would have preferred another main field for his activities, since his literary interests were genuine and strong.[101]

These interests were manifested throughout his journalistic career in his writings on the formative arts, on music, on education, and even in the slight causeries for what might be called today "the woman's page." Belles-lettres, however, hold a first place in his interest, and within them above all the dramatic arts and consequently the theater.

This is hardly surprising in view of the influence exercised by English and French drama upon German writing at that time, the English being represented by Shakespeare, the French by Racine and Corneille. There is also the influence of Gottsched and of Lessing's and Nicolai's earlier endeavors. There is the belief that the stage could be converted into a "moral" or, rather, "morally uplifting" institution of the greatest potential educational value.[102] There is further the incontestable fact that prior to the existence of various modern recreational facilities, the theater played a much larger role in social life than it does today. Last, the psychological ethnic factor must not be overlooked, for nowhere in German-speaking lands to this very day is interest in the theater greater than in Austria, a phenomenon reflected in the whole Baroque tradition, be it the Jesuit court drama, the Italian opera in Austrian style, or the popular Baroque comedy.

The majority of Sonnenfels' studies on literature, and particularly dramatic literature, are contained in the third part of

Joseph von Sonnenfels

Der Mann ohne Vorurteil of 1767 and his extensive *Briefe über die wienerische Schaubühne* between 1767 and 1769.[103] This means that they were written almost simultaneously with Lessing's famous *Hamburgische Dramaturgie*. Almost, but not quite. Certain references in *Der Man ohne Vorurteil* indicate that the general plan of Lessing's work as well as the early part of it were known to Sonnenfels when he started his undertaking. This means only that the Austrian borrowed from Lessing the form of his writing, a running commentary on the theatrical production of the day.[104] Even this form was not entirely new. Certainly in content the two works differ very much.

One characteristic feature of these letters on the Viennese stage is revealed at the outset on the title page. The author signs himself "A Frenchman." This pseudonym, one of many used in the literature of the German Enlightenment, deceived nobody. Sonnenfels indeed did not want to conceal his identity. He intended rather to protest against the still-prevalent scorn of domestic accomplishments and respect for foreign patterns and criticism, particularly French criticism. In view of the standard of German literary development in the first half of the eighteenth century, as compared with that of the French and English, this attitude was by no means as unreasonable as it appeared in the light of the accomplishments of the following generation. Thus Sonnenfels writes, "The author of these letters about the Viennese stage was handed over to the clowns at their pleasure when he discussed this subject with his countrymen in his own name. . . . As a Frenchman, as long as he was believed to be one, he was forgiven for what was called charming archness, but which amounted almost to insolence. To be read, to be celebrated in society, one has to be a foreigner."[105] In these reflections he anticipates and endeavors to promote a development, which, outstanding exceptions notwithstanding, could hardly have been generally recognized at the time. Here again like Gottsched rather than Lessing, Sonnenfels severely criticized the preponderance of French taste, though actually he himself was still very much under its influence, and just at the point where it was least warranted.

In his "lady's journal," *Theresie und Eleonore*, Sonnenfels had already criticized the overemphasis on French language and customs in higher education. In contrast to the taste of one of his chief protectors, Prince Kaunitz, he attacked the excessive French influence on the German play of higher style. This does not mean that, like Lessing, he called for a reversion to Shakespeare's pattern. Neither did he renounce the outmoded triad of time, place, and character. He merely revised it, and here indeed he is, if not at his worst, certainly at his most tedious. He does, it is true, admit that entertainment is a legitimate function of the theater. Yet this entertainment must never question the legitimacy of existing institutions, must never show virtue in a disadvantageous position. In short, controversial issues must be banned from the stage. Thus, as Schiller put it later in a witty criticism of the prolific playwright Kotzebue:

> *Wenn sich das Laster erbricht,*
> *Setzt sich die Tugend zu Tisch.**

In setting forth these noble principles, Sonnenfels of course acted fully in accord with the enlightened spirit of an absolutism that wanted to prove continuously that its appeal to reason would produce an even stricter moral climate than had the waning era of submission to feudal-ecclesiastical standards. This applied in particular to the fight against the obscene, the ribald jest on the stage. Here Sonnenfels was on solid ground indeed.[106] In fact, the obscenities of the popular Baroque comedy illustrated a phenomenon observable in other periods as well: the cultivation of the sexy, sometimes in its lewdest form, as an outlet for inhibitions created by curbs on freedom of expression. Such ideas were of course quite foreign to Sonnenfels. He did not want to combat lasciviousness with greater freedom but with greater austerity of thought, which resulted inevitably in dullness of topic, plot, and dialogue. A "cleaning-up" of the stage would have been fully justified if he had understood the genuine psychological necessity for true and decent entertainment, the need to improve moral standards by arousing the interest of the audience. Instead, he ignored these legitimate interests and tried to impose a straight jacket of literary rules.

Only a few of these rules can be touched upon here by way of illustration. The Aristotelian dramaturgy for all its limitations was entirely consistent. It was moreover based on the social and ideological conditions of its age. If one did not recommend the obvious—that this dramaturgy be abandoned altogether as anachronistic, as in fact had already been done in the English Elizabethan age—it had to be recognized as the absolute standard.

*After Vice has collapsed, Virtue sits at the table.

That had been the logical position of the scholastic era. But what could be said in defense of the hollow revisionism of a Sonnenfels, who for example, recommended the following change of the strict rule of unity of place? "The poet may lead the spectator from one room of the house into another, from one square of the town into another. Yet these changes must take place only in the intermissions between the acts. The changes of place must be changes of vista rather than of setting."[107]

As to the strict and, from the point of immanent criticism, not illogical unity of time (day and night, twenty-four hours) Sonnenfels generously proposes an extension to thirty-six hours to give both logic and imagination their fair share.[108] "If our poets follow these 'and similar' observations they will travel the middle road between French *politesse* and English *ruggedness*; their plans won't be as adventurous as those of Shakespeare, who throws me like a ball from one corner into the other. Now he makes me the witness of military preparations in France and in another moment the witness of the countermeasures at the British coast. Now in the palace of Theseus he makes me the confidant of the discussions between the king and his bride, and a moment later he forces me to watch Peter Quince's rehearsal behind a fence." Yet the playwright need not be as artificially correct as Corneille either, who for the sake of unity of place has Cinna and his fellow conspirators deliberate in the anteroom of Augustus.[109] Hence Sonnenfels proposes a limited revision of the Aristotelian rule as to the unity of place.

Though pedantic to the point of being ridiculous, Sonnenfels is by no means stupid. His reflections abound in sometimes sound and usually at least well-reasoned observations and proposals as to how stage management could be improved, how a genuine ensemble theater without stars could be created, how the actor should make himself clearly understood without endangering the naturalness of his performance. But all these and many similar reflections are marred by the insistence of the Enlightenment upon imposing rules on everything and allowing little leeway for common sense.

Yet if one makes allowance for the vogue of his time and some grave errors of judgment on his part, it should be granted that Sonnenfels had decidedly better than average literary taste. But while rightly critical of the stilted hollowness of Gottsched's prolific dramatic production, he blindly rejected the charming

Italian *commedia dell' arte*. It seemed to him dangerously similar to the Viennese burlesque that he fought so bitterly. On the other hand he fully appreciated the genius of Molière. At a time when such praise was by no means common, he rated Lessing's *Minna von Barnhelm* and *Emilia Galotti* highly, some well-reasoned criticism of detail notwithstanding. His inordinate respect for the plays of the mediocre Austrian playwright Ayrenhoff was certainly due in part to patriotic pride. In any event, his misjudgment in regard to one of them, *Der Postzug*, was shared by no less a man than Frederick II of Prussia.

That Sonnenfels could not fully comprehend the unique phenomenon of a Shakespeare is less surprising than the fact that he had some perception of his greatness. Sharply critical of what appeared to him the undue liberties that Shakespeare took with all dramatic rules, he still admitted, for instance, that Macbeth "had many of the daring and beautiful features so characteristic of this poet."[110] It is notable too that Sonnenfels was not oblivious of the significance of the fool in Shakespeare's tragedies and of the sudden change in dramatic style that takes place whenever he is on stage. As he puts it in this context, "Shakespeare's plays are always monsters when the hero, a moment before clad in gold and purple, is suddenly heading for the inn, discoursing in vulgar language, when mores and decency are trodden upon against all probability. Shakespeare's plays, in spite of all the fire of the tragic genius, should be admired rather than copied."[111] If one reads these and many other controversial but not trite observations, one cannot help thinking that Sonnenfels was at heart a pedant who at certain points sacrificed common sense, warmth of feeling, and individualism to an artificially created, ossified monster of reason.

o. Drama and the "Hanswurst" Fight

From what sometimes appears to be a welter of confusing tirades, two factors emerge clearly in Sonnenfels' writing: He never took a pragmatic approach to any social problem. He always endeavored to be systematic, though sometimes with indifferent success and by resorting to ridiculous means. Even in regard to what appear comparatively trifling issues, he never deviated from a peculiar utilitarian ideology measured by absolute standards. The idea of research for its own sake, the notion of the pursuit of truth irrespective of its immediate application in the service of reform, was entirely alien to him. Tedious, sterile, and controversial as this approach of enlightened absolutism can be at times, its consistency is impressive. The *Hanswurst*, or harlequin, controversy concerning the legitimacy of the harlequinade on the Austrian stage, wherein he fought with the most passionate stubbornness for the most controversial objective, is a good illustration of this.[112]

Without going into the broad literary ramifications of the issue, the history and meaning of this conflict, insofar as it reflects Sonnenfels' position, is the following. The first German theater of a more permanent nature in Vienna was built in 1708 under Joseph I, who like his father Leopold I and his brother Charles VI, but very much unlike his niece Maria Theresa, had a considerable interest in the dramatic arts. This, however, did not include German drama. Leopold, the most musically gifted among the Habsburg rulers, was almost exclusively concerned with the Italian opera, the attention of Joseph and, after Joseph's untimely death, that of Charles VI were focused on the Italian *commedia dell' arte*. Essentially the new theater, or rather the *stagiones* that were allowed to perform in Vienna, employed the style of the Italian comedy in a German Baroque setting. Italian texts were not translated, however, since the plays given by such troops of author-actors and actors generally did not follow any written text. The Italian *commedia dell' arte*, and to a much greater extent its German replica, were based on improvisation. The manager of the group would outline a scenario. He had at his disposal a number of standard characters, Pantalon, the buffoon, Colombina, and Harlequin—i.e., the highly controversial Hanswurst. This type of comedy—in spirit very much like a Punch and Judy show, acted, however, by people, not puppets—offered the actor an unparalleled opportunity to display his charm and wit. The temptation to poke fun at odd customs and characters in the public limelight, though frequently at the risk of short-term jail sentences, was almost irresistible. Advantage was also taken of the opportunity to earn applause by ribald jests and sometimes by even outright obscenities. Obviously here too sanctions on the part of the authorities were threatened. This threat was not very serious, however, since the institution itself was not taken very seriously by the government. The improvised comedy was too flimsy, its social criticism too superficial, the display of talent too charming, to arouse grave governmental concern. At least subconsciously, it was perhaps felt that this innocent pleasure provided a good outlet for popular dissatisfaction on more weighty matters.

In any case, all these factors tended to further this kind of entertainment, which for half a century flourished unmolested under the symbol of the "green hat" and wooden sword of the harlequin. A change in that perhaps not entirely happy but quiet state of affairs was presaged by the fact that in 1741 Maria Theresa assigned a small building connected with the Hofburg, the imperial palace, to theatrical entertainment. It could hardly be foreseen at that time that out of this would grow Joseph II's National Theater of 1776, the famous Burgtheater, for well over a century and perhaps to this very day the leading German theater in the field of dramatic arts. Maria Theresa, who took a dim view of literature in general and of the theater in particular, consented to setting up the new institution chiefly because etiquette and representative duties required the existence of a court theater. Within its bounds the Italian decorative opera and the French classical drama, then favored by court and aristocracy, played a far more important part than the popular German comedy.

However, things did not work out quite that way. The new theater was far too small to provide a satisfactory setting for the lavish opera performances, which soon were transferred to a new and larger house. French drama, alien to Viennese taste and already in a period of decline at that time, had little drawing power. The German comedy conducted by such brilliant actors and witty extemporizers as Stranitzky, Weiskern, Prehauser, and Kurz (Bernardon), favorites of the Viennese people, tipped the scale in public interest and drawing power.[113] Naturally it now received much greater and, from the point of view of actors and public, rather undesirable governmental attention. Its association with the court demanded greater dignity and respectability. In 1751 theatrical censorship was imposed, and since its enforcement in regard to improvised texts was obviously technically difficult, extemporizing was severely restricted, though not entirely forbidden.[114]

It is this understandable concern of an absolutist government and court, not literary considerations, that form the background of the *Hanswurst* conflict. However, literary considerations developed by enlightened taste and thought became manifest at about the same time. The interplay of both despotic absolutism of the old school and enlightened absolutism of the new resulted in a struggle of unexpected consequences. In the 1750's the literary Germany of the old Gottsched and young Wieland had already condemned the "green hat" and looked contemptuously on its chief domicile, Habsburg Vienna.

The first literary attack against poor Harlequin's Viennese reign from the enlightened quarter was made in a truly Gottschedian, supremely doctrinaire fashion in 1760 by Heyden and Engelschall. At a time when the literary rule of the bombastic Saxon Gottsched was already shaky, this criticism could not prove successful. A year later a more subtle attack was launched by Klemm in the first Austrian literary weekly, *Welt*, closely associated with the new Deutsche Gesellschaft. It was directed not so much against the *Hanswurst* himself as against the obscene aberrations forced upon him by crude popular taste.

In *Welt* Sonnenfels took up the question in 1762, and immediately his doctrinaire and arrogant approach to the problem lost him much sympathy for his cause. Yet he injected a notable new social thought into what to that time had been treated chiefly as the issue of refined literary taste versus a vulgar popular one. Sonnenfels in his first writings on the issue actually defended the actor or actor-creator. (In view of the character of these plays one can scarcely speak of an author.) It is the low level of public taste that determines the slapstick, immoral, and obscene character of the popular comedy, as he saw it. Reform must begin with the education of the public to higher standards, not by taking the easy way of putting the blame on the comedian. As to the comedian himself, he points out that, in accordance with the rise of general standards of taste, a better theater would have to give him his due in the form of higher pay and above all an increase in social prestige.[115]

When Sonnenfels took this line and consistently upheld it, he did not espouse a cause pleasing to the supreme authority. Maria Theresa, in answer to a report of Sonnenfels, wrote: "The comedians are rabble; Mr. von Sonnenfels could do something better than to write reviews."[116] Yet in spite of the creditable independence of Sonnenfels' position in this argument, his record in the later stages is marred by chicanery and worse. As soon as he started to engage in the controversy in his own journals, first

A Study in Austrian Intellectual History

Der Vertraute, later *Der Mann ohne Vorurteil*, he began to display his peculiar gift for making enemies. This is so disturbing that all too frequently one forgets how interesting, though by no means necessarily correct, many of his ideas on the subject are. To begin with the worst aspects of his doctrine. Seen from an artistic standpoint, Sonnenfels' greatest weakness is his lack of imagination. He simply cannot understand that something that does not conform to strict principles can have any positive value. The idea that the artist is in some ways subject to a different set of laws from that which pertains in other honorable professions is alien to him. A particularly striking result of this lack of insight is that in his aesthetic rules he does not make any allowance for the specific character of a literary work, its author, or the actor whose function is to interpret it. The actor must always act the same character in all his roles. Once a hero always a hero, once a villain, noble, father or mother of the hero, sweetheart, confidant, the dramatic artist must stick forever to his "specialty." There should be only one main line of action. The attention of the public must not be diverted by any side issue, however fascinating, or by any minor character, however colorful. Critical as Sonnenfels is in some respects of the formalism of the French *tragédie classique*, it obviously measured up more nearly to his requirements than either the English Shakespearean theater or burlesque comedy.[117]

While Sonnenfels and his enlightened friends were firmly convinced that they were right in these matters, the public unfortunately was not. When the (according to Sonnenfels) most irreproachable plays were given, like the dull tragedies of Ayrenhoff, the theater—alas—was empty. The audience just did not understand what was good for it and its taste must therefore be educated. One means of doing this was to acquaint the public beforehand in literary journals with plot, qualities, and objectives of a play.[118]

One of Sonnenfels' main points, which he consistently attempted to drive home, is that high purpose and noble style are entirely compatible with a legitimate desire for entertainment on the part of the audience. Here he is as often right in principle as he is wrong in practice. As to the noble purpose, virtue must always triumph; vice must be defeated and punished. This, of course, is hardly news in the history of the theater. Yet Sonnenfels goes further.

Joseph von Sonnenfels

The opposing moral forces must never be juxtaposed in such a way that the issues they stand for are not perfectly clear-cut; neither side can be partly right or partly wrong. In short, the very core of the dramatic, the conflict of controversial issues, is taboo. Nobody could assert, of course, that the popular comedy throve on the analysis of highbrow conflicts between love and power, ambition and obedience, contradicting loyalties, etc. It had an insidious way of poking fun at the priggish. In a rather subtle and yet undoubtedly superficial way it ridiculed the sublime, though it did so through form rather than through content. This comedy snatched the cothurnus from the hero; it showed the king in his dressing gown—in other words, it seemed to undermine the existing order. These, presumably, are the real grounds for the war on the harlequin. His undeniable obscenities and vulgarities simply provided a convenient and obvious target for attack and were not the main issue. For Sonnenfels the theater had a mission to defend the good, to fight evil, to uphold authority, to obviate subversion, however well camouflaged under the false naïveté of slapstick comedy.

But where does entertainment come in? To Sonnenfels the deplorable lack of popular appeal of high tragedy was due largely to the fact that it was so full of unpleasant characters. A Titus, as Sonnenfels saw him, rather than a Nero or a Don Giovanni should be the hero of the tragedy. The pleasant, or, rather, avoidance of the unpleasant, is thus identified with the interesting or the stimulating, a notion actually much more commonly held than one might suppose from this naïve example.[119]

Sonnenfels did not expound these and similar odd theses in a straight axiomatic way. He first presents both sides of an argument in a quite fair and lucid manner. Yet frequently the doctrinaire, outmoded view predominates over the voice of individualism, and little understanding is shown of the freedom of the artist and of the organic growth of the artist's work in its traditional setting. Frequently (by no means always) Sonnenfels quite sensibly took up the cause of a restrained and modified naturalism that must be freed from the strait jacket of the French-Gottschedian aesthetic code. He severely criticized the artificiality of the role of the confidant in the *tragédie classique*, whose uninspiring lot it is to listen passively to the narration of past events. He was insistent in his demand that the happenings in a dream must be acted, not simply related, that the characters should thus be portrayed in action, not by description. He rejected the long-drawn-out formal dialogue as unnatural and felt that the monologue, if justified at all, should be a means of revealing emotions rather than of presenting intellectual reflections and facts.

In this he went not only beyond Greek and French tragedy but to a certain extent beyond Lessing and Schiller. He did so in another respect as well. Not before Hebbel and Ibsen was it clearly recognized in dramatic literature that what is really unexpected will fall flat in its effect because it will always appear psychologically false and implausible. The audience, according to Sonnenfels, has to be prepared for a sudden turn of events, though of course it must not be expressly told of it in advance.

In line with this reasoning, Sonnenfels also rejected the artificiality of the preposterous *deus ex machina* solution. On the other hand, he is again at his most tedious when he lays down certain rules of dramatic structure, as for example that in the three-act play the plot must be complicated in the first two acts and unraveled in the third, whereas in the five-act play the complication and unraveling ought to take place in the first three and the last two acts, respectively.[120]

Sonnenfels also overshot his mark in his scathing criticism of the Italian opera, the artificial character of *bel canto*, the bad acting of the singers, all of which he compared unfavorably with the composition and performance of the operas of Gluck. He did not realize at all that the character and needs of the opera should be judged by entirely different standards, of which he as a critic of indifferent musical knowledge and ability knew but little. Yet it is likely that his rejection of the great Italian opera was influenced by his far more violent distaste for the comic *opera buffa* and the *commedia dell' arte,* including Goldoni's charming plays. No wonder he traced the rise of the *Hanswurst* burlesque historically to this Italian influence.[121]

He bitterly denounced the coarseness of these plays, particularly their crude and repellant naturalism. Yet he did not reject naturalism without qualifications. In the dramaturgy of Sonnenfels and of most of his contemporaries, the common man plays at best an insignificant part on the stage. When he does appear, usually as a peasant or a servant, he must not be represented in his natural vulgarity, but decently—that is, by means of a purified and streamlined naturalism that elevates him but still sets him clearly off from the exalted dignity of the noble hero.[122]

Joseph von Sonnenfels

While Sonnenfels intended to accomplish his reform partly
by raising the status of the actor, he did so not only to promote
better taste but also because he fully realized that the protagonists of the burlesque in Austria were extremely gifted in their
vocation and thus worthy subjects of reform. He went even
farther and admitted that Stranitzky, Prehauser, and particularly
Kurz (Bernardon) were comedy writers of considerable talent as
well.[123]

This point must be stressed in order to make it clear that,
contrary to various assertions, personal animosity played no part
in Sonnenfels' literary crusade. When he later became the butt
of comedians' ridicule, which quite naturally did not please him,
his position was already unmistakably clear. *Hanswurst* had to
go because, though the actors might raise their standards, the
improvised burlesque farce was beyond remedy, as he saw it. The
great National Schaubühne, the national theater of Joseph II
which he had zealously promoted and which he lived to see in
its first glory, could not be realized so long as extemporizing was
the vogue of the day.[124]

Sonnenfels' standpoint in this respect is indeed fully comprehensible, as far as the question of the cultivation of higher
literary taste was concerned. Yet he weakened his case considerably by linking the issue of extemporizing with that of censorship. According to him, the extemporaneous play is and must be
crude, vulgar, and obscene not only because of the literary taste
of the audience but also because technically it cannot be subject
to advance censorship. The enlightened writer, the academic
teacher in his precomposed lecture texts, the literary playwright,
had to submit to censorship, yet the improvising actor and playwright for obvious technical reasons could not be subjected to
the same rules. Should he therefore be free from the fetters of
censorship, and should the improvement of literary standards be
left exclusively to the long-drawn-out process of education? By
no means. To kill the rat, Sonnenfels was quite ready to burn
the barn by means of rigid censorship.

What is right for the one is right for the other, and censorship, the pillar of the authoritarian absolute state, is always right.
To refute this is of course easy enough, but in so doing one must
not forget that to abolish censorship would have been to strike
at the very core of the governmental machinery. Who could in
all fairness expect the faithful servant of an authoritarian system

to oppose its most basic principles? One should not forget further that in upholding, indeed in insisting on, censorship of the theater[125] Sonnenfels defended an institution from which he had to suffer as much as any contemporary Austrian writer. He was simply a man of his time who could not jump over his own shadow.

In the same context belongs another important factor, on which however it is more difficult to condone Sonnenfels' intention—the issue of standards of literary taste. He was rightly and seriously concerned with its cultivation. He fully realized that reform must be focused first of all on this broadest aspect of the problem. But how does this frequently expressed view of his tie in with the following statements?

> Displeasure on the part of the great and the noble would be sufficient to drive the shameless monsters from the stage, just as perhaps—in confidence—their pleasure has been sufficient to keep them there.
>
> An expedient has to be used to raise national poets. This benefit again must be received from the hands of the nobility. Don't ask for purses filled with gold and diamond rings as reward for your national poets. That always has been the remuneration for those who have no merits. There are rewards which have not thus been deflated in their value by self-interest; there are rewards which are more pleasant and more creditable to the genius. [And now he proceeds thus:] A single word in praise of the poet by a [Prince] Kaunitz, a smile of a benevolent [Prince] Liechtenstein must be considered as more of an incentive, more of a reward, than all the gold of the world. . . . The honor is preserved to nobility . . . to free us in regard to products of intellect and wit from the hitherto-existing slavery.[126]

Can it be said in defense of these extraordinary observations that Sonnenfels really believed in a superior discriminating ability on the part of the nobles? Hardly! As noted frequently before, he was highly critical of the lack of true literary interests on the part of the great.[127] How then are these views to be interpreted? Hermann Hettner, one of the most distinguished German literary historians dealing with the eighteenth century, makes some interesting observations on this point. In an otherwise rather favorable evaluation of Sonnenfels he states: "Sonnenfels is free, daringly progressive, often even challenging in the fight against encroachment of the clergy, against the Junker greed of the nobility, whose hereditary character appears to him rather as injustice against the contemporaries than as justice against the ancestors. . . . If one looks closer, however, it shows how right Nicolai was when he answered that letter of Lessing praising Austrian freedom of the press with the ironical observation that if Sonnenfels tells the lower nobility a few true things, he bows all the more deeply before the higher nobility and the empress."[128] And with a subtle sense of irony Nicolai remarked in the letter referred to: "To write in general terms against despotism and for the freedom of the people is gladly permitted here. . . ." The application to specific Austrian conditions is, however, quite a different matter.[129]

The true meaning of these remarks requires an explanation. Sonnenfels made the distinction between high and low nobility, that is, between the aristocracy and that of the nobility of letters to which he himself belonged. Whenever he refers in the quoted statement to "true nobility," to the benevolence of the Princes Kaunitz and Liechtenstein, he actually means "aristocracy." These great aristocrats, in particular those at court who rallied around the sovereign and performed noble service in the army, in administration, and in diplomacy, were in his eyes the genuine leaders of the state. According to Sonnenfels, aristocracy should set a shining example in the arts as well. Yet as Hettner rightly points out, Sonnenfels was at the same time fully aware of the shortcomings of this narrow class.

Is it justifiable to conclude that he is a mere opportunistic hypocrite? This question is not as easy to answer as it seems. For one thing, the facts as Sonnenfels presents them are largely correct. The Austria of Maria Theresa, and only to a lesser extent that of Joseph II, Leopold II, and Francis I, was ruled by the aristocracy under the directives of the sovereign. Bartenstein, Van Swieten, Gebler, Sonnenfels, Felbinger, and later Gentz and Adam Müller,* and others were important public servants in administration and in council. They were even more important as ideological pioneers of reform, but they did not actually govern the

---

*Johann Christoph von Bartenstein, vice-chancellor of the Bohemian court chancellery; Friedrich von Gentz and Adam Müller, aides of Metternich and distinguished writers, respectively, under Francis I (II).

state. The chief executives, though strongly influenced by such men, were still members of the aristocracy. This applies on the whole to cultural activities hardly less than to high politics. The supreme administrators, though of course not the actual managers of the imperial theaters, art galleries, and palaces in the Habsburg empire, were and remained the great nobles long after Maria Theresa's reign. Sonnenfels could not change this and indeed did not attempt to do so. But as in his academic teaching, he wanted those who were candidates for leadership by reason of birthright to secure office on the basis of earned qualifications of merit. To look for the approval of that class was not simply an expression of Byzantinism. It represented rather the contradictory compromise between the demands of an enlightened philosopher and reformer and the intangible premises of the authoritarian absolute state.

This should help to explain Sonnenfels' strategic position in the *Hanswurst* conflict. The empress, as noted before, showed no particular interest in the matter and rather frowned upon Sonnenfels' interference in a controversy that at its outset was obviously not within the scope of his official duties. Joseph II shared her opinion on this point, but it was his general agreement with Sonnenfels' basic ideas that finally saw the reform through. Kaunitz and some of the great nobles resented Sonnenfels' criticism of French and Italian plays and his only thinly camouflaged slurs on their own taste. They could not, however, interfere openly with a movement the aim of which was to improve the standards of the court theater. Thus Sonnenfels did not have to worry about any counteraction on the part of the authorities.

He had, of course, to face the opposition of the comedians and the antagonism of an audience that did not want to be deprived of its traditional pleasures. In the end, also, he had to bear the more or less subtly expressed resentment of his fellow writers, who were greatly displeased by what they considered his inordinate zeal or, in more vulgar language, pushiness. None of these factors was strong enough to cause Sonnenfels, as the representative of the authoritarian state, to deviate from a once-adopted course, but all these combined forces sufficed to put him in a somewhat precarious and—considering the subject—ridiculous position.

In February, 1767, the so-called German comedians (as distinguished from the French and Italian actors) performed a play *Der auf den Parnass erhobene grüne Hut,* "The Green Hat Elevated to Parnassus." Unlike the usual pieces in which Harlequin performed, this play, though still partly extemporized on the stage, was completely written out and was printed shortly afterwards. What is more, it was written by Klemm, Sonnenfels' former companion in the fight against *Hanswurst,* who had now turned traitor to the cause. In this *Green Hat,* a comedy not without charm and wit, Sonnenfels, impersonated by the brilliant Prehauser, appears on the stage as an intolerable pedant and busybody and delivers himself of such statements as the following: "I tell the author without hesitation that he is a bad writer because he did not take my advice." Being asked, "And what if he seeks your advice?" Sonnenfels counters, "Then I criticize it [his play] so much that he will have no use for it any more." Being asked, "What is good taste?" he answers, "What I declare it to be."[130] The play ends with a glorification of Hanswurst, who is admitted to Parnassus as the tenth muse. It is obvious from the foregoing that Sonnenfels had no sense of humor, least of all when he was at the receiving end of the wit of others. He immediately turned for assistance to the police and requested that further performances of the embarrassing play should be suppressed. Not only did the authorities ignore this demand, but his own highly exaggerated criticism of the comedy, printed as a separate leaflet and later included in *Der Mann ohne Vorurteil,* was actually censored.[131]

Doubtless the fact that here Sonnenfels was attacking censorship for its failure to prohibit the play, the general tendency of which was known beforehand, gave the authorities a proper excuse for their inactivity. The underlying reason was most likely that they were at least secretly pleased to see the busy reformer, whose inordinate zeal carried him into so many fields, taken down a peg.

This was Harlequin's last triumph. The attacks on the stage were finally stopped. In the end authoritarian government could not permit a man of Sonnenfels' official position and prestige to become the butt of general ridicule. There was no need any longer to worry about too much popular opposition against prohibitive measures. Contrary to expectations, the success of the *Grüne Hut* play was transitory and meager. The popularity of the burlesque comedy had after all passed its peak. The fame of the rising great German literature had begun to spread to broader strata. The outstanding interpreters of Harlequin, Weiskern and Prehauser, died in 1768 and 1769. There was, at the time when the literary repertoire theater was growing in popularity, nobody either able or, as a matter of fact, willing to replace them. The actors themselves for obvious reasons of social prestige refused now to heed the call of Harlequin as long as others with increasing success were able to work in a theater of better repute.

Thus Sonnenfels saw his chance and seized it. In a passionate appeal for a German national literary theater, which should free itself just as clearly from the farcical influence of the burlesque as from the antiquated pattern of the French court theater, Sonnenfels, supported by State Councilor von Gebler, turned once more in 1770 to Joseph II. His request was granted. Improvised comedy was banned from the court stage, which was soon to become a true national theater. Foreign *stagiones*, whether French or Italian, were likewise to terminate their activities, very much against the wishes of the high nobility.

This last ordinance in particular was of course highly controversial. Yet from a long-range point of view it can be argued that this action, under then existing conditions, helped to raise the German literary theater from its inferior status. Thus it became possible to raise dramatic standards and at the same time to attract the interest of the burgher. The course could be steered from the burlesque show and the aristocratic court theater to the genuine national stage. Its doors were for the best part of its proud history open to the best of the Western world's dramatic production. The well-founded charge that this wholesome change was brought about not merely by education and persuasion but partly by compulsory action as well can hardly be laid specifically at Sonnenfels' door. This method, for better or for worse, is after all an intrinsic feature of enlightened absolutism and accounts for both its failure and its success. Sonnenfels played an important part on the morrow of the victory of his cause. He practically, though not technically, became for a short time the chief executive of the imperial city's theatrical production. In terms of his time, place, and philosophy, he obtained the task and title of dramatic censor.

Neither his office nor his character endeared him to the authorities in this new function. After only a few months' tenure he was replaced, probably largely because of the influence of Kaunitz, who resented his campaign against the French theater.[132] This, however, proved to be a victory in form rather than in substance. Sonnenfels' dismissal may have been a cause for personal satisfaction among his opponents, but Harlequin was already gone, and the French *stagione* followed him two years later. Sonnenfels' decisive influence on the German and Austrian stage and its further development was an accomplished fact at the time he was called to office in 1770. His discharge did not alter the course of a development that by that time had become inevitable.

The theater thus created became known officially within a few years as the German National Theater—today the Burgtheater. Like any other theater it could not of course live on the gems of the new great literature alone. Nevertheless, apart from the performance of a number of mediocre comedies and routine conversation plays, it shortly became the home of the drama of Lessing, Goethe, and Schiller. It acquainted the Viennese public with Shakespeare, Calderón, and Lope de Vega. The literary standards of this theater almost immediately caught up with the developments of the stage abroad. In quality of acting, it soon surpassed any other German theater.

What was Sonnenfels' share in this development? Undoubtedly in spite of all his hit-and-miss techniques, his zealous activities merely accelerated an evolution long overdue, an evolution that probably would have come about sooner or later without his interference. The same can be said, of course, of others of Sonnenfels' activities, yet with some difference. His action in the torture question likewise only accelerated the development of what appeared to be inevitable, yet this prompting which pushed the calendar of reform ahead meant a great deal in terms of fighting and overcoming human sufferings for a number of years. The same certainly cannot be said of the outcome of the *Hanswurst* feud. No great harm would have been done if Harlequin's precarious reign had been protracted by a few years. Was Sonnenfels' action then worth the trouble it created? Would it not have been better to wait for an organic change in public taste rather than to impose new literary standards by decree from above? One is tempted to answer this question in the affirmative; yet to do so would mean the adoption of a fatalistic interpretation of history. To scan the horizon, to read the signs of historical change, and to act accordingly is to trust in the spirit of evolutionary progress. To wait and see, even with the benefit of a better understanding of tradition, means stagnation and decay, with the possible final consequence of an unexpected and unpredictable revolution. Even the most likely development is not a certain development. Furthermore, the conclusion that something would have happened anyway is drawn after the event. It is merely a tentative explanation of why something happened, not a mathematical prediction that it will happen. The inevitability of the change of literary taste by organic growth at that time and place appears clear to us, but it could not have been known to Sonnenfels. Who can blame him, then, for acting in accordance with his principles rather than with the predictions of others?

One might go farther. Sonnenfels and his fellow reformers did better than just foretell a new development and propose adjustment to impending change. By their activities they actually helped to shape the new forms, the new taste. They were not merely heralds; they were architects of change as well. This, in spite of their glaring deficiencies, is the final vindication and justification of their work.

As in the case of his activities in many other fields, such considerations have been frequently and greatly misunderstood. Older critics have usually (with some exceptions of undisguised political bias) given full credit to Sonnenfels' merits in his fight for the new stage. Hettner praises him highly. So do the standard Austrian biographers, Franz Gräffer and Konstantin von Wurzbach. While the first, in a hyphenated clause, still regrets the demise of Hanswurst, the second calls his defeat somewhat comically the deed of a "spiritual Hercules." Yet both agree that Sonnenfels accomplished for Austria what Lessing did for Germany.[133]

This comparison between the work of an intellectual genius like Lessing and that of a man who as a literary writer was nothing more than at best a sound and constructive critic does little service to Sonnenfels' reputation. The ironic feature here is the fact that Lessing, the adamant and incisive judge of literary merits, actually liked Harlequin and considered him an innocent, humorous, and charming adornment of German literature. He asks, "Why should we be more critical, why should we be more choosy in our pleasures and more conforming to cold reason, than—I won't say the French and the Italians—but even the Romans and the Greeks were? Was their parasite anything but Harlequin? Didn't he too have his own peculiar costume, in which he appeared in many a play? Did not the Greeks have a drama in which satyrs were interwoven, whether they fitted into the plot or not? A few years ago Harlequin defended this case before the court of true criticism with just as much humor as thoroughness."[134]

Lessing's observation, true as it is, actually proves little against Sonnenfels. For one thing it would hardly be fair to measure Sonnenfels' literary efforts by the standards of one of the unchallenged master critics of world literature. Second, when Lessing wrote these lines in Hamburg in 1767, Harlequin's German reign had already come to an end. He could afford to be more generous toward a waning institution than Sonnenfels toward one which in Austria not only was very much alive but still exercised an influence that, even in its heyday, it had hardly enjoyed in northern Germany.

Modern criticism, however, has rather indiscriminately taken up Lessing's line. The late nineteenth century rediscovered the charm, the humor, the colorfulness of popular Baroque literature. Quite naturally it went as far in its post-mortem defense as the preceding age had gone in its rejection. Thus Erich Schmidt in his monumental Lessing biography, after heaping much abuse on Sonnenfels' character, declares flatly: "One may say whatever one wants about the bottomless decay of the popular stage, its roughness, obscenity, lack of culture and form—but Hanswurst was basically the most gifted, the only full-blooded character of Austrian eighteenth-century literature. The Viennese popular poetry was a wonderful treasure, which demanded refining care and not pedantic extinction." And the German-Austrian literary history of Nagl and Zeidler states, "The expulsion of the Viennese *Hanswurst* was basically a real anachronism at the very moment when it seemingly succeeded."[135] There is a mixture of truth and error in these reflections. That the *Hanswurst* comedy had its strong points, which Sonnenfels did not fully realize (or entirely deny either), is correct. It is correct also that higher dramatic literature in Austria had very little to offer at that time, certainly less than Sonnenfels assumed. Yet he did not drive Hanswurst from the stage merely to replace him with mediocre dramatic production. He did it to open the gates to Lessing and Shakespeare and indirectly to Goethe, Schiller, Kleist, and Grillparzer. He did it primarily not for the sake of the Austrian literature of his time but in the expectation that reform would open the way for a greater Austrian literature of the future. His expectation proved to be right. He lived to see the first drama of Grillparzer performed on a Viennese stage. His fight against the burlesque did not hamper the rise of the great and truly popular Austrian play of Raimund and Nestroy, which likewise came out in his lifetime. He fought against the rather vulgar spirit expressed in the words of a widely known writer of the day, Mozart's librettist Schikaneder, who observed that he would not trade Lessing's collected works for the first act of the slapstick comedy *Tirolerwastl*.[136] With all his honest tries and manifest errors, Sonnenfels here too should be judged not merely from the comfortable vantage of hindsight but as the agent of an historical evolution.

p. The Formative Arts

In 1811 Sonnenfels was appointed vice-president and curator of the Academy of Formative Arts, a position that carried little practical authority, though of course a certain prestige. The only fairly well-known fact about the tenure of this, his last office, the honorable sidetrack on which his colorful career ended, is the already mentioned incident of 1814, when he canceled a speech at the academy rather than submit it to preventive censorship.[137] It is not known whether this refusal should be considered entirely as a protest against inhibition of thought or whether it was at least partly a mere act of wounded vanity that can easily be explained on the grounds of his known conceit and the stubbornness of old age. In view of his general attitude toward the institution of censorship, the second interpretation indeed seems more likely. But while one could expect little initiative from a man of eighty—his age when he obtained this last position—the appointment itself was not an arbitrary one. Sonnenfels in the prime of his life had given a great deal of attention and thought to the formative arts, particularly etching, engraving, and above all painting. His activities in this respect were far less polemic in character, far less controversial in his time, than his literary campaigns. Yet they too shed additional light on the character of the man and his time.[138] It is most impressive that at a time when

Joseph von Sonnenfels

Sonnenfels carried a heavy load as academic teacher and text-book writer, when he was engaged in the torture campaign and the *Hanswurst* polemic, he still managed to draw up three lectures on the subject of formative arts. He was as seriously concerned with the social prestige of the formative artist as with that of the actor. From its rise he expected greater achievements. He strongly rejected a mere *l'art pour l'art* attitude on the part of the engraver and the painter while he stressed the point that the artist, as in Greece, must appeal to the higher levels of taste of the general public.[139] This, however, would be difficult. "One cannot impress upon the common man, upon a certain class of burghers, the refined perception necessary for the evaluation of works of art. Education which lays the foundation for this perception, some instruction in the arts themselves, guidance through a continuous experience of seeing the beautiful, of becoming so well acquainted with beauty that the ability is developed to perceive it at first glance, not to miss the smallest deviations from it, these are the enviable prerogatives of nobility. . . . If one speaks of promotion or decay of the arts, praise and blame will chiefly fall on the nobility. In works of taste it represents the nation."[140] The student of Sonnenfels' literary criticism will readily recognize that here again while referring to nobility Sonnenfels actually means aristocracy. Indeed, even more important than aristocracy is to him the benevolent promotion of arts by exalted sovereigns like Charles V, Francis I of France, and of course Maria Theresa. What has been said previously in explanation of Sonnenfels' evaluation of aristocracy as the guardian of literary taste is in a way pertinent to an analysis of the view given above. In regard to formative arts however, Sonnenfels is on more solid ground. Literary taste after the Renaissance was associated largely with the aristocracy because they were the holders or representatives of power in public life. As to the formative arts—particularly architecture, sculpture, and only to a somewhat lesser extent painting—aristocrats were indeed among their undisputed patrons. With the transition from the German Renaissance to Baroque and into the later Maria Theresan Rococo period the mainstream of formative arts was fed by two principal sources, the Church, particularly the great non-urban monasteries, and secular princes and aristocrats. This applies to the great works of Fischer von Erlach, Hildebrandt, Carlone, Prandauer, Martinelli, in architecture, to only a somewhat lesser extent to those of Raphael

Donner and Mattielli in sculpture, and to Rottmayr, Gran, Altomonte, Troger, and Maulpertsch in painting.

In the history of art there is scarcely any style that lends itself
as fully as does the Baroque to the grand, the spectacular, the
luxurious—its deeper spiritual meaning notwithstanding. To a
point this is true even for the Rococo. In any case, only "the
Great" and great temporal and ecclesiastic institutions of the
realm could afford to support these particular features of art. This
certainly holds true of the whole period from the early seventeenth
century to the beginning of the second half of the eighteenth. It
is hardly necessary to add that Baroque also created fine works of
bourgeois culture in architecture, sculpture, interior decoration,
and painting. Yet these works are perhaps only fully appreciated
today, since they lacked the ostentatiousness associated with the
Baroque period at its height.

Sonnenfels with some vision might have foreseen the social
changes that would come about in this respect in the Empire-
Biedermeier style, the simple and noble art of the Josephine and
Franciscan era. Yet for a long time he was on solid ground when
he maintained that there was an integral connection between the
formative arts and aristocracy.

Unfortunately his other perceptions in regard to contemporary arts were not very meaningful. What he chiefly condemned is a kind of beautified semi-naturalism, of which the
work of the German court portraitist Balthasar Denner (1689-
1749) rightly appeared to him as an outstanding example. This
artist was in favor of a return to the grand spirit of Rubens, as
exemplified in Rubens' Decius Mus series. But Sonnenfels had
little understanding of the daring composition, verve, and virile
strength of the great Fleming. He admired him as the successful
artist who, like Titian before him, had become the friend of a
great sovereign, and this not merely in an ordinary materialistic
sense. Rubens, Titian, and in a way also Leonardo, Michelangelo,
Raphael, Correggio, Van Dyck, and even Rembrandt—a strange
"assortment" indeed—represented to him the ideal of the cultured,
historically minded, and aesthetic painters who were well acquainted with the allegoric meaning of their subject and, it may
be added, with the institutions and leading actors of the world
stage as well. "Invention, wealth of thought, composition where
fire and poetic spirit rules, judgment in the arrangement of the
subject, nobility of figures, expression that reveals their passion

and psychological situation and forces me to feel with it, the costume, as the Italian calls it, that is the closely observed pattern in dress, way of life, mores, buildings, tools, even in animals, nature, state of the country, of time and conditions where the action of the painting takes place—in all these the greatness of the artist manifests itself...."[141] Indeed a tall order! The lack of discrimination that Sonnenfels exhibits in his praise of the greatest artists of late Renaissance and early Baroque is certainly anything but impressive. Yet there is a kind of leitmotiv in this paean, which includes both a Phidias and an Apelles. One may truly say that if Faust sees Helena in every woman, Sonnenfels sees every genius as an academician, rhetorical references to soul and passion notwithstanding.

This becomes even clearer in his lecture on the merits of the portraitist. There, with reference to illustrious examples, he fights the prejudice of his time that the portraitist is not the equal of the painter of great allegorical and historical compositions or, to inject a disrespectful German term, big *Schwarten*. Actually a real connoisseur of art, even in the late Baroque period, would have immediately recognized that Sonnenfels' defense was so much waste motion. His line of argument is noteworthy; his thesis is not. According to Sonnenfels, the portraitist is considered inferior by many because he is usually interested only in producing a mere, so to speak, "photographic" likeness of his model. Does this mean that the critic Sonnenfels was a forerunner of expressionist tendencies? By no means! The failure of the portraitist is not due to lack of understanding of the feelings, emotions, psychological state, and actions of his subject. Sonnenfels pays little attention to all this. The artist's ignorance of composition, his scant regard for the aesthetically pleasing, for the decorativeness of the subject, are to blame. Anticipating the vogue of a not distant future, he recommends that the model be clad in Greek garments with pleasing contours. Truth and beauty should go hand in hand, "since body and figure represent truth ... the soft contours express beauty perfectly."[142] And somewhat comically, with reference to the classicist doctrine as exemplified by Winckelmann's theory of "noble simplicity and quiet greatness" and Raphael Mengs' practice, he advised the artist as follows: "The general proportion of the parts to the whole is the only thing he has to observe. Furthermore, he may flatter his beauties [i. e., his beautiful models] by way of a reference to the heaving bosom of Venus and the lovely rejuvenated fingers of dawn [Eos]. Art entitles him to do so; honor demands it of him."[143] "Let us follow the Greeks," he exclaims, "who by portraying their models as more beautiful [than they actually were] gave them at the same time likeness, by implication even greater likeness."[144] Indeed, to praise the great does not necessarily mean to understand them! Yet even here it is easier to poke fun at Sonnenfels than to do him justice. He is dreary and doctrinaire; he was in command of a fairly comprehensive though hodgepodge collection of facts concerning the history of arts; but he obviously lacked the key to its true appreciation. And yet even here, where he is almost at his worst, he is no fool.

First, in his frequent exhortations to the aristocracy to further the arts and the artist, he followed the precedent of the Renaissance and the Baroque, where in painting, sculpture, and architecture the very greatest achievements were inseparably linked with patronage. Since in the highly visual Baroque period respect for the formative arts on the part of the mighty was much greater than their regard for literature (the promotion of which was less easily demonstrable and possibly politically and socially controversial), such sponsorship demanded little change in their attitude. Maria Theresa would never have referred to the formative artists as "rabble," as she did to actors. Not even the Italian singers and the performers of the French comedy, let alone Harlequin, Bernardon, and Colombina, had anything like the social prestige of the great builders, painters, and sculptors of the Baroque and the Rococo.

Sonnenfels somehow realized that the age of spectacular patronage of the formative arts was on its way out. The heir Joseph II and his contemporaries looked for economy and reform rather than magnificence and opulence. His lesser successors wanted comfort and modest dignity rather than impressiveness and brilliance. They were hardly aware that with these changing preferences they opened artistic opportunities for the burgher as builder and customer rather than as patron and sponsor.

From a social standpoint Sonnenfels foresaw the change in taste and artistic climate. Even his bizarre defense of the modest portraitist as compared to the ambitious fresco-painter is an example of the new austerity. He could not imagine, however, that the more prosaic character of future art would be based on a social tradition different from the one in which he had been reared. Again he was the almost accidental pilot of a changed future; again he was also fettered by the tradition of the past.

q. Sonnenfels and His Contemporaries

Sonnenfels the eloquent speaker and prolific writer is on the whole commendably reticent concerning domestic relations. Thus a direct testimony of his wife as to his character, biased as it may be, has at least the value of rarity. Actually there is far more to it.

In a letter of January 21, 1769, from Sonnenfels to Christian Adolf Klotz, professor of archaeology at the University of Halle, his friend by correspondence and more widely known as the unequal opponent of Lessing,[145] there are two strange passages. To give Klotz a true picture of Mrs. von Sonnenfels, he sketches her character in very flattering terms and invites her in turn to describe his own character. This is what she has to say: "He [Sonnenfels] must have made his career by pertinacity, since the nobles have no worse enemy than he, who tells them straight out and repeatedly in a clear and unvarnished way that their parchment titles mean nothing. Nobility and others too have been allied against him for a long time. Many say, beware, that fellow is a freethinker. I don't know whether he is one, but he is a good head of family. . . ."[146] The whole idea of reciprocal character sketches on the part of the Sonnenfels couple is in rather poor taste. It is easily understandable in view of the reformer's notorious vanity. The validity of Mrs. von Sonnenfels' alleged portrait of her husband is quite a different matter. In fact, it is quite likely that these lines were not written by the modest, unassuming housewife who is rarely mentioned in the reformer's correspondence. Sonnenfels may well have drafted them himself; and even if he did not, it can be taken as fairly certain that his wife would never have written this passage without his approval. This means that it reflects the picture that Sonnenfels wanted a supposedly impartial witness to give of him. As such, this brief sketch is of considerable interest. We know from Nicolai's shrewd observations that Sonnenfels' criticism of the nobility— meaning again aristocracy—must be taken *cum grano salis*.[147] We know further that in his correspondence with Klotz, the then famous "enlightened" scholar of the Protestant North, he wanted to be considered as an arch foe of feudal privilege. A little more subtle but hardly less clear is the suggestion that he really did not care to be regarded as a freethinker, but in general as a courageous fighter against established privilege. Abroad he was quite willing to have such a reputation, but this is not the way he would have dared to express himself publicly on his home ground. Altogether this passage proves that Sonnenfels wanted to pose before his enlightened contemporaries and posterity in the toga of a spiritual hero—without running unnecessary risks at home. This may have been a vain, a childish feature, but it is a human one. Did he, as far as his contemporaries go, succeed in this effort?

There is first of all the empress's attitude toward Sonnenfels, on the whole benevolent within her deeply conservative limitations. The opposition of the high clergy as represented chiefly by Cardinal Count Migazzi and of the traditionalist administrators such as Counts Chotek and Kolowrat has been sketched. The support given Sonnenfels by enlightened statesmen and reformers —by Prince Kaunitz and Count Blümegen a somewhat qualified support and by Van Swieten and Gebler a rather more direct one—has been reviewed. In all these and many similar cases one fact stands out clearly: opposition to Sonnenfels (with the possible exception of the empress) is always directed against the ideas of the man as well as against his personality.

As to friends, promoters, and sponsors who shared his ideology the situation is different. They support his cause, but—and here they are in accord with his opponents—they have little liking for the man. With the exception of his most respected student, the political scientist Ignaz de Luca, who refers to him as his second father,[148] and a very few others, those of his contemporaries who quite frequently praised the man unreservedly did not know him personally.

This applies to the literary sphere no less than to the political. It can be seen in the ridicule heaped on him by his former collaborators, the playwrights Klemm and Heufeld. It can be discerned in the subtle praise of that discerning observer Friedrich Nicolai.[149] The brief comments of this controversial and shrewd character are noteworthy in two respects. First, he tells us that Sonnenfels observed to him that the good German style, for which he so ardently strove, was called Lutheran German in Vienna. Considering the anti-Protestant tradition in Catholic Austria, this remark sheds considerable light on the kind of difficulties Sonnenfels had to face. Every single issue that he took up, however apolitical it might appear, was connected by his adversaries with a general hostility to established tradition.

Was their feeling wrong? Arthur Schnitzler observes in his play *Der einsame Weg* that "rumor never knows where we are going, but always knows in what direction we are driven." Sonnenfels was certainly not a Lutheran, but just as certainly he was moving away from the political-cultural synthesis between Church and State. Thus his opponents were better psychologists than critics. Possibly the shrewd Nicolai had some dim notion of all this when, though seemingly with the intention of praising the successful efforts of a self-made man, he referred to Sonnenfels' Jewish background.[150] Such references are common among the later enemies of Sonnenfels' philosophy, but they are anxiously avoided by his ideological friends and in his lifetime by his enemies as well. Yet while, in line with the ideas of their time, these friends consciously though not always emotionally separated religion from the racial-ethnic background, Nicolai felt that the "alien corn" theme played its part in the life work of Sonnenfels. Nicolai, as mentioned previously, observed also the apparent contradiction between Sonnenfels' outspoken criticism of the lower nobility and his respect for the aristocracy. Most of these seeming or real problems have escaped the charming Austrian encyclopedist Franz Gräffer (1785-1852), who refers to Sonnenfels as "our Montesquieu and something more. Sonnenfels, fighter in life, fighter through life, and all that by and through himself. He is for Vienna and the monarchy what Lessing was for Hamburg and Germany, prosecutor of inhumanity, bad taste, torture, Hanswurst (one is sorry for him after all!); reformer of literary and business language, administrator, genius; educator of our most famous public servants, teacher!"[151] And in his *Österreichische National-Encyclopädie*, Gräffer expresses the same thought: "The pragmatic biography and characterization of him—who solely by his genius and creative energy has accomplished such great things in his field of activities as no single person before him and probably not after him either—would be a noble subject for a prize contest."[152]

This strange glorification reads almost like an epitaph on a tombstone or a monument, and to Gräffer, though technically still Sonnenfels' contemporary, he was already a monument of a bygone era, the Austrian Enlightenment. He could glorify Sonnenfels unhesitatingly because many of his ideas on civil service and criminal-law reform and on the purification of language and literature had been generally accepted and were no longer considered controversial. The same could not, of course, be said of the enlightened spirit itself. Yet its ideas were so far removed from the realities of the pre-March era that it was hardly dangerous to praise the heroes of the past, as long as their work and ideas were not intentionally associated with the different programs of a not-distant future. Sonnenfels for a time was thus removed from the field of action to the exhibition hall of an Austrian historical museum.

That process of mummification—a phase but not the final one of Sonnenfels' influence on history—becomes rather clearly visible during the brief reign of Leopold II, when Sonnenfels resigned his professorship and was relegated to the field of compilation and technical codification of statutes.[153] This becomes even clearer under Francis I, when Sonnenfels was showered with practically meaningless distinctions and decorations, but when he became still further removed from the field of action.[154]

It is true of course that Sonnenfels' further contribution to editing the legal codification work had a quite significant, indirect influence on the subject matter itself. It is further true that his position as vice-president and curator of the Academy of Formative Arts had some connection with his previous work, but in comparison to his influence in the era of Maria Theresa this narrowed field of action amounted to little.

Considering the intellectual atmosphere of the Franciscan reign, and even of the transition period from Josephinism to that later age (the brief reign of Leopold II and the very first years of Francis's rule) this is hardly surprising. Yet it seems paradoxical that the great break in Sonnenfels' position should have occurred at the beginning of the exclusive rule of Joseph—that is, at the very time when the chances for realization of most of Sonnenfels' reform ideas appeared to be better than ever before. Yet the high tide of Josephinism marks not in form but in actuality the termination of Sonnenfels' influence. The explanation of this seemingly bizarre fact, as reflected in the personal relationship between emperor and reformer, gives a good bit of insight into Josephinism itself, as far as Joseph II's personal attitude is concerned.

There is no evidence whatsoever that Sonnenfels was a less loyal "servant" to the emperor than to his mother. Frequent references to Joseph, the ruler who wanted to brighten the fate of his people, the emperor who was proud to be called a "fellow citizen," [155] are not lacking in Sonnenfels' writings. If these enlightened rhapsodies do not quite fit the complex character of Joseph, others in a similar vein were certainly even less appropriate for that of Maria Theresa. Yet undoubtedly under her regime Joseph had backed Sonnenfels in a number of issues ranging from populationism, censorship, judicial reforms, to the *Hanswurst* fight.[156] Sonnenfels had every reason to be grateful for the co-regent's support against powerful conservative forces at court and in the Church. Conversely, Joseph must have realized that his limited influence on the Maria Theresan reform program could never have been maintained without the efforts of the few men of Sonnenfels' purpose, energy, and efficiency.[157]

There is no doubt, however, that Joseph did not like him, and the personal reasons for that attitude are easily established. He resented Sonnenfels' persistence, his tactlessness, arrogance, and vanity, the magisterial manner in which he expressed his opinions, his tendency to teach where he should merely have advised and to give the impression of criticizing those with whom he basically agreed.[158] As Mitrofanov puts it, "Joseph could not stand people who always talked about the then fashionable love for humanity; business should not be transacted according to their advice, but according to his own well considered ideas."[159]

All this is clear enough. Yet it is more difficult to comprehend why a man of Joseph's grand principles, ambitions, and energy did not disregard these personal feelings in the case of a man of Sonnenfels' eminent and proved usefulness. Still there are keys to explain the imperial attitude. Most probably the emperor did not think that Sonnenfels was nearly as useful during his own reign as he had been during that of his predecessor. And here we come upon a basic difference between the regimes of Maria Theresa and Joseph. The empress, because of her conservative leanings and her intellectual limitations, both of which were frankly recognized by herself, was anxious to receive advice as well as instruction on controversial matters of state. Frequently she would overrule those whose basic philosophy differed from hers. She was nevertheless quite ready to acknowledge that she had obtained more elucidation from those who (though only cautiously) opposed her course than from the statesmen of the old order who acquiesced to the conditions of "a world they never made." Within such a setting the zealous pen and voice of a Sonnenfels was an invaluable asset to the reform party, all the more so since the empress seemed to have a certain personal regard for him. His function was not so much, if at all, that of introducing reform as that of explaining its necessity and of keeping the issues, once injected, alive. He did so not only with loyalty and energy but also with great skill. The fact that such a voice of enlightened reason was raised at a lower echelon of government made it all the more useful. It could be approved, modified, rejected, or even ignored without causing the kind of embarrassment to imperial authority and prestige that a direct clash of opinion with the co-regent, Kaunitz, or other statesmen of high rank would inevitably have involved. They might well have measured imperial sentiments by the reaction to Sonnenfels' voice below. They might conveniently have repudiated it, if necessary. They might, on the other hand, as they often did, have used it as an *avant-garde* to press a reform issue gradually to the fore.

The situation was quite different during the reign of Joseph. Obviously the emperor was as superior to Maria Theresa in intellect as he was inferior to her in common sense and political acumen. While fully, indeed, all too fully, conscious of his intellectual strength, he was painfully lacking in that kind of self-knowledge that the empress, all her prejudices notwithstanding, possessed, and so he was quite blind to his own glaring limitations. He certainly did not need elucidation regarding enlightened principles, yet just as surely he did need advice on policies. It would be unjust to say that he did not call for such counsel. Yet it was not the advice of philosophers of reform he was looking for, but that of expert consultants on the pursuit of policies, the principles of which had already been decided.

Sonnenfels was not primarily the technical expert in any field. Yet by virtue of his experience, industry, intelligence, and knowledge, further contributions on his part could have been substantial in this respect as well. They proved so in the limited area of language purification and the editing of statutes—i.e., as vice-president of the Commission for the Compilation of Laws even under Joseph. But this and his academic teaching are only single leaves in what had previously been a fully rounded wreath of intellectual pioneer work. To be sure, if Sonnenfels had been a different public servant and Joseph a different sovereign, Son-

Christoph, Cardinal Archbishop Count Migazzi

Emperor Joseph II

nenfels would have dropped his annoying academic instructions to the emperor and would have kept to technical matters; the emperor would have taken the one and ignored the other. Yet Sonnenfels was first and foremost a kind of missionary writer, and Joseph was primarily an absolute ruler and only secondarily the ardent champion of enlightened ideals. Each man according to his personality had to act as he did.

Even if they could have changed some of their personal traits it would have altered matters little. The decisive factor did not lie in the personal relationship—in Joseph's utter lack of political instinct and Sonnenfels' failure to adjust to the new regime. It was rather the fact that the reign of Joseph represented an altogether new era.

The time had passed for the gradual evolution and cautious introduction of reform ideas; an age had dawned in which they were hastily and often brutally pursued. The struggle for the preservation of the old, rambling Habsburg realm had given place to a brief, harsh, and febrile attempt to expand and streamline them into a mighty germanized empire. A rather effective defense had been transformed into an inefficient offensive, only to give way very shortly before a far more powerful offensive from abroad. The incongruous and yet in so many ways harmonious colors of the dying Rococo were to be replaced by an aggressive austerity. Tempo, direction, and atmosphere had changed. All three were alien to the reformer Sonnenfels, who looked for the new and could not fully shake off the irresistible forces of the old. He who had fought a reactionary tradition stubbornly and valiantly was, in fact, far more deeply rooted in it than he ever realized. The brief Josephine period, wherein that tradition was violently shaken for the first time, found him spiritually bewildered and politically sidetracked. Yet when that brief era, so much more significant in its repercussions than in its achievements, had passed, Sonnenfels' time was over. He who under Joseph had failed to be the tool of a revolution was no longer the herald of Maria Theresan reforms but a monument of the past.

The intrinsic cause of Sonnenfels' shattering disappointment under Joseph and with Joseph is that calm and unruffled evolution had come to the end of its course—just when the outlook seemed most propitious.

A Study in Austrian Intellectual History

r. Greatness Versus Sonnenfels

Concerning what may be called "the museum period," or in less respectful terms the period of the ossification of Sonnenfels' fame, we have the interesting testimony of Mirabeau. In his shattering criticism of the miscarriage of Josephine reforms, the great radical states that Austria could boast of only three really famous men, Jacquin, Stoll,* and Sonnenfels, the last insufficiently appreciated as academic teacher by the students.[160] One might easily argue that this reference, which links Sonnenfels with two distinguished members of the University of Vienna whose work had little effect on Austrian public life, does scant justice to Sonnenfels' fame. Still, the reference to Sonnenfels by a controversial political genius whose knowledge of Austrian political conditions was hazy, but whose insight was rather keen, indicates that Sonnenfels was one of the few Austrian intellectuals whose name was known beyond the German-language borders.[161] And Mirabeau's criticism of the rather slight attention paid to Sonnenfels' academic endeavors merely confirms the fact that his influence was on the decline under Joseph even in this field. In fact, two years later he relinquished the chair of political science altogether.

If Mirabeau can testify to Sonnenfels' international reputation, Beethoven can bear witness to his national fame. As is known to students of Beethoven, he dedicated his Sonata in D Major, Opus 28, of 1802 to Sonnenfels. The Beethoven literature gives practically no information as to the reason for this extraordinary honor—from a long-range point of view, probably the greatest ever bestowed upon Sonnenfels. In fact, it is not even definitely known whether Beethoven was personally acquainted with Sonnenfels, though it is quite likely that they met through Sonnenfels' brother-in-law, who was a friend of the composer.[162]

It can be safely assumed that in honoring Sonnenfels Beethoven was not prompted by musical considerations. After all, Sonnenfels was not even an amateur musician, though he had dabbled in musical criticism. Yet his condemnation of the Italian opera and his praise of Gluck as set forth in the *Briefe über die wienerische Schaubühne* applied chiefly to dramatic problems, stage direction, and acting, in which he was very much interested. They were in no sense musical analyses.

---

* Nicolaus J. Jacquin, as noted before, was professor of botany; Maximilian Stoll, professor of medicine.

When Klotz censures Sonnenfels for his ignorance of these matters, Sonnenfels defends himself meekly by stating that he has after all a musical ear and a reliable feeling for what is really beautiful.[163] In view of Sonnenfels' self-confidence, this is indeed an admission of ignorance that practically rules out the possibility of a musical relationship between him and Beethoven.

There remains, in fact, only one possible interpretation for the dedication, and it is not difficult to recognize, if one looks at Beethoven's life work and political sentiments during this period. Only two years later Beethoven dedicated the *Eroica* to Napoleon as the supposed savior and champion of the liberal achievements of the French Revolution. As is generally known, he crossed out the inscription when he learned of Bonaparte's assumption of the imperial dignity. The dedication as well as its withdrawal is indeed considered to be strong evidence of Beethoven's liberal spirit. Unquestionably the dedication to the septuagenarian Sonnenfels, the lonely monument and symbol of the bygone Austrian Enlightenment, is another example. It is all the more convincing and impressive since any personal relationship between the young master and the old reformer could only have been most tenuous. It is perhaps the one absolutely incontrovertible fact that permits Sonnenfels to quote the proud words of Horace *non omnis moriar....*

The foundations of Sonnenfels' glory appear far less solid if one turns to the judgment of the greatest figures in German, and indeed in European, literature of the period, Goethe and Lessing. The relationship of these two men to Sonnenfels is of great interest, though only in the case of Lessing was it based on a kind of personal contact. Considerable data are available on this point.[164] Sonnenfels, in his *Briefe über die wienerische Schaubühne* of 1767-68, had expressed a rather high though, in view of some of his other literary preferences, not a sufficiently high opinion of Lessing as a playwright. Lessing in turn, at the time of the creation of the *Hamburgische Dramaturgie*, in a previously quoted letter to Nicolai of 1769 expressed envy and admiration for the frankness of Sonnenfels' writings on conditions in Vienna, the like of which would not be tolerated in Berlin.[165] In the following year, 1770, he felt compelled to accept the rather unsatisfactory position of court librarian in the small principality of Brunswick-Wolfenbüttel. His letters of October 25 and November 27 of that year to the person closest to him, his future wife

A Study in Austrian Intellectual History

Eva König, indicate a notable change of attitude toward Sonnenfels. He now criticizes Sonnenfels' questionable principles of
theater management. A particular case in point is the *Hanswurst*
question, in which he disagreed with Sonnenfels' doctrinaire
views.[166]

At the same time Lessing's negotiations with the Austrian government regarding the possible directorship of the Burgtheater
came to naught. Was it possible that Gebler, and particularly
Sonnenfels, who seemed to support his appointment as the best
solution for reform of the theater, worked against him behind the
scenes? Lessing certainly believed so.

He was strengthened in his suspicion by Eva König, who then
resided in Vienna and acted at times as Lessing's unofficial agent.
Mrs. König, who as Lessing's companion, loyal friend, and future
wife deserves an honorable place in his biography, was however
anything but an impartial observer. She was clearly envious of
lesser literary men who, like Sonnenfels, enjoyed much greater
social prestige and influence than her friend. Anyway, she made
entirely unproved accusations, laying the failure of Lessing's
Viennese negotiations at Sonnenfels' door. The fact, for example,
that Sonnenfels had received her most cordially in his home
appeared to her as a probable act of hypocrisy.[167] Thus the flames
were stirred. On January 13, 1771, Lessing wrote to her: "I have
to take it that Mr. von Sonnenfels wants to be my good friend
and protector. I just cannot stand any longer his intolerable
braggings about his alleged capital of the German empire
[Vienna] and his friendship with Messrs. Klotz . . . Anyone who
clings to such miserable people must be badly in need of praise.
It will serve him right if he is humiliated a little in Vienna."[168]
Worried about his chances in Vienna, Lessing tries to assuage his
feelings by further letters to Eva König in which he expresses the
belief that Sonnenfels would have little influence anyway on the
question of his appointment. While still accepting his support—
though grudgingly—he took the questionable step of sharply
criticizing Sonnenfels in matters of the theater in a letter to State
Councilor von Gebler.[169]

The whole development to this point shows the anguish of a
great artist of high sensibility, tied down to an unworthy position
and forced into a situation in which he can make a change for
the better only by the sacrifice of his pride. Clearly this sacrifice
did not consist in any intentional humiliation imposed by Son-

nenfels upon Lessing. Yet Lessing had to ask for the support of a fellow writer whom he rightly did not consider his intellectual equal, but whom he was forced to recognize as his superior socially. The suspicion that Sonnenfels' seemingly benevolent support of Lessing's Viennese endeavors was a mere camouflage for the intrigues of a hypocrite poisoned the atmosphere further.

Long-standing and barely suppressed resentment thus set the stage for a break, the final and trivial cause of which would appear almost incomprehensible without some understanding of the antecedents. An unauthorized edition of the correspondence of Klotz, Lessing's inferior literary opponent, was published in 1772 by his widow, and some letters of Sonnenfels referring to the literary Klotz-Lessing feud were included.[170] In one of them Sonnenfels remarked that Klotz might risk his great fame in this feud but Lessing hardly the reputation of a good man.[171] Lessing's worst suspicions thus seemed confirmed. And now, probably with some emotional relief, he "let go." In a further letter to Eva König of December 3, 1772, he called Sonnenfels "a deceitful and base man" and declared that he would demand a public explanation from him.[172] Meanwhile the Klotz correspondence had become known in Vienna, even in imperial circles. All of Sonnenfels' opponents saw with glee the embarrassing position in which the arrogant reformer had put himself by his own fault. Considering this state of affairs, including, one can assume, the fact that Sonnenfels could hardly be asked to apologize for a private letter published without his approval, Lessing wrote to Eva the famous words: "Who is attacked by everybody will have peace from me."[173]

From what we know of Lessing's character, it can be taken for granted that he sincerely believed in the noble principle expressed here, though certainly he did not adhere to it in his further conduct. Several months later he had the opportunity to meet the nephew of Sonnenfels' arch-opponent, Cardinal Migazzi. He reports as follows on this discussion to Eva König, who continued to stir up that tempest in a teapot: "You can well imagine that the conversation touched upon Sonnenfels. I did not hesitate in the least to show my feelings and contempt for him. I wish only that he could have heard part of what I said, so that he would know what he [Sonnenfels] should expect from me." And in a further letter of April 8, 1774, to his future wife he declares that Sonnenfels should know what he, Lessing, thinks of him, and people should not hesitate to spread his opinion of Sonnenfels.[174]

It was hardly necessary to give Eva König, then still residing in Vienna, this generous permission. Her voluminous correspondence is filled with abusive language on the subject of Sonnenfels. He is berated for his arrogance, vanity, and insincerity. Opposition and, more often, mere rumors of opposition to him at court and in literary circles are gleefully recorded. What gives these letters a peculiar character is the fact that most of them were written before the Klotz episode, at a time when Eva frequently visited Sonnenfels' house and was, according to her own repeated statements, most cordially received there and promised every support.[175]

The correspondence, as indeed the whole Sonnenfels-Lessing affair, does not present a pretty picture. The following facts, however, stand out clearly. Sonnenfels had made a regrettably slighting remark, though only in a confidential letter to Klotz. Even this remark, however, questions neither the honesty nor the ability of Lessing, but refers rather to the impetuousness and harshness of the great writer. Certainly this alleged defect had nothing to do with Lessing's character. Thus through the remark that Lessing was not a good man was certainly ill chosen, under the circumstance it was of little consequence. The more important charge that Sonnenfels worked against Lessing's appointment is not substantiated. Even Schmidt, a severe and not unprejudiced critic of Sonnenfels, does not in the end make it in so many words. Nagl and Zeidler, equally critical of Sonnenfels, reject it outright.[176] There is, in fact, some evidence to suggest that Sonnenfels actually favored Lessing's appointment before 1772 and no definite proof that he opposed it when Lessing came to Vienna in 1775 as a highly honored guest to conduct negotiations personally.[177]

It is however true that Sonnenfels, in spite of his recognition of Lessing as an outstanding modern dramatist, did not fully comprehend his greatness.[178] Sonnenfels judged Lessing as a contemporary and not through the eyes of posterity. *Nathan der Weise* and *Die Erziehung des Menschengeschlechtes* were still unborn; the full significance of *Hamburgische Dramaturgie* and *Laokoon* had not yet been recognized. Lessing's fame was rising but was by no means fully established. Moreover, Sonnenfels looked upon Lessing as "a mere man of letters," whereas he saw himself as a leading figure in the broad realm of social reform. It is from this standpoint that his apparently condescending attitude must be judged.

Less easy to comprehend is Lessing's attitude in this sorry relationship. His frustration and resentment are quite understandable, but they still do not justify a hostile campaign, which in many ways, particularly prior to the Klotz affair, was based on mere gossip. It is even more difficult to understand how the trivialities of the Viennese episodes could occupy a Lessing so interminably, and how, in spite of his judicial position as Germany's first critic, he could remain so completely oblivious to Sonnenfels' merits in very many fields. It is conceivable, though of course not proved, that the one important factor never referred to in the whole affair, Sonnenfels' Jewish background, played its part. Lessing, the liberal who more than any other contemporary German man of letters stood for the emancipation of the Jews, the friend of Moses Mendelssohn,[179] the author of *Nathan*, may still have resented the fact that he had to deal with a man of Jewish descent not as a protector or as an equal but as a petitioner. This subconsciously may have strained the relationship between him and the noble of Jewish origin from the very beginning. Lessing respected and admired the Jewish image in the humble and unworldly Mendelssohn, scorned by his gentile environment and defended by the enlightened heroes. He glorified this image in the guise of Nathan, the sage *procul negotiis*, in a world of violent strife. Yet he may have rejected it in the form of what appeared to him the busy and pliant bureaucrat and petty courtier, the ennobled pseudo-enemy of nobility. He presumably saw in Sonnenfels the vainglorious man of letters with comfortable government backing, as compared to himself, the free writer of the North struggling with much harder external conditions.

The fact is that Lessing expected more of Sonnenfels than of others. He judged him by the rigid standards of the enlightened brotherhood of free-lance writers. Ignoring the demands of Sonnenfels' official position, he may have considered his ambivalent status as permanent civil servant *and* writer a betrayal of the spirit of the new age. He was unwilling to perceive that Sonnenfels, both in his strength and in his weakness, should be judged by the standards of his contemporaries—that is, in the light of the modest reality of the Maria Theresan era, not according to

Platonic ideals. Thus, whether or not in this case his error of judgment had an ethnic connotation, he yielded to a typical human prejudice.

More enlightening in intellectual history than the whole puny Lessing affair is Goethe's relationship with Sonnenfels, or, rather, his evaluation of Sonnenfels. It is extremely brief, a mere drop in the ocean of Goethe's life work, but it shows the spark of genius. Important as a contribution to the understanding of Goethe's own political philosophy, it sheds at the same time a penetrating light on Sonnenfels' ideas.

Goethe's works contain two references to Sonnenfels. Both were published in the *Frankfurter gelehrte Anzeigen*. The first deals with the *"Theateralmanach für das Jahr 1773, verfasst von einigen Liebhabern der deutschen Schaubühne,* part II, Vienna 1773."[180] Sonnenfels is only casually mentioned here as the target of camouflaged attacks in an insignificant comedy of Weisse. The review, however, is of great interest in that it deals with the whole reform and "purification" of the theater undertaken in Vienna. Critical of the Viennese stage on several points, Goethe fully supports the reform idea itself, including the termination of further French-comedy performances. In fact, he complains that the opera buffa, at the expense of the German reformed play, still occupies too much space in the repertoire.* Controversial as the whole issue may be, this is no small testimony in favor of Sonnenfels, a testimony all the more valuable as it was rendered by a man fully conscious of the power of tradition and popular humor. Yet whatever satisfaction Sonnenfels might have derived from this judgment, it was more than canceled by Goethe's review of his "Über die Liebe des Vaterlandes," of 1771.[181]

Several aspects of this work, in a way Sonnenfels' most important non-academic treatise in the field of political science, have been touched previously in regard to social stratification, religion, patriotism, and form of government. Seen with the eye of the contemporary historian who tries to form his judgment within the frame of reference of the past, this study had its good points as well as shallow and dreary stretches of argumentation. Viewing it from the vantage of the comprehensive evolutionary

---

*This testimony is all the more noteworthy since Wieland had ridiculed Sonnenfels for his exaggerated Germanism. (See J. W. Nagl and J. Zeidler, *Deutsch-österreichische Literaturgeschichte*, II, 39.)

philosophy of life of the genius, one gets a different picture. According to Goethe the question "Do we have a fatherland?" posed by Sonnenfels with exaggerated seriousness and pathos is artificial and makes little sense. The same is true of Sonnenfels' complaint that German-speaking peoples were lacking in patriotism, which Goethe answers as follows: "If we find a place in the world to settle with our possessions, a field to feed us, a roof to shelter us, don't we have a fatherland? Do not thousands and thousands have it in every state? Don't they live happily under these modest conditions? Why should we vainly reach out for an emotion which we neither can have nor want to have and which was and is only with certain peoples and at certain times the result of many happily converging factors?"[182]

He denounces Sonnenfels' unhistoric glorification of a Roman patriotism unsuitable for contemporary German conditions; he ridicules the attempt to perceive qualities such as egotism, pride, modesty, and loyalty as the specific national characteristics of certain peoples. He derides the notion that patriotism is related to such occupations and geographical features as hunting and fishing, cattle-breeding in plains, mountainous regions, and nonfertile soil. "Not the soil but the institutions of a people, of which it is true many are the product of the soil where they settle, determine the nation. Thus the Jews have more of a nation and more patriotism than hundreds of generations of serfs."[183] He further shows how Sonnenfels presents the ancient lawgivers Solon and Lycurgus as dreary pedants who merely teach the formal tricks of their trade: "In the . . . life of these great men . . . one sees always principles, political principles, objectives. The [Sonnenfels] treatise argues with the clarity and dead-sureness of the craftsman who, sitting at his glass of beer, explains cabinet secrets, state relations, intrigues. . . . Mysteries (which great historical data are after all not mysteries?), to be touched only by the deepest spirit with his presentiment, are discussed superficially! Things are getting worse every day. Previously one showed off erudition in such writings. No harm was done this way to humanity. Now the gentlemen mistreat common sense and feeling!"[184] Statutes are treated summarily. Laws are picked from artificial categories with blatant disregard for or misunderstanding of historical conditions, emotions, family relations. We must frankly admit that we can see nothing in the author's pictures but arbitrarily scribbled strokes. After all, they are still as characteristic as the twelve apostles in woodcuts, which, all venerable distortions notwithstanding, may still be recognized by their keys, swords, crosses, and saws."[185]

If one regards Sonnenfels' political writings as the only key to his philosophy and as the basis of his actions in public life, this verdict certainly would not be fair. It overemphasizes the antiquated form of Sonnenfels' magisterial admonitions; it disregards the salutary practical influence of their contents. Yet if this expression of Goethe's views is taken simply as the review of a treatise that must be judged on its own merits, irrespective of those of its author, it is a stroke of genius. With one brief gesture it tears aside the curtain and exposes the hollow pretentiousness of enlightened doctrinarism, its schematic and unhistorical applications of the treasures of Western civilization of the past to a present which does not conform to the classifications of a primer of politics.

This, of course, is only one facet of the Enlightenment, only one facet of Sonnenfels' work. Also, it must be added, it is only one facet of Goethe's political philosophy. The skepticism expressed in this masterpiece does not represent his final verdict on fatherland, patriotism, and nation. But he persisted in his view that political relations must be judged not on the basis of principles expounded in an historical vacuum but within the context of the historical evolution and the institutional setup of a people. It is no accident that this review was written in the Strassburg period of Goethe's life, when he was under the influence of the herald of that triad of humanitarian, evolutionary, and historic nationalism, Herder. But neither is it an accident that this whole new line of thought, which paved the way for Romanticism, remained for Sonnenfels a sealed book.

Sonnenfels in his old age, and in fact throughout a whole generation well beyond his lifespan, managed neither unsuccessfully nor dishonestly to create the impression that he was the enlightened warrior fighting against a world of privilege and prejudice. But viewed through the piercing eyes of the genius, the foundation of his ideas, though not the honest efforts and achievements of the man, are reduced to their proper proportions.

s. *Man and Image*

The evaluation of the status of a man in history is obviously not dependent on the greatness of his achievement alone. Change is necessarily more rapid in the political-social sphere than the literary-aesthetic. The work and personality of Goethe, Tolstoy, or Shakespeare, or for that matter even of Confucius, Horace, or Euripides, are still before us essentially unchanged. In the political-social sphere there is a clear difference between the few areas of civilization which, temporary periods of friction notwithstanding, have enjoyed a steady evolutionary adherence to the same political philosophy and the many where, because of repeated political friction, systems of values have been in constant flux. The evaluation of Washington, Jefferson, Gladstone, or even Cromwell and Lincoln has undergone far less change than that of Frederick II of Prussia, Robespierre, Napoleon, or Bismarck. In the first case we deal essentially with men as they were; in the second, primarily with their image as it has evolved through the passage of time.

Sonnenfels' Austria was not one of those fortunate exceptions where uninterrupted evolutionary continuity in political ideas has prevented the change from life to image within the course of a generation. His life work, his ideas, while not wholly extinct, were certainly paralyzed in his country within his own lifetime. This was by no means due entirely to the reaction to Jacobinism. While the spirit of the ensuing wars of the anti-Napoleonic coalitions, and particularly of that unique popular war that the Habsburg power fought singlehandedly in 1809, was not directly opposed to the doctrines of the Austrian Enlightenment, it necessarily put an end to major reform beyond the limited objectives of the judicial sphere. What is far more important, as it turned out after 1814, this meant the end not merely of what by and large had been progressive action but of the progressive spirit as well, and for a long time to come. The Congress of Vienna took place within Sonnenfels' lifetime. The Carlsbad Decrees were issued only one year after his death. To be sure, neither the restoration of Austria's Great Power position nor even the establishment or, rather, remodeling of the Austrian police state ran counter to the technical aspects of Sonnenfels' action. But it seems to have been an intrinsic though subconscious part of Sonnenfels' work that the pursuit of his reform ideas would sooner or later have stretched, if it did not actually burst, the strait jacket of the authoritarian state. The censorship regulations, the educational-administrative measures, the handling of political refugees according to the Carlsbad decisions, the subsequent foreign policy of counterrevolutionary, anti-national, and anti-liberal intervention, as formulated at Aachen, Troppau, Laibach, and Verona between 1820 and 1822 and executed accordingly, are compatible with the legal framework but not with the spirit of the Austrian Enlightenment.

True, Sonnenfels had endorsed censorship; his state was a police state; his loyalty to the Habsburg imperial idea in its preconstitutional meaning was unswerving. Yet censorship, as well as police power, were to him primarily tools of the neo-mercantilist enlightened state, the rise of which to the level of what appeared to him as Western civilization at its best he ardently desired. Neither must it be forgotten that his basic ideas were formulated prior to the American and the French revolutions.* In a positive sense there exists no ideological program formulated by Sonnenfels on Austrian foreign policy. Unquestionably, however, his strongly implied endorsement of a German cultural union† and his social philosophy, which after all was related to Rousseau's ideas, were incompatible with the ideology of the Quadruple Alliance of 1815 and the spirit of the German Confederation.

From the intellectual trends of the period Sonnenfels is farther removed even than from the political. He might have enjoyed the patriotic songs of a mediocre poet like Collin, but the essentially dramatic art of the young Grillparzer and Raimund certainly was "Greek" to him—and he did not understand Greek at all. The generally held notion that Romanticism and Enlightenment represent antipoles of intellectual development perhaps requires some revision. They have after all in common a certain visionary, basically naïve belief in perfection, though the one looks to the future while the other casts yearning eyes toward

---

* Brunner for once is on solid ground when he ridicules the aged Sonnenfels' claims that the French revolutionary principles of freedom and equality, if rightly understood, were actually in operation in the Austria of Emperor Francis. (See the Introduction to Sonnenfels' *Handbuch der inneren Staatsverwaltung mit Rücksicht auf die Begriffe und Umstände der Zeit* [Vienna, Camesina, 1798], I, quoted from S. Brunner, "Sonnenfels nach der französischen Revolution," in his *Die Mysterien der Aufklärung in Österreich, 1770-1800* [Mayence, 1869], 81 ff.)

†It is interesting to note that Wieland had already ridiculed what appeared to him as Sonnenfels' exaggerated Germanism. (See J. W. Nagl and J. Zeidler, *Deutsch-österreichische Literaturgeschichte* [Vienna, 1889-1914], II, 33.) It may be noted here that Sengle's assertion that Sonnenfels may have not only prevented Lessing's call to Vienna but Wieland's as well is entirely unsubstantiated. (See Friedrich Sengle, *Wieland* [Stuttgart, 1949], 268 ff.)

the medieval past. Such considerations, however, hardly apply to a man of Sonnenfels' type. He does not represent the visionary character of the Enlightenment but exclusively that of a not always practical but certainly never fanciful social reformism. Where is the middle ground between the utilitarian eclectic of classic virtue and pseudo-classic spirit and the aesthetic and social philosophy of converts to Austro-Romanticism, the fatalism of a Zacharias Werner, the universalistic art philosophy of a Friedrich Schlegel, the mystic animistic and altogether pretotalitarian political theory of an Adam Müller? Where indeed is the middle ground? There is none and never will be between that spirit of mysticism imported from abroad and the conscious striving for cognition. Sonnenfels' chalky-white dreariness still holds its ground nobly against the bewildered and ambivalent champions of a twilight of ambiguous spiritual revival.

The victory of the later spirit did not bring with it any direct attack on Sonnenfels' work, let alone the destruction of the reforms themselves. Rather to the contrary. To point out only one remarkable illustration, the *Austrian National Encyclopedia* of 1835-37 still gives Sonnenfels the highest praise.[186] No contemporary statement of importance to the contrary is known. The reasons are not difficult to see. The regime of Francis I and what may be properly called the regency, the reign of the feeble-minded Ferdinand, under Metternich's and Kolowrat's guidance —that is, the whole pre-March period up to 1848—had renounced the spirit of the Enlightenment. It had established an ideological foreign and domestic policy, but it had *not* revoked the specific Maria Theresan reforms themselves. In fact, except for the changes during the brief reign of Leopold II and the very first years of Francis' regime, it had left intact the bulk of the Josephine legislation outside of Hungary.

This applies as much to the reforms of the educational system as to Church-State relations, the basic trends of judicial change, and the principles of a partly state-controlled economic policy. It applies above all to the further development of what may properly be called the system of German centralism in the Austrian government—that is, the entrenchment of a German-directed though not consciously German national, fairly uniform administrative system of centripetal tendencies. These tendencies, which, had the reign of Joseph II been longer, might have developed in a German national direction, were arrested, except during relatively brief intervals. They were arrested, though only in terms of governmental action, not in political thought. In any case, the transition period from the semi-feudal to the almost fully bureaucratic Austrian state system was over. Apart from sudden intermittent shifts resulting from the pressure of political events, the power of the German-directed centralistic administration was never seriously threatened until 1867.[187]

Certainly there are tremendous ideological differences between reformism under Joseph II, which launched a rapid, semiconscious development in a potentially liberal direction, and the conservative philosophy of the pre-March era. In the first case we face evolution, in the second stagnation. Here we have reform as a means to achieve a still-distant, still-changing end; there we are confronted in political practice with terminal, limited objectives. On the basis of accomplished facts, however, there is no reason why the regimes from Leopold II to Ferdinand should have repudiated the Josephine reformer Sonnenfels. They might have done so if they had proceeded from the reform legislation of Maria Theresa and Joseph to an analysis of the underlying philosophy of that era, a philosophy to which Sonnenfels had made so significant a contribution. But philosophical analysis was certainly not the strength of those regimes that ignored the enlightened ideas and misunderstood those of their own brilliant intellectual allies, the would-be Austro-Catholic Romantics. Sonnenfels' image, though in a withered and faded form, was thus "safe" until 1848.

Then and only then did radical change set in. The March revolution has a long ideological background history, but its political impact in German Austria was more sudden than that of the national struggles of some of the Slavonic groups and of the Magyars in their respective territories. There the revolution represents primarily a late stage of an ancient political conflict. It does not resemble too closely the issue of constitutional Liberalism raised in Vienna, or the national-union fight in Frankfurt revolving around the German-Austrian position at St. Paul's Church. The new German-Austrian policies had no Hus, Žižka, Kościuszko, no Rákóczi or Bethlen Gabor, not even a Sžechenyi or pre-March Kossuth, to connect their platform with an ancient and still-virile political tradition.

Neither the mystical concept of a Holy Roman Empire nor the complex German national idea offered such possibilities. The natural though not logical thing to do was to assume some sort of connection with the past—if possible, with the more recent past. The privileged Austro-German centralistic position ruled out such a connection in the national sphere, yet there appeared to be a link in the liberal one—the Austrian Enlightenment. Tenuous as this limit was, if one thinks of the direction in which Josephinism might well have been going, had it been subjected to a less restricting external strain, this line of thought does not sound wholly unreasonable. Valjavec probably goes too far in referring to this evaluation as *Vulgärjosephinismus*.[188] If a connection between Josephinism and the Austro-German liberal revolution is assumed to exist, then it is impossible to confine it to the narrow grounds of the intellectual movement in Vienna university circles, the new academic legion, the briefly mushrooming revolutionary journalistic press and pamphlet literature. Yet this is exactly what has been done not only by the revolution itself but, with far less historical and psychological justification, by the weak blossom of neo- and pseudo-Liberalism of the 1860's and early '70's, which followed the counterrevolutionary neo-absolutist era. Contemporary interpretation stresses the link between Josephinism and the emancipation of the Jews rather than that of the peasants, freedom of the press rather than utilitarian educational objectives in general, renunciation of clericalism rather than co-ordination of Church-State relations. Thereby it presages and invites the inevitable reaction. Austro-German Liberalism was exposed at its weakest point—its social blindness, its narrow and unhistorical national philosophy, its ignorance of psychological motivation.

The spirit of that era of liberal twilight, which has no premonition of its impending doom, has perhaps done more to mar the image of the enlightened hero Sonnenfels than the hostile opposition to it that was inspired by much broader and deeper emotions.

Thus Feil, with the well-known predilection of nineteenth-century Liberalism for outworn metaphors (a characteristic that it shares with the Enlightenment), chants the hackneyed light-darkness theme: "The name of Sonnenfels will never be forgotten in Austria as a shining star in the days of transition from dusk to the light of intellectual development and humanizing ennoblement."[189] What is one to say further of the evaluation of that standard Austrian biographer, the otherwise so meritorious Wurzbach, who calls Sonnenfels in his *Hanswurst* fight an "intellectual Hercules . . . who after he had chopped off one head of the hydra, burned out the bloody trunk"? Sonnenfels, "through battle to victory, through night to light, hardly anybody else would deserve this motto written on the pedestal of his monument in golden letters more justly than he."[190] And Willibald Müller, one of Sonnenfels' uninspiring biographers, plays exactly the same tune when he describes Sonnenfels as the representative of Liberalism in its broadest sense.[191] Rollett's evaluation, or rather glorification, of Sonnenfels is written in a similar vein.[192] Again Sonnenfels' other chief biographer, Kopetzky, sings the beloved refrain "the glorious and determined striving [of Sonnenfels] . . . offers one of the most attractive monographs of his time, which, to put it briefly, was a transition from night to day, from dark to light, from fight to victory."[193]

Five times the same theme is heard in similar words in the period between 1858 to 1882—a period, that is, which stretches from the heights of the neo-absolutist period to the twilight of German political Liberalism. Does this exaggerated and bombastic praise of Sonnenfels mean that he has really been accepted as part of a common Austrian cultural heritage, since his work has been recognized by different ideological trends? Such a conclusion would be precipitate. It is true that the neo-absolutist Bach regime erected his monument in 1857, yet in rendering him this honor it merely paid its respect to the reformer who had helped set up the more efficient, the more streamlined, in fact the more absolutist Austrian state. The government celebrated the memory of the man who had helped to forge the Josephine frame within which the new regime operated. It conveniently ignored the intrinsic Josephine spirit and Sonnenfels' ideological contribution to it.

In 1855, the year of the new Austrian Concordate, Feil again, though in necessarily cautious words, praised Sonnenfels quite clearly as the man who had stood for the Josephine separation of Church and State, but he ignores the fact that Sonnenfels cannot be directly associated with the demands for constitutional representative government desired by the opponents of the new regime.* He speaks here in a historical situation the horizons of

* See Josef Feil, *Sylvesterspende* (Vienna, 1858): "May the swingings of the pendulum of the wide course of historic progress touch presently the extreme contrast of what was striven for and on the whole achieved in his [Sonnenfels']

which were in some respects narrower than those that had confronted Sonnenfels. Thus his identification of Sonnenfels' enlightened philosophy with a desired liberal renaissance is at least psychologically understandable, though historically not quite correct. The same identification on the part of Wurzbach, Müller, and Kopetzky is completely without basis in history or reality. The so-called Austrian *Liberalismus* of the 1860's and '70's and its sorry disintegration in the 1880's is on the whole as far removed from true Enlightenment as from true Liberalism. Sonnenfels of course was not a genuine Liberal, but neither is he to be associated ideologically with Liberalism's later nineteenth-century replica, that hodgepodge of genuine enlightened thought, class franchise, big-business philosophy, boom-and-bust speculations, German centralistic arrogance, all dressed up in shallow and high-sounding phraseology.

Yet these pseudo-Liberals, who were equally oblivious to the rising forces of an integral Pan-Germanism, of the petty bourgeois' Christian Social movement, and of the new power of organized Social Democratic Labor, claimed Sonnenfels as theirs. In doing so, they gave a shred of justification to the abuse heaped on him by the exponents of the new and broader social and political currents. It would, of course, be naïve to assume that the rising radical political forces, which made short shrift of the neo- and pseudo-liberal era in Austria, would in any case have stopped short of the attack on Sonnenfels' image. The unfair identification of Sonnenfels with the threefold shortcomings of Austro-German neo-Liberalism—blindness and ignorance in the social field, arrogance and sterility in national questions, misunderstanding of the Austrian historic tradition—virtually invited an attack on Sonnenfels' image.

There can be hardly any doubt about the specific injustice, vulgarity, and crudeness of many of these attacks. The popular literary historian of integral German nationalism, Adolf Bartels, calls Sonnenfels insincere, vain, aesthetically retarded, and shallow. "Thus after one has credited him with certain local merits, one may pass him over quickly."[194] However, Bartels recognizes

---

day. Just, impartial judgment will know that nature and significance of the great merits of the man must be valued according to the highest standards of mature opinion of his time, not ours. . . ." This statement of the "mature opinions" of Sonnenfels' time obviously conceives true Josephinism as Liberalism, very much in contrast to the spirit of the writer's own time.

at least Sonnenfels' local merits. The canon Sebastian Brunner (1814-93), in his earlier writings a decidely unsympathetic but keen critic of Sonnenfels' obvious human frailties, twenty years later made short shrift of Sonnenfels in a book, the title of which speaks for itself: *Lessingiazie und Nathanologie.*[195] The arguments brought forward against Sonnenfels here may easily be reduced to plain anti-intellectualism and vulgar anti-Semitism.[196]

The essence of the Bartels and Brunner type of attack is taken up far more skillfully by Joseph Nadler. He sees Sonnenfels as the typical uprooted product of the Enlightenment imported from the German North to become a slavish and loud imitator and admirer of trivial foreign ideas. He looks upon him as catering to the whims of the aristocracy and oblivious of the true values and achievements of the Austrian soil, and as such deservedly exposed to the public contempt of his own and of our times.[197]

Some of these and similar arguments might be supported if applied impartially to specific issues and in specific contests. Here, presented as they are against the black background of German totalitarianism, they betray bias and superficiality. As such they deserve attention not because they are based on expert knowledge, but simply as typical examples of the spirit of which they are an expression. It is the synthesis of a pseudo-traditional and pseudo-religious philosophy, increasingly infected with a National Socialist *Blubo* doctrine,* which in recent years, not altogether without success, has tried to crawl back under cover.

The distinction so generally made between a religious-social anti-Semitism promoted by the Christian Social movement and the racial-national one spread by Schönerian Pan-Germanism, though on the basis of episcopal encyclicals certainly correct and on that of party platforms at least arguable, loses much of its practical significance in the light of later developments. All brands of anti-Semitism ultimately merge in the murky stream of National Socialist ideas, despite the clear record of the Church and specifically that of the Austrian episcopate as well.

Yet just as the Church cannot be held responsible for the party movement which she did not organize but which rallied around her, so also Liberalism cannot be held accountable for its sorry epigones in the 1860's, '70's and '80's. In fact, serious

---

* *Blubo*: the widely accepted term for the so called *Blut und Boden* (blood and soil) literary interpretation.

adherents of genuine Austrian Liberalism have questioned the soundness of the image of the enlightened Sonnenfels. Rudolf Lothar sees in him "the earliest type of that rare political human species which in Austria is called the Liberal party. The word 'liberal' roughly corresponds to the word *freiheitlich* much as do Sonnenfels' endeavors to those of Lessing."[198] Here Sonnenfels is regarded as the model of the pseudo-liberal business politician, in contrast to the upright Liberal, the *freiheitliche* of 1848, who had his roots in the true Enlightenment, who had thus a genuine tradition behind him, unlike his successors of the neo-liberal period in Austria. This judgment by a cultured Austrian writer of intellectual integrity is not substantiated, as indeed it cannot be. How would it be possible to establish a direct connection between Sonnenfels and his alleged ideological friends, separated from him as much by the lapse of time as by changes in the Austrian intellectual climate? Yet the obvious question arises as to why Sonnenfels should invite an impartial observer to make such a comparison.

Hans Tietze, on the whole one of the most discriminating historians of Judaism in Vienna, indirectly answers this question. His argumentation, controversial as it is, warrants close scrutiny.

In the struggle of the rising Austrian Enlightenment "a baptized Jew played a big part. He was the first [Jew] who influenced the intellectual life of Vienna; the thin atmosphere of a new culture without tradition was the premise for the activities of an uprooted man like Joseph von Sonnenfels." After a brief, on the whole somewhat less than just, survey of Sonnenfels' manifold activities, Tietze continues, "Nevertheless the Austrian ways were alien to him and remained so. Because the tradition at home meant nothing to him, he made a fashion out of the senseless veneration of average achievements [imported] from abroad."

Tietze, however, denies neither the genuineness of Sonnenfels' convictions nor some of his specific merits in matters of reform. Yet he continues, "Nevertheless the uprootedness of his character is as terrifying as his pathos is repulsive. . . ." This is, says Tietze, what Goethe condemned in his famous criticism of "Über die Liebe zum Vaterlande," Sonnenfels' abstract evaluation of men and mores, his flouting of the demands of tradition and soil in history. "What Goethe criticizes in Sonnenfels is exactly what he [Sonnenfels] is proud of. He really is what he called the most important of his periodicals, *Der Mann ohne Vorurteil*. Was he aware of the price he had to pay for this sublime vantage point? Persistent assimilant to the culture which he wanted to serve with no mean abilities, the loquacious Sonnenfels has kept quiet about this point all his life; he forgot his Judaism as he forgot his mother. With both feet he jumped into general humanitarianism. . . ."[199]

Comparing him to another Jewish descendant, the celebrated contemporary painter Anton Raphael Mengs, Tietze concludes: "Both deemed it wise not to stop where they were thrown by the blind accident of fate, but to strive for a new home which they believed they had obtained by honest labor. Yet they keep the stigma of the forced separation from their native soil. The amiable and politely smiling Rococo mask of Joseph von Sonnenfels covers only imperfectly a sad Ahasverian face."[200]

Much of this evaluation of Sonnenfels is surely out of focus, though the soundness of the criticism of Sonnenfels' vanity, loquacity, pathos, and disregard for tradition cannot be denied. Yet in making the basic assumption that the key to Sonnenfels' character is the insecurity, the inferiority complex resulting from the chasm between his native Jewish milieu and his laboriously achieved and defended position in society, Tietze is viewing the problem from the point of view of the assimilated Austrian Jew in the period shortly before and between the two World Wars.

There is much more naïveté in Sonnenfels than Tietze realizes. Unlike the assimilated twentieth-century Austro-German Jew or Jewish convert, he did not have to look back on a long range of hills and dales, ups and downs, advancements and setbacks, in the history of the Jews. He was in many of his character traits and in his ability the true son of his people, but he was to an equal degree the true offspring of the Enlightenment. And both Judaism and the Enlightenment, in earlier modern times, shared in common the belief in a universal law of reason by virtue of which the new era was expected to last forever. Sonnenfels did not think of himself as riding precariously on the crest of a wave. Rather, he saw himself steadfastly marching along an infinite road into an ever more widely unfolding realm of progress.

Wrong as Tietze is in the main in his evaluation of Sonnenfels' character, the whole question appears in a very different light if one passes from the historical Sonnenfels to his image. Here the insecurity of his position amid the ideological cross currents cannot be disputed. Yet this insecurity is not just that of the enlightened Jew who emerges from the atmosphere of scholarly seclusion, and therefore friendly toleration enjoyed by a Moses Mendelssohn, into the arena of political action. Such insecurity is produced by something more than the precariousness of the Jewish position in general, which again becomes apparent in each new era of spiritual and political tension and crisis. It is the insecurity of the liberal position itself.

The genuine Liberal in German Austria does not occupy a firm middle ground between the party ideologies of political Catholicism, integral nationalism, and Socialism. He is at times —more often than not erroneously—to some extent associated with one of them, but generally attacked by all of them. His position is further weakened by the fact that, unlike in England, France, and America, Liberalism in Austria, even in its heyday in 1848, could not look back on a tradition of constitutional doctrine, let alone a history of liberal practice. The liberal position is even more seriously jeopardized by its later failure to cope with social, national, and historical traditional problems. Above all, it has never had a social group support equal in strength to that of any of the other groups mentioned.

Does this fact account at least in part for the attraction that Liberalism has always, though particularly in nineteenth-century Austria, possessed for the fully assimilated Jewish middle and upper middle class? But if so, it is not so much because Liberalism before the rise of the labor movement constituted the only political refuge for this assimilated Jew, as because of the affinity between Jewish emancipation and political relativism itself. In this sense the confounding of emancipated Judaism with Liberalism, at least in part, is justified.[201]

Sonnenfels, to be sure, was neither a relativist nor a Liberal, and biased attacks on Judaism for its Liberalism and on Liberalism for its inordinate proportion of Jewish support are in his case doubly fallacious. Yet they are fallacious only insofar as directed against the man himself as distinguished from his image. The innate trend of the Enlightenment was in the direction of a liberal program. The liberal program, however, in the particular Austrian setting of rather clear-cut social group interests tends to become relativistic. For better and for worse! For better in the sense that rigid social and ideological claims are thereby modified; for worse because insecurity within the body politic is further enhanced. It is in this sense that the image of Sonnenfels is deeply connected with the liberal spirit. It seems to fade into oblivion under the impact of totalitarian ideologies; with all its faults and virtues it will rise again in saner periods. Thus far it has not entirely disappeared from the Austrian earth.

Sixty-five years ago Lustkandl sketched the ideological setting of Sonnenfels' life as follows: "Sonnenfels, born in the year 1732, just a hundred years after Spinoza, Pufendorff, and Locke, three years after Lessing, three years before Beccaria, seventeen years before Goethe, lived and acted in a time which received its imprint from Immanuel Kant."[202] To this it may well be added: he died 100 years before the Bolshevik Revolution, 101 years before the disintegration of imperial Austria, 115 years before Hitler's rise to power, and 127 years before Hitler's downfall. Fascism and Bolshevism, either directly or indirectly, are the powers that prevented the stabilization of his image in the contemporary world.

Far less strong in a technical sense are those forces that tend to establish this image more firmly in history. Rash as it would be to assert that the survival of Liberalism in the ideological and geographical area of German Austria where Sonnenfels lived is assured, it cannot be denied that there exists a strong and in many ways substantiated expectation to that effect. One thing, however, appears to be certain on the strength of a vast array of unrefuted historical facts: the permanent recognition of Sonnenfels and his significance depends above all on the victory of evolutionary over revolutionary methods. This is the premise on which a lasting revival of the Sonnenfels image and his greatness would have to be based.

Thus it is only at the very end of this study that the name of Sonnenfels has been linked with the quality of greatness. This judgment has been arrived at after much hesitation, but eventually with great assurance. What after all makes for the recognition of greatness in history?

Is it ability? In this respect the biographer of Sonnenfels is on solid ground. Sonnenfels was an able, a brilliant, and above all a creative man. What is often held against him, that he lacked originality, is only partly true, and insofar as it is true it does not preclude creativeness in its true sense. The task of connecting Austria with the intellectual and social development in the West was a formidable one which required no less ingenuity but much more energy and courage than the formulation of new doctrines did. To inject new Western ideas into Austria was an essential first step. That Sonnenfels took this step for much broader and deeper reasons than did the seventeenth-century Austrian neo-mercantilists can hardly be challenged. That he partly failed in the second step of adapting these ideas to a different environment is true. His failure was far more his misfortune than his fault. His time was up before the new ideas had a chance to mature in the new environment. But even where he can be personally blamed for faulty methods, such blame rests on the naïve assumption that one man in Austria should have taken over the combined functions of Voltaire and Rousseau, Quesnay and Turgot, Locke and Berkeley, Adam Smith and Bentham. This is obviously absurd.

One thing is true, however; Sonnenfels, seen in the light of today, was a much poorer communicator of his and others' ideas and reform plans than his intellectual predecessors in England and France. No one can tell how much more successful he could have been had he possessed the colorful brilliance of Abraham a Sancta Clara or had he been endowed with the irony of a Voltaire, the passion of a Rousseau. The colorless, humorless, shallow, and doctrinaire character of his pathos is only partly his own, however. It is rather the product of literary sterility, the inevitable result of the transplantation of foreign ideologies in not yet fully receptive ground. To be sure, the example of a Lessing will always be held against him, but aside from all the differences between the Protestant North and the Catholic South, Lessing was a free-lance writer, Sonnenfels primarily a civil servant. After all these factors have been taken into consideration, his accomplishments, imperfect as they are, remain substantial. His abilities are undisputed.

Ability, however, is not enough. History requires character of its leading men. None of the numerous flaws in Sonnenfels' attitude—some of them, like his vanity and pomposity, more comic than serious—are important enough, either separately or in combination, to mar the general trend of his life work. Nevertheless, this life work is one of zealous effort and struggle, sometimes at personal risk, for what he deemed right. History has not put him in the position of the hero, but the Austrian Enlightenment required him to perform the task not of a hero but of a reformer. He had neither the opportunity nor the duty to fight and to command, but rather to suggest, to persuade, and to prompt. This he did, and on this basis he must be judged.

History, in evaluating its great men, also considers their influence on future developments, and here one treads on more uncertain ground. The impact of Sonnenfels on the Enlightenment and the Enlightenment's effect on further Austrian history can never be denied. This holds true in spite of the era's profound lack of foresight concerning all the great national and some social problems of the Austrian future.

Still, any single measure initiated or supported by Sonnenfels, including the judicial reforms and "purification" of the theater, presumably would have been taken without his personal efforts. All of his reform ideas were already, so to speak, in the air, and if the test of greatness is whether the course of history would have been entirely different without the action of a single man, Sonnenfels probably fails to meet it. Perhaps it must even be conceded to his opponents that his most spectacular direct influence is the seemingly ineradicable ideological association between Jewish intellectualism and radical reformism or pseudo-reformism in Austria.

This, however, puts the whole problem in a wrong context. Intellectual influence should not be measured according to the specific impact of a man on specific events far beyond his lifetime, an influence which can never be readily gauged. It is far more important to determine whether ideas represented by him are connected with those of later generations. In this wider sense the content of the philosophy of the Enlightenment, its methods notwithstanding, is definitely linked with those of evolutionary social and cultural reform. Insofar as evolution is based on a liberal premise, there exists a non-spectacular but deep and irrefutable connection between the enlightened philosophy of progress and later disappointments, illusions, and new hopes.

In this sense the world of today has every reason not to disregard the image of Sonnenfels, but to recognize his work as a link between past, present, and future. In this sense we are justified in seeing in Sonnenfels' image not merely the specter of the past but a living reality. In this sense we salute him as the great son of the Austrian Enlightenment.

V

THE SWING OF THE PENDULUM

Era of Francis I, 1792-1835

a. *Government and Change*

In a lecture on Lessing, Thomas Mann observes that in the German sphere Catholicizing Romanticism offers the only example of a reactionary period endowed with intellectual brilliance.[1] Whether this is a unique phenomenon, and whether Mann was entirely justified in terming this period, without qualification reactionary, are certainly controversial questions. Yet various flaws in the intellectual history of Catholic Romanticism notwithstanding, that period of Austro-German history in which romantic ideas played so important a part was certainly one of great intellectual brilliance. Recognition of this fact, as will be discussed more fully below, has a decisive bearing on the conclusions of this study.

It should help much to refute one of the most widely held misconceptions about the Franciscan era. Well-established liberal, pseudo-liberal, and German national historiography has generally perceived the political, social, and intellectual currents of that period as merging into one murky stream of narrow reaction.[2] Actually the character of this chapter of Austrian history is far more complex than it appears to such historians, several of them of distinguished rank. In the first place, a distinction has to be made between the era of Francis I and the regime itself. The intellectual concepts and scope of the two are by no means identical, in some ways are not even similar. Although many aspects of the emperor's regime cannot be defended, this much should be

259

clearly stated at the outset: throughout this era, major ideological trends prevailed and were openly expressed in German Austria which were in theory greatly at variance with the political principles of the Austrian government. This applies not only to moderately liberal and more or less vague German national tendencies—in short, what would have been considered at that time (in modern terminology) "leftist" trends. It is also true to some extent of the evolution of conservative Romanticism, German Catholic unionism, and religious reform ideas in general, as well as of the promotion of Estates' autonomy on a historic-traditional basis. These ideological differences between Franciscan regime and Franciscan period were thus apparent not only in the era of advancing French Jacobinism, Directorate, Consulate, the Napoleonic wars, but also, even increasingly so, in the Restoration period after 1815, throughout the Latin-American and Greek crises, the French July revolution and the Polish uprising of 1830.

When in 1797 Emperor Francis prohibited anti-revolutionary propaganda because it helped to spread revolutionary principles as well,[3] he acted according to his own lights, not foolishly but quite consistently. His whole philosophy of government, as expressed throughout his reign, implies unmistakably that the influence of public opinion on governmental action is at the bottom of all social change. Such motivation, except in the emergency situation of Austria's singlehanded war of 1809, was considered *ipso facto* of a potentially revolutionary character. Thus the influence of public opinion is the primary revolutionary force; Jacobinism, Liberalism, and democracy are only specific and dangerous consequences. According to the imperial system, they are only one set of consequences, though verging closely on revolution. Potentially the influence of the intellectualism of the Catholic Romantics Friedrich Schlegel, Zacharias Werner, the universalist political philosopher Adam Müller, the religious reformer Clemens Maria Hofbauer, even to a point the statecraft of Gentz, are only one step farther removed from the prospects of potential revolution. Independent thought has an inveterate tendency to spread to lower and broader echelons. The force of public opinion thus created may be controlled only with difficulty. However "innocent" in its original intentions, it may easily change its character in an unpredictable direction. Unpredictable thought may well be nonconformist, and behind nonconformism lurks the danger of revolutionary tendencies. Even the most laudable expression of public opinion that never deviates from the prescribed path appears suspicious. The government expects the people to obey its decrees because it has so ordered, and for no other reason. An appeal for the support of public opinion would imply that a law lacking this support would be less valid, and this indeed would imply a dangerous concession to the allegedly revolutionary principle of popular sovereignty. All this helps to explain the suspicion, the at best lukewarm support, and sometimes the harassing of even conservative intellectual forces.

It helps to explain something else too. A regime that above anything fears change will be wary of shifting suddenly from one system of government to another, even though it may be a change from comparative radicalism to conservatism. The revolutionary dangers inherent in the sudden impact of the Josephine reforms had been stopped by the brief reign of Leopold II. The general policies of Joseph II's regime in regard to domestic administration, civil service, economic-military organization, Church-State relations, and even to a point public education were, however, transmitted for the most part unaltered to the Franciscan era. What is more, they were largely preserved under that long regime. Naturally in a social order harassed by internal crisis and external wars and revolution, weighty reasons of political expediency forbade return to the antiquated policies of the pre-reform era that had prevailed at the beginning of Maria Theresa's reign. Probably of equal importance was an ideological consideration: the era spiritually characterized by the Maria-Theresan–Josephine reforms and their Leopoldinian modifications represented the *status quo* to the new government. This status may have appeared in many ways undesirable to the early Franciscan regime, but it seemed even less desirable to set a new example of radical change, the consequences of which were unpredictable.

After all, Josephinism, highly concentrated as it was under Joseph, is only one component factor of a much larger ideological unit. At the outset it was conditioned by the gradual evolutionary reforms of Maria Theresa's long reign and blunted by the brief rule of Joseph's successor Leopold at the end. Its spirit had already been altered at the time of Francis's accession. It would be reversed in many, though by no means in all, respects under the new administration.[4] Yet in its pragmatic contests the legislative and administrative structure of the Franciscan era deviates only cautiously and not always in a strictly reactionary way from the preceding regime.

It may well be held, however, that the spirit, the intellectual and ideological foundations of an era, weigh more heavily in its evaluation than the technical structure of the government does. This line of argument is perfectly legitimate. Yet it should not be forgotten that if the body of the social order is preserved intact, an inevitable change in intellectual climate will facilitate an evolutionary transition to a new reform period. That the revolution of 1848 and the reform era linked to it produced no widespread and violent Jacobin transgression can be largely attributed to the relative moderation with which the Franciscan regime operated in domestic affairs.

This restraint, however, applies only to the cautious attitude toward institutional change, not to the profoundly altered spirit of governmental policy. Thus the following tentative conclusions seem to be warranted: As to political theories, and indeed to the generally prevailing ideologies, the rift between principles of governmental philosophy and contemporary intellectual trends was much greater in Austria in the heyday of Catholic Romanticism and neo-conservatism than during the previous era of Enlightenment. True, even the Josephine reform regime met the demands of enlightened theory only to a limited extent in governmental practice. But by and large it was faithful to its principles. The same does not hold true of the Franciscan government, not primarily because it was more conservative but because it was basically opposed to the influence of the ideologies of independent thinkers on the theory of government. "Theirs not to reason why" but to obey is the Franciscan motto; theirs to reason, but then to compromise with the demands of the existing state in its reality, is the line of thought of the Austrian enlightened government.

Differences in governmental attitude toward political theory is one thing. Political practice is another. Here the difference between administrative actions and specific and concrete programs proposed for the pursuit of such actions was far smaller under Franciscan conservatism than under enlightened government.

b. Conservatism and Romanticism

Further pursuit of these assumptions leads to an evaluation of the main ideological forces developed in the Franciscan era. The reform concepts of unrestricted enlightened rationalism, even in their most specific practical application, paid little heed to the traditional realities of the day. In the Franciscan era the situation changed. As great as the differences in theory were between broad intellectual currents and the narrow philosophy of the government, in practice they moved closer and closer together.

Here a difference between Romanticism and conservatism is obvious. Early Romanticism, particularly in its attitude toward the French Revolution, in an emotional sense had a radical past though not a radical program; indeed, in a specifically political sense it had no program at all. This lack is in fact a connecting link with the rising forces of conservatism, particularly after 1815. Both were influenced by the shocking experience of Jacobin intolerance and concomitant imperialism. Yet conservatism was most reluctant to subscribe to rigid doctrinaire programs of any kind. As to furthering its interests, it relied on political expediency. On the other hand, not only is conservatism determined to defend the *status quo* and to bring about the return of the social order to this status, but it is prepared to take practical steps to this end. Conservatism is quite flexible as to where the line or, rather, lines for the defense of the old order are to be drawn. Principle determines the issue of the defense itself, expediency that of procedure.

Expediency, however, was little valued in early Romanticism. Like conservatism it rejected and abhorred the phenomenon of Jacobinism. Yet it became increasingly opposed to it not so much because of its violation of established interests but because of the injury done to highly esteemed ideas. Romanticism became repelled by the spiritual dreariness and the potential political danger of exaggerated rationalism. Further, it became cruelly disappointed by the Jacobin conversion of the tenets of loudly proclaimed individualism to semi-totalitarian intolerance. The deep spiritual roots of Romanticism inevitably led to an idea of religious revival, for which neither Jacobinism nor early political Liberalism had any use. Romanticism and Jacobinism had in common a new and positive attitude toward the concept of the cultural and political nation. But like the Jacobin conversion and distortion of the idea of individualism, French revolutionary nationalism moved with ever-increasing speed into the sphere of imperialism, while the early German-Austrian national romantic idea was still a tender bud groping toward the light of political recognition, but chilled by the specter of revolutionary wars.[5]

A Study in Austrian Intellectual History

By virtue of these ideas and the fact that both a more mature and less naïve Romanticism and an experienced conservatism became disappointed with crude reality, they were drawn together. They met eventually on the platform of historical tradition. Yet to conservatism tradition primarily meant established right; to Romanticism it was originally not a value in itself but rather the rediscovered soil from which its social, religious, and political values derive. These differences appeared very real in theory, though they gradually became less distinct in political practice. Almost nowhere did they emerge as clearly as in the relationship between the two immigrant intellectual champions of the Metternich system from the North, the rationalist neoconservative diplomat Friedrich von Gentz and the literary-political theorist and Romantic Catholic convert Adam Müller. To Müller, the romantic zealot, the Revolution, including "all the endeavors and all the products" from its very beginnings to the restoration, was an unmitigated evil. Gentz, the conservative, considered it as wholly evil only in a specific historical situation, the Jacobin era, but possibly as something of a blessing once the danger had passed. It is not flights of imagination but the facts of stark reality that must govern political action.[6]

The implications are obvious. Romanticism developed original and brilliant—though in practice frequently odd—ideas. A conservative might have found it difficult to bring many of them in line with existing political conditions. Conservatism, sure of its intentions, stood above any specific ideological programs in its fight for very real objectives. Theories were always subordinated to the contingencies of the contemporary situation. The conservatives, entrenched in a long-standing tradition, were considered "safe" from the standpoint of the anti-revolutionary regime—even if they were willing to compromise on various issues. The emotional romantic attitude, whose outlook had considerably changed under the impact of the hectic years from 1789 to 1815, had to prove its dependability by clearly defined action. Consequently the disillusioned Romantics and romantic ideological converts were and had to be as adamant in their new-won outlook as the conservative realists could afford to be flexible in their political programs. The Romantics merely wished for what they felt to be right; the conservatives knew precisely what they wanted. Both, however, by force of obvious necessity were bound to the past, though not to the same past. Conservatism looked back to the enlightened reforms in the spirit of a realism that was strong and determined as far as its interests are concerned, but frequently rather broad-minded in regard to principles and procedures on specific issues. Reform that touched upon the industrial, commercial, legal, and administrative needs of an expanding society was not *a limine* rejected, but only where it directly implied a shift in economic and political power.

Romanticism, on the other hand, even in its political manifestations, did not consciously represent the specific interests of any social group. It stood for a way of life and thought that is directly opposed to that of the Enlightenment, its Jacobin consequences, and its potentially even more radical future. As to the problem of a more or less qualified "restoration," this politically homeless ideology faced the question "Restoration of what?" The answer is vague in civic terms. Yet this much is clear. Return to the recent pre-revolutionary past, so closely connected with spiritual sterility, was not acceptable. Spiritual frustration—such as Romanticism saw in the Enlightenment—was to be feared above anything else. Somehow the strength of emotional-spiritual forces as pillars of the social order must have been lost in the course of modern civilization. Greek-Roman civilization, the Renaissance and its consequences, were too obviously connected with the enlightened spirit to be of any help. The Baroque era seemed too diffuse in its ideas and their manifestations too spectacular to appeal to the Romantics. Thus by a process of elimination, the Christian medieval heritage remained the only safe anchor in a world of spiritual dissolution. The Middle Ages, however, were chosen for strong and profound reasons and not by the process of mere elimination. The choice was also motivated by something stronger than a fondness for romantic chivalry and mysticism. The high Middle Ages, as Romanticism saw them, do not represent a society in flux directed toward yet unknown social, political, and intellectual goals, but a permanent though not perfect order based on firm spiritual concepts. Trust and faith in these foundations, rather than their social-political emanations, lie at the root of romantic neo-medieval tendencies.

No doubt a political philosophy as impractical, unrealistic, and unworldly as that which Romanticism had to offer could never take the lead in that era of violent crisis from 1789 to 1815 and in the following Restoration period, with its less stormy but hardly less complex problems. Naturally in the German-Austrian orbit intellectual political leadership was in the hands of the straight rationalist, yet not unimaginative conservative realists, like Gentz, and not in those of a romantic, emotional, though also subtle Friedrich Schlegel or Adam Müller. The realists knew where they were going; the Romantics (eventually) only where they stood.

Yet the contribution of Romanticism to the operations and achievements of the anti-Jacobin, anti-Liberal coalition is not negligible. This holds true not only in the realm of ideas but in that of action as well. Conservatism by itself could never have rallied the masses to the fight against Napoleonic imperialism. Since Liberalism appeared to be inextricably allied with Jacobinism, Romanticism offered the only acceptable set of values to be raised in the "Wars of Liberty"—soon to be changed to mere "Wars of Liberation" from a foreign threat. Here Romanticism made a very real contribution to the rise and even to the organization of a true mass movement of wide and well-justified popular appeal.

This central position between liberal and conservative tendencies could not be held after 1814-15. And what is more, expressions of disappointment in the domestic results and consequences of the great struggle, disillusionment with the status of political rights that lagged far behind even those of the French Bourbon restoration, could be suppressed but not satisfied by the romantic influence, even if it had crystallized in a definite political program. Conservatism, feebly supported by an indifferent crew, would have to man the bridge alone, with the odds wholly against a safe voyage for the ship of state. Romanticism could not change those odds to an appreciable degree, but it could delay and soften the effects of a potential rise of popular opposition to the new course. It did so by the promotion of two main values, a Christian revivalism on broader and deeper foundations than those of the established hierarchy alone, and a new, not merely renewed, emphasis on a cultural and political nationalism still free from aggressive proselytizing tendencies. The German governments and the Austrian regime did not react favorably to these ideas, which, at least in regard to the national issue, were incompatible with their terminal aims. Neither, considering their precarious position, could they repudiate them as strongly as they might have wished, had the situation been less tense.

Thus the political and ideological course of the Austro-

Emperor Francis I (II)

Clemens Lothar, Prince Metternich-Winneburg

German generation grown to manhood since 1789 and active in public, or rather quasi-public, life after 1815 was largely formed by two component main factors. There was a conservatism committed to the defense of the order of the Congress of Vienna and, by the Carlsbad Decrees of 1819, to increasingly tightened domestic controls. Yet conservatism was not bound to reverse the enlightened bureaucratic centralization of government, the supremacy of the state in church relations, nor was it in the economic field committed to repudiate neo-mercantilist policies. Conservatism remained firm in intent but flexible in method, except for the clear rejection of any appeal for articulate popular support in pursuit of its policies.

There was, secondly, a political Romanticism, more uncompromising in its rejection of the recent past, but on the other hand by no means opposed to the use of mass media in the service of its ideas. By ironic contradiction, it tended increasingly toward a medieval heritage of little popular appeal. Conservatism and Romanticism to a wide degree shared general political objectives. Yet at the end of the Franciscan era, and in a sense of the Restoration period in general, Romanticism and Liberalism in their search for popular support meet on common ground. Eventually, as particularly conspicuous in the French July revolution and the Polish insurrection of 1830-31, romantic and liberal ideas merge to a large extent. However, the Austrian evolution of enlightened Josephine concepts to liberal-democratic ideas was only dimly visible in the literary-scientific field and was not yet of much political significance.

The domestic course of the Austrian government was thus the resultant of these conservative-romantic, not yet liberal trends and the reaction to the bygone enlightened reform era. Oblivious and, indeed, even hostile to any kind of dynamic ideology, conservatism in action was limited by the expediencies of Great Power administrative policies that had outgrown their semi-feudal foundations. This course was further limited by aversion to any implications of radical change that the full reversal of the reformism of two past generations would represent. This meant a certain anti-intellectual political attitude but, appearances to the contrary, not the lack of an intellectual political strategy. Nobody who believes that anti-intellectualism necessarily means the nonexistence of intellectual concepts in the minds and the actions of leading statesmen of the period can satisfactorily explain the consistency and determination of Austrian governmental action, at least in foreign policy. Nobody who thinks that opposition to popular programs necessarily means lack of any ideological foundation can explain the wide and not altogether short-lived success of the governmental system.

c. Philosophy of the Metternich System

What is commonly referred to as "the Metternich system" is simply the resultant of the main currents of political thought of the period, as shaped by recent political experience. The Metternich system intended to establish the equilibrium between a positive conservative principle of perseverance and a negative destructive principle of excessive motion. Thus while it evaluated these principles rather differently, it nevertheless did not intend to eliminate the force of motion completely. It did not believe, however, that political standstill in a society in flux —and what society is actually not in flux?—leads inevitably to retrogression. But this is a conclusion which is supposed to be drawn from practical experience alone. In theory the concept of equilibrium recognizes the significance of slow evolutionary motion. This means moderate reform, without which equilibrium can never be reached, since otherwise a force of retrogression would throw it off balance. In practice, it is true, the Metternich system held that the equilibrium had been seriously disturbed by too great an influence of the principle of motion since the beginning of the revolutionary period—in fact, ever since the late Enlightenment. Yet while such diverse concepts as revolution, nationalism, Liberalism, inordinate individualism, constitutional monarchy, and popular sovereignty were rejected as excessive emanations of the *Zeitgeist*, their *raison d'être* as formative forces in history, without which the balance can never be established, was by no means flatly denied.[7] In practice the interpretation of the concept of excessive motion might thus be arbitrary and harsh, still in principle the concept of slow evolutionary progress was affirmed.

Here we find a connecting link between conservatism in its intellectual form and the more subtle but also more obscure concept of political Romanticism as formulated in Austria principally by Adam Müller. In a way his work represents the compromise between the conservatism of Burke and the early, purely emotional concept of the state as set forth by Novalis. The allegedly balancing forces of the Metternich system correspond very well indeed with Müller's *Lehre vom Gegensatz*, the antithesis of opposing, though not—as in Hegel's doctrine—conflicting principles. Müller's unity achieved through multiplicity—but, again unlike the Hegelian thesis, not elevated to a higher synthesis —resembles in its universalist concept Metternich's equilibrium. His state, which in theory "represents the totality of human affairs, their fusion into a living whole,"[8] approximates actually the dreary reality of Metternich's police state.

To be sure, the reduction of universalism to equilibrium, of the total though not totalitarian state to the police state, brings a philosophical doctrine down to the somber realities of the body politic. Yet we are concerned here precisely with the connection between Austro-romantic political concepts and the realities of the governmental course. This reality is palpable indeed. It is the reality of the legal community of the conservative states—which Metternich's Concept of Powers, with its right of intervention against revolutionary action, attempted to materialize—rather than the superstate at the apex of the universalist political doctrine.[9] It is the reality of the anti-individualistic Estates-group representation in lieu of the democratic general representation of the individual subjects. Though the Metternich system, as victor over the Enlightenment, had little use for the political Estates' organization, it was also Enlightenment's heir and still subscribed fully to its different social hierarchy. Finally, the oversophisticated glorification of basic features of medieval economic feudalism by Müller was, though with a far more modest rationalization, reflected in the passive agricultural policy of the ruling system.

Here and in other fields the differences between Müller's doctrines and Metternich's system are even more important than the similarities. Müller was not only against a competitive society, free trade, and division of labor.[10] He crusaded against the separation of political powers. Though with some qualifications, he affirmed on principle the medieval Estates ideas. He considered war a creator of invigorating spiritual and emotional values for the state. Finally, he conceived of this state as neither a legal body nor a union of individuals, but as a structure composed of what might be described as minute cells of political-social relationships. This rules out the notion that any part of man's activities may be considered as exclusively his own private concern. This romantic philosophy, unlike the Metternich system, does not hew to the line of compromise between rest and motion. It aims at a very different compromise between a sometimes badly misunderstood medieval past and an equally distorted romantic concept of the present. It results, though unintentionally, not in gradual motion but in a standstill—actually in social and political reaction. These differences between the system's flexible conservative realism and Müller's brand of romantic dogmatism may be obscured in political practice. In theory they are fundamental. Historians do and would have done well not only to consider the obvious relations between Austro-romantic and Austro-conservative ideas, but to pose the equally important question: What would the Franciscan era have been like if it had taken over completely the philosophy of a Müller?

Realistic conservatism is not represented by a theorist who advocated its ideas in as comprehensive, as subtle, as brilliant, but also as deeply controversial a manner as Adam Müller did in his program of political Romanticism. Were it otherwise, this Austrian conservatism could not have had its feet as solidly on the ground as it did. It could hardly have warded off war and revolution as long as it did. Yet since the Metternich system does not represent conservatism pure and simple but rather a resultant of the conflicting forces of past, present, and future, the search for the true character of the Metternichian compromise must go beyond strict conservatism to the ideas of an intellectual mediator and representative of the regime's *Realpolitik*. This chief intellectual promoter, Friedrich von Gentz, personifies not only important ideas and actions of the system, not only the conflict between conservatism, Romanticism, and their heritage, but the basic nature of the Franciscan regime in the war as well as the postwar periods.[11]

Gentz was a most determined advocate of the anti-Napoleonic European coalition. Yet after the danger of Jacobinism had passed, he took this position not so much in the name of a definite political ideology as in the service of the concept of political equilibrium itself. Very characteristic of Gentz, and in a way of Metternich as well, is the idea that the state and the whole traditional order, including the enlightened reforms, even to a point some of the French revolutionary reform ideas, should be the foundation of governmental philosophy.[12] This implies a stand against the evolving romantic concept of the nation as the core of the political structure. It denies also the belief that not merely a specific system but a specific set of rigid ideas should govern the body politic. Also significant is recognition of the inheritance of enlightened absolutism, the concept of government for the people but not by the people. This surely is a doctrine very different from the democratic ideal, a doctrine which, after the withering of the enlightened spirit, tended in the direction of a most undesirable police state. It is still not the concept of the totalitarian state, which imposes not only its own decrees but its own values on the people.

The system imposes its order on the subjects, but it does not require of them the active, vociferous support so characteristic of totalitarianism of any brand. From this self-enforced limitation of governmental functions and by no means merely from political expediency, it naturally follows that this doctrine is essentially defensive, essentially opposed to zealous conversion. It is not basically opposed to evolutionary reform, however, once the idea of reform has become part of an established tradition. This implied qualification, while it does not shut the door to gradual change, may however restrict reform severely in practice.

d. *Metternich System and Franciscan Government*

As to specific issues, the difference between the Metternich-Gentz compromise and Catholic Romanticism comes out particularly clearly in the religious sphere. For political reasons, in order to preserve state power, the government pursued with modifications the line of Maria Theresan State-Church relations. These modifications led to recognition of religious orders such as the Redemptorists (Liguorians) and eventually to readmission of the Jesuits. Church supervision of education was gradually restored. The supreme control of the state, however, including that in the field of ecclesiastical education, remained unshaken. The new governmental course meant only recognition of the Church and of religious life in general as the basic foundation of a sound and stable political order. It did not imply any general idea of religious revival. The system, being opposed to any potentially popular movement, even of a strictly spiritual nature, viewed both allegedly liberal and missionary-crusade tendencies with suspicion that was different only in degree. Thus the Catholic rationalist theologians Bernard Bolzano and Joseph Michael Fesl lost their lectureships. A romantic Catholicism—the sweeping intellectual

271

principles and objectives of which conflict with the concept of domestic equilibrium—did not fare well either. The powerful apostle of domestic mission and broad religious revivalism, Clemens Hofbauer, had to suffer from much administrative chicanery. Nevertheless, while the policies of the Metternich system in the religious sphere were dictated by expediency, this was not the same as Machiavellian cynicism. Religion, while interpreted in a rather mundane fashion, remained a primary aim of policy, not merely a means of ensuring its success.[13]

If religious revival as a spiritual movement was suspect not because of its ideological content but because of the potentially dangerous implications of any kind of mass appeal, an intellectualism based not primarily on religious, or even necessarily on liberal, tenets appeared even more dangerous. In the broad sphere of restriction or suppression of intellectual freedom it was indeed most difficult to recognize the existence of a concept of equilibrium encompassing the heritage of the Enlightenment.

If the system is viewed from the standpoint of a (so to speak) merely quantitative analysis, it can be admitted, however, that the system did not infringe indiscriminately upon the extent of public education. On the contrary, one can even recognize here in a limited area a moderate expansion. Contrary to popular belief, this expansion applied particularly to higher education. As to general elementary education, the parish priests regained supervision of village schools, the ecclesiastic deans that of school districts. They in turn were supervised by the diocesan bishops. Over-all control remained, however, with the government. In regard to elementary public education this meant, even in a purely administrative sense, a step backward from the concept of public education as shaped by the Maria Theresan and Josephine reforms.

As to higher secondary education the number of *Gymnasien* with a strictly humanistic curriculum, largely but not exclusively under ecclesiastic superintendents, was increased. The university character of the *lycées* in Graz, Innsbruck, Lwów, and Olomuc was definitely established. Technical institutions of university rank were set up in Prague (1812) and Vienna (1851). The curriculum of the law schools benefited appreciably from the promulgation of the outstanding legislative works of the period, the code of criminal law of 1803 and the superb civil code of 1811. As pointed out previously, a large measure of the credit for these reforms goes to the preparatory work of the Josephine era.[14]

In regard to the more important question of the spirit of education, in particular higher education, free research, and the closely connected question of civil liberties, the following considerations raise serious problems. As Srbik rightly points out, the government was here primarily concerned with three issues—the activities of the secret societies, academic freedom in the broadest sense, as well as freedom of the press.[15] The first problem is undoubtedly outright political in character. The government in regard to true or alleged revolutionary dangers—particularly in German, Italian, and Polish affairs—took precautionary preventive as well as more active measures. We know from the diaries or the memoirs of Anton von Prokesch-Osten, Gentz, Grillparzer, J. F. Castelli, and many others that here the mere desire for privacy was very often taken as highly suspicious secrecy. We know too, on the other hand, that the stern measures against the *Burschenschaften* all over the Germanies only exaggerated actually existing dangers. We know above all, as was pointed out clearly enough by Gentz and Prokesch in particular, that it was rather naïve to regard the activities of secret societies as the main source of political Liberalism and nationalism. Certainly there is little evidence of governmental compromise and of the equilibrium policy here. Nevertheless, it is true that the national issue, particularly among the national groups with an independent political history, was to a certain degree fed and directed by secret organizations. If this was not true to the same extent of the liberal-constitutional currents, recognition of the difference was not easy, though certainly it was possible for more brilliant political thinkers even in the early Restoration period.

As to the larger issue of intellectual freedom in general, Metternich declared in 1838 with impressive frankness:

I distinguish between thinking, speaking, writing, printing. Thinking? Yes, that is free; man is born free. Speaking? Here the distinction must be made as to whether one intends to exchange ideas or to teach. In the first case, one has to determine whether one speaks before many, in the second case [presumably that of talking before large audiences and teaching] the state always has to exercise rigid control. Writing is free like thinking; it is merely a recording of thought. Yet it is a differ-

ent and quite peculiar thing with printing. There the
state has to draw the narrow restrictions which we call
censorship. Either freedom of the press or the most
severe censorship. Nothing in between, as it exists
abroad. When Louis XVIII proclaimed freedom of the
press in the Charter, I said: Either it is an inborn right
or it is not: if it is the first, one need not [expressly]
concede it; if it is not, one must not [concede it]. *Sic.*[16]

This precious piece of dialectics—which dissects the general concept of thought into a permissible because not provable liberty
of thinking, a private and public speech, free recording for one's
own "consumption," and strictly controlled printing—might
easily be considered an example of that hypocrisy which Schopen-
hauer calls the bow of vice to virtue. Such an interpretation is
based chiefly upon the sad effect of the Metternich policy in regard to the suppression of free intellectual communication between Austrian and foreign, particularly German scholarship,
strict university control, rigid preventive censorship with a corollary of objectionable police supervision, and denunciations by
confidential informers.

Yet the sincerity, indeed the whole *raison d'être*, of the Metternich system in the intellectual sphere must be measured primarily not by its effects but by its motivations. In its unequivocal
opposition to radical change and the disturbance of the equilibrium in domestic and foreign politics, the system feared two
main forces—liberal, democratic, Jacobin, or outright national
mass movements, as well as intellectual programs leading potentially to such movements. That the second danger should appear to
be greater than the first seems paradoxical, but actually it is not.
Austria in her stage of political development under Francis I
(except for the irredenta of Polish and Italian frontier territories)
could hardly have been considered a likely soil for mass uprisings
such as those of the French Revolution. In any case, the social
stratification of the empire, with its scanty middle-class representation, the discrepancy between the cultural standards of the
various national groups, and the lack of appeal of Western
political reform philosophy, in depth as well as in breadth could
hardly be said to offer favorable conditions for widespread Jacobin
uprisings.

As to the true or alleged dangers deriving from genuine or

seemingly radical intellectualism, the situation looked quite different. According to the government, the possibility could not be excluded that movements directed by small radical circles might claim to represent a nonexistent conscious *volonté générale* as actually happened in 1848. Thus they would gain an inordinate influence, which could eventually give them control of the body politic. To be sure, neither Gentz nor Metternich in opposing these forces meant to defend the true will of the people against that of small pressure groups. They thought quite consistently in terms of the interest of the state, not of majorities of people. To them the two were quite different. In any case, they considered themselves sincere defenders of the common good, which must not be disturbed by the influence of radical minorities. Thus while the policy of the Metternich regime in regard to the problem of intellectual freedom was harsh, at times cruel, and on the whole detrimental to the evolutionary development of Austrian culture, it lacked neither consistency nor even sincerity. Even the weakest link in the system, the fight against true or alleged intellectual radicalism, could be defended, not merely rationalized, as an outgrowth of the concept of equilibrium as diametrically opposed to that of radical change.

Another line of thought brought forward in the intellectual sphere presents a more baffling problem. The Franciscan era was in many ways one of cultural brilliance in Austria. Metternich's policies, the dialectics of Gentz, the philosophy of Adam Müller, the aesthetic theory of Friedrich Schlegel, are controversial, though their intellectual level to say the least is respectable. Yet the literary production of Grillparzer, Stifter, Raimund, Nestroy, Lenau, is neither controversial nor merely respectable but clearly admirable. Even lesser literary lights of the pre-March periods, like Anastasius Grün, Zedlitz, Feuchtersleben, and Charles Sealsfield (Postl) rank higher than the writers of the enlightened and the early Franciscan era before the Metternich system took definite shape. The cultural rise would appear even more impressive if this analysis covered the period up to 1848 and was not confined to the earlier pre-March period—that is to say, roughly up to the July revolution of 1830. Even so, the entire work of Beethoven and Schubert falls within that earlier Austrian pre-March period.

Nobile and Kornhäusel, leading architects of the Austrian Biedermeier style (to mention only a few names in other fields), do not of course belong in the same class, even in their own spheres, but their work also compares well with the achievements of the past generation. The earlier paintings of the young Schwind, as well as those of Waldmüller and the sculptor Zauner, definitely surpass them in the formative arts. The same applies to the well-deserved early fame of the Austrian Medical School and the even earlier achievements of the great codifiers and commentators of the Franciscan legislative works. The last, with the possible exception of certain works of architecture, are the only chief and major creations of the period directly associated with the Josephine tradition.

In hardly any other field does either the character of the cultural contribution of Josephinism or its limited influence on the Franciscan era help much to explain how such great cultural attainments were reached under Francis I in an intellectual climate that was so unfavorable to independent thought. It may be held that great achievements in certain spheres, above all in music, could be explained as isolated phenomena only vaguely connected with the *Zeitgeist*. This line of reasoning could be accepted if such outstanding cultural achievements had come to the fore only in specific areas. The high general level of cultural creation requires also a general explanation.

Two superficially suggestive theories may be easily dismissed. One is that intellectual progress in Austria is to be interpreted as a protest movement against the system, stimulated by ideological friction; the other, diametrically opposed, is that it is the cultural outgrowth of the system. The first assumption is clearly refuted by the facts. While the major philosophical, religious, and literary trends of the time certainly do not reflect faithfully the ideology of the system, they do not oppose it directly. By and large they lean more to the conservative than to the liberal side. Even severe critics of the regime, like Grillparzer, show a far more detached attitude than does the radical liberalism of the German *Jungdeutsche* movement.[17] Only the work of lesser literary figures like Anastasius Grün could be classified as direct protest literature against the spirit of the system. The earlier, faintly liberal, moderately nationalist literature is directed against Bonapartist rather than Franciscan absolutism.[18]

As to the second supposition, it would be equally wrong to assume that the regime intentionally furthered cultural activities, except those of a strictly professional character and in a modest way the formative arts. In this connection the interests of some aristocratic and now also patrician burgher families must be mentioned, limited as their active support of the arts appears if compared to that of the aristocracy and ecclesiastical hierarchy in the Baroque era. It is not any decline in the cultural interests of the top strata of society that is to blame here, but a change in the whole social structure. Sponsorship of art by the great of the realm as the main source of cultural activities had declined with the definitive ascendancy of bureaucratic centralism over political feudalism. The effects of the rising Industrial Revolution on urban society made this development very obvious. Gradually aristocratic and high ecclesiastical leadership began to be replaced in furthering the arts by the healthy development of cultural interests in the middle class.

The situation in regard to general literary and scholarly endeavors is more complex. Here the restrictions imposed by the regime were strong enough to bar almost completely from Austria the influence of as vigorous a movement as that of Young Germany and to curtail the free pursuit of historical and philosophical studies severely. The well-known fact that Heine's poetry and his and Börne's political writings were practically unobtainable in Austria while they were secretly enjoyed by Metternich and Gentz represents a cynical flaw in the policy of the regime's "brain trust" that is in a way more disturbing than the intellectual narrow-mindedness of the emperor and his immediate entourage.

The practical effect of these differences in aesthetic judgment within the regime's top leadership was, however, negligible. In any event, the many administrative chicaneries, of which the admittedly rather sensitive Grillparzer complains in his autobiography and diaries, cannot be excused simply by the fact that the quietism of the pre-March period provided a kind of sheltered existence for nonpolitical literature. It is senseless to say that Grillparzer could hardly have created greater works than he did even in a freer atmosphere. What counts is not what he might have done under other circumstances but that he was prevented from writing all he wanted and in the way that he wanted. After all, it is the specific curse of a system of preventive censorship that the harm it inflicts on those subjected to its rules can never be measured, since the ideas suppressed by it may never see the light of day. To be sure, this harm might have been far greater if the cultural policy of the regime had been more ruthless than it actually was. Yet this is not the issue at stake. The fact that the system in the cultural field might have been more harmful does not obscure the fact that it was harmful.

It is a commonplace truth that the literary flowering of German Romanticism and Classicism did stimulate literary activities in Austria. On the other hand (a fact which is less frequently recognized) the exemplary prose style cultivated in Austrian administration, law, free professions, and social relations in general also stimulated German literary conditions. But over and above this, the cultural achievements of the Austro-Germans are in a very real sense the products of the specific conditions of the Austrian soil, products ripened in a setting certainly not favorable to the promotion of free thought, but nevertheless quite congenial to the evolution of the Austrian tradition. This means simply that the impact of this cultural heritage of Austria, situated as she was at the crossroads of many lands, peoples, institutions, mores, and ideas, must be fully recognized. Of all the great currents of ideas that have blown across the Alps, the Enlightenment was particularly unfit to honor this heritage. This is not, as a truly reactionary interpretation will have it, primarily due to the content of the enlightened reforms, though the excess of enlightened zeal at points is obvious. It is rather a consequence of the Enlightenment's methods of intellectual operation. Any movement primarily concerned with the subject matter of change —i.e., in the content of reform—will necessarily take a dim view of reflection, contemplation, and quiet observation, of the study of phenomena as they are. Its attention is focused almost exclusively on the question of how these phenomena ought to operate. Such a movement is, in the terminology of a great political scientist Hans Kelsen, concerned with the *Soll Ordnung*, the "thou shalt" order, not the *Seins Ordnung*, the order of "being."[19]

The significance of this kind of thought, "enlightened" thought, in the evolution of mankind—in its positive aspects deeply connected with the development of the great religious systems—should by no means be denied. Such phases of thinking unquestionably play a vital part in human history. Yet whatever the merits of these periods and whatever the obvious spiritual and political dangers they may have to face, they are by their very nature uncongenial to great secular literary-artistic achievements. They definitely lack the elements of reflection, contemplation, and quiet observation, which are and always will remain intrinsic elements of artistic creation. These elements will have their day in the eras of human activities that precede or follow those of reforming zeal, in the periods when the order of "being" and not the order of "shall be" is the focus of artistic attention. This is a major reason why the late post-counterreformatory Baroque as well as the Classic-Romantic era surpasses the literary-artistic achievement of the Enlightenment in aesthetic value. Restrictions imposed by any regime on freedom of thought may to some extent divert the process of artistic creation from its course, but short of physical destruction, they will not destroy the flower of creation based on the aesthetic supremacy that the study of the order of "being" holds over the order of "shall."[20]

While the general level of cultural pursuits under the Metternich system is on the whole determined by much larger issues than that of the specific merits or demerits of the regime itself, the situation in the legal-administrative field is rather the reverse. Here it is quite obvious that the government has a very direct responsibility. However, it should be clear that this responsibility rests not primarily with the system as characterized above. Long before the elevation of Metternich to the position of State Chancellor in 1821, and even prior to his appointment as Minister of Foreign Affairs in 1809, the basic course of the regime in legal-administrative questions was firmly though not always consistently established. The Metternich system is an intellectual concept instrumental in the pursuit of domestic and foreign policies according to specific experiences and predictions. Its legal administrative foundations are based, however, on a curious combination of merely pragmatic and to a point also experimental expediency, held together under the more paralyzing than unifying bond of Franciscan absolutism as developed in the first decade of the emperor's reign.[21] Krones, with little exaggeration, puts it quite succinctly: "Metternich cannot be held responsible for the regime of state absolutism. He was not its creator, but merely its agent in foreign affairs. In the internal administration the emperor kept a firm hold on the oar. Metternich, the diplomatic 'virtuoso,' would also have put up with a constitutional regime; but to prepare the ground for it would have been quite foreign to his nature. Habit and the belief in its usefulness tend to become the strongest power. Out of them grows the maxim, the dogma: It must be this way and not otherwise."[22] This remark certainly does not represent the entire intellectual range of Metternich's influence, but it indicates his actual and potential flexibility as to means to be employed to preserve and strengthen the system of equilibrium. To Metternich and Gentz, the system was an end in itself, a terminal goal. To the emperor, it was merely a device to preserve the principle of absolutism, which antedates the ideas of his leading statesman and that statesman's principal intellectual adviser. Beyond this aim to preserve the imperial power intact and to secure the Great Power position of Austria, there is no dominant idea traceable in the emperor's personal policy.

To be sure, this aim of imperial domination and Great Power claims was not a negligible one. But the complete indifference to strengthening the *raison d'être* of the regime in line with the religious and social reformulation of the conservative position, in which this era of Central European brilliance otherwise abounds, paralyzed Austrian conditions more than any other aspect of the Metternich system. The emperor's philosophy (if it can be called a philosophy) penetrated only the surface of institutions and social concepts, and anyone might serve the policy of government as long as he did not threaten the principle of legitimate absolutism. This helps to explain the curious zigzag course of Austrian administration, with its intermittent resort to Josephine forms of institutions, mercantilist doctrines, and semi-feudal decrees. As long as these and other devices served imperial absolutism, they might be employed at discretion, since their ideological foundations in themselves were meaningless to the sovereign.

The Franciscan administrative regime in its early period is actually more closely linked with Josephinism than with the even briefer regime of Leopold II. In its reaffirmation and strengthening of Hungarian autonomy, in its concessions to Transylvanian and Serb-Illyrian demands for self-rule, in its limited and transitory pledges to the Bohemian Estates and to the historic claims of the crownlands in general, as well as in its abandonment of the German state-language idea, the Leopoldian government had already decisively reversed the trend toward the unified-empire concept. No leading political doctrine but the sound determination to save the Habsburg lands from impending revolution was involved in these changes.

With the ascent of Francis, the Josephine concept of the centralized Habsburg empire was taken up again. The reason for this new reversal of policy was not primarily the fact that Francis had received his training in the art of absolutist government from Joseph rather than from his father,[23] but in the desire to refortify absolutist government. There was more likelihood of achieving this through a would-be streamlined centralism than through a regime reverting to the idea of the historical Estates' rights. What appeared to be better even than Josephine centralism was a political structure that would preserve the Josephine absolutist form but at the same time would separate it from its enlightened ideological content. This, in a nutshell, is the philosophy of early Franciscan centralism.

Reform merely for the sake of preservation, lacking as it does any specific ideological direction, is a poor incentive for improvement in any field. Hence the unsystemmatic but not merely pragmatic efforts of the Franciscan administrative reforms under Counts Colloredo, Saurau, and in a way the elder Stadion, who were by no means incompetent but, in their powers, severely restricted chief advisers in domestic affairs.* In the very first year of Francis's reign the administration of the Bohemian and Austro-German hereditary lands, and the Hungarian-Transylvanian administrative-financial agenda as well, were subordinated under supreme central agencies. It was actually planned to have this centralization go even farther than the Josephine reforms. Because of pressing political expediency, governmental affairs in the Austrian Netherlands and the Austro-Italian territories were, however, expressly exempted in 1793 from this co-ordination process. Between 1793 and 1797 the supreme political and financial administrations in the bulk of the Habsburg lands were again separated. On the other hand, political and judicial matters were linked together. In 1801—the high-tide period of Franciscan centralism—the supreme financial-political and judicial administrations were merged; the state council was abolished and replaced by a state and conference ministry divided roughly into departments of foreign affairs, defense, and domestic administration. Yet as early as 1802 judicial agenda were again separated from the general political-financial administration. The state and conference ministry was abolished in 1808 and the state council restored. In 1814 it was supplemented by a conference council that was to handle problems which the state council felt unable to settle. Also specific issues of major importance were to be assigned to that body directly by the emperor.

*Count Francis Colloredo, Minister of State, former tutor of the emperor; Count Francis Saurau, Minister of Police Agenda; Count Philipp Stadion, Minister of Foreign Affairs and in charge of general administrative reforms.

The supreme decision in everything still rested with the emperor, whose decisions were usually handed down to the administrative agencies without explanatory comment. This perhaps more than anything else impeded the conduct of a policy according to strict utilitarian principles. The emperor unquestionably was a man of great industry, of not less than average ability, and was endowed with a good deal of common sense. Yet the task he wanted to perform would have overtaxed the strength of a man of qualities far superior to those of even a Joseph II. Joseph, whether one agrees or, as is more often the case, disagrees with his policies, had the ability to see the problems of government in the context of definite principles and ideas. Francis I, except on the all-important issue of absolutist rule, was singularly incapable of this and, it must be added, unwilling as well. Beyond the overall objective of his rule, Francis did not want to see issues in the light of ideas—any ideas, whether enlightened, liberal, or conservative—but only the facts of the case. Thus he was unable to give directions and to steer a steady course in those most difficult times. Actually, the best that can be said of this reign is that in its second half the emperor yielded sufficient influence to Metternich, Gentz, and eventually in a more pragmatic way in the domestic administration to Count Kolowrat, to provide the regime with broader ideological foundations.

As to the earlier Franciscan regime, before Metternich's influence became strong, the only major sphere of governmental activities wherein the situation was somewhat brighter is the judicial sphere. The Josephine judicial administration remained on the whole intact, and the range of patrimonial jurisdiction was actually further restricted. On the truly impressive legislative achievements previously noted, the code of criminal law of 1803 and that of civil law of 1811, much preliminary work had been done under Joseph. But some very telling acts must be recognized here. The continuation and completion of the Josephine judicial reforms, unlike the work in many other fields, did not merely preserve the frame of the reform ideas; it developed and crystallized their content more clearly. The major exception pertains to certain parts of the criminal legislation. Yet this is a positive and creditable exception. The final version of the Franciscan code was more humane than Josephine legislation, which, with an often callous disregard for the dignity of the individual, sacrificed without any mercy the life of the guilty to what Joseph deemed to be the common good. Even the more than questionable methods of Franciscan criminal procedure cannot obscure this change for the better.

Nor is the positive character of Franciscan civil legislation accidental—in glaring contrast to so many aspects of the regime's actions. It is based on the needs of an increasingly urbanized society in which the burgher played a more important part. It offered this burgher full protection as to his civil status and property. At the same time the regime was anxious to limit this strictly to the domain of private affairs—hence the term *Privatrecht*. The laudable principles of the civil code were not, to be sure, applied to that of civil liberties in general—i.e., to political freedom in the sense of the citizenry's evolutionary participation in governmental affairs, whether of a political or merely an economic nature.

As to this economic sphere, the record of the government is again largely unsatisfactory. True, the difficulties that the regime had to face during the war period from 1792 to 1815 were enormous. The wear and tear of that era on the Austrian economy could not have been prevented by anybody. Yet the lack of planning in the matter of war expenses and repair of war damages is depressing. Since neither foreign nor domestic loans could help to any appreciable degree, the government took the easy course of outright inflation. Between 1762 and 1795 the amount of money bills in circulation increased by 300 per cent; in 1806 it had increased by not less than 3,700 per cent.[24] A consequence of these conditions, accentuated by the outcome of the war of 1809, was the notorious state bankruptcy of 1811, which reduced the paper money in circulation to one-fifth of its nominal value. However, the war of 1813 led to a new increase of money bills. Inflation, but not the general impoverishment following in its wake, was stopped only with the end of the war period, reduction of military expenses, and receipt of indemnities from France.

Criticism of the way in which the state bankruptcy of 1811 was handled is widespread. It includes charges not only of glaring inefficiency but of corruption as well. Even if the second are entirely discounted, the fact remains that the main burden in 1811 was put on the shoulders of the lower urban classes, including many white-collar workers, whereas the big-estate owners were let off relatively easily. The obvious method of fighting inflation primarily by an equitable income tax was not resorted to. Neither could the queer mixture of direct and indirect taxes levied during the war period in the form of head, trade, general-property taxes and a crude consumption duty on edibles solve the desperate financial situation. The final solution was expected to be found in a general land tax proclaimed in 1817 and introduced with great and cumbersome regional differentiations on a provisional basis in 1819. The problem of recognition of personal services, servitudes, and tithes paid by the peasants to the lords as general tax deductions was not permanently settled until 1848. In general, the great Maria-Theresan–Josephine reform work in regard to the emancipation of the peasants, though it was not completely undone, remained a truncated torso up to the time of the revolutionary legislation of 1848 and that of the following neo-absolutist period.

Indirectly, the introduction of general conscription, necessitated by the war period, alleviated the lot of the peasant at least in a specific sphere. To make this stringent innovation more acceptable, lifetime military-service obligations for the common soldier now had to be reduced to terms ranging from eight to fourteen years. Even more important, the service exemptions for a substantial part of the higher and middle strata of society were restricted, though not eliminated. On the other hand, some new exemptions were created for landowning peasants and in general for young men on whose work the livelihood of their families depended. The Austrian peasant benefited at least indirectly from this transformation of the army into a socially somewhat more representative force. However, these reforms, which were born only of understandable military necessity and not yet in line with much farther-reaching measures of a similar kind in Prussia, did not and were not intended to strike at the core of the fundamental problem of lord-peasant relations.[25]

It is quite clear that the evolution of a free peasant class did not fit into the Franciscan system. It is more difficult to understand why the industrial and commercial policy of the regime did not progress beyond the neo-mercantilist theories of Sonnenfels. Austrian expansion of industry and communications under Francis was not negligible. In a way the realm had even benefited for a short time from the Napoleonic Continental Blockade, which temporarily eliminated powerful British competition from overseas. The fall of Napoleon and the end of the war period brought the cessation of a somewhat artificial boom. The government hoped to prolong it, however, by a consistent policy of high protective tariffs. By and large, however, Austrian industrial economy, still based primarily not on large industrial plants but on the work of small craft shops, had not reached a productive capacity that could seriously compete with British industry and commerce. It was not so much the import from foreign markets as the Austrian intrastate custom lines that impeded industrial development.* A great Austrian customs union, with moderate tariffs to give room and time for gradual development and to keep prices of needed foreign raw materials and industrial goods relatively low, would have been the need of the time rather than the mechanical application of economic principles developed under different conditions in the West. Yet just here, where a more conservative policy in regard to internal commercial relations would have been largely justified, the government in spite of Gentz's† warnings could not extricate itself from the Josephine pattern.[26]

e. *The Metternich System and Nationalism*

The same is in a way true of the complex problem of rising nationalism, in regard to which Josephinism had so conspicuously failed. A chief extenuating factor in the evaluation of the indiscriminate German, though not yet German-nationalist-controlled, centralization effort under Joseph is that Josephinism in the national sphere was treading on new and entirely unfamiliar ground. The same excuse cannot be made for the Franciscan regime. Radical Jacobin nationalism, the rise of German nationalist sentiment during the Napoleonic wars, and academic national radicalism after the wars, political Romanticism, early Pan-Slavonic trends, the whole Slavonic cultural Renaissance, and

---

*Hungary and her *partes adnexae (regna socia)*—Croatia-Slavonia, Transylvania, and Fiume—and also Istria, the Austro-Italian free ports, and the territory around Brody in Galicia formed separate customs areas. The Austrian-Galician and Austro-Italian (Lombardy-Venice) customs lines were, however, abandoned in 1828.

†Gentz, an early and enthusiastic adherent of Adam Smith, had modified many of his views, especially in regard to the specific conditions of the Austrian empire. In particular he denied the danger of British industrial competition and retaliatory tariffs. More controversial are his later preferences for indirect taxation and his opinion that the elimination of internal customs lines within the German confederation would be impractical. (On Gentz's economic theories and reflections see W. Roscher, *Geschichte der Nationalökonomik in Deutschland* [Munich, 1874] 756-63.)

A Study in Austrian Intellectual History

Magyar reform claims had come into the open. Even prior to the Greek, Belgian, and Polish independence uprisings and the Italian irredenta activities, no European government could plead ignorance in these matters. It would be an unfair oversimplification to assume that the Metternich system disregarded entirely their political significance. Yet it is not unfair to say that it either did not understand their true psychological character or, where it comprehended, failed to act on its insight. This applies far more to domestic than to foreign policies. The fight against the national issue in international relations can hardly be separated from the concept of the conservative equilibrium of powers. To condemn it flatly would mean to judge it on the basis of principles that were in direct contradiction to those for which the regime stood. A more appropriate criticism would have to be based primarily on methods and procedures. The great lines of thought, as applied (not without flexibility) in regard to time and place, will hardly be approved in the light of today. Yet, on the whole, notwithstanding the controversial military interventions in revolutionary national-liberal movements, they can be comprehended as emanations of over-all policies intended to ensure peaceful Great Power equilibrium.

The domestic problem is quite different. Here from the standpoint of immanent criticism two basic lines of policy would have been compatible with the philosophy of the regime. One might have led to an evolutionary modification of Josephine centralism, with national representation under the supreme German-directed authority of the crown and its councils. The other alternative would have been to establish a firm link with the older Estates tradition and to build a national organization within the historically well-established frame. To be sure, a rejuvenation of the medieval Estates idea in a more modern representative setting would still have been based on the concept of the old historic-political entities of the once independent or semi-independent Habsburg lands. The concepts of ethnic nationalism crossing ancient boundaries would have been little heeded in any case. Yet again it could not be expected that early-nineteenth-century political thought and practice would be able to take cognizance of problems fully recognized only two generations later.

Either the concept of modified centralism or a rejuvenated Estates idea, as promoted by the German-Austrians Andrian-Werburg and Möring in the later pre-March period and by

Hartig in and after 1848,* would have been firmly linked to a strong Austrian political tradition. Neither of them would have collided with the basic philosophy of the system. Yet the government by implication rejected both of them. Neither did it look for a conceivable compromise between the two ideas. Following more or less the motto that no solution is better than any solution, it let things run their course, resorting only under the pressure of events to haphazard measures.

Francis I undoubtedly was deeply conscious of the imperial dignity of his House and person. Yet in this one respect, not unlike Joseph he valued the specific historical traditions of his individual realms but little. A centralized absolutism separated from its enlightened Josephine tradition probably appeared to him the best way to tackle the national problem as well as the administrative one. It has been noted that Franciscan administrative centralism in the early part of his reign failed. This was not due to mere technicalities but was primarily a consequence of the fact that, in view of the great historical experience of the Maria-Theresan–Josephine reform era, strict centralism could no longer be linked with despotic absolutism in its late-seventeenth- and early-eighteenth-century sense. In other words, the emperor could not build up centralism without including Josephinism. Since he rejected the spirit of that, he had to modify centralism, and here the Estates idea obviously suggested itself as the possible solution. While the Estates concept could be separated from the dominant influence of enlightened ideology, the problem arose as to whether it might not lead to a deviation from the concept of absolutism.

The government proceeded under the shadow of this specter, the most terrible that could be raised in the reign of Francis I. The Estates institutions, though formally still recognized, were thus further reduced in power. In doing so, the government, it is true, was merely following a path opened not by the Josephine but even earlier by the Maria Theresan reforms. Yet need for reforms was precisely the reason why the empress and her eminent son had restricted Estates rights. As in other aspects of his regime, Francis followed in many ways the formal pattern of the Maria-Theresan–Josephine administration but reversed its spirit. The old Estates, composed of secular and ecclesiastical lords, lower

*Victor von Andrian-Werburg, vice-president of St. Paul's Church Assembly; Artillery Captain Karl Möring, also a member of the assembly; Count Francis Hartig, governor of Lombardy and later "state and conference minister." All three were distinguished political writers.

nobility, and town representatives, had impeded reform, hence the previous curtailment of their functions in the enlightened reform era. Later restrictions of their limited functions, as they were introduced by administrative practice rather than by law, were based on fear not of their actual power but of their potential expansion in the direction of a more representative composition. The declining political significance of the Estates since the beginning of administrative defeudalization under Ferdinand II and their very limited popular appeal facilitated the further curtailment of their rights under Francis. The people knew something about the character and composition of the socially unrepresentative Estates; they were hardly aware of the possibility of their reform on a broader basis and the implications of that reform.

The exception that in a way confirms these facts is Hungary. The far-reaching autonomy wrested by the Hungarian Estates from Leopold II could quell the revolutionary threat produced by the precipitate Josephine reform. Yet the Hungarian Estates could succeed only if these rights were not to be rescinded at an opportune moment in the only country where they truly represented the will of the political nation—even though this political nation stood only for a segment of the Hungarian peoples as a whole. Francis I lacked the power but not the will to revoke or at least to circumvent these rights. The convocation of the Diet in 1825, thereafter to be called into session at regular three-year intervals after an unlawful thirteen-year recess, was certainly not evidence of a reversal of the general imperial Estates policy. It proved only that, with the spirit of early Kossuthianism in the offing, the crown had to yield where the Estates stood for something more than a medieval tradition. The Hungarian experience explains but does not justify the Franciscan Estates policy in the emperor's other realms.[27]

It is one of the most characteristic features of the whole Franciscan regime that such simple and narrow considerations as those outlined above frequently led to the same result as do the subtle, often brilliant thoughts of the champions of the Metternich system. This does not represent primarily a victory of self-assured obstinacy over intellectual programs. The emperor as well as the architects of the system knew quite clearly what they wanted and why. But Francis often did not realize fully the implications and obstacles that the imperial policy might have to face. It was quite different with Metternich, Gentz, and even to a point with the far less brilliant representative of the territorial aristocracy, the Bohemian aristocrat Count Kolowrat. These men realized the dangers that beset their course, and "thus the native hue of resolution is sicklied o'er with the pale cast of thought." This is particularly true in the case of the national issues. In the end Metternich returned to the imperial policy of inactivity. But this policy, where the emperor was concerned one of simple predetermined conviction, was for Metternich one of resignation. After much subtle and often brilliant deliberation he did not dare to take the risk of action.

The State Chancellor was faced with the difficult task of settling the gradually evolving problem of political nationalism without impairing the key position of an Austrian empire in the center of a European combination of powers. Whether rightly or wrongly, but certainly not without reasons worthy of careful consideration, he believed that the German element in the monarchy would be the most likely to hold together the heterogeneous realms of the Habsburg power. Living as he did in a time that was not yet familiar with the devices and implications of various systems of national autonomy and the character of ethnic nationalism, he knew at least that neither a system of streamlined Josephine centralism nor one of federalism on the basis of the historic-political entities crossing national boundaries could offer a fully satisfactory solution. He realized further that the Hungarian question represented problems per se which could not be treated on the same basis as those of lesser entities. He has been frequently, and on the whole rightly, criticized for his profound disregard of the Italian national issue and at points, with less justification, for his uninspiring attitude toward the complex problem of the German Confederation. In fairness to Metternich it should be pointed out that the Austro-Italian provinces, Galicia, and the Germanies could not be seen by him primarily from the angle of the national issue but as outposts and bastions of the precarious Austrian Great Power position hemmed in by Russia, Prussia, and France. Neither should the positive element of an in many ways passive and unimaginative nationality policy be overlooked: a timid and suspicious attitude in regard to the national problem in general prevented at least an equally dangerous deviation in the opposite direction—that is, subservience to any specific national force, to the detriment of the others. In the light of the sinister Pan-Slav ideologies then emerging in Russia and the possible dangers of a Pan-German course, which in Metternich's time would have been emotionally much stronger than in Joseph's, this point must not be overlooked.

Early vacillations notwithstanding, Metternich also avoided the error of assuming the existence of an Austrian nation to be promoted almost inevitably by way of an artificial over-all Austrian national idea in a Jacobin or ethnic sense. In the foreground of the Chancellor's political thinking appeared now the concept of the Austrian state and the Austrian-state idea embracing many nationalities, bound together by a German-directed cultural and administrative superstructure under the supreme union of the crown. This may still have appeared as a controversial concept to many, but nobody could claim that it was an arbitrary one. It certainly was not a constructive approach to the national problem; on the other hand, this concept did not eliminate the historical realities of the traditions of the Habsburg lands. It denied the notion of the integrated, fully centralized state, but in Srbik's words, "we can call the Austria which Metternich looked for the decentralized unified state."[28] Metternich finally denied in the political sphere the whole evolutionary idea of constitutional government in the modern sense. This held true not only on the central level but on the lower one of the historical political entities as well—partial concessions in the administrative field notwithstanding. As Srbik again rightly points out, the Hungarian exception and the concessions to Magyarism imply here only recognition of an existing force, a force based on traditional constitutional government, but not on popular sovereignty.[29] It may be added that it means only a concession to a force too strong to overcome; it does not mean insight into the necessity of reform but insight into the limitations of executive central power.

This lack of spiritual readiness for genuine reform applies of course not only to the Hungarian question. Only feeble attempts were made to create an imperial consultative council in legislative affairs in conjunction with a ministerial conference to deal with administrative agenda. Metternich's provisions for separate advisory consultants in Hungarian affairs and a division of a Ministry of Interior into Bohemian-Moravian-Galician, Austrian (i.e., German-Austrian), Illyrian (Southern Slav and Italian) chancelleries quite apart from the autonomous Hungarian administration did not succeed either. They were weakened in their organization by imperial ordinance, and even more so by imperial practice. Yet even if the projects of the State Chancellor had been fully realized, they would by no means have resulted in national autonomous and constitutional government in the modern sense. Again from the standpoint of immanent criticism, Metternich cannot be blamed for the rejection of principles that collided with the basic philosophy of his system. It was naïve to assume, however, that a feeble and soul-less approximation to a separation-of-power system and federal-representative organization could bridge the abyss between the principles of the system and the rising demands of modern ideas. It is not in the formulation and execution of the policy of his system, which will always be respected in its way as a model of clear thinking, but in his pseudo-concessions and attempts to compromise superficially with new conditions that the Chancellor was at his worst.

This applies also to the unsuccessful attempts to revise rather than to reform the Hungarian Estates constitution, the failure to co-operate in time with the enlightened and moderate leaders of the nation, Count Stephen Széchenyi and Francis Deák. Though perhaps in a less conspicuous way, the same is true of the series of lost opportunities to support the Bohemian and German-Austrian moderate enlightened reformers Count Leo Thun, Francis Palacký, Victor von Andrian-Werburg, and others of equally distinguished rank. In Metternich's time, far-reaching, though to be sure imperfect solutions based on a modified concept of the historical-political entities might still have been feasible. Necessary evolutionary revisions of these solutions later on might still have been technically difficult but, since the factor of national pressure would have been greatly relieved, by no means impossible. Neither feasible nor possible, however, was the notion of tolerating up to a point the evolution of cultural-humanitarian nationalism among the empire's Slavonic peoples as a counterweight against Magyarism and Eastern Pan-Slavism, and of expecting that such movements could be stopped short of the evolution of political rights. Here the system profoundly lacked insight into the factor of continuity in history which, in several aspects of foreign policy, was one of its assets. Piecemeal reforms like the Hungarian-language regulations of 1846, which still had to resort to the Latin expedient, and the temporary and in a revolutionary way backfiring support of Ruthenian national rights against Polish nationalism do not change this picture substantially.[30] Thus altogether, many of the Chancellor's and his advisers' subtle reflections notwithstanding, the practical results of the system's sophisticated national policy flowed into the same channel as the emperor's simple and stubborn rejection of the whole issue.

Two main arguments can be brought forward here, however, in defense of the system's policy. For one thing, the results of the experiments of the two following generations in the field of Austrian nationalism cannot claim better results than Metternich's negative policy. If measured by the tragic final outcome, they are in a way far worse. In the light of the principle of continuity in history, this line of reasoning is deceptive. The problem of nationalism in Metternich's time in the monarchy was not yet the deadly issue that it was to become for later generations. There was probably no real chance of settling it even then. But there was a better chance of easing it and keeping it under control before it had assumed its integral character and had become more ominously linked with increased external imperialist pressure from abroad. The system cannot be condemned for having failed to find nonexistent perfect solutions. It can be blamed, however, for having underrated the dangerous potentialities of the national problem.

The second point to be considered in defense of Metternich on this particular issue carries much greater weight. The national question, as a genuine or alleged expression of the will of the people, is inextricably linked with the problem of popular sovereignty. Many a champion of the national idea had acted quite sincerely in the service of this issue; some others, particularly in the period of integral nationalism, have exploited it for dictatorial purposes. Yet everyone has paid at least lip-service to it. That Metternich was above such hypocrisy is certainly to his credit. Here the observations made by Heinrich Heine in 1852, though intended in a more general sense, are pertinent:

> Indeed, we might fight against Austria and fight heroically until death, sword in hand; yet most deeply we feel that we are not justified in abusing this power in words. Austria was always a frank, honest enemy, who has never denied her fight against Liberalism and who has never stopped it intermittently. Metternich has never flirted with the goddess of freedom; never in the fear of his

heart has he played the demagogue. He has never sung
Arndt's songs to Berlin beer; he has never practiced gym-
nastics on the Hasenheide;* he has never affected sancti-
monious piety. He has never shed tears with the political
prisoners while he held them in chains. One always knew
where one stood with him; one knew that one had to
watch out for him, and one did. He was always a reliable
man who neither deceived us by gracious looks nor infuriated us by private malice. One knew that he did not
act out of either love or petty hatred, but grandly in the
spirit of his system, to which Austria has remained faithful for three centuries. This is the system for which
Austria has fought against the Reformation; this is the
system for which Austria has opened the fight against
the revolution. . . .[31]

This is no negligible testimony to the character of Metternich the man on the part of one whose political philosophy was
diametrically opposed to that of the Chancellor. In a way it is
even more than that. It is by implication a testimony to the work
of Metternich the statesman as well. As a statesman he could not
be expected to act against his principles, even though it would
have shown foresight on his part if he had made serious compromises not only in the case of the national issue but in other issues
as well. He could have gone along with national reforms on the
basis of the historical-political entities without seriously endangering the *raison d'être* of his system. But nobody would have
been able to guarantee him that reform could be stopped at this
point. Even in Metternich's time such a contingency seemed
questionable. Further evolution in the direction of ethnic
nationalism linked to the organization of popular representation
within the frame of democratic constitutional government might
have prevented revolution, but, according to Metternich's philosophy, only at the price of heavy ideological sacrifice. Moreover, the whole subtle system of foreign relations so brilliantly
executed in regard to France, so precariously maintained in view
of the development of the problems of the German Confederation,
Greece, Naples, Russo-Polish aspirations, and other conflict zones,
might well have been upset. Could Metternich really have been
expected to be willing to take such a course, which might have

*An allusion to Friedrich Jahn.

diminished the dangers of an as yet uncertain revolution but which would inevitably have entailed changes that to Metternich were hardly less objectionable and dangerous than revolution itself? The answer to this question is a clear "no," a "no" that exonerates Metternich the man, justifies him even as statesman from the standpoint of immanent criticism, but in this instance condemns the system, which by implication considers both evolutionary democratic reform and revolution as equally objectionable alternatives, possibly even as equally great dangers. Metternich rightly rejected and feared revolution and its possible consequences, but he would have considered the reformed Austria that might have prevented revolution with a certain degree of probability not worth fighting for and well worth fighting against. This is the true, inevitable, and tragic impasse into which Metternich's leadership had steered Austria in regard to the most important issues facing the body politic.

f. *Nature of the Cycle*

Here it is necessary to turn back to the cyclical development in Austrian intellectual history, the central subject of this study. At the point where this analysis starts, the crisis of the later Austrian Baroque era under Leopold I, the pattern of semi-feudal government was no longer fit to serve the great administrative, economic, military, and educational needs of the time. Many of the existing institutions, therefore, had gradually to be revised. The spirit that directed these reforms was still that of the era of the religious wars, that of a feudal ideology. Reform, however, by historical necessity more than by individual volition opened the gate for the Western influence of the Enlightenment. By degrees the new philosophy of government was able to co-ordinate the political needs and will of that small part of the body politic that had a voice in public affairs.

To be sure, it was a co-ordination by degrees only. Strong opposition on the part of the Church and the landed aristocracy impeded the progress of the Enlightenment, though often for different reasons. On the other hand, the spirit of enlightened absolutism, in a way until 1780 a force of opposition as well, accelerated its pace. On several specific weighty issues it definitely threatened the evolutionary development of existing traditions. Yet both kinds of opposition, seen in retrospect, often unwittingly serve the same on the whole rather beneficial purpose. Conservative traditionalism, particularly on the part of the Church, put the brakes on a development that otherwise in the course of a century might eventually have followed the pattern of Jacobinism. Yet the policy of radical Josephine absolutism had the same effect, in a different sense. In many instances it created avoidable or unavoidable conflict, but what is more important, it also relieved pressures that under a less dynamic regime might again have exploded in the form of revolutionary Jacobinism. The fact that different currents of opposition existed in Austria did not prevent the swing of the pendulum from Baroque to Enlightenment, but each trend in its own way certainly helped limit and shorten this swing.

The brief regime of Leopold II and the earlier part of the Franciscan era still accepted this process of the institutional conversion of Austria, which had started with Leopold I and had reached its height under Joseph II. Yet in its fight against the French Revolution, the new regime reversed the spirit of the enlightened reform period. The pendulum swung back again in the other direction. It was to swing still farther back in the second part of Francis' reign, the early pre-March period. Contrary to well-established views, this was by no means due exclusively to the so-to-speak "official" political philosophy of the Restoration period. It was also largely a consequence of the fact that by this time, under profoundly changed political and intellectual conditions, the institutional pattern of Josephinism had become outworn and outdated. We now face the dominance of a regime that was conservative in spirit and embedded in an increasingly stale institutional setting.

Allowing for a limited degree of generalization, we thus face the following development: The Baroque crisis represented incipient new institutional forms controlled by conservatism. The Enlightenment injected a new spirit into these gradually reformed patterns. The early part of the reign of Francis I, resembling the Baroque period, goes back to the old spirit that henceforward should control the new institutions. In the early pre-March period the controlling conservative spirit had by and large remained the same, but the institutions had grown old. Yet by this time a dynamic force of opposition had again clearly come into the open, though it was still far from representing political power. Its diverse forms of church reformism, political Romanticism, romantic and liberal nationalism, as well as reform Liberalism of the English type, cross and recross the common party lines of right and left. All of them, however, in different ways press against the stable forces of traditional conservatism in the direction of dynamic change. The pendulum will soon reverse itself again. And again the swing of the new trends will be slowed down and checked by the rigorous forces of a conservative tradition until the pendulum once more reverses its course.

No analogy between the physical forces of nature and the forces of history is perfect. It would be a dull and shallow world indeed if the grandiose laws of inanimate nature could be applied mechanically to the inscrutable world of the human spirit. In the mind of the observer the physical pendulum is primarily associated with movement in space, the historical in time. The segments of the arc through which the mechanical pendulum passes back and forth are equal to each other in spatial distance as halves of a full swing. The distances in time through which the historical pendulum passes on either side of the nadir are by no means equal to each other. According to Newton, "actions and reactions are equal and opposite." In the realm of history, however, these forces, though opposite, are in general not equal.

As already noted in the Introduction to this study, the periods of dynamic change in Austrian history are briefer than those of quiet development on a traditional basis. The Baroque in its more stable phases—that is, after the Counter Reformation has passed its peak—lasted on for almost a century, the Austrian Enlightenment only about half that time. Whether one regards the revolution of 1848 merely as a brief though highly important interlude in a continuous political development, or as a phase in its own right, the Franciscan period and its aftermath—certainly until 1848 and possibly including the neo-absolutist period to the end of the 1850's—far outlasted the preceding enlightened and the ensuing neo-liberal period ending in the 1870's. The reasons for the unevenness of the cycle are not difficult to comprehend. In the specific setting of the Austrian tradition, the enlightened and liberal dynamic forces, conflicting as they did with established institutions and ideas, had to face an uphill fight. They encountered opposition that was not only vigorous and spontaneous but also broad and tenacious. It sapped their strength and diminished their appeal. Furthermore, the always-existing danger that dynamic evolutionary movements might lose control of their own policies and often unwittingly fall prey to unpredictable and dangerous radical tendencies played a part in stiffening the opposition. The Jacobin precedent is only one example, which was followed later by even more brutal experiences. Neither can the intangible yet certainly very potent influence of a simple historical law of inertia, working in favor of the *status quo*, be denied. There is a further point to be considered: that in times of dynamic reforms the conservative traditional forces cleared their house to some degree of anachronistic ideas and institutions and became gradually less vulnerable to attack. Even more important is the consideration that because of the pressure of radical extraneous ideas—as for instance the pressure on Josephinism at the time of the French Revolution—Austrian reform movements were forced to call a halt to such influences and moved into a precarious center position. Reform at this point had revealed the force of the radical dangers to which it might easily succumb by further continuation of its course. Its ability to resist them was widely questioned. Consequently the task of defense against these dangers gradually shifted to the trusted forces of the traditional order. All these factors limited the supremacy of reformism in time.

The conservative traditional regimes, which in consequence of such a process came to power, could expect a longer rule. The tradition that supported them may in many ways have lacked spontaneous appeal, but the penetration into depths of popular feelings was much greater and of longer standing than that of the dynamic forces in history. This penetration was wider, too. Reformism, chiefly inspired by intellectual concepts introduced from the West, had to face a serious problem of communication and could only very gradually gain broader appeal. Conservatism, on the other hand, did not rely merely on the support of those forces that held entrenched power in society, though even their backing was based not on mere social strength but to a large extent on ability to compromise at times and thus to relieve pressures. The chief stronghold of conservatism was the passivity of the teeming millions, who could not be reached, let alone be convinced, by the controversial message of reform in the brief span of time at the disposal of the reformers.

All these advantages served to strengthen another factor of great importance. Since conservatism had the advantage of time on its side, it could avoid the pitfalls of reform particularly conspicuous in the character of the Josephine era, which pressed for overhasty change as long as the going seemed good and by that nervous speed strengthened rather than hurt the challenged traditional forces. Reformism often accomplished less than it might have if it had not acted so precipitately. It did so because it felt the element of time working against it. Conservatism with time, though not unlimited time, on its side could go farther, because it moved more slowly.

The problem of the inequality of the forces of action and reaction in history does not necessarily mean that the impact of conservatism, though longer-lasting in time, was also stronger in effect than that of reformism. Neither of them should be identified simply with the concepts of political right or left, but rather with those of more stable or more dynamic forces and counterforces. Contrary to the tenets of a materialistic interpretation of history, it is assumed here that the dynamics of the reform start out not primarily from a change or from the desire for a change in social-economic conditions. The whole history of European enlightened philosophy in the eighteenth century, though connected with specific social demands, was basically heir to far more fundamental changes in the intellectual seventeenth-century world of Descartes, Hobbes, Pascal, Spinoza, Leibniz, Newton, and many others of their kind, though very few of their rank. The course of none of these men was to a measurable degree influenced by rising mercantilism, the evolution of the standing armies, the political issues of the religious wars, and other problems of profound social change, but rather by the preceding fifteenth- and sixteenth-century transition in intellectual climate. On the other hand, all future changes in the social world were strongly influenced by the methods and ideas of the great seventeenth-century philosophers and scientists.

This primacy of the spiritual forces as motivating factors gives intellectual history a dominant position in human development. The general influence of these forces outlasts and far outgrows their pale reflections and repercussions on the specific policies of any regime. Social reform in a way is just such a dim reflection and repercussion of great intellectual concepts, and so also is conservatism. The simple reason for this lies in the fact that these great intellectual concepts are not bound up with any existing or specific desired social situation, but are connected with the whole human spiritual heritage. No era in human

Le Chevalier Gentz

Friedrich von Gentz

Adam Heinrich Müller

history can thus claim that it alone has been entrusted with the monopoly of this great heritage.

It is true, however, that the leading spirits of one era or regime may have their ears closer to the ground of ideological developments than those of another do. Then and only then will the reflection of the intellectual heritage in the social order be clear and profound. The Austrian Enlightenment, in spite of its glaring political and social deficiencies, was such an era to a certain degree, and thus the intellectual influence of that period outweighs its brief duration in time. Considering its brief hey-day, the effect of its action was not commensurate with that of the preceding Baroque and coming Franciscan conservative-romantic eras. In the same way, the effect of this preceding Baroque era outweighed by far that of the still earlier Renais-sance period in Austria. Likewise, the impact of the coming Franciscan regime, the whole pre-March and the neo-absolutist periods, was much stronger than that of neo-Liberalism of the 1860's and '70's, which but for the disconnected, controversial overture of the revolution of 1848 was only a feeble, revised replica of vigorous eighteenth-century trends. Here conservatism had its ears closer to the ground on which the shining romantic, Christian, national ideas blossomed. Action and reaction again are not commensurate.

There is still another historical connection between action and reaction that carries great spiritual significance. If we dis-tinguish between the concrete institutional facts and conditions of any era and the spiritual forces which, often quite unknown to the actual rulers, control them and which are remote but clear causes, we find the following relationship: Barring extreme revo-lutionary change, the institutions and customs of any age are of course primarily influenced by the preceding one. Gradual evo-lutionary change may not alter the basic structure of established conditions substantially, and in wide fields of human activities even hardly touch upon them. This observation must be qualified to some degree in relation to the era since the industrial and agri-cultural revolutions, but it appears rather obvious in previous periods of far less rapid changes in technology. Thus the economic policies, military organization, the legal system, agricultural-production methods, to give only a few examples, were in practice changed only slightly from the late Baroque to the heights of the Maria Theresan reform period. Likewise the Franciscan administrative setup, Church and educational organization, and trade policies deviated technically not too much from those of the Josephine era. The future is built on the foundations of the recent past, though it is obviously not an exact replica of the recent past.

As to intellectual-spiritual influences in a new era, the situation is quite different. Here the future development is not simply the outgrowth of a straight and simple evolution from the recent past; it develops ideas as reaction to that past—that means, of course, to some degree in opposition to prevalent thought. One does not necessarily have to subscribe to an ontological method of thinking to acknowledge that new thought is not conceivable without a relationship with past thought. Yet as to the specific character of new phases of intellectual history, it is held here that, contrary to the true or alleged meaning of Hegelian notions, such phases owe part of their ideological heritage not so much to the recent past to which they stand in opposition as to one prior to it.

Such periods of the past are not arbitrarily chosen. Since the course of human development in time, to a point, will affect the validity of intellectual concepts in the social world, those dating back to a very remote past often can no longer serve as a practicable basis for new intellectual experiences. Furthermore, the problem of the communication of ideas after many centuries is a big stumbling block in establishing ideological connections with ancient times. Hence, more often than not new ideas thrive on the ground of the era just preceding the recent past. Again, as is *not* the case with Hegelian notions, the influence of that phase of history would then appear not equal to another and completely synthesized in a third one. It would preserve a primordial importance for future development. In this way, neo-Liberalism reveals an obvious ideological connection with the Enlightenment, Franciscan conservatism with the Baroque, the Enlightenment with the Renaissance, and the Renaissance in a wide sweep across the Middle Ages with classic Hellenic and Roman history.

To be sure, only some elements of new thought are connected with established ideas, and even here one can note only similarities and analogies, not identities. The political concepts of Liberalism are very different from those of the Enlightenment, but their relationship as to basic philosophies is close. The affinity between the Franciscan era and the Baroque age lies chiefly in the similar social-political outlook and the emotional element in both Romanticism and Baroque. The literary-artistic ideals of the two eras are entirely different. The same differences exist in the kinship between Renaissance and Enlightenment. Here one cannot even speak of a similarity of philosophical concepts, but there does exist at least a similarity of intellectual outlook, and to a certain point of political concepts as well. Further affinities between Baroque and high-medieval emotions are as obvious as their differences. Rather commonplace, but actually quite controversial, is the assumption of a kindred spirit between Renaissance and classical antiquity. It is obviously necessary to beware of the danger of treating the long intervening period all too summarily. Still in certain spheres, and not only in that of Humanism, there is a sufficient affinity between these two eras to respect the Burckhardian concept of the evolution of the Renaissance.

Recognition of the particularly strong relationship between the ideas of an era and the one immediately preceding the period just passed is of far-reaching spiritual significance. The fact that intellectual boundaries between historical periods are necessarily not clear-cut rather enhances this significance. It strengthens the conviction that spiritual achievements and ideas are not molded and determined by any specific set of thoughts, but that they grow and rise as the product of a compromise between different sets of ideas, developed in different times and under different conditions.

Such a compromise is again no mathematically balanced resultant of forces of equal strength. It is the product of the beautifully varied inequality of organic human life. By reason of this inequality, the intellectual influence of the period preceding the one just passed will be stronger than that of the intervening period. Yet the danger of its assuming an inordinate supremacy will be checked by the ideas of the recent past as well as by those of the one antedating this preceding era. Thus the effect of the Enlightenment will be furthered by that of the Renaissance and even classical antiquity, yet it will be checked by those forces that hem it in in the future as well as in the past, i.e., Baroque and, in the case of the Renaissance, the high-medieval spirit. The strength of Franciscan conservatism is controlled by neo-Liberalism in the future and by that of Enlightenment in the past. Its supporting force, the Baroque era, in the past is again checked by Enlightenment and Renaissance, strengthened by the medieval spirit but impeded in effect by classical antiquity. And so it goes back and forth in past and future in an unending chain, which connects every human achievement with the whole cultural heritage of mankind and its prospects for new horizons. Achievements brought forward in this unending chain are thus subject to everlasting change; sufferings evolving from the clash of ideologies, cruel as they may be, are not interminable.

Here again we face a decisive distinction between the physical and the historical pendulum. The pendulum in the physical world swings back and forth through exactly the same orbit at exactly the same speed, and it would do so endlessly—except for the force of friction. Friction shortens its amplitude, diminishes its speed, and brings it eventually to a stop. Friction, the encounter and conflict of ideas, has exactly the opposite effect on the pendulum of history. It does not shorten, slow down, and finally stop its motion. On the contrary, it is actually the stimulus for the continuity of its motion and the increase of its speed.

It changes its orbit, its amplitude, as well. And here we face the final and supreme difference between the physical and the historical pendulum. This pendulum of history moves neither in an ideal physical world without friction from the same starting point to the same point of destination, nor in the actual physical world of friction in between the extreme points, between which the motion started. Prompted by ideological conflict, it moves forward in the form of human action, backward again in that of human reaction to it, but never backward as far as the original starting point, forward always farther than the previous point of destination. Its retreat is shorter than its advance, its trials and errors briefer than its progress. Yet steadily, though not without setbacks, continuously, though not straight or at an even speed, it does progress as long as friction, the element of free controversy in the realm of the spirit, is not eliminated by totalitarian conformism. This is the premise of the evolution of human freedom as illustrated in this brief study of Austrian intellectual history.

Bibliographical Notes

CHAPTER I

1. *The Life of Leopold, Late Emperor of Germany* (London, 1708), Preface. (Author unknown.)

2. As to the character of Leopold I, see Oswald Redlich, *Das Werden einer Grossmacht* (Vienna, 1942), 49, 359 ff., and the literature quoted there; Hugo Hantsch, *Die Geschichte Österreichs* (Graz, 1947-50), II, 26 ff., 43; F. M. Mayer, *Geschichte Österreichs* (Vienna, 1909), II, 238; A. F. Pribram, *Franz Paul Freiherr von Lisola* (Leipzig, 1894), 267-69, 389-90, 412; H. von Srbik, *Wien und Versailles, 1692-97* (Munich, 1944), 25-28.

3. Redlich, *op. cit.*, 137-42, 239-42.

4. A speech by Count Szécsen in the Reichsrat in 1860 as quoted in L. Eisenmann, *Le Compromis Austro-Hongrois de 1867* (Paris, 1904), 227. See also Josef Redlich, *Das Österreichische Staats- und Reichsproblem* (Leipzig, 1920, 1926), I, part 1, 198 ff., and the quotations there. See further Eisenmann, *op. cit.*, 227 ff.; Joseph von Eötvös, *Die Garantien der Macht und Einheit Österreichs* (Leipzig, 1859), 85 ff.

5. MAGYAR SOURCES: See E. Csuday, *Die Geschichte der Ungarn* (Vienna, 1898), II, 126-211; D. G. Kosáry, *A History of Hungary* (Cleveland, 1941), 102-37, 257-67; J. Szekfü, *Etat et nation* (Paris, 1945), on Transylvania, 150-77; H. Marczali, *Hungary in the Eighteenth Century* (Cambridge, 1910), 1-16.

GERMAN SOURCES: Mayer, *op. cit.*, II, 206-30; O. Redlich, *op. cit.*, 148-217; R. Kralik, *Österreichische Geschichte* (Vienna, 1914), 151-85; Hantsch, *op. cit.*, II, 44-47, 56-58; F. Krones, *Handbuch der Geschichte Österreichs* (Berlin, 1881), III, 556-61, 583-628, 649-84; IV, 22-39, 55-69, 95-108, 112-20. It should be noted that Krones' most accurate and impartial general political survey of the problem conforms to a much greater extent to the views of Magyar historiography than almost any other presentations of Magyar and Austro-German history referring to later periods.

303

A Study in Austrian Intellectual History

As to Slovak problems, which at this point must be studied in the context of Hungarian rather than Czech history, see R. W. Seton-Watson, *A History of the Czechs and Slovaks* (London, 1943), 254-57; A. Szana, *Die Geschichte der Slowakei* (Bratislava, 1930), 76-79. A comparative study of Magyar and German sources cited above gives a fair evaluation of the situation in Transylvania and Croatia.

6. Seton-Watson, *op. cit.*, 110-42; S. H. Thomson, *Czechoslovakia in European History* (Princeton, 1953), 111-52; Krones, *op. cit.*, III, 425-45; Kralik, *op. cit.*, 122-50; Mayer, *op. cit.*, II, 262-68, 415-19; Herman Münch, *Böhmische Tragödie* (Braunschweig, 1919), 75-87.

7. Mayer, *op. cit.*, II, 292-303.

8. A. Huber and A. Dopsch, *Österreichische Reichsgeschichte* (Vienna, 1901), 192-94, 205-24; F. C. Helbling, *Österreichische Verfassungs- und Verwaltungsgeschichte* (Vienna, 1956), 244-46; Krones, *op. cit.*, IV, 399, 422 ff., 490; Mayer, *op. cit.*, II, 275-79, 300-303; J. B. Wolf, *The Emergence of the Great Powers, 1685-1715* (New York, 1951), 135-37; E. Heischmann, *Die Anfänge des stehenden Heeres in Österreich* (Vienna, 1925), 55 ff., 135 ff., 181 ff.

9. Mayer, *op. cit.*, II, 193; Srbik, *op. cit.*, 28.

10. Huber and Dopsch, *op. cit.*, 180-205; Helbling, *op. cit.*, 239-83; Krones, *op. cit.*, III, 562-70, 631-42; H. F. Schwarz and J. I. Coddington, *The Imperial Privy Council in the Seventeenth Century* (Cambridge, 1943), see particularly 3-46, 143-90; Srbik, *op. cit.*, 25-44.

11. Krones, *op. cit.*, III, 361-65, 616-22; Mayer, *op. cit.*, II, 206-10, 303-12; Seton-Watson, *op. cit.*, 130-38, 255-57; Huber and Dopsch, *op. cit.*, 230-33; Helbling, *op. cit.*, 267-70; Hantsch, *op. cit.*, II, 15, 16, 21, 22.

12. Ferdinand Tremel, *Der Frühkapitalismus in Innerösterreich* (Graz, 1953), 141-55; Huber and Dopsch, *op. cit.*, 208-12; Mayer, *op. cit.*, II, 282-92; Eva Priester, *Kurze Geschichte Österreichs* (Vienna, 1949), II, 1-50; Wilhelm Roscher, *Geschichte der Nationalökonomik in Deutschland* (Munich, 1874), 263-70.

13. Roscher, *op. cit.*, 275.

14. Roscher, *op. cit.*, 263-304; Mayer, *op. cit.*, II, 335-40; Hantsch, *op. cit.*, II, 65-71.

15. See *Allgemeine deutsche Biographie* (Leipzig, 1875-91),

I, 201-03, on Becher; XIII, 157-58, on Hörnigk; XIX, 405-07, on Marperger; XXXI, 530-32, on Schröder, Klenck, and Leeb; see further on Becher, H. Hassinger, *Johann Joachim Becher* (Vienna, 1951), 138-96.

16. See *Allgemeine deutsche Biographie*, I, 701-03; XIII, 157-58; XXXI, 530-32; Mayer, *op. cit.*, II, 289-92, 335-45; Priester, *op. cit.*, II, 1-49.

17. See Hantsch, *op. cit.*, I, 211-23, 271-72; K. Krofta, *Geschichte der Tschechoslowakei* (Berlin, 1932), 72-74; Kosáry, *op. cit.*, 84-91; Mayer, *op. cit.*, II, 355-86.

18. Kralik, *op. cit.*, 173-79; Mayer, *op. cit.*, II, 369-73; Anna Coreth, *Österreichische Geschichtschreibung in der Barockzeit (1620-1740)* (Vienna, 1950), 152-61.

19. Kralik, *op. cit.*, 167-70, 179-80; H. von Srbik, *Geist und Geschichte vom deutschen Humanismus bis zur Gegenwart* (Salzburg, 1950-51), I, 91, 92; Eduard Castle, *Dichter und Dichtung aus Österreich* (Vienna, 1951), 5-16; Mayer, *op. cit.*, II, 373; Coreth, *op. cit.*, 15 ff., 23 ff., 72-78, 99, 105 ff., 136, 141.

20. Otto Brunner, *Adeliges Landleben und Europäischer Geist* (Salzburg, 1949); Mayer, *op. cit.*, II, 333; Kralik, *op. cit.*, 172, 173.

21. Hantsch, *op. cit.*, II, 140-43; Mayer, *op. cit.*, II, 395-96; Ludwig Reiter, *Österreichische Staats- und Kulturgeschichte* (Klagenfurt, 1947), 141 ff.; P. H. Lang, *Music in Western Civilization* (New York, 1941), 327-72, 392-408.

22. See Karl Wörmann, *Geschichte der Kunst . . .* (Leipzig, 1913-22), IV, 359-430; Werner Hagen, *Die Bauten des Deutschen Barock* (Jena, 1942), 71-98; H. Tietze, *Wien* (Leipzig, 1917), 127-207; Oskar Schürer, *Prag* (Munich, 1935), 213-57, 395-98; Bruno Grimschitz, *Wiener Barockpaläste* (Vienna, 1944); Justus Schmidt, *Die Donau von Passau bis zur Reichsgrenze* (Berlin, Vienna, 1942).

23. A similar though not identical thought is expressed in Egon Friedell, *Kulturgeschichte der Neuzeit* (London, 1947), II, 138. See also Arnold Hauser, *The Social History of Art* (New York, 1951), I, 423, 424.

24. Brunner, *op. cit.*

25. Franz Borkenau, *Der Übergang vom feudalen zum bürgerlichen Weltbild* (Paris, 1934), xii.

CHAPTER II

1. The quotations in this chapter are chiefly from the following selection of Abraham a Sancta Clara's numerous works and the extensive literature about him.

a. Works by Abraham a Sancta Clara

Auf, auf Ihr Christen (Vienna, 1883; first ed., Vienna, 1683).

Lösch Wien (Passau, 1836; first ed., Vienna, 1680).

Gack, Gack, Gack a Ga! (Lindau, 1846; first ed., Munich, 1684).

Grosse Todten Bruderschaft (Passau, 1836; first ed., Salzburg, 1684).

Grammatica Religiosa (Passau, 1842; first ed., Vienna, 1690).

Heilsames Gemisch-Gemasch (Lindau, 1846; first ed., Würzburg, 1703).

Mercks Wien (Passau, 1836; first ed., Vienna, 1679).

Hui und Pfui der Welt! (Passau, 1836; first ed., Würzburg, 1707).

Etwas für alle, I; *Sämtliche Werke*, XIV (Passau, 1841; written presumably 1698; first ed., Würzburg, 1711 [?]).

Judas der Ertzschelm, ed. Felix Bobertag, in *Deutsche National-Literatur*, XL (Berlin, Stuttgart, 1883; first ed., Salzburg, 1685-95, 1710).

Abrahamisches Gehab dich wohl; Sämtliche Werke, XI (Lindau, 1862; written 1706-09; published first, Nürnberg, 1729).

Geistlicher Kramladen; Sämtliche Werke, XXI (Lindau, 1867; completed 1709; first ed., Würzburg, 1710).

If not otherwise stated, quotations are taken from *Abraham a Sancta Clara, Sämtliche Werke* (Passau-Lindau, 1830-72). This, however, is not a regular, co-ordinated edition of his works, but rather a collection of monographs. The badly needed standard edition of Abraham's work has not yet been published. Thus his works listed above—all of them among his more important writings—represent a limited chronological cross section of his entire literary production from 1679, when he first began to write, to his death in 1709.

Quotations from Abraham's works are usually given in English, except in certain instances where the quotations in the text are in German and an English translation is provided in the footnotes. The purpose of this is to illustrate Abraham's inimitable technique of puns and alliteration. Even the reader entirely unfamiliar with German will be able to recognize the sound effect and may thus form a clearer impression of Abraham's style.

For unpublished primary sources see Section I of the Bibliography at the end of this volume.

b. *Literature on Abraham a Sancta Clara*

This literature on the whole does not do full justice to Abraham's literary significance, certainly not to his ideological influence. The major full-length biography is still Th. von Karajan, *Abraham a Sancta Clara* (Vienna, 1867), somewhat outdated and of limited critical value, but very useful for the facts that it contains. Since most of Abraham's numerous works exist only in completely outdated editions, and since their loosely organized subject matter has never been made accessible by means of indexes or concordances, this old-fashioned biography still renders an essential service.

Bertsche, Karl, *Abraham a Sancta Clara* (Munich-Gladbach, 1918, 1922).

Bianchi, L., *Studien zur Beurteilung des Abraham a Sancta Clara* (Heidelberg, 1924). Interesting survey.

Capanaga, Victorio, *Un celebre predicatore umorista, Abrama da san Chiara* (Catania, 1934). Novel.

Danszky, Edward Paul, *Pater Fabelhans: Der Lebensroman Abrahams a Santa Clara* (Moedling, St. Gabriel, 1950). Novel.

Loidl, Franz, *Menschen im Barock: Abraham a Santa Clara über das religiös sittliche Leben in Österreich in der Zeit von 1670-1710* (Vienna, 1938; typescript).

Scherer, Wilhelm, "Pater Abraham a Sancta Clara," in *Vorträge und Aufsätze zur Geschichte des geistigen Lebens in Deutschland und Österreich* (Berlin, 1874), pp. 147-92. One of the most important contributions to the subject. See also—

Scherer, W., "Abraham a Sancta Clara," in *Allgemeine deutsche Biographie* (Leipzig, 1885), XXI, 178 ff.

Scheid, N., "Abraham a Sancta Clara," in *Catholic Encyclopedia* (New York, 1907), I, 56 ff. A clear, objective interpretation.

Nagl, J. W., and J. Zeidler, *Deutsch-österreichische Literaturgeschichte* (Vienna, 1899-1914), I, 621-51.

A number of monographs deal with specific aspects of Abraham's literary work, among them the following:

Bertsche, Karl, "Abraham a Sancta Clara und die Bücher," *Sankt*

Wiborada, Annual V (Augsburg, 1938), 72-77. On Abraham's literary interests.

Bertsche, Karl, "Die Handschriften Abraham a Sancta Clara's in der Wiener Nationalbibliothek," from *Jahrbuch für Landeskunde von Niederösterreich* (1936), 125-39.

Buchwald, Renate, *Abraham a Sancta Clara's Stellung zu den sozialen und wirtschaftlichen Problemen seiner Zeit* (Vienna, 1949; diss., typed).

Hocker, Ambros, *Echtheitsfragen bei Abraham a Sancta Clara* (Weimar, 1929). An important contribution to the question as to which of Abraham's writings are to be considered apocryphal.

Loidl, Franz, "Abraham a Sancta Clara als Vorkämpfer für deutsche Art wider Türken und Fremdländerei: Ein Beitrag zum süddeutschen Barock," in *Unsere Heimat,* Jahrgang XIV (Vienna, 1941).

Loidl, F., "Abraham a Sancta Clara und das Judentum" in *Studie über das Judentum in Wien und Österreich im Barock* (Vienna, 1941).

Mener, Joseph, *Forschungen zur Beurteilung Abrahams a Sancta Clara: Eine Untersuchung seines homiletischen Schrifttums nach Inhalt und Anlage* (Bottrop i. W., Postberg, 1938).

Michel, Max, *Die Volkssage bei Abraham a Sancta Clara* (Leipzig, 1933). An interesting study of the question of Abraham's superstitions; informative also on the problem of style.

Schulz, Hans, *Studien zu Abraham a Sancta Clara* (Freiburg im Breisgau, 1910). On Abraham's relationship to the German "fool's literature."

Schmid, Karl, *Studien zu den Fabeln Abrahams a Sancta Clara* (diss.; Munich, 1928).

Spielmann, Elisabeth Marie, *Die Frau und ihr Lebenskreis bei Abraham a Sancta Clara* (Vienna, 1944; diss., typescript).

Vosatka, Stephanie, *Die Predigten von Abraham a Sancta Clara* (Vienna, 1946; diss., typescript).

On the problem of style—a most important aspect of Abraham's work—see also:

Blankenburg, Kurt, *Studien über die Sprache Abrahams a Sancta Clara* (Halle, 1897).

Cladder, Eleonore, *Der Wortschatz des Abraham a Sancta Clara im Bereich des Verstandes* (Bottrop i. W., Postberg, 1940; diss., Münster).

Hoffmann, Helmut, *Die Metaphern in den Predigten und Schriften Abrahams a Sancta Clara* (Düsseldorf, 1933; diss., typescript.

Lutz, Friedrich, *Dramatische Elemente im Stile des Abraham a Sancta Clara* (Vienna, 1947; diss., typescript).

Strigl, Hans, "Einiges über die Sprache des Paters Abraham a Sancta Clara," *Zeitschrift für deutsche Wortforschung,* VIII (1906-07).

Works of a more general character concerning the Abraham a Sancta Clara problem are referred to in the notes below.

Appendixes IV and V of Karajan's biography give a detailed though, regarding the question of authenticity, outdated bibliography of his works. More up to date but confined to early editions is the bibliography by Karl Bertsche, *Die Werke Abrahams a Sancta Clara in ihren Frühdrucken* (Schwetingen bei Heidelberg, n.d.).

2. W. Scherer, "Pater Abraham a Sancta Clara," 151.

3. N. Scheid, "Abraham a Sancta Clara," in *Catholic Encyclopedia,* I, 56-57.

4. See Scherer, *op cit.,* 155-61. On Abraham's education in general, see also Th. von Karajan, *Abraham a Sancta Clara,* 18-69. See also the Introduction in F. Bobertag (ed.), *Judas der Ertzschelm,* ii ff.

5. Scherer, *op. cit.,* 163. See also Karajan, *op. cit.,* 9 ff.

6. See Karajan, *op. cit.,* 27.

7. See on this point, E. M. Spielmann, *Die Frau und ihr Lebenskreis bei Abraham a Sancta Clara.*

8. Scherer, *op. cit.,* 171. Karajan, *op. cit.,* 15 ff., submits evidence that Abraham's mother was several times required to appear before the magistrate on charges of quarreling, of abusive language, and so forth.

9. See Richard von Kralik, *Geschichte der Stadt Wien und ihrer Kultur* (Vienna, 1926), 217. See Abraham a Sancta Clara, "Prophetischer Willkomm," in *Geistlicher Kramladen,* 233 ff.

10. As to the question of authenticity of the writings bearing Abraham a Sancta Clara's name, see the conclusions in A. Hocker, *Echtheitsfragen . . .* 93 ff. See further Karl Bertsche, "Die Handschriften Abraham a Sancta Clara's in der Wiener National-

bibliothek," from *Jahrbuch für Landeskunde von Niederösterreich* (1936), 125-39.

11. See for instance H. Pirchegger, *Geschichte und Kulturleben Deutschösterreichs von 1526 bis 1792,* 72 ff.; F. M. Mayer, *Geschichte Österreichs,* II, 363 ff. Certain late-sixteenth- and early-seventeenth-century preachers, notably Johann Nas, Peter Muchitsch, and the Jesuit Georg Scherer, are forerunners of Abraham in their literary style. The language of Scherer, however, is far more moderate than Abraham's.

12. On Abraham's education, see the abundant but highly uncritical data in Karajan, *op cit.,* 29 ff., 95 ff., 112 ff. To Karajan the mere mention of a writer or of foreign words, institutions, etc., constitutes evidence of a knowledge of it on the part of his hero. Karajan's contention that Abraham had good instruction in history is, however, to some extent borne out by his writings. See also Scherer, *op. cit.,* 156 ff., 175 ff.; K. Bertsche, *op. cit.,* 72 ff.; S. Vosatka, *Die Predigten von Abraham a Sancta Clara,* 6-18. See also J. Mener, *Forschungen zur Beurteilung Abrahams a Sancta Clara.*

13. See *Geistlicher Kramladen,* 315 ff.; *Gehab dich wohl,* 270 f. See Scherer, *op. cit.,* 177 ff., who mentions also a case where Abraham, on the occasion of a funeral oration, gives the biographies of all the saints who died on the same day of the year as the deceased.

14. See Scherer, *op. cit.,* 156; Karajan, who surveys the major writers known to Abraham, *op. cit.,* 112 f., does not mention these names either.

15. *Geistlicher Kramladen,* 628 ff.

16. See Karajan, *op. cit.,* 77 ff., and the sources quoted by him. Instead of many, see further *Geistlicher Kramladen,* 242, 245; *Gehab dich wohl,* 116, 118, 413. On the whole problem of superstition in Abraham's writings, see particularly M. Michel, *Die Volkssage bei Abraham a Sancta Clara.*

17. See *Judas,* 10; *Hui und Pfui der Welt!* 17; Michel, *op. cit.,* 62 ff.; K. Schmid, *Studien zu den Fabeln Abrahams a Sancta Clara.*

18. See particularly F. Lutz, *Dramatische Elemente im Stile des Abraham a Sancta Clara,* 13-162; Vosatka, *op. cit.,* 100-139; E. Cladder, *Der Wortschatz des Abraham a Sancta Clara;* H. Hoffmann, *Die Metaphern in den Predigten und Schriften Abrahams a Sancta Clara.*

19. Mayer, *op. cit.*, II, 363.

20. See *Hui und Pfui*, 311 f.

21. See particularly R. Buchwald, *Abraham a Sancta Clara's Stellung zu den sozialen und wirtschaftlichen Problemen seiner Zeit;* Franz Loidl, *Menschen im Barock: Abraham a Sancta Clara und das religiös sittliche Leben in Österreich in der Zeit von 1670-1710* (Vienna, 1938).

22. See at this point also Michel, *op. cit.*, 65 f.

23. Scherer, *op. cit.*, 163; Loidl, *Menschen im Barock*, 97-111; Buchwald, *op. cit.*, 8, 9, 37-40, 45-47.

24. See Karajan, *op. cit.*, 209 f. and the evidence quoted there; *Bescheid-Essen* (1719), 121, 127; *Centifolium stultorum* (1709), 274 f. See also *Auf, auf Ihr Christen*, 41. See further F. Loidl, *Abraham a Sancta Clara als Vorkämpfer für deutsche Art wider Türken und Fremdländerei*, 18 ff.

25. For far more extreme examples of this technique, see, e.g., *Mercks Wien*, 32 ff., 116 ff.; *Etwas für alle*, 467 ff.

26. Karajan, *op. cit.*, 188-89, quoted from *Mercks Wien*, 313-14. (Obviously this reference to the eighteenth century is taken from a later early-eighteenth-century edition.)

27. Karajan, *op. cit.*, 187 ff., 205 ff., and the passages quoted there from *Mercks Wien*, 313 f., 46, 105 ff., 239 ff.; *Gehab dich Wohl* (ed. 1729), 40 ff., 446, 372, 8, 39, 69-77, 122 ff.; *Lösch Wien* (ed. 1680), 30, 57 f., 40 f., 48, 55, 77 f.; *Etwas für alle* (ed. 1711), I, 486; *Judas* (first ed.), IV, 277, 303 f.; I, 303 ff.; II, 91; I, 590, 104, 323, 428; IV, 412 f.; II, 88; I, 320; IV, 513; III, 308; *Wohlangefüllter Weinkeller* (ed. 1710), 141 f.; *Auf, auf Ihr Christen* (1683) 43 f.; *Bescheid Essen* (ed. 1719), 94 ff., 99 f.; *Lauberhütte* (ed. 1721-23), II, 359; I, 124; *Centifolium stultorum* (ed. 1709), 368; *Hui und Pfui* (ed. 1707-10), 77, 8 f.

28. *Mercks Wien*, 22 ff.

29. See also on the plague *Mercks Wien*, 22 ff., 148 ff.; *Lösch Wien*, 208; *Geistlicher Kramladen*, 308 ff.; Karajan, *op. cit.*, 265 ff.

30. On the background history of the Turkish siege, see Onno Klopp, *Das Jahr 1683 und der folgende grosse Türkenkrieg bis zum Frieden von Carlowitz 1699* (Graz, 1882); Reinhold Lorenz, *Türkenjahr 1683* (Vienna, 1933); A. P. von Camesina, *Wiens Bedrängnis im Jahre 1683* (1868). See also E. Castle, *Dichter und Dichtung aus Österreich* (Vienna, 1951), chapter I (5-16), "Johann Constantin Feigius."

31. See *Geistlicher Kramladen*, 233 ff.; Karajan, *op. cit.*, 255 ff.; Scherer, *op. cit.*, 166 ff.

32. On the Austrian court, see Karajan, *op. cit.*, 262 ff.; Mayer, *op. cit.*, II, 395 ff.; H. Tietze, *Wien* (Leipzig, 1918), 145 ff.; Loidl, *Menschen im Barock*, 208-11; Buchwald, *op. cit.*, 63-66. For an interesting contemporary account see S. Pufendorf, *Bericht über Kaiser Leopold, seinen Hof und die österreichische Politik, 1671-77* (ed. G. Helbig; Leipzig, 1862).

33. See for instance Karajan, *op. cit.*, 219.

34. *Gehab dich wohl*, 153.

35. On the Jesuits and Holy Orders in general, see *Mercks Wien*, 36 ff.; *Geistlicher Kramladen*, 63 ff.; Scherer, *op. cit.*, 167 ff.; Loidl, *Menschen im Barock*, 135-67.

36. See particularly *Grammatica religiosa*, 210 ff.; *Gehab dich wohl*, 365 ff.

37. *Hui und Pfui*, 312, 347 ff.; *Gemisch-Gemasch*, 258 ff.

38. See also (h) "The Free Professions," below.

39. For other of Abraham's reflections on the clergy see further *Etwas für alle*, 16 f., 186 f.; *Gehab dich wohl*, 155 ff., 206 f.; and particularly many references in the main work on the subject, *Grammatica religiosa*. See further Loidl, *Menschen im Barock*, 236-43; Buchwald, *op. cit.*, 15-82.

40. *Auf, auf Ihr Christen*, 127; Karajan, *op. cit.*, 166 ff.; Loidl, *op. cit.*, 211-17.

41. On Abraham's criticism of the treatment of serf-tenants see further Karajan (ed. 1710), *op. cit.*, 160 ff., and the quotations listed there from *Judas*, II, 80 f., and *Grosse Todten Bruderschaft* (1684), 16. See also Loidl, *Menschen im Barock*, 218-24; Buchwald, *op. cit.*, 45-47.

42. *Gehab dich wohl*, 71 ff.; Karajan, *op. cit.*, 163 ff.; Loidl, *Menschen im Barock*, 296-303; Buchwald, *op. cit.*, 26-36; Spielmann, *op. cit.*, 27-53.

43. On money and wealth see *Auf, auf Ihr Christen*, 108 f.; *Gehab dich wohl*, 14 ff., 162 ff.; *Gack, Gack*, 44 f.

44. See for instance *Etwas für alle*, 76 ff. See also Loidl, *Menschen im Barock*, 236-42; Buchwald, *op. cit.*, 80-82.

45. *Gehab dich wohl*, 401 f.; see also 84, 169 f., 426, 172 ff.; *Etwas für alle*, 54 ff.; *Hui und Pfui*, 319; *Gack, Gack*, 147 ff.; Karajan, *op. cit.*, 173-80. Contrary, i.e., favorable to lawyers, see *Lauberhütte*, I, 119 ff.; *Etwas für alle*, 49 ff.; see also Buchwald, *op. cit.*, 76-79.

46. *Etwas für alle,* particularly chapters VIII, IX, XVI, XXII, XXVII, XXXI, XXXV–LXXXII, LXXXIV–LXXXVII, XC–XCIII, XCV–XCVII, on the various trades; here Abraham reveals an impressive knowledge of manufacturing processes. *Gehab dich wohl,* 77 ff., 67 ff.; *Auf, auf Ihr Christen,* 97 ff.; Karajan, *op. cit.,* 180 ff.; Loidl, *Menschen im Barock,* 225-36; Buchwald, *op. cit.,* 82-89.

47. On the peasant question see *Etwas für alle,* 441 ff., 480 ff.; Karajan, *op. cit.,* 186 ff.; Scherer, *op. cit.,* 163; Loidl, *Menschen im Barock,* 218-24, 97-111; Buchwald, *op. cit.,* 45-47.

48. See also Loidl, *Menschen im Barock,* 69-70, 315-25, 97-111; Spielmann, *op. cit.,* 150-95; Buchwald, *op. cit.,* 37-40.

49. *Hui und Pfui,* 225.

50. *Etwas für alle,* 483 ff.; *Gehab dich wohl,* 22 ff.; *Grammatica religiosa,* 265 ff.; Loidl, *Menschen im Barock,* 97-111; Buchwald, *op. cit.,* 37-40.

51. *Gehab dich wohl,* 62; *Auf, auf Ihr Christen,* 37, 72 ff.; Karajan, *op. cit.* 172; Loidl, *Menschen im Barock,* 243-45; Buchwald, *op. cit.,* 91-94.

52. *Etwas für alle,* 62.

53. *Auf, auf Ihr Christen,* 27. See also Loidl, *Menschen im Barock,* 7-10; Loidl, *Abraham a Sancta Clara als Vorkämpfer für deutsche Art,* 3 ff.

54. *Auf, auf Ihr Christen,* 13.

55. *Ibid.,* 14, 101.

56. *Ibid.,* 101-06; *Lösch Wien,* 234 f.

57. *Auf, auf Ihr Christen,* 107; *Lösch Wien,* 234 f.

58. *Auf, auf Ihr Christen,* 96.

59. *Ibid.,* 113 ff. See also Karajan, *op. cit.,* 152 f.

60. On the history of the Jews in Vienna during that period see particularly Hans Tietze, *Die Juden Wiens* (Leipzig, Vienna, 1935), 41-78.

61. *Heilsames Gemisch-Gemasch,* 464 ff.; *Hui und Pfui,* 362. See also Loidl, *Menschen im Barock,* 290-93; Loidl, *Abraham a Sancta Clara und das Judentum.*

62. *Mercks Wien* (ed. 1680), 347 f., quoted from Karajan, *op. cit.,* 149 ff.

63. *Mercks Wien,* 112 f.; *Judas,* 27 f.; *Heilsames Gemisch-Gemasch,* 467 f.

64. *Hui und Pfui* (1707), 305, quoted from Karajan, *op. cit.,* 149 ff. See also *Gehab dich wohl,* 55.

65. *Gehab dich wohl,* 12 f., 62; *Auf, auf ihr Christen,* 111; *Hui und Pfui,* 470; Loidl, *Abraham a Sancta Clara und das Judentum,* 23 ff.

66. Karajan, *op. cit.,* 150 f., quoting D. Fassmann, *Gespräche im Reiche der Toten,* 74; *Entrevue,* 695; *Centifolium stultorum* (1709), 343; *Judas,* I, 58 f.

67. On the Protestant issue see Karajan, *op. cit.,* 143 ff. See further *Gehab dich wohl,* 366 f.; *Auf, auf Ihr Christen,* 100 f.

68. See as examples for many similar reflections *Lösch Wien,* 212 f.; *Mercks Wien,* 63; *Gehab dich wohl* (a particularly rich source on feminine weakness), 71 ff.; *Hui und Pfui,* 434 ff.; Karajan, *op. cit.,* 192 ff.; Loidl, *Menschen im Barock,* 168-87; Spielmann, *op. cit.,* 10-26, 60-97; Buchwald, *op. cit.,* 100-101.

69. See above all "Von der Weiber Bosheit," *Gehab dich wohl,* XII, 219-35, from which the foregoing quotations are taken. See further *Gehab dich wohl,* 289 f., 367 ff.; *Judas,* 24 ff.

70. *Lösch Wien,* 244 ff.; *Gehab dich wohl,* 68 ff., 402 ff., 410, 108 f.; *Etwas für alle,* 135 ff.; *Hui und Pfui,* 435 f., 233 ff. Karajan, *op. cit.,* 119 ff.; Loidl, *Menschen im Barock,* 69-70, 296-311, 315-25; Spielmann, *op. cit.,* 27-59; Buchwald, *op. cit.,* 26-36.

71. *Auf, auf Ihr Christen,* 101 f.; for a slightly different version of this passage see *Judas,* 28 f.

72. *Judas,* 172 ff.; Loidl, *Menschen im Barock,* 168-201; Spielmann, *op. cit.,* 98-149; Buchwald, *op. cit.,* 101-03.

73. *Judas,* 168.

74. *Ibid.,* 166 f.

75. *Ibid.,* 167, see also 165 ff.; *Gehab dich wohl,* 510; *Mercks Wien,* 131 f.

76. *Mercks Wien,* 133; *Lösch Wien,* 234; *Gehab dich wohl,* 190 ff. On the whole problem of education see also Karajan, *op. cit.,* 202 ff.; Loidl, *Abraham a Sancta Clara als Vorkämpfer,* 10 ff.; Buchwald, *op. cit.,* 41-44.

77. See *Etwas für alle,* chapter XXXIII (203-08), "Der Schulmeister." On another aspect of the youth problem, that of guardianship and the protection of wards and orphans from its abuse, see *Gehab dich wohl,* Discourse XVII, 301-14, and particularly 314 f.

78. *Gehab dich wohl,* Discourse XXVI, "Die billige Sünder- und Kinderstraf," 445-54, see 454 ff. See also *Hui und Pfui,* 399.

79. *Gehab dich wohl,* Discourse XXX, "Die scharfe Strafruthen," 496-516. See 498, 502 ff.

80. *Ibid.*, 506 f.

81. *Gehab dich wohl,* Discourse XXVII, "Die Betrachtung des Todes," 459-74; see 464.

82. See the first section *c* of this chapter, above. See at this point also S. Vosatka, *Die Predigten von Abraham a Sancta Clara,* 100-139; E. Cladder, *Der Wortschatz des Abraham a Sancta Clara im Bereiche des Verstandes,* 7 ff.; H. Hoffmann, *Die Metaphern in den Predigten und Schriften Abrahams a Sancta Clara,* 99 ff.; F. Lutz, *Dramatische Elemente im Stile des Abraham a Sancta Clara,* 13-168; Lorenzo Bianchi, *Studien zur Beurteilung des Abraham a Sancta Clara.*

83. See also Hans Schulz, *Studien zu Abraham a Sancta Clara,* 4 ff.; Karl Bertsche, "Abraham a Sancta Clara und die Bücher," 74.

84. *Gehab dich wohl,* preface to ed. 1729; quoted from Th. von Karajan, *Abraham a Sancta Clara,* 219.

85. See the reference to Abraham in J. W. von Goethe, *Aus meinem Leben, Wahrheit und Dichtung,* Part Three, chapter XIX, in which Goethe compares Abraham to the mystic physiognomist J. K. Lavater.

86. See footnote on page 65: letter of Schiller to Goethe of October 9, 1798. The translation of this passage is from the article "Abraham a Sancta Clara" in Volume I of the *Catholic Encyclopedia.* On Goethe's and Schiller's evaluation of Abraham, see also J. W. Nagl and J. Zeidler, *Deutsch-österreichische Literaturgeschichte,* I, 621-51.

87. Josef von Eichendorff, *Sämtliche Werke* (Regensburg, 1911), X, 376; Jean Paul (Johann Paul Friedrich Richter), *Vorschule der Aesthetik,* chapter VIII, par. 36; W. Scherer, *Vorträge und Aufsätze,* 154.

88. Scherer, *loc. cit.*

89. K. Goedeke, *Grundriss zur Geschichte der deutschen Dichtung* (Dresden, 1862), I, 500; G. Gervinus, *Geschichte der deutschen Dichtung* (Leipzig, 1853), III, 396 f., with its rough rationalistic rejection of Abraham's life work.

90. Nagl and Zeidler, *op. cit.,* I, 650; R. von Kralik, *Das unbekannte Österreich* (Vienna, 1917), 63.

91. Hugo Hantsch, *Geschichte Österreichs* (Graz, 1947), II, 71; see also 49, 72; Josef Nadler, *Literaturgeschichte Österreichs* (Linz, 1948), 164-68.

92. *Catholic Encyclopedia,* I, 57.

93. *Der grosse Herder* (Freiburg im Breisgau, 1931), I; *Allgemeine deutsche Biographie* (Leipzig, 1885), XXI, 178 ff. See also *Allgemeine Realencyklopädie, oder Conversations-lexikon für das katholische Deutschland* (Regensburg, 1846), I, 57.

94. See particularly F. Loidl, *Abraham a Sancta Clara und das Judentum*. It may be noted also that the National Socialist *Reichsstatthalter* and *Gauleiter* Baldur von Schirach in Vienna sponsored the three-volume edition of the thus-far unpublished works of Abraham, edited for the Akademie der Wissenschaften in Vienna, 1943-44, by Karl Bertsche.

95. Heinrich Suso-Waldeck, *Lese aus Abraham a Sancta Clara* (Brixlegg, 1938), 8.

96. Herbert Cysarz, *Deutsche Barockdichtung* (Leipzig, 1924), 219.

97. Richard von Kralik, *Geschichte der Stadt Wien und ihrer Kultur,* 216 f.

98. Scherer, *Vorträge und Aufsätze,* 186.

99. R. M. Werner (ed.), *Der Wiener Hanswurst (Wiener Neudrucke,* No. 1; Vienna, 1883-86), xi ff., cii ff.

100. See at this point also H. Tietze, *Wien,* 260.

101. On Stranitzky and the fight against the harlequin issue, see Werner, *op. cit.,* Nos. I, X; K. von Görner, *Der Hans-Wurst Streit in Wien und Joseph von Sonnenfels* (Vienna, 1884); R. Lothar, *Das Wiener Burgtheater* (Vienna, 1899), 4 ff.; Otto Rommel, *Die Wiener Volkskomödie* (Vienna, 1952), 153-582.

102. See at this point Karajan, *op. cit.,* 243 f. and the sources quoted there. See further Hantsch, *op. cit.,* II, 49; R. Lorenz, *Türkenjahr 1683,* 390 f.; Nadler, *op. cit.,* 164 ff.; Rommel, *op. cit.,* 194, 339.

103. Cysarz, *op. cit.,* 221.

104. Ambros Hocker, *Echtheitsfragen bei Abraham a Sancta Clara* (Weimar, 1929), see particularly 93 ff. See also Rommel, *op. cit.,* 194, 339.

105. Scherer, *op. cit.,* 188.

106. Ferdinand Kürnberger, quoted from Herman Bahr, *Wien* (Stuttgart, 1906), 116 ff.

107. M. Michel, *Die Volkssage bei Abraham a Sancta Clara,* 66.

108. See on this point Karl Bertsche, "Abraham a Sancta Clara und die Bücher," 72 ff. Here this nerve-shattering technique is connected with the misunderstood prescriptions of Abraham's Jesuit intellectual education. See also Vosatka, *op. cit.,* 5-18.

109. It is obviously impossible in this essay to go into the theoretical aspects of the question of the correct religious interpretation of the principles misunderstood by Abraham. Ample reference should be made at this point to the standard work, Josef Mausbach, *Katholische Moraltheologie* (Münster, 1936). See particularly I, 373-414, "Die sittlich bösen Handlungen und Zustände"; II, 239-59, "Die religiöse Weihe der Zeit," and the whole of III, dealing with *Spezielle Moral, II: Der irdische Pflichtenkreis.*

110. Scherer, *op. cit.,* 188. If Scherer had written his essay fifty years later, he probably would have said "subconscious" instead of "unconscious."

111. Michel, *op. cit.,* 64–65 ff. See also Cladder, *op. cit.,* 7; Lutz, *op. cit.,* 157-68.

112. See at this point also F. M. Mayer, *Geschichte Österreichs,* II, 312-415; H. Pirchegger, *Geschichte und Kultur Deutschösterreichs von 1526 bis 1792,* 180-90, 242-81; Cysarz, *op. cit.,* chapter VII.

113. Excellent illustrations of this spirit can be found in the socially as illuminating as politically insignificant literature dealing with the Viennese scene around the time of the Congress of Vienna. See, for instance, August de la Garde, *Gemälde des Wiener Kongresses,* with the significant subtitle "Erinnerungen, Feste, Sittenschilderungen, Anekdoten" (2 vols.; Munich, 1914). See also Countess Lulu Türheim, *Ein Leben, Erinnerungen aus Österreichs grosser Welt, 1788-1852* (4 vols.; Munich, 1913), or J. F. Castelli, *Memoiren meines Lebens* (4 vols.; Vienna, 1861). As to the political literature, with one of its dominant themes, namely, the lack of response to new ideas on the part of the people (i.e., primarily the urban population), see the illuminating volume by O. Rommel (ed.), *Der Österreichische Vormärz, 1816-47* (Leipzig, 1931).

114. See A. Jenks, *The Austrian Electoral Reform of 1907* (New York, 1950), 11-26; R. A. Kann, *The Multinational Empire* (New York, 1950), I, 89-103.

115. Friedrich Gundolf, *Caesar's Mantle* (New York, 1938), 101.

CHAPTER III

1. On the personality of Charles VI, see A. von Arneth, *Geschichte Maria Theresias* (10 vols.; Vienna, Braumüller, 1862),

I, 55 ff.; Eugen Guglia, *Maria Theresia* (2 vols.; Munich, 1917), I, 3 ff.; H. Kretschmayr, *Maria Theresia* (Gotha, 1925), 12 ff.

2. See particularly W. Roscher, *Geschichte der National-ökonomik in Deutschland* (Munich, 1874); M. Adler, *Anfänge der merkantilen Gewerbepolitik in Österreich* (Vienna, 1903); M. von Merzi, *Die Finanzen Österreichs von 1701 bis 1740* (Vienna, 1890); P. von Radics, *Kaiser Karl VI als Staats- und Volkswirt* (Innsbruck, 1886).

3. F. M. Mayer, *Geschichte Österreichs* (Vienna, 1909), II, 352 ff.

4. *Ibid.*, II, 452. See on this issue above all Arneth, *op. cit.*, IX, chapter XII (334-88); F. Walter, *Die Theresianische Staatsreform von 1749* (Vienna, 1958).

5. Arneth, *op. cit.*, IX, 148 ff.; F. Maass, *Der Josephinismus: Quellen zu seiner Geschichte in Österreich, 1760-1790* (Vienna, 1951—), I, 1-105; II, 3-126; III, 10-41; E. Winter, *Der Josefinismus und seine Geschichte* (Brünn, 1943), 11-126.

6. Arneth, *op. cit.*, IX, 90 ff.; Winter, *op. cit.*, 67 ff.

7. See here the critical position of Arneth, otherwise an ardent admirer of the Maria Theresan regime, Arneth, *op. cit.*, IX, 261 ff.

8. On the educational reforms see particularly Arneth, *op. cit.*, IX, chapters VIII-IX (225-60); IV, 109-32; Mayer, *op. cit.*, II, 595 ff.; F. Krones, *Handbuch der Geschichte Österreichs* (4 vols.; Berlin, 1880, 1881), IV, 466 ff.; G. Strakosch-Grassmann, *Geschichte des österreichischen Unterrichtswesens* (Vienna, 1905).

9. Arneth, *op. cit.*, IX, 237; quoted from Emperor Joseph's comments of July 15, 1772.

10. Instruction of 1776, Arneth, *op. cit.*, IX, 241 ff.; see also Strakosch-Grassmann, *op. cit.*

11. On Van Swieten see particularly W. Müller, *Gerhard van Swieten* (Vienna, 1883); Arneth, *op. cit.*, IV, 117 ff.; F. Walter, *Männer um Maria Theresia* (Vienna, 1951), 123 ff.

12. Erich Schmidt, *Lessing* (Berlin, 1909), II, 139 ff.

13. At this point see F. Valjavec, *Der Josephinismus* (Vienna, 1945); F. Valjavec, *Die Entstehung der politischen Strömungen in Deutschland, 1770-1813* (Munich, 1951); Maass, *op. cit.* I, II; Winter, *op. cit.*; F. Fejtö, *Un Habsburg révolutionnaire, Joseph II* (Paris, 1953), 146-55, 232-46.

14. See particularly A. Fischel, *Sprachenrecht* (Brünn, 1910), and his *Materialien zur Sprachenfrage* (Brünn, 1902).

15. On the evolution of the concept of Josephinism, see also F. Engel-Janosi, "Josephs II Tod im Urteil der Zeit," *Mitteilungen des österreichischen Instituts für Geschichtsforschung*, XXX (1944), 325-46; Valjavec, *Josephinismus*, particularly 122 ff.; Georg Franz, *Liberalismus: Die deutschliberale Bewegung in der habsburgischen Monarchie* (Munich, 1955), 11 ff.; Karl Eder, *Der Liberalismus in Altösterreich* (Vienna, 1955), 40-56.

16. As specimens of such Communist and National Socialist evaluations see Eva Priester, *Kurze Geschichte Österreichs* (Vienna, 1949), II, 202 ff.; Ernst Fischer, *Österreich* (Vienna, 1946), 26 ff.; J. Bibl, *Kaiser Joseph II: Ein Vorkämpfer der deutschen Idee* (Vienna, 1943).

17. Bibl, *op. cit.*, 307-08, 7-8.

CHAPTER IV

1. On Sonnenfels' family background see particularly Franz Kopetzky, *Josef und Franz von Sonnenfels: Das Leben und Wirken eines edlen Brüderpaares* (Vienna, 1882), vi ff.; Willibald Müller, *Joseph von Sonnenfels* (Vienna, 1882); K. von Wurzbach (ed.), *Biographisches Lexikon des Kaiserthums Österreich* (Vienna, 1877), XXXV. For the only fairly comprehensive bibliography on Sonnenfels see Michael Holzmann and Max Portheim, "Materialien zu einer Sonnenfels Biographie," *Zeitschrift für die Geschichte der Juden in der Tschechoslowakei* (Brünn), Annual 1930-31, 198-207, and Annual 1931-32, 60-66. Ignaz de Luca, *Das gelehrte Österreich* (Vienna, 1776-78), one volume published in two separate parts. Pages 143-81 contain a brief biography of Sonnenfels until 1775. The first part of this entry, until roughly 1761 (pp. 143-70), is an autobiography; see especially 144-51.

See also Sonnenfels' memorandum of 1763 to the Empress Maria Theresa concerning his unsalaried assistance to his father's work as interpreter in the Hebrew language. See Österreichisches Staatsarchiv, Allgemeines Verwaltungsarchiv, Polizei- und Cameralwissenschaften, Fascicle 10, 1763–84. (In the following notes the archives are cited as "AV" or "AVPC, Fasc. ...")

For unpublished primary sources on Sonnenfels, see also the Bibliography, Section I, following these notes.

2. See Sonnenfels in de Luca, *op. cit.*, 144-47; see also Müller, *op. cit.*, 3 ff.; J. W. Nagl and J. Zeidler, *Deutsch-österreichische Literaturgeschichte* (Vienna, 1899-1914), II, 260 f.

3. See A. von Arneth, *Geschichte Maria Theresias* (Vienna, Braumüller, 1862), IX, 203-05.

4. Sonnenfels in de Luca, *op. cit.*, 148; Müller, *op. cit.*, 13 ff. Sonnenfels refers here to the already outdated German Baroque poets.

5. Wenzel Lustkandl, *Sonnenfels und Kudler* . . . (Vienna, 1891).

6. Müller, *op. cit.*, 16.

7. Sonnenfels in de Luca, *op. cit.*, 150 ff.; Müller, *op. cit.*, 16.

8. Wurzbach, *op. cit.*, XXXV, 319.

9. See for example *Der Mann ohne Vorurteil,* written 1765-67, in Sonnenfels' *Gesammelte Schriften* (Vienna, 1783), I, 285-87; Sonnenfels in de Luca, *op. cit.*, 152-56; AVPC, Fasc. 15, "Über den Geschaftsstil," memorandum of 1784 on literary style for newly appointed public servants. See also F. M. Mayer, *Geschichte und Kulturleben Deutschösterreichs* (Vienna, 1929-37), II (ed. by H. Pirchegger), 351; Arneth, *op. cit.*, IX, 269; Müller, *op. cit.*, 50; Lustkandl, *op. cit.*, 5, 55, particularly on Sonnenfels' correspondence with the great philosopher of language Johann Christoph Adelung and the terms introduced by Sonnenfels into the German language.

NOTE: References to the various volumes of Sonnenfels' *Gesammelte Schriften* will hereafter be abbreviated as "S:GS," followed by volume number and other relevant data. For example, the citation at the beginning of Note 9 would hereafter be "S:GS I, 285-87."

10. AV, Hofkommission in Gesetzessachen, CCXIX, proceedings of 1798-99.

11. On Sonnenfels' career see principally his autobiography and biography in de Luca, *op. cit.*, previously cited works of Kopetzky, Müller, and Lustkandl, and the articles in Wurzbach, XXXV, and in *Allgemeine deutsche Biographie*, XXXIV. See also Arneth, *op. cit.*, IX, 201-11.

12. AVPC, Fasc. 10, decrees by the empress concerning Sonnenfels' salary and salary rises of 1764, 1765, and 1769, and conferment of the title government counselor *(Regierungsrat)*; see further Fasc. 15, memorandum of 1776 by Sonnenfels regarding his salary.

13. See Note 12, above, particularly Sonnenfels' memorandum of 1776.

14. Nagl and Zeidler, *op. cit.*, II, 258.

15. Kopetzky, *op. cit.*, 361; see also section *p* of this essay, below.

16. On the history of the Jews in Austria from Leopold I to the beginning of the reign of Maria Theresa see particularly Simon Dubnow, *Die Geschichte des jüdischen Volkes in der Neuzeit* (Berlin, 1930), VII, 264-84; H. Graetz, *History of the Jews* (Philadelphia, 1895), V, chapters IV-VII; M. Grunwald, *Vienna* (Philadelphia, 1936), 113-38; H. Tietze, *Die Juden Wiens* (Vienna, 1935), 65-98; S. Mayer, *Die Wiener Juden, 1700-1900* (Vienna, 1918), 71-101.

17. J. A. Mahan, *Maria Theresa of Austria* (New York, 1932), 255; on the Jews under Maria Theresa and Joseph II see further Dubnow, *op. cit.*, VII, 284-92, 372-84; Grunwald, *op. cit.*, 139-65; Tietze, *op. cit.*, 98-122; Arneth, *op. cit.*, IV, 41 ff.; Sebastian Brunner, *Joseph II* (Freiburg i. B., 1885), 137-48.

18. Eugen Guglia, *Maria Theresia* (2 vols.; Munich, 1917), I, 363; see also Mahan, *op. cit.*, 255.

19. On Sonnenfels' personal relationship with the Austrian rulers, primarily Maria Theresa and Joseph II, see AVPC, Fasc. 10, 15, and Österreichisches Haus-, Hof- und Staatsarchiv, Vertrauliche Akten der Kabinettskanzlei, Fasc. 41. See further Kopetzky, *op. cit.*, 78 ff.; Lustkandl, *op. cit.*, 16 ff.; F. Mencker in *Allgemeine deutsche Biographie*, XXXIV, 634; P. Mitrofanov, *Joseph II* (Vienna, 1910), I, 92 ff.; Sebastian Brunner, "Joseph von Sonnenfels," in *Die Mysterien der Aufklärung in Österreich, 1770-1800* (Mayence, 1869), 54 ff.

In the case of Leopold II, by reason of the shortness of his reign, and of Francis I because of the change of ideological atmosphere, the relationship with Sonnenfels was of less importance. Some material is to be found, however, in Haus-, Hof- und Staatsarchiv, Vertrauliche Akten der Kabinettskanzlei, Fasc. 41, and in Haus-, Hof- und Staatsarchiv, the fascicle "Sonnenfels, Miscellanea."

20. S:GS VIII, "Rede auf Marien Theresien," 25; see also Brunner, *Die Mysterien*, 68 ff.

21. S:GS VIII, "Die letzten Tage Theresiens," 65 ff.

22. See particularly AVPC, Fasc. 10, the cardinal's and Count Chotek's long memoranda of 1767 to the empress on Sonnenfels' anti-religious attitude in his *Lehrbuch der Polizey- und Cameralwissenschaften*. None of the official documents refers to Sonnenfels' family background. See Arneth, *op. cit.*, IX, 203; Mitrofanov, *op. cit.*, II, 740, 804, 827, on Migazzi's opposition.

See Müller, *op. cit.*, 104 ff.; on Migazzi's personality see also C. Wolfsgruber, *Kardinal Migazzi* (Saalgau, 1890).

23. Kopetzky, *op. cit.*, 61; Grunwald, *op. cit.*, 330.

24. See for instance Friedrich Nicolai, *Besprechung einer Reise durch Deutschland und die Schweiz im Jahre 1781* (Berlin, 1784), III, 353, and the Viennese historian of the pre-March period Franz Gräffer, *Kleine Wiener Memoiren* (Vienna, 1848), II, 73, 74.

25. Max Pirker, "Joseph von Sonnenfels," in *Österreichische Rundschau*, LI, 72, 73; as to Gebler on Lessing, see Note 169, below; on Van Swieten see AVPC, Fasc. 10. Van Swieten's memoranda to the empress of 1767, however, support Sonnenfels in substantive matters. On Van Swieten see further W. Müller, *Gerhard van Swieten* (Vienna, 1883), and Guglia, *op. cit.*, II, 79; on Kaunitz see Alexander Novotny, *Staatskanzler Kaunitz* (Vienna, 1947), 119, 156.

26. At this point see particularly Fritz Valjavec, *Der Josephinismus* (Vienna, 1948), 133, 168; G. Franz, *Liberalismus* (Munich, 1955), 11 ff., 186 ff.; Karl Eder, *Der Liberalismus in Altösterreich* (Vienna, 1955), 26 ff., 222; Brunner, *op. cit.*

27. See preceding Note 26.

28. See particularly the significant pamphlet "Aloysis von Sonnenfels Des uralten und weltberuehmten Wienerischen Universitaet Mitgliedes, JUDISCHES BLUT-ECKEL oder das von Gebrauch des unschuldigen Christen Bluts angeklagte, untersuchte und unschuldig befundene Judenthum. Als Teil der Wahrheit an Tag gegeben. Mit Erlaubnis hoher Obrigkeit Anno Domini, 1752" (Vienna); see also Dubnow, *op. cit.*, VII, 143, 144, who erroneously refers here to Joseph but obviously means Alois (Berlin), the father.

29. See Müller, *Sonnenfels*, 28 ff.

30. See for instance S:GS VIII, 153, 154.

31. Gräffer, *op. cit.*, II, 73, 74. In connection with these installations, the charge was made that Sonnenfels had improperly employed his brother as contractor. See Sebastian Brunner, *Lessingiasis und Nathanologie* (Paderborn, 1890), refuted by Kopetzky, *op. cit.*, 244 ff. In this context it is worth noting that Sonnenfels, after more than half a century of government service, left an estate of only 3,000 guilders. See Müller, *Sonnenfels*, 43.

As to Sonnenfels' widely criticized conceit, see for instance his memorandum to the empress of 1776, AVPC, Fasc. 10, and Sonnenfels in de Luca, *op. cit.,* 154. See also R. M. Werner (ed.), "Geblers und Nicolais Briefwechsel während der Jahre 1771-1786," *Aus dem Josephinischen Wien* (Berlin, 1888), 64 (letter by Gebler of February 14, 1775); 109, 130 f. (letters by Nicolai of February 15, 1783, and March 6, 1785).

32. Such a line of argument is well reasoned in Tietze, *Die Juden Wiens,* 107-11.

33. See particularly Tietze as referred to in Note 32.

34. See particularly the ideas of Rousseau as expressed in his *Consideration sur le gouvernement de Pologne* (1772).

35. Wilhelm Roscher, *Geschichte der Nationalökonomik in Deutschland* (Munich, 1874), 533.

36. S:GS IV, *Der Mann ohne Vorurteil,* Appendix, 31 ff. See also Lustkandl, *op. cit.* 27.

37. S:GS III, *Mann ohne Vorurteil,* part III, 282.

38. Sonnenfels, *Politische Abhandlungen* (Vienna, 1777), 101-09. See also Sonnenfels' undated memorandum (presumably directed to the emperor Leopold II) on the basic principles to be submitted to the Bohemian Estates, Vertrauliche Akten der Kabinettskanzlei, vol. XLI/XVIII.

39. See for example his last treatise, with the characteristic title *Über die öffentliche Sicherheit oder die Sorgfalt, die Privatkräfte des Staates in einem untergeordneten Verhältnisse zu erhalten* (Vienna, 1817).

40. S:GS VII, "Über die Liebes des Vaterlandes," 107 (chapter V, 88-133); S:GS II, *Der Mann ohne Vorurteil,* 41-46; see also Kopetzky, *op. cit.,* 74, 75.

41. S:GS VII, "Über die Liebes des Vaterlandes," 91.

42. *Ibid.,* 108, 109.

43. *Ibid.*

44. "Das Bild des Adels," introductory lecture at the Theresan Academy in 1770. For the whole lecture, see S:GS VIII, 147, 153, 154, 176. See also the following lecture, "Über den Beweggrund der Verwendung," given in 1768, 177-204; see particularly 188, 191. See further "Vorschläge über die Reform des Studiums der Cameralwissenschaft" of 1771, AVPC, Fasc. 15.

45. As to other references to the Jewish question, particularly as to Jewish exclusiveness and claims of spiritual superiority, see S:GS VIII, "Über die Liebes des Vaterlandes," 172-75. This cautious defense of Judaism against prejudices significantly acknowledges no specific personal interest of Sonnenfels in the

question. See further on his chairmanship in the commission for the purification of the Talmud, which he owed to his knowledge of Hebrew, Kopetzky, *op. cit.*, 353. Here again he avoids expressing any personal interest in this problem.

46. Kopetzky, *op. cit.*, 74, 75; Brunner, *Die Mysterien*, 76 ff.

47. See S:GS III, *Der Mann ohne Vorurteil*, part III, 250-60; S:GS VII, "Über die Liebe des Vaterlandes," 133-78.

48. S:GS IX, "Über die Ankunft Pius VI. in Wien," 215-42.

49. See E. Winter, *Der Josefinismus und seine Geschichte* (Brünn, 1943), 188, 189.

50. See for instance AVPC, Fasc. 10, rescripts by the empress as to the immoderate character of Sonnenfels' writings of January 18, February 5, June 13, and November, 1767, as well as of December 4, 1772. Neither in any of these rescripts nor in any others does one find an outright suppression of Sonnenfels' writings.

51. See Roscher, *op. cit.*, 601; on Justi, 444-65; on Sonnenfels, 533-52. Roscher's in many respects outdated treatise still gives the most comprehensive picture of Sonnenfels' economic ideas. See also Lustkandl, *op. cit.*, 23-26. See further Felix Spitzer, *Joseph von Sonnenfels als Nationalökonom* (diss.; Berlin, 1906), 122 ff.

52. A fair but not complete bibliography of Sonnenfels' economic writings is contained in Georg Deutsch, "Joseph von Sonnenfels und seine Schüler: Ein Beitrag zur Geschichte der Nationalökonomie," *Österreich-Ungarische Revue*, 1888, 65-85; see 82.

See further Roscher, *op. cit.*, 533-52; Spitzer, *op. cit.*, 122 ff.; and in particular out of an impressive number, the following works by Sonnenfels: The textbook *Grundsätze der Polizei-, Handlungs- und Finanzwissenschaft*, published first in 1765, re-edited eight times, and in use in Austrian universities until 1848. See further "Von der Theuerung in grossen Städten, und dem Mittel derselben abzuhelfen," "Von Mauten und Zöllen," and "XXXX Sätze über die Bevölkerung" (all 1764) and " Von dem Zusammenflusse," all in S:GS X of 1787; see particularly "Von der Theuerung in grossen Städten," 69 ff., 89 ff.; "Von dem Zusammenflusse," 103 ff., 171 ff., 184; "Von Mauten und Zöllen," 287 ff.; "XXXX Sätze über die Bevölkerung," 398 ff., 414 ff.

See further the volume *Joseph von Sonnenfels, Politische Abhandlungen,* edited by his former student Ignaz de Luca (Vienna, 1777), which contains among other essays "Versuch über das Verhältnis der Stände," "Vom Maut- und Zollwesen" (a somewhat different version of "Von Mauten und Zöllen"), "Über das Wort Bevölkerung" (another version of the "XXXX Sätze . . ."); see particularly "Vom Maut- und Zollwesen" 191; "Über das Wort Bevölkerung," 254 ff.

See also AVPC, Fasc. 10, Sonnenfels' memorandum of 1767 as to the principles embodied in his textbook on police and cameral sciences.

53. See Müller, *Sonnenfels,* 104-14.

54. See AVPC, Fasc. 10, memorandum by Cardinal Count Migazzi to the empress and the imperial rescript to Count Chotek of January, 1767, in which the empress sustains the cardinal. See further the official reprimand to Sonnenfels of February 5, 1767. Lustkandl, *op. cit.,* 16 ff.; Arneth, *op. cit.,* IX, 204.

55. AVPC, Fasc. 10, imperial rescript of November, 1767. See also Kopetzky, *op. cit.,* 78 ff.

56. See S:GS III, *Der Mann ohne Vorurteil,* part III.

57. See S:GS II, *Der Mann ohne Vorurteil,* part II, 109 ff., and Sonnenfels, *Politische Abhandlungen,* "Versuch über das Verhältnis der Stände," 110 ff. See also *Von der Verwandlung der Domänen in Bauerngüter* (Vienna, 1773); Lustkandl, *op. cit.,* 29 ff., 34; Müller, *Sonnenfels,* 110 ff.; Roscher, *op. cit.,* 558 ff.

58. See particularly the following Sonnenfels' treatises with the highly significant titles "Über die Aufgabe: Was ist Wucher und welches sind die Mittel demselben ohne Strafgesetze Einhalt zu tun?" (On the problem: What is usury and which are the means to check it without resorting to criminal law? [Vienna, 1791]) and "Abhandlung über die Aufgabe der Wuchergesetze" (Treatise on the abolition-of-usury legislation [Vienna, 1791]), "Vom Wucher" (Vienna, 1791, polemic *contra* Kres), "Abhandlung von der Theuerung in grossen Städten und dem Mittel derselben abzuhelfen" (Leipzig, 1769). See also AVPC, Fasc. 10, Sonnenfels' memorandum to the empress of 1767 in defense of his *Grundsätze der Polizeywissenschaft;* Roscher, *op. cit.,* 543; Müller, *Sonnenfels,* 110 ff.

59. S:GS II, *Der Mann ohne Vorurteil,* part II, 236, 238; see also Lustkandl, *op. cit.,* 29, on guild restrictions.

60. Sonnenfels, *Politische Abhandlungen,* "Versuch über das Verhältnis der Stände" (study of the relationship between the Estates), 131 ff., 143 ff., 117 ff.

61. See in *ibid.,* "Aus den Anfangsgründen der Handlung,"

9 ff., 20 ff., 30 ff.; S:GS X, "Betrachtungen über die neun Handlungsgrundsätze Englands," 185 ff.; see also S:GS X, "Von dem Zusammenflusse," 103 ff.; Müller, *Sonnenfels*, 110 ff.

62. S:GS VIII, "Die erste Vorlesung im Jahre 1782," 128-29.

63. S:GS II, *Der Mann ohne Vorurteil*, part II, 191 ff.; Roscher, *op. cit.*, 550; Eva Priester, *Kurze Geschichte Österreichs* (Vienna, 1949), 164.

64. S:GS III, *Der Mann ohne Vorurteil*, part III, 284, see also 279-83.

65. See also AV, Hofkommission in Gesetzessachen, CCXIX, on Sonnenfels' substantial contribution to drafting an Austrian code of criminal law.

66. See Roscher, *op. cit.*, 558 ff.; Kopetzky, *op. cit.*, 351 ff.

67. See F. M. Mayer, *Geschichte Österreichs* (3d ed.), II, 456 ff., 486 ff.; Guglia, *op. cit.*, II, 362 ff.; H. Hantsch, *Die Geschichte Österreichs* (Graz, 1947-50), II, 247 ff.; Arneth, *op. cit.*, IX, 198 ff.; Kopetzky, *op. cit.*, 351 ff.; Mitrofanov, *op. cit.*, II, 503-78; E. von Kwiatowsky, *Die Constitutio Criminalis Theresiana* (Innsbruck, 1904).

68. See Arneth, *op. cit.*, IX, 198 ff.; Guglia, *op. cit.*, II, 362 ff.; Mitrofanov, *op. cit.*, II, 511, 524, 592 ff.; Lustkandl, *op. cit.*, 16. Sonnenfels, however, even in his contribution to the criminal code of 1803 still advocated "minor corporal punishment" for domestic servants, apprentices, journeymen, and day laborers. See his *Grundsätze der Polizey-, Handlungs- und Finanzwissenschaft* (5th rev. ed.; Vienna, 1787), part I. See also F. Simonson, *Joseph von Sonnenfels und seine Grundsätze der Polizey* (Berlin, Leipzig, n.d.), 30, 45 ff.

69. S:GS VII, part II, 24 ff., *Über die Abschaffung der Folter*, first published 1775. See also AVPC, Fasc. 10, Sonnenfels' memorandum to the empress of 1772.

70. See Note 54, above, and AVPC, Fasc. 10; see also the memorandum by Count Chotek of 1767 to the empress against Sonnenfels' views on capital punishment. Mitrofanov, *op. cit.*, II, 740, 827; Lustkandl, *op. cit.*, 16.

71. S:GS VII, part II, 27, *Über die Abschaffung der Folter*, and Note 70 above.

72. See Mitrofanov, *op. cit.*, II, 521-36.

73. For Sonnenfels' major writings on the torture problem, see *Über die Abschaffung der Folter* and his *Sätze aus der Polizey-, Handlungs- und Finanzwissenschaft* (both Vienna, 1765-67—i.e.,

preceding the *Constitutio Criminalis Theresiana*). See further AVPC, Fasc. 10, Sonnenfels' great memorandum of 1772 to the empress.

For monographic literature, see Josef Feil, *Sonnenfels und Maria Theresia* (Vienna, 1859); C. von Hock, *Der österreichische Staatsrat* (Vienna, 1879); W. Wahlberg, *Gesammelte Kleinere Schriften*, II, 265 ff.; W. Lustkandl, *Die Josefinischen Ideen* (Vienna, 1881), 15, 97. See further Müller, *Sonnenfels*, 128 ff.; Arneth, *op. cit.*, IX, 199 ff.; Kopetzky, *op. cit.*, 79, 199-218; Guglia, *op. cit.*, II, 362 f.; Mayer, *op. cit.*, II, 456 f.; Kwiatowsky, *op. cit.*; Brunner, *Die Mysterien*, 59 ff., 79 ff.

74. See the memoranda by Count Chotek and Cardinal Migazzi of 1767 in AVPC, Fasc. 10; see *ibid.*, the rescripts of the empress of February, June, August, and September, 1767, and of 1772. See also Arneth, *op. cit.*, IX, 202; Brunner, *Die Mysterien*, 75.

75. AVPC, Fasc. 10, Sonnenfels' memorandum of 1772; Arneth, *op. cit.*, IX, 207-08. For the text of Sonnenfels' presentation to the empress, see also Feil, *op. cit.*, 24-33.

76. AVPC, Fasc. 10, memorandum by Count Blümegen and rescript by the empress of December 4, 1772.

77. Arneth, *op. cit.*, IX, 213.

78. S:GS III, *Der Mann ohne Vorurteil*, part III, 353; see also 337 ff.

79. *Ibid.*, 356.

80. *Ibid.*, 376-96.

81. *Ibid.*, 427-32, 446-76; Kopetzky, *op. cit.*, 260 ff.

82. S:GS III, *Der Mann ohne Vorurteil*, part III, 476-97.

83. Ludwig Anzengruber, *Das vierte Gebot* (1878).

84. S:GS III, 497-508.

85. *Ibid.*, 553 ff.

86. S:GS IV, *Theresie und Eleonore*, 11-20, 521 ff.

87. *Ibid.*, 117.

88. Müller, *Sonnenfels*, 124.

89. See S:GS VIII, "Über den Nachteil der vermehrten Universitäten," introductory lecture in 1771, 245 ff.; S:GS X, "Von der Theuerung in grossen Städten und dem Mittel derselben abzuhelfen," 86-93; Guglia, *op. cit.*, II, 77 ff.; Arneth, *op. cit.*, IX, 215-24.

90. S:GS VIII, "Über den Beweggrund der Verwendung,"

lecture before the young nobility of the Savoyan Academy in 1768, 182, 183, 188.

91. *Ibid.,* 188-90. See also 191-93; see further S:GS VIII, "Das Bild des Adels," the lecture of 1770, 174-76, and "Von der Bescheidenheit im Vortrage seiner Meinung," that of 1772, 205-42. See further AVPC, Fasc. 10, *Vorschläge über die Reform des Studiums der Cameralwissenschaften* (1771), and Fasc. 15, "Über den Geschäftsstil . . ." written in 1784; Österreichisches Haus-, Hof- und Staatsarchiv, Vertrauliche Akten der Kabinettskanzlei, XLI, in an undated memorandum of Sonnenfels, the remarks pertaining to the status of nobility in modern society.

92. Herman Hettner, *Geschichte der deutschen Literatur im achtzehnten Jahrhundert* (Leipzig, 1928), II, 221. See also Rudolph Lothar, *Das Wiener Burgtheater* (Vienna, 1899), 22-24; Karl von Görner, *Der Hanswurst Streit in Wien und Joseph von Sonnenfels* (Vienna, 1884), 79 ff.

93. Franz Muncker, "Sonnenfels," in *Allgemeine deutsche Biographie,* XXXIV, 628-35. For *Der Mann ohne Vorurteil* see S:GS I-IV. See also Hermann Rollett (ed.), *Briefe von Sonnenfels* (Vienna, 1874), which contains nine letters to Klotz written between 1768 and 1770.

94. J. von Sonnenfels, *Theresie und Eleonore* (separate edition; Leipzig, 1765); also in S:GS IV.

95. Görner, *op. cit.,* 11.

96. Erich Schmidt, *Lessing* (Berlin, 1909), II, 137.

97. Kopetzky, *op. cit.,* 60.

98. *Allgemeine deutsche Biographie,* XXXIV, "Sonnenfels," 631.

99. See at this point H. K. Kettler, *Baroque Tradition in the Literary Enlightenment, 1700-1750* (Cambridge, n.d.).

100. See *ibid.,* 26-92, 129-31; W. H. Bruford, *Theatre, Drama and Audience in Goethe's Germany* (London, 1950), 40 ff.

101. See Sonnenfels in I. de Luca, *Das gelehrte Österreich,* 152-64.

102. See S:GS V, *Briefe über die wienerische Schaubühne,* part I, Introduction; Rollett, *Briefe von Sonnenfels,* particularly letters I, III, VI, VIII, IX; Sonnenfels in de Luca, *op. cit.,* 167-70, and de Luca in *ibid.,* 173-76; Görner, *op. cit.,* 86; Bruford, *op. cit.,* 40 ff., 86 ff.

103. S:GS III, *Der Mann ohne Vorurteil,* part III; S:GS V-VI, *Briefe über die wienerische Schaubühne,* parts I and II.

104. Görner, *op. cit.*, 55, 56.

105. S:GS V, *Briefe über die wienerische Schaubühne,* part I, 3-4.

106. S:GS III, *Der Mann ohne Vorurteil,* part III, 122-26.

107. *Ibid.,* 175.

108. *Ibid.,* 179, 180.

109. S:GS VI, *Fortsetzung der Briefe über die wienerische Schaubühne,* 109.

110. *Ibid.,* 184-88; on Sonnenfels' critical evaluation of dramatic literature as discussed here see also S:GS V, *Briefe über die wienerische Schaubühne,* 308 ff.; Görner, *op. cit.,* 58-63.

111. S:GS VI, *Fortsetzung der Briefe über die wienerische Schaubühne,* 32-34.

112. For the principal literature on the question see, as to Sonnenfels' own writings, particularly S:GS III, *Der Mann ohne Vorurteil,* part III; S:GS V, *Briefe über die wienerische Schaubühne;* S:GS VI, *Fortsetzung der Briefe über die wienerische Schaubühne.* See also R. M. Werner (ed.), *Der Wiener Hanswurst: Stranitzky und seiner Nachfolger ausgewählte Schriften* (Vienna, 1883-86), "Wiener Neudrucke," Nos. IV, VI-VII, X; Görner, *op. cit.;* Lothar, *op. cit.;* Nagl and Zeidler, *op. cit.,* I; E. Schmidt, *op. cit.,* II; Otto Rommel, *Die Alt-Wiener Volkskomödie* (Vienna, 1952); H. Rollett (ed.), *Briefe von Sonnenfels,* see letters I, III, IX. R. M. Werner (ed.), *Aus dem Josephinischen Wien* (Berlin, 1888), 29, 51, 52, 138, 142 (letters by Gebler of February 17, 1772, and December 13, 1772); Bruford, *op. cit.,* 60 ff.

113. See Lothar, *op. cit.,* 6 ff.; Görner, *op. cit.,* 1 ff.; Rommel, *op. cit.,* 153 ff.

114. For the text of the imperial order see Görner, *op. cit.,* 4-5.

115. S:GS III, *Der Mann ohne Vorurteil,* part III, 99 ff.; Görner, *op. cit.,* 16 ff.; Müller, *Sonnenfels,* 50 ff.; see here also the references to *Der Mann ohne Vorurteil.*

116. Görner, *op. cit.,* 74 ff.; see also Hantsch, *op. cit.,* II, 201 ff.; Guglia, *op. cit.,* II, 220 ff.; Werner, *Aus dem Josephinischen Wien,* 29, 51 ff., 138, 142.

117. S:GS III, *Der Mann ohne Vorurteil,* part III, 106 ff., 167 ff.

118. S:GS V, *Briefe über die wienerische Schaubühne,* 189 ff.; S:GS III, *Der Mann ohne Vorurteil,* 117 ff.

119. S:GS III, *Der Mann ohne Vorurteil,* 120 ff., 154 ff.

120. *Ibid.,* 184 ff., 194 ff., 197 ff.; S:GS VI, *Fortsetzung der*

Briefe über die wienerische Schaubühne, 232 ff.

121. S:GS V, *Briefe über die wienerische Schaubühne,* 148, 161 ff., 167 ff., 176 ff., 248 ff., 285 ff.; S:GS VI, *Fortsetzung der Briefe* . . . 310 ff., 428 f.

122. S:GS VI, *Fortsetzung der Briefe* . . . 232 ff.

123. *Ibid.,* 141 ff., 232 ff., 314 ff., 371-83.

124. *Ibid.,* 29 ff., 80 ff.; Sonnenfels in de Luca, *op. cit.,* 169; de Luca in *ibid.,* 175.

125. S:GS III, *Der Mann ohne Vorurteil,* 135 ff.

126. *Ibid.,* 112-13, 115.

127. See for instance S:GS V, *Briefe über die wienerische Schaubühne,* 196 ff.; Görner, *op. cit.*

128. See Hettner, *op. cit.,* II, 220-21.

129. The quoted letter of Nicolai to Lessing, *de dato* Berlin, 8–2–1769, is fully published in G. E. Lessing, *Sämtliche Werke* (Leipzig, 1904), XIV, 305. As to Nicolai, see also Werner, *Aus dem Josephinischen Wien,* 51 f. (letter of December 12, 1773).

130. Görner, *op. cit.,* 47, see also 45-54; Rommel, *op. cit.,* 386. Ch. G. Klemm, *Der auf den Parnass versetzte grüne Hut* (1767), "Wiener Neudrucke," IV (Vienna, 1883); on Sonnenfels' own criticism of the *Grüne Hut* see S:GS III, *Der Mann ohne Vorurteil,* 313-26. See also his letter to Klotz of February 25, 1769, in S:GS VI, *Fortsetzung der Briefe über die wienerische Schaubühne,* 410-37, and de Luca, *op. cit.,* 174 ff.

131. Klemm, *op. cit.;* S:GS VI, *Fortsetzung der Briefe über die wienerische Schaubühne,* 410-37; de Luca, *op. cit.,* 174 ff. See also Werner, *Aus dem Josephinischen Wien;* Rollett, *Briefe von Sonnenfels.*

132. For the final history of the *Hanswurst* conflict, see Görner, *op. cit.,* 74-86; Lothar, *op. cit.,* 17-25; Rommel, *op. cit.,* 337 ff.

133. Hettner, *op. cit.,* II, 220; Gräffer, *op. cit.,* II, 73, 74; Wurzbach, *op. cit.,* XXXV, 326 f.

134. G. E. Lessing, *Hamburgische Dramaturgie,* part I, section XVII.

135. Schmidt, *op. cit.,* II, 137-39; Nagl and Zeidler, *op. cit.,* I, 816.

136. Schmidt, *op. cit.,* II, 139.

137. Kopetzky, *op. cit.,* 311 ff.

138. The three principal treatises in which Sonnenfels deals with problems of formative art are "Ermunterung zur Lektüre an junge Künstler," a lecture given on the occasion of the distribution of prizes in the new Academy for Engravers in 1768, "Von

der Urbanität der Künstler," a lecture delivered at the same occasion in 1771, and "Von dem Verdienste des Porträtmalers," a lecture read there in 1768. For all three lectures, see S:GS VIII, 273-96, 297-324, 349-410.

139. "Von der Urbanität der Künstler," 319 f.

140. "Von dem Verdienste des Porträtmalers," 363-64.

141. "Ermunterung zur Lektüre an junge Künstler," 282; see also 281, 283-87.

142. "Von dem Verdienste des Porträtmalers," 380 (quoted from Maximus Tyrius, oratio XVI); see also 374 ff.

143. *Ibid.*, 382.

144. *Ibid.*, 393–94.

145. Lessing's *Briefe antiquarischen Inhalts* comprise his writings against Klotz.

146. Rollett, *Briefe von Sonnenfels,* letter V, 15 f.

147. See Hettner, *op. cit.,* II, 221.

148. De Luca, *Das gelehrte Österreich,* quoted from Rollett, *Briefe von Sonnenfels.* See also the introduction to Sonnenfels, *Politische Abhandlungen* (Vienna, 1777), by de Luca. See also Leopold Alois Hoffmann, professor at the University of Vienna, *Höchst wichtige Ereignisse über einige der allerernsthaftesten Angelegenheiten dieses Zeitalters . . .* (Vienna, 1795), 1: "Mr. von Sonnenfels has no reason to consider it a flattery if one lists him among the classical writers of Germany. With particular regard to Austria he is entitled to call himself a literary Prometheus."

149. See also Note 24, above.

150. Nicolai, *op. cit.,* III, 353-56.

151. Gräffer, *op. cit.,* II, 73–74. Gräffer in the same context, however, in two anecdotes previously referred to mildly satirizes Sonnenfels' vanity and self-esteem. On the second point see also Nagl and Zeidler's references to Gebler's estimate of Sonnenfels' vanity, *op. cit.,* II, 252.

152. Franz Gräffer and Czikann, *Österreichische National-Enzyklopädie,* V, 1835-37.

153. See Haus-, Hof- und Staatsarchiv, Vertrauliche Akten der Kabinettskanzlei, XLI/XVI, memorandum by Sonnenfels to the emperor, July 22, 1790. Here Sonnenfels complains about his forced inactivity during the reign of Joseph II and asks for greater responsibilities in the field of administration. See also Kopetzky, *op. cit.,* 321; *Allgemeine deutsche Biographie,* XXXIV, 634.

154. Nagl and Zeidler, *op. cit.,* II, 258; Pirker, *op. cit.;*

Österreichische Rundschau (Vienna, 1917), LI, 74; Kopetzky, *op. cit.,* 321-67.

155. See for instance S:GS VIII, "Die erste Vorlesung in dem akademischen Jahrgange 1782," 144 f.

156. See for instance AVPC, Fasc. 110, rescript by the emperor of November, 1769, in which he gives Sonnenfels thanks and praise for the controversial *Lehrbuch der Polizey- und Cameralwissenchaften.*

157. The limitations of this influence as well as that of Sonnenfels' position become apparent in the letter of the emperor to his brother Leopold, November 14, 1779. See A. von Arneth (ed.), *Maria Theresia und Joseph II: Ihre Correspondenz samt Briefen Josephs an seinen Bruder Leopold* (Vienna, 1867-68), III, 235 f.

158. See the Sonnenfels memorandum cited in note 153, and particularly Mitrofanov, *op. cit.,* 92, 93, and the references quoted there; see also *Allgemeine deutsche Biographie,* XXXIV, 634, 262 f., 283; Brunner, *Die Mysterien,* 66 ff. His assumption that an impropriety on the part of the brothers Sonnenfels may have been responsible for the emperor's attitude is not substantiated. See also Note 31, above, and S. Brunner, *Joseph II,* 85-88.

159. Mitrofanov, *op. cit.,* I, 93; see particularly the references in his Notes 1 and 2; F. Fejtö, *Un Habsburg Révolutionnaire, Joseph II* (Paris, 1953), 154 ff.

160. Gabriel Honoré, Conte de Mirabeau, *Réflexions sur l'éducation de la jeunesse surtout aux Pays Bas—Autrichiens, tirées en plus grande partie des meilleurs auteurs* (Liège, 1788), *Recueil bleu,* CXVII, No. 15, quoted from Mitrofanov, *op. cit.,* 834, 835.

161. As to Sonnenfels' relationship to another brilliant and even less scrupulous Frenchman, Caron de Beaumarchais, see A. von Arneth, *Beaumarchais und Sonnenfels* (Vienna, 1768).

162. W. Nagel, *Beethoven und seine Klaviersonaten* (Langensalza, 1903), I, 227, 228; A. W. Thayer, *The Life of Ludwig van Beethoven* (New York, 1927), I, 293.

163. S:GS VI, *Fortsetzung der Briefe über die wienerische Schaubühne,* Appendix, letter to Klotz of February 25, 1769, 425-26.

164. See the standard biography of Lessing, Erich Schmidt, *Lessing* (2 vols., 3d ed.; Berlin, 1909), I, 493 ff., 598 f.; II, 133 f., 137 ff., 147; Nagl and Zeidler, *op. cit.,* II, 32; Lustkandl, *op. cit.,* 8; Görner, *op. cit.,* 85; Kopetzky, *op. cit.,* 60; Lothar, *op. cit.,*

24-26; Müller, *Sonnenfels*, 90 ff. For Lessing's evaluation of Sonnenfels see above all G. E. Lessing, *Sämtliche Schriften,* quoted here from the third edition by Karl Lachmann (Leipzig, Göschen, 1904-07), XVII-XXI. For Sonnenfels on Lessing see further numerous references in S:GS V-VI, *Briefe über die wienerische Schaubühne* and *Fortsetzung der Briefe über die wienerische Schaubühne,* as quoted before; as to personal relations, see also Rollet, *Briefe von Sonnenfels,* letters II, VII, VIII; J. J. A. von Hagen, *Briefe deutscher Gelehrter an den Herrn Geheimrat Klotz* (Halle, 1773); Werner, *Das Josephinische Wien.*

165. Lessing, *op. cit.,* XVII, 272; Kopetzky, *op. cit.,* 60. Kopetzky mistakenly names Gleim as the recipient of this letter.

166. Lessing, *op. cit.,* XVII, 351, 352, 368, 369; *Hamburgische Dramaturgie,* part I, section XVII.

167. See Lessing's letter of October 25, 1770, Lessing, *op. cit.,* XVII, 344.

168. Letter to Eva König of January 13, 1771, *op. cit.,* XVII, 368–69.

169. *Ibid.,* XVIII, letters to Eva König of January 23, 1771, and April 10, 1772, 8, 30–31. Lessing, however, was understandably piqued by the fact that Sonnenfels left a letter unanswered in which he aired his wishes and worries concerning the impending performance of *Emilia Galotti* in Vienna. Letter to Tobias Philipp, Baron Gebler, of October 26, 1772, *ibid.,* 55, 56.

170. For the Lessing-Klotz controversy see G. E. Lessing, *Briefe antiquarischen Inhalts;* Rollett, *Briefe von Sonnenfels* (to Klotz); Werner, *Aus dem Josephinischen Wien.*

171. Schmidt, *op. cit.,* I, 675. The Sonnenfels letters are included in J. J. A. von Hagen, *Briefe deutscher Gelehrter an den Herrn Geheimrat Klotz,* and in Rollett, *op. cit.;* see particularly letter VII, also letters II, VIII.

172. Lessing, *op. cit.,* XVIII, 65.

173. Letter to Eva König of December 30, 1772, Lessing, *op. cit.,* XVIII, 71, 72. See further Werner, *Aus dem Josephinischen Wien,* 43 f., 47, 68, 140, 146 (letters by Gebler to Nicolai of May 1 and December 13, 1773, July 15, 1775). Gebler condemns Sonnenfels' attitude. His unfavorable opinion of Sonnenfels' character is reciprocated by Nicolai. See *ibid.* 109, 130 f. (letters of January 29, 1783; March 1, 1785). It is characteristic of Sonnenfels' vanity but also perhaps of his basic kindness that he consist-

ently conceived of Gebler as a genuine friend and the sponsor of his career. See Sonnenfels in de Luca, *op. cit.,* 168 f.

174. Lessing, *op. cit.,* XVIII, 73, 107.

175. See Eva König's letters to Lessing of October and December, 1770, January, 1771 and 1772, April, May, June, October, December, 1772, January, February, August, October, 1773, March, 1774, in Lessing, *op. cit.,* XIX, 392, 428; XX, 4, 13, 118, 119, 156, 167, 172, 185, 199, 207, 225, 230 f., 279, 283 f.; XXI, 19.

176. See Schmidt, *op. cit.,* II, 132: "Yet his [Sonnenfels'] influence was not strong enough to prevent the offer of an appointment for Lessing in Vienna and he let things go"; Nagl and Zeidler, *op. cit.,* II, 32.

177. See the above-quoted Lessing-König correspondence; Lothar, *op. cit.,* 24-26; Schmidt, *op. cit.,* II, 130-49.

178. See for instance his letter of September 3, 1769, to Klotz, Rollett, *op. cit.,* letter VIII.

179. On Mendelssohn and Sonnenfels' rather superficial relationship see Moses Mendelssohn, *Gesammelte Schriften* (Berlin, 1844), V, 620-23; this correspondence of 1784–85 (two letters) deals with the invitation extended to Mendelssohn by Sonnenfels to become a member of the Gesellschaft der Wissenschaften in Vienna.

180. *Goethe's Werke* (Grandduchess of Saxony edition; Weimar, 1896), XXXVII, 239-42.

181. S:GS VII, *Über die Liebe des Vaterlandes,* 1-223. For Goethe's review see *Frankfurter gelehrte Anzeigen* in *Goethe's Werke* (Grandduchess of Saxony ed.), XXXVII, section I, 269-73.

182. *Ibid.,* 270.

183. *Ibid.,* 271.

184. *Ibid.,* 272.

185. *Ibid.,* 273.

186. See Note 152, above.

187. See R. A. Kann, *The Multinational Empire* (New York, 1950), I, 51-68; Valjavec, *Der Josefinismus,* 69 ff.

188. *Ibid.,* 141 ff.; see also Franz, *op. cit.,* 41 ff.; Eder, *op. cit.,* 105 ff.

189. Josef Feil, *Sylvesterspenden* (Vienna, 1858).

190. Wurzbach, *op. cit.,* XXXV, 326.

191. Müller, *Sonnenfels,* 114.

192. Rollett, *Briefe von Sonnenfels,* i–xii.

193. Kopetzky, *op. cit.,* vi.

194. Adolf Bartels, *Geschichte der deutschen Literatur* (Berlin, 1897), 297.

195. Sebastian Brunner, *Lessingiazie und Nathanologie* (Paderborn, 1890), 182-85. For Brunner's earlier, much better substantiated criticism of Sonnenfels, see his essays "Joseph von Sonnenfels" and "Sonnenfels nach der französischen Revolution" in *Die Mysterien der Aufklärung in Österreich, 1770-1800*.

196. For a brief survey of the anti-Semitic currents as far as they can be traced back directly to the Josephine setting, see again Valjavec, *Der Josephinismus*, 157-61; Franz, *op. cit.*, 186 ff., 193 ff.; Eder, *op. cit.*, 222-34.

197. Josef Nadler, *Literaturgeschichte der deutschen Stämme*, III, 344, 345. In his *Österreichische Literaturgeschichte* (Linz, 1948), published after the war, Nadler takes a notably different—in this case indifferent—attitude toward Sonnenfels; see p. 206.

198. Lothar, *op. cit.*, 20; see also 18 ff.

199. Tietze, *op. cit.*, 107-09.

200. *Ibid.*, 110.

201. See also Rudolf Bienenfeld, *Die Religion der religionslosen Juden* (2d ed.; Vienna, 1955).

202. Wenzel Lustkandl, *Rede auf Josef von Sonnenfels und Josef von Kudler*, 4.

CHAPTER V

1. "Rede über Lessing" in the collection of essays, Thomas Mann, *Adel des Geistes* (Stockholm, 1948), 25.

2. For representative examples, see A. Springer, *Geschichte Österreichs seit dem Wiener Frieden 1809* (Leipzig, 1863), I, 1-440; H. Friedjung, *Österreich von 1848 bis 1860* (Stuttgart, 1908), I, 1-13; V. Bibl, *Der Zerfall Österreichs* (Vienna, 1922-24), I: *Kaiser Franz und sein Erbe;* A. J. P. Taylor, *The Habsburg Monarchy, 1809-1918* (London, 1948), 20-46.

3. F. Valjavec, *Die Entstehung der politischen Strömungen in Deutschland, 1770-1815* (Munich, 1951), 320, 321.

4. For the ideological history of Josephinism after 1790, see particularly F. Valjavec, *Der Josephinismus* (Vienna, 1945); E. Winter, *Der Josefinismus und seine Geschichte* (Brünn, 1943); G. Franz, *Liberalismus* (Munich, 1955); K. Eder, *Der Liberalismus in Altösterreich* (Vienna, 1955).

5. See Valjavec, *Entstehung der politischen Strömungen*, 324, 411, 412; Paul Kluckhohn, *Die deutsche Romantik* (Bielefeld,

1924), 154-73; E. Ruprecht, *Der Aufbruch der romantischen Bewegung* (Munich, 1948), 59-101; J. Ch. Allmayer-Beck, *Der Konservatismus in Österreich* (Munich, 1959), 33 ff.

6. *Briefwechsel zwischen Friedrich Gentz und Adam Heinrich Müller, 1800–29* (Stuttgart, 1857), see letters of 1816, 211, 217; see further *Briefe von Friedrich von Gentz an [J. von] Pilat* (Leipzig, 1868), I, 270, also of 1816. For an interpretation of these and similar references, see Paul R. Sweet, *Friedrich von Gentz* (Madison, Wisconsin, 1941), 77, 78, 209, 210, 224, 225; Golo Mann, *Secretary of Europe* (New Haven, 1946), 245. On Gentz and Müller see also notes 8, 10, 11.

7. See Heinrich von Srbik, *Metternich* (Munich, 1925–54), I, 317-420; II, 517-68; Walter Tritsch, *Metternich und sein Monarch* (Darmstadt, 1952), 644-55; Otto Rommel, *Der österreichische Vormärz, 1816-1847* (Leipzig, 1931), 9, 10. Allmayer-Beck, *op. cit.,* 25 ff. As for Metternich's own presentation, see Prince Richard Metternich (ed.), *Aus Metternich's nachgelassenen Papieren* (8 vols.; Vienna, 1880-82). See particularly vol. VII: *Mein politisches Testament.*

8. Adam Müller, *Die Elemente der Staatskunst* (Vienna, 1922), see particularly I, 37; see further A. Müller, *Ausgewählte Abhandlungen* (Jena, 1931); A. Matz, *Herkunft und Gestalt der Adam Müllerschen Lehre von Staat und Kunst* (Philadelphia, 1937), 40-53, 87-88. Of the several studies of the leading authority on Müller, Jacob Baxa, *Adam Müllers Philosophie Aesthetik und Staatswissenschaft* (Berlin, 1929), gives the most succinct brief presentation of his ideas. The standard biography is J. Baxa, *Adam Müller* (Jena, 1930); see further Louis Sauzin, *Adam Heinrich Müller, Sa vie et son oeuvre* (Paris, 1937).

9. Srbik, *op. cit.,* I, 342, 373-74, believes, on the other hand, that Metternich's theory of equilibrium remained alien to Müller. Yet Srbik is concerned primarily with Müller's ambiguous theories, not with their practical implications.

10. For a brief and lucid presentation of Müller's economic theories, see W. Roscher, *Geschichte der Nationalökonomik in Deutschland* (Munich, 1874), 763-78; see also Baxa, *Adam Müller,* 83-98; O. Spann, *Die Hauptheorien der Volkswirtschaftlehre* (Leipzig, 1918), 86-91.

11. A standard edition of Gentz's writings including his letters and diaries, though badly needed, does not exist. The idea referred to in this chapter may be found in Gustav Schlesier (ed.),

Schriften von Friedrich von Gentz (5 parts; Mannheim, 1833–40); F. C. Wittichen (ed.), *Briefe von und an Friedrich von Gentz* (3 vols. in 4; Munich, 1909-13); F. von Gentz, *Tagebücher von . . . Gentz* (Aus dem Nachlass Varnhagen's von Ense; 4 vols.; Leipzig, 1873-74); *Briefwechsel zwischen Friedrich Gentz und Adam Müller* (Stuttgart, 1857). See further Friedrich von Gentz, *Fragmente aus der neuesten Geschichte des politischen Gleichgewichtes in Europa* (Leipzig, 1806); *F. von Gentz on the State of Europe Before and After the French Revolution . . .* (London, 1803); K. Mendelssohn-Bartholdy, *Friedrich von Gentz* (Leipzig, 1867); E. Guglia, *Friedrich von Gentz* (Vienna, 1900); P. Reif, *Friedrich Gentz, An Opponent of the French Revolution and Napoleon* (Urbana, 1912). As noted, the two most recent biographies are Paul R. Sweet, *Friedrich von Gentz, Defender of the Old Order* (Madison, 1941), and Golo Mann, *Secretary of Europe* (New Haven, 1946).

12. See Note 6, above.

13. See A. Huber and A. Dopsch, *Österreichische Reichsgeschichte* (Vienna, 1901), 322, 323; Srbik, *op. cit.*, I, 307, 383-85. On the anti-missionary, anti-romantic governmental policies in the religious sphere see particularly Rudolf Till, *Hofbauer und sein Kreis* (Vienna, 1951), 24-26, 31-32, 39-46, 67-77, 85-94; Sebastian Brunner, *Klemens Maria Hofbauer* (Vienna, 1858). On the measures taken against Catholic rationalism, see Bibl, *op. cit.*, I, 259-74.

14. See Huber and Dopsch, *op. cit.*, 323, 324; H. Hantsch, *Die Geschichte Österreichs* (Vienna, 1950), II, 281, 282; P. Mitrofanov, *Joseph II* (Vienna, 1910), 503-78; A. Strakosch-Grassmann, *Geschichte des Österreichischen Unterrichtswesens* (Vienna, 1905).

15. See Srbik, *op. cit.*, I, 393-401; Valjavec, *Entstehung der Politischen Strömungen*, 315-24.

16. *Max von Löwenthals Tagebuch* in H. Bischoff, *Nikolaus Lenaus Lyrik*, II (Vienna, 1921), 201, quoted by Srbik, *op. cit.*, I, 397-98.

17. See particularly Rommel, *op. cit.*, 5-19; Franz Grillparzer, *Selbstbiographie, Briefe und Tagebücher* (various editions); O. Hellmann, *Joseph Christian von Zedlitz* (Glogau, 1910). As to the later post-Franciscan, pre-March period see also E. Castle, *Nikolaus Lenau* (Leipzig, 1902); E. von Bauernfeld, *Aus Bauernfelds Tagebüchern 1819-79* (2 vols.; Vienna, 1895-96); J. F.

Castelli, *Memoiren meines Lebens* (4 vols.; Vienna, 1861).

18. See, for example, Walter C. Langsam, *The Napoleonic Wars and German Nationalism in Austria* (New York, 1930).

19. Hans Kelsen, *Über Grenzen zwischen juristischer und soziologischer Methode* (Tübingen, 1911). The significance of this terminological distinction is further developed in many later writings by Kelsen.

20. Of the wide literature dealing with general cultural-artistic-literary, though hardly specific intellectual-scholarly achievements in the period under discussion, only a few of a general nature can be listed here: J. Nadler, *Literaturgeschichte Österreichs* (Linz, 1948), 172-352; Castle, Nagl, and Zeidler, *Deutsch-österreichische Literaturgeschichte* (Vienna, 1914), II; F. M. Mayer, *Geschichte Österreichs* (Vienna, 1909), II, 595-639; E. Leisching (ed.), *Der Wiener Kongress: Kulturgeschichte der bildenden Kunst und des Kunstgewerbes, Theater, Musik, 1802-25* (Vienna, 1898); H. Hantsch, *Die Geschichte Österreichs* (Graz, 1950), II, 301-45; Bibl, *op. cit.*, I, 254-99, stresses almost exclusively the negative aspects of the Franciscan regime's cultural policy; H. Tietze, *Wien: Kultur, Kunst, Geschichte* (Vienna, 1931); H. Tietze, *Wien* (*Berühmte Kunststätten*, LXVII; Leipzig, 1918).

21. Th. Fellner, *Die österreichische Zentralverwaltung,* completed by H. Kretschmayr (3 vols.; Vienna, 1907); see Huber and Dopsch, *op. cit.*, 284-89, 302-22; J. Beidtel, *Geschichte der österreichischen Staatsverwaltung (1740-1848)* (Innsbruck, 1897), II; J. Ulbrich, *Das österreichische Staatsrecht* (Tübingen, 1909), 30-34; F. von Krones, *Handbuch der Geschichte Österreichs* (Berlin, 1881), IV, 544-51, 617-20, 627-32; H. Marczali, *Ungarisches Verfassungsrecht* (Tübingen, 1911), 19-21.

22. Krones, *op. cit.*, IV, 619-20.

23. On the education of Francis, see particularly, W. C. Langsam, *Francis the Good* (New York, 1949), I; see also Tritsch, *op. cit.*, 17-114. A far less favorable, in many ways biased, interpretation is given by Bibl, *op. cit.*, I, 49-61; and by the same author, *Kaiser Franz* (Vienna, 1938); see also W. Tritsch, *Franz von Österreich* (Leipzig, 1937).

24. See Huber and Dopsch, *op. cit.*, 312-15; Bibl, *Kaiser Franz und sein Erbe,* 194-201, 307-13; Springer, *op. cit.*, I, 139-77, 304-22; A. Beer, *Die Finanzen Österreichs im 19. Jahrhundert* (Prague, 1877); P. Stiassny, *Der österreichische Staatsbankrott vom Jahre*

1811 (Vienna, 1911); E. C. Helbling, *Österreichische Verfassungs-und Verwaltungsgeschichte* (Vienna, 1956), 332-35.

25. See Huber and Dopsch, *op. cit.*, 243-46, 312-17; Helbling, *op. cit.*, 340-41; K. Grünberg, *Studien zur Österreichischen Agrargeschichte* (Leipzig, 1901); Jerome Blum, *Noble Landowners and Agriculture in Austria 1815-1948* (Baltimore, 1948).

26. On Austrian industrial development during the Franciscan era see particularly Mayer, *op. cit.*, II, 579-95; A. Beer, *Die österreichische Handelspolitik im 19. Jahrhundert* (Vienna, 1891); F. Engel-Janosi, "Über die Entwicklung der sozialen und wirtschaftslichen Verhältnisse im deutschen Österreich, 1815-48," *Vierteljahrschrift für Sozial- und Wirtschaftsgeschichte,* XVII (1924), 325-46.

27. Huber and Dopsch, *op. cit.*, 212-25, 255, 256, 284-86, 318-21; Springer, *op. cit.*, I, 178-99, 323-62, 509-50; Marczali, *op. cit.*, 17-21; see also as background reading, F. von Krones, *Ungarn unter Maria Theresia und Joseph II* (Graz, 1881).

28. Srbik, *Metternich,* I, 434.

29. *Ibid.,* 435.

30. On the national issue, see *ibid.,* I, 402-10, 424-436, 456-468; II, 32-39, 182-96; Valjavec, *Entstehung der politischen Strömungen,* 328-42; Springer, *op. cit.*, I, 323-61, 509-49; II, 1-35; H. Schlitter, *Aus Österreichs Vormärz* (Vienna, 1920), I–IV; O. Rommel (ed.), *Der Österreichische Vormärz,* 5-19; R. A. Kann, *The Multinational Empire* (New York, 1950), I, 59-68, 118-23, 152-68, 224-29, 238-51, 274-77, 285-86, 309-10, 321-24; H. Kohn, *The Idea of Nationalism* (New York, 1944), 329-579; H. Lemberg, *Geschichte des Nationalismus in Europa* (Linz, 1950), 172-85; C. J. H. Hayes, *The Historical Evolution of Modern Nationalism* (New York, 1931), 1-163; Hantsch, *op. cit.*, II, 301-23.

31. Heinrich Heine, *Französische Zustände* (1852), Preface.

Selected Bibliography

The following bibliography is restricted to an enumeration of unpublished primary sources and to a limited number of important works that contribute to the knowledge of German-Austrian intellectual history in general. Consequently, neither the bibliographical material on specific problems nor most of the general background readings on various other aspects of Austrian history are included in the list. References pertaining to these important topics, including the biographies of Abraham a Sancta Clara and Joseph von Sonnenfels, will be found in the preceding bibliographical notes to the individual chapters. On the other hand, a few general histories as well as biographies are listed here. The reason for their inclusion is not to give general information on Austrian history or individual personalities, which has already been attempted in the notes supplementing the text, but solely because these works contribute to our knowledge of broad phases of intellectual history in the German-Austrian cultural orbit.

The conclusion is warranted at this point that none of the works included here, however distinguished many of them are, discusses more than certain aspects—frequently only piecemeal aspects—of the subject. Historians of the future will still have to meet the challenging task of writing the comprehensive German-Austrian intellectual history.

I. UNPUBLISHED PRIMARY SOURCES

A. Austrian State Archives

1. HAUS-, HOF- UND STAATSARCHIV.—Several "printing privileges" for Abraham a Sancta Clara's works between 1683 and 1695 as well as Abraham's personal petition for permission to have the tract *Auf, Auf ihr Christen* published in 1683 (RHR, *Impressorien,* Fascicles 1, 27).

The fascicle "Sonnenfels, Miscellanea," containing an application by Joseph von Sonnenfels regarding a *Kameral* professorship in Tyrnau, 1799 (*Wissenschaft und Kunst,* Fascicle 1); several letters regarding legislation in criminal affairs, March, 1799 (*ibid.*); one private letter of March, 1817 (*ibid.*).

Vertrauliche Akten der Kabinettskanzlei, XLI, contains several memoranda by Sonnenfels on general administrative policies and a letter referring to his membership in the masonic lodge Zur wahren Eintracht.

2. ALLGEMEINES VERWALTUNGSARCHIV.—Polizei- und Kameralwissenschaften, 1763–84, Fascicles 10, 15, contain numerous documents dealing with Sonnenfels' participation in the work of the Studienhofkommission. These documents pertain in particular to (*a*) organization of the commission, (*b*) judicial techniques (*juristische praktische Geschäftskunde*), (*c*) *Kameralwissenschaften,* populationism, capital punishment, police administration, etc.

For various documents pertaining to Sonnenfels' participation in the work of judicial government commissions, see also Hofkommission in Gesetzessachen, CCXIX.

B. Archive of the University of Vienna

Appointment of Aloys von Sonnenfels (father of Joseph von Sonnenfels) as official interpreter for the Hebrew language, March, 1757.

Five documents (1763, 1765, 1769, and 1803) pertaining to Joseph von Sonnenfels' appointment to professor of *Polizey- und Cameralwissenschaften,* the conferment of the degree of Doctor of Philosophy on him in 1763, of *Regierungsrat* in 1769, appointment as senior professor of the faculty of philosophy and member of the University Senate, 1803.

II. SECONDARY SOURCES AND PUBLISHED PRIMARY SOURCES

(See also notes to Chapters II-V)

A. Works Pertaining to the Whole Period Under Discussion

Hantsch, H. *Die Geschichte Österreichs,* 2 vols. Graz, 1947-50.

Helbling, E. C. *Österreichische Verfassungs- und Verwaltungsgeschichte.* Vienna, 1956.

Helfert, J. A. von. *Die Österreichische Volksschule,* 3 vols. Prague, 1860.

Selected Bibliography

Huber, A., and A. Dopsch. *Österreichische Reichsgeschichte.* Vienna, 1901.

Kralik, Richard von. *Österreichische Geschichte.* Vienna, 1919.

Kralik, Richard von, and Hans Schlitter, *Wein: Geschichte der Kaiserstadt und ihrer Kultur.* Vienna, 1911.

Krones, Franz von. *Handbuch der Geschichte Österreichs,* 4 vols. and index vol. Berlin, 1880, 1881.

Loesche, Georg. *Geschichte des Protestantismus in Österreich.* Tübingen, 1902.

Lux, Joseph A. *Ein Jahrtausend österreichischer Dichtung.* Vienna, 1948.

Mayer, F. M. *Geschichte Österreichs mit besonderer Rücksicht auf das Kulturleben,* 2 vols. Vienna, 1909. See II.

Mecenseffy, Grete. *Geschichte des Protestantismus in Österreich.* Graz, 1956.

Nadler, Josef. *Literaturgeschichte Österreichs.* Vienna, 1948.

Nagl, J. W., W. Zeidler, and E. Castle. *Deutschösterreichische Literaturgeschichte,* 4 vols. Vienna, 1899–1937. I covers literary history until 1750, II from 1750 to 1858.

Rommel, Otto. *Die Alt-Wiener Volkskomödie.* Vienna, 1952.

Roscher, Wilhelm. *Geschichte der Nationalökonomik in Deutschland.* Munich, 1874.

Schindler, F. M., ed. *Das soziale Wirken der Katholischen Kirche in Österreich,* 12 vols. Vienna, 1896–1903.

Schulmeister, Otto, ed. *Spectrum Austriae.* Vienna, 1957.

Strakosch-Grassmann, G. *Geschichte des Österreichischen Unterrichtswesens.* Vienna, 1905.

Tietze, Hans. *Wien: Kultur, Kunst, Geschichte.* Vienna, 1931.

Tietze, Hans. *Wien.* Series *Berühmte Kunststätten,* LXVII; Leipzig, 1918.

Wolfsgruber, Cölestin. *Kirchengeschichte Österreich-Ungarns.* Vienna, 1909.

Zenker, E. V. *Geschichte der Wiener Journalistik.* Vienna, 1892, 1893. See I.

B. Late Baroque

Cysarz, Herbert, ed. *Hoch- und Spätbarock.* Leipzig, 1937.

Cysarz, Herbert, ed. *Schwund und Kirchenbarock.* Leipzig, 1937.

Ginhart, Karl, ed. *Die bildende Kunst in Österreich, Renaissance und Barock.* Vienna, 1939.

Hettner, Hermann. *Geschichte der deutschen Literatur im achtzehnten Jahrhundert.* Leipzig, 1928.

Liess, Andreas. *Wiener Barockmusik.* Vienna, 1946.

Pirchegger, H. *Geschichte und Kulturleben Deutschösterreichs von 1526 bis 1792.* Vienna, 1931.

Vietor, Karl. *Probleme der deutschen Barockliteratur.* Leipzig, 1928.

C. Enlightenment

Arneth, A. von. *Geschichte Maria Theresias,* 10 vols. Vienna, 1863–79.

Arnold, R. F., ed. *Vor dem Untergang des alten Reiches 1756-95.* Series *Politische Dichtung;* Leipzig, 1930–39.

Blumauer, Aloysius. *Beobachtung über Österreichs Aufklärung und Literatur.* Vienna, 1883.

Bruford, W. H. *Theatre, Drama and Audience in Goethe's Germany.* London, 1950.

Brüggemann, F. *Das Weltbild der deutschen Aufklärung.* Leipzig, 1925.

Eder, Karl. *Der Liberalismus in Altösterreich.* Vienna, 1955.

Franz, Georg. *Liberalismus: Die deutsch-liberale Bewegung in der habsburgischen Monarchie.* Munich, 1955.

Guglia, E. *Maria Theresia,* 2 vols. Munich, 1917.

Hettner, H. *Op. cit., supra.*

Lothar, R. *Das Wiener Burgtheater.* Vienna, 1899.

Lustkandl, Wenzel. *Die Josephinischen Ideen und ihr Erfolg.* Vienna, 1881.

Maass, Ferdinand. *Der Josephinismus,* I: *Ursprung und Wesen des Josephinismus;* II: *Entfaltung und Krise;* III: *Das Werk des Hofrat Heinke;* IV: *Der Spätjosefinismus.* Vienna, 1951-1957.

Mitrofanov, Paul von. *Joseph II.* Vienna, 1910.

Padover, Saul. *The Revolutionary Emperor Joseph the Second, 1741–1790.* New York, 1934.

Pirchegger, H. *Geschichte und Kulturleben Deutschösterreichs von 1526 bis 1792.* Vienna, 1931.

Valjavec, F. *Der Josephinismus.* Vienna, 1945.

Valjavec, F. *Die Entstehung der politischen Strömungen in Deutschland, 1770–1815.* Munich, 1951.

Walter, F. *Männer um Maria Theresia.* Vienna, 1951.

Wangermann, Ernst. *From Joseph II to the Jacobin Trials.* London, 1959.

Selected Bibliography

Werner, R. M., ed. *Aus dem Josephinischen Wien: Staatsrat Geblers und Nicolais Briefwechsel.* Berlin, 1888.

Winter, Eduard. *Der Josephinismus und seine Geschichte.* Brünn, 1943.

Wolf, G. *Das Unterrichtswesen in Österreich unter Joseph II.* Vienna, 1880.

D. Conservatism and Romanticism

Allmeyer-Beck, J. Ch. *Der Konservatismus in Österreich.* Munich, 1959.

Arnold, R. F., ed. *Fremdherrschaft und Befreiung 1795–1815.* Series *Politische Dichtung;* Leipzig, 1930–39.

Baxa, Jakob. *Einführung in die romantische Staatswissenschaft.* Jena, 1923.

Bibl, Viktor. *Der Zerfall Österreichs,* 2 vols. Vienna, 1922–24. See I.

Bietak, Wilhelm. *Lebenslehre und Weltanschauung der jüngeren Romantik.* Leipzig, 1936.

Bolzano, Bernard. *Selbstbiographie.* Salzburg, 1936.

Castelli, J. F. *Memoiren meines Lebens,* 4 vols. Vienna, 1861.

Eder, Karl. *Der Liberalismus in Altösterreich.* Vienna, 1955.

Frankl-Hochwart, Ludwig August von. *Erinnerungen.* Prague, 1910.

Franz, G. *Op. cit., supra.*

Gräffer, Franz. *Wiener Dosenstücke,* 2 vols. Vienna, 1852.

Gräffer, Franz. *Kleine Wiener Memorien,* 5 vols. Vienna, 1845, 1846.

Grillparzer, Franz. *Briefe und Tagebücher,* ed. K. Glossy and A. Sauer. Stuttgart, n. d.

Hevesi, Ludwig. *Österreichische Kunst, 1800-1900,* 2 vols. Leipzig, 1903. I covers the period from 1800 to 1848.

Kluckhohn, Paul. *Die deutsche Romantik.* Bielefeld, 1924.

Langsam, W. C. *The Napoleonic Wars and German Nationalism in Austria.* New York, 1930.

Leisching, E., ed. *Der Wiener Kongress: Kulturgeschichte der bildenden Künste und des Kunstgewerbes, Theater, Musik, 1800-1825.* Vienna, 1898.

Lothar, R. *Op. cit., supra.*

Pichler, Karoline. *Denkwürdigkeiten aus meinem Leben.* Vienna, 1844.

Prokesch-Osten, Count Anton. *Aus den Tagebüchern des Grafen Prokesch von Osten.* Vienna, 1909.

Rommel, Otto, ed. *Der Österreichische Vormärz, 1816–47.* Leipzig, 1931.

Schmidt-Weissenfels, Eduard. *Fürst Klemens Metternich und sein Zeitalter,* 2 vols. Prague, 1860.

Schreyvogel, Joseph. *Tagebücher, 1810-23,* ed. K. Glossy, 2 vols. Berlin, 1903.

Sealsfield, Charles (Karl Postl). *Österreich, wie es war.* (Various editions.)

Springer, Anton. *Geschichte Österreichs seit dem Wiener Frieden (1809–49),* 2 vols. Leipzig, 1863–65.

Srbik, Heinrich von. *Metternich,* 3 vols. Munich, 1925–54.

Till, Rudolf. *Hofbauer und sein Kreis.* Vienna, 1951.

Valjavec, F. *Opera cit., supra.*

Winter, E. *Op. cit., supra.*

Wittner, Otto. *Briefe aus dem Vormärz.* Prague, 1910.

E. Reference Works

Allgemeine deutsche Biographie, 55 vols. Leipzig, 1875-1912.

Charmatz, Richard. *Wegweiser durch die Literatur der Österreichischen Geschichte.* Stuttgart, 1912.

Dahlmann, F., and G. Waitz. *Quellenbuch der deutschen Geschichte.* Leipzig, 1931.

Günther, Franz. *Bücherkunde zur deutschen Geschichte.* Munich, 1951.

Hormayr, Joseph von. *Österreichischer Plutarch,* 20 vols. Vienna, 1807-20.

Katholische Deutschland, Das. Augsburg, 1933–.

Mischler, Ernst, and Joseph Ulbrich. *Österreichisches Staatswörterbuch,* 4 vols. Vienna, 1905-09.

Neue deutsche Biographie. Berlin, 1953–.

Neuve österreichische Biographie, ed. A. Bettelheim. 1923–.

Österreichisches biographisches Lexikon, 1815-1950. Graz, 1954–.

Uhlirz, V. *Handbuch der Geschichte Österreichs und seiner Nachbarländer Böhmen und Ungarn,* 3 parts in 4 vols., ed. M. Uhlirz. Graz, 1927-31.

Wurzbach, Konstantin von. *Biographisches Lexikon des Kaisertum Österreich,* 60 vols. Vienna, 1856–91.

Index

Abele, Christoph von, 22

ABRAHAM A SANCTA CLARA: anti-intellectualism of, 67-69, 71, 102; appeal to lower middle class by, 71; background of, 51, 82*n*; Baroque and, xxi; career of, 52-54; Catholic action program and, xvi; Catholic and Counter Reformations and, xxi; clergy and, 66, 67, 112*n*; as critic of society, 61-65; as court preacher, 53, 54, 106, 107; death of, 54; on education, 51, 55, 56, 84-88, 312; erudition of, 55, 56, 102, 108; free professions and, 69, 70; homiletics of, 54-56, 66, 67, 90, 96, 97, 99, 100, 102, 107, 108, 112, 113; image of, xv, 136, 146; influence and appeal of, 90, 94-115, 131; Jews and, 57, 62, 77-79, 83, 96, 104, 104*n*; Leopold I and, 53, 66; literary standing of, 37, 50, 90-94; literary style of, 58-60, 93, 97, 100, 103, 107, 108, 308-09; Luther and, 65, 66, 72, 79; on peasants, 52, 67, 71, 72, 106, 108, 109; personality of, 88, 89, 103-05, 257; plague of 1679 and, 54, 54*n*, 64, 65, 78; on pleasures, 82-84; the poor and, 61, 71-73, 101-03; as prior of Augustinian monastery, 54; Protestants and, 62, 72, 79, 80, 96, 104; siege of Vienna of 1683 and, 54, 63, 65; superstition and, 56-58, 104; on trades and crafts, 70-71; Turks and, 74-76, 96; on urban burgher class, 106-14; Vienna and, 63, 64; on virtues of the antichrist (Moslems and Jews), 75, 76, 78, 83; on women and marriage, 80-82; works of: *Auf, auf Ihr Christen,* 54, 63, 64, 65*n*, 74, 83, 91; *Etwas für alle,* 70-74, 106; *Gehab dich wohl,* 68, 69, 80, 81, 87, 88; *Hui und Pfui,* 58, 72, 73, 84, 85; *Judas der Ertzschelm,* 58, 80, 81, 83, 88, 89, 106; *Lösch Wien,* 74, 75; *Mercks Wien,* 54, 63-67, 78, 104*n*

Absolutism, despotic, 2, 5, 6, 23, 182; French pattern of, 23, 24, 126, 287

Absolutism, enlightened, 120, 126, 127, 165-72, 182, 203; bureaucratic, 139, 140; Gentz and, 271; totalitarianism and, 140; under Joseph II, 136-45, 295

Act of Settlement of 1701 (England), 5

Addison, Joseph (ed. *Spectator*), 198

Administration, 19-23; commercial directory of, 124; court chamber for financial affairs of, 21; general court chancellery of, 21; German-directed centralism of, 141, 247-49; in Bohemian and Hungarian lands, 22; in hereditary lands, 19; local, 124; of police state, 245, 246; reforms of, under Ferdinand I, 1, 19; —under Maria Theresa, 124; Secret Conference of, 118; state chancellery of, 124; training and selection of government officials for, 22, 23; transition of, to centralized bureaucratic state, 23, 267; under Charles VI, 118

Agricultural revolution, 299

347

Index

Index

Index

352

Index

Index

Index

Index

Jahn, Friedrich, 293, 293n
James II, King of England, 5, 24
Jansenism, 23, 24
Jacquin, Nicolaus L., 135, 236n; and Mirabeau, 236
Jean Paul (Friedrich Richter), 92
Jefferson, Thomas, 245
Jesuit Order, 2, 22, 58, 66, 98; architecture and, 3, 46; control of universities by, 35; curriculum in secondary schools of, 35, 36; dissolution of Province of, in Austria, 128, 133; education and, 35, 36, 51, 52, 107; homiletics of, 59; in Bohemia, 16; in France, 23, 24; literature and theater and, 120, 204; readmission of, under Francis I, 271
Jews: Abraham a Sancta Clara and, 57, 76-79; assimilation of, 254, 255; emancipation of, under Joseph II, 11, 138, 139, 163, 249, 253, 254; expulsion of (1421), 77; (1669-70), 25, 79, 157; —from Bohemia (1745), 158; Ferdinand II and Ferdinand III and, 77; Goethe and, 243; in Prussia, 147, 150, 158; Leopold I and, 25, 77, 157; Liberalism and, 254; restrictions on peddlers who were, 29; under Charles VI, 157, 158; under Maria Theresa, 157-59, 253, 254; see also Anti-Semitism
Joseph I, Holy Roman Emperor (1705-11), 54, 117; foreign trade and, 118; Viennese theater and, 209
JOSEPH II, Holy Roman Emperor (1765-90): agricultural reforms and serfdom under, 119, 139, 140, 249, 284; Church and, 137-39, 172-74; civil legislation under, 184, 185, 282, 283; co-regency of, 96, 122, 136, 185; criminal law under, 184, 282, 283; cultivation of German language under, 152, 153; economic policy of, 130, 176, 285; Estates system and, 17, 109, 287; Francis I and, 280, 282, 287;

formative arts and, 226, 228; German nationalism under, 141-44; Germanization attempts under, 141; image of, 145; Jews and, 77, 138, 139, 163; judicial reforms under, 140, 184, 282; mercantilism and physiocratic practices under, 31; opposition of, to educational reformers from abroad, 133; —to education of soldiers' children, 132, 133; personality of, 185, 233, 234; philosophy of Enlightenment and, 123, 131, 139, 167, 234; Protestants and, 138, 139; reign of, 44, 136-45, 171, 217, 247, 248, 261, 262, 295; Sonnenfels and, 155, 156, 159, 171, 172, 174, 184-86, 188, 232-36; theater and, 210, 218, 220; Tolerance Edict of (1781), 129
Josephinism: Austrian tradition and, 142; bureaucracy and, 140-42; concept of, 136, 137, 139, 141-43, 232, 247, 250, 287; evaluated as *Vulgärjosephinismus*, 249; Ferdinand I and, 247, 248; Francis I (II) and, 142, 232, 247, 248, 261, 262, 280, 295; French Revolution of 1789 and, 297; German-directed centralism and, 247, 248; Jewish emancipation and, 249; Leopold II and, 142, 232, 247, 248; Liberalism and, 137, 141-45, 157, 162, 267; nationalism and, 141, 143, 144, 285; opposition to, 137; totalitarianism and, 140, 143-45
Judicial reforms: under Maria Theresa, 134, 135, 154, 155, 181-89; under Joseph II, 140; under Francis I, 272, 273, 276, 282, 283
Jungdeutsche movement, 276, 277
Justi, Johann Heinrich von, and populationism, 175

Kant, Immanuel, 256
Kaunitz, Wenzel Anton, Prince, 118, 216, 217; Church-State relations and, 173, 230; French literary

Index

Mozart, Wolfgang Amadeus, xvi, 41, 224

Müller, Adam, 217; between Burke and Novalis, 268, 269; Estates and, 269; French Revolution (1789) and, 264; Hegel's dialectics and, 269; Metternich and, 217n, 269; Metternich system and, 264, 270; political philosophy of, 260, 268-70; reactionary influence of, 270; romantic philosophy of, 247, 266, 275

Müller, Paul, 22

Müller, Willibald, and Sonnenfels, 250, 251

Muncker, Franz, on Sonnenfels, 200

Murner, Thomas, 90

Music: in Baroque period, 40, 41; opera, 40, 41, 209, 214, 236; opera buffa, 242; social setting of, 41

Mustafa, Kara, 5

Nadler, Joseph, 92, 93; on Sonnenfels, 252

Nagl, Johann Willibald, 92, 223, 240

Nantes, revocation of Edict of, 5, 23

Napoleon I, Emperor: Beethoven and, 237; Continental Blockade and, 284; Gentz and, 270; imperialism and, 266

Napoleonic Wars, 259, 260, 266, 284; and German nationalism, 285

Nationalism: cultural-humanitarian, 291; Czech, 9, 10, 15, 16; ethnic, 9, 248, 286, 289, 290, 293; historico-political entities and, xviii, 9, 10, 286, 289; Italian Irredentism and, 9, 289; Jacobin, 285, 290; Josephinism and, 141-45; liberal, 286, 296; Magyar, 9, 10, 291; Polish, 291; romantic, 296; Rumanian, 9; Ruthenian, 291; Slovak, in Hungary, 13, 24; Southern Slav, 8, 9

National Socialism: see Nazism

National Theater of 1776: see Burgtheater

Nation concept: Metternich rejects Austrian, 290; political and cultural, 263; rejected by Gentz, 270, 271; shared by Jacobinism and Romanticism, 263

Natural Law, 73, 76; Sonnenfels and, 168, 183

Natural sciences: education in, 35, 36; under Maria Theresa, 135

Nazism, 93, 112, 252, 256; Blubo doctrine of, 252, 252n; Joseph II and, 143-45

Neo-absolutist period, 249, 250, 296, 299

Nestroy, Johann, and Austrian literature, 95, 224, 275

Newton, Sir Isaac, 36, 43, 296, 298

Nicolai, Friedrich, 202, 204; on German language in Austria, 152; on intellectual climate, 165, 199, 237; Sonnenfels and, 217, 229-31

Nobile, Peter von, and architecture, 275, 276

Nobility, 39, 67-69; lower, 217, 231; of letters, 217; see also Aristocracy

Novalis and Adam Müller, 269

Nürnberg trials, 183

Opera: Sonnenfels and, 214, 236; under Leopold I, 40, 41, 209; under Maria Theresa, 210, 214

Opera buffa and Goethe, 242

Opitz, Martin, 37

Oppenheimer, Samuel, 32, 33

Oriental academy, 133

Orsini, Domenico, 42

Ottoman empire: administration of, in Hungary, 11, 14; evangelical churches in, in Hungary, 11; in Baroque period, 6, 7; wars of, with Habsburg power, 6, 7

Painting in Baroque period, 42

Palacky, Francis, and empire reform, 291

Palatine: see Hungary

Pan-Germanism, 8, 251, 252, 255, 290; associates Jews with Liberalism, 162

Pan-Slavism, 8, 285, 289, 291

Pascal, Blaise, 2, 36, 43, 298

Passarowitz, treaty of (1718), 7

Index

Index

Renaissance in Austria (*Cont.*)
formative arts in, 45-46, 225; Greek-Roman civilization and, 300; Humanism and, 301; limited influence of, 299; literature in, 38; patronage of arts in, 227
Restoration period after 1814, 110, 260, 265, 267, 295
Revay, Peter, Count, 38
Revolution of 1848, 110, 262, 296, 299; and Liberalism, 248, 255
Richelieu, Armand Jean du Plessis, Cardinal, 6
Richter, Friedrich: see Jean Paul
Riegger, Paul Joseph: legal education and, 134, 183; legal reforms and, 135, 152
Rinek, Gottlieb Eucharius, 38
Robespierre, Maximilien de, change of image of, 245
Robota system: Joseph II and, 139, 140; under Charles VI, 119; under Leopold I, 17, 71, 119; under Maria Theresa, 124-27, 178, 180, 181
Robot Patent of 1775, 126
Rollett, Hermann, and Sonnenfels, 250
Rococo, 44; decline of, 235; formative arts in, 225, 226, 228; literature in, 201
Roman law, *Rezeption* of, 70
Romanticism: Austro-German cultural tradition and, xvi, xx, 99, 166, 195, 247, 260, 278; Baroque and, 300; Catholic trend of, 248, 259, 260, 262; Christian national trends of, 299; Christian revivalism in, 266, 272; common grounds of Liberalism and, 267; conservatism and, 262-69; Enlightenment and, 246; French Revolution (1789) and, 263; Middle Ages and, 265; political, 285, 295, 296
Roscher, Wilhelm, on Sonnenfels, 167, 175
Rottmayr von Rosenbrunn, Johann, and painting, 42, 226
Rousseau, Jean-Jacques: Eugene of Savoy and, 121; intellectual cli-

mate and, 165, 167, 257; social contract of, 168, 246; Third Estate and, 125; tradition and, 164
Rubens, Peter Paul, 226
Rudolf II, Holy Roman Emperor (1576-1612), Letter of Majesty of, 25
Rumanians, 25: see also *Vlachs*

Sachs, Hans, 91
St. Francis Xavier, 105
St. Gotthardt, battle of (1664), 8
St. Ignatius: see Loyola, St. Ignatius of
St. Paul of Tharsus, 72
St. Paul's Church assembly: see Frankfurt assembly
St. Thomas Aquinas, 56, 72
Salzburg, eviction of Protestants from, 25
Sancta Clara, Abraham a: see Abraham a Sancta Clara
Saurau, Francis, Count, and Francis I, 281
Savonarola, Girolamo, 105
Savoyan academy, lecture by Sonnenfels in, 193, 194
Scheffler, Johannes: see Silesius, Angelus
Scheffler, Karl, 2
Scheicher, Josef, 112, 113
Scheid, N., on Abraham a Sancta Clara, 50, 93
Scherer, Georg, 59, 311; *Lutherischer Bettlermantel*, 59
Scherer, Wilhelm, on Abraham a Sancta Clara, 50, 52, 56, 61, 82n, 89, 92-94, 98, 99, 99n, 105
Schikaneder, Emanuel, and burlesque comedy, 224
Schiller, Friedrich von: Abraham a Sancta Clara and, 65, 65n, 91, 92; Burgtheater and, 221, 224; Kotzebue and, 206; *tragédie classique* and, 214
Schlegel, Friedrich, 266; philosophy of art of, 247, 260, 275
Schmid, Erich, 136; on *Hanswurst* comedy, 223; on Sonnenfels, 198, 223, 240

Index

Index